Dynamic and Safe Economy in the Age of Smart Technologies

Hamed Nozari
Independent Researcher, Australia

IGI Global
Scientific Publishing
Publishing Tomorrow's Research Today

Vice President of Editorial	Melissa Wagner
Managing Editor of Acquisitions	Mikaela Felty
Managing Editor of Book Development	Jocelynn Hessler
Production Manager	Mike Brehm
Cover Design	Phillip Shickler

Published in the United States of America by
IGI Global Scientific Publishing
701 East Chocolate Avenue
Hershey, PA, 17033, USA
Tel: 717-533-8845
Fax: 717-533-7115
Website: https://www.igi-global.com E-mail: cust@igi-global.com

Library of Congress Cataloging-in-Publication Data

LCCN: 2025020109 (CIP Data Pending)
ISBN13: 9798369343692
EISBN13: 9798369343708

British Cataloguing in Publication Data
A Cataloguing in Publication record for this book is available from the British Library.

Table of Contents

Detailed Table of Contents

The rapid advancement of digital technologies has transformed economic systems, shifting from static models to dynamic, adaptive frameworks. This research explores the evolution of economic optimization, highlighting the role of artificial intelligence, machine learning, blockchain, and real-time analytics in shaping the smart economy. It examines the impact of digital disruption, adaptive optimization, and dynamic decision-making in enhancing economic resilience, efficiency, and sustainability. The study also discusses challenges related to cybersecurity, fairness, and regulatory concerns in the era of digital transformation.

The rapid advancement of financial technology (FinTech) has revolutionized the financial sector by integrating artificial intelligence, blockchain, quantum computing, IoT, and digital payments. These innovations enhance efficiency, security, and accessibility while introducing new cybersecurity challenges such as fraud, identity theft, and ransomware attacks. This research explores emerging FinTech trends, cybersecurity risks, and mitigation strategies to ensure a secure and transparent financial ecosystem. Future advancements in AI-driven automation, decentralized finance (DeFi), and quantum encryption will further shape the financial industry's digital transformation.

The chapter investigates the convergence of sustainable smart economies, green technologies, and circular business models, underscoring their vital contributions to promoting environmental sustainability and economic resilience. As global issues such as climate change and resource scarcity become more pressing, incorporating innovative green technologies spanning renewable energy initiatives to sophisticated waste management solutions becomes essential. These technologies not only improve resource efficiency but also play a significant role in diminishing ecological footprints. Concurrently, implementing circular business models is crucial for reimagining value creation in ways that reduce waste and encourage sustainable practices. Enterprises can shift from conventional linear models to more regenerative frameworks that harmonies with ecological objectives by emphasising systems that focus on recycling, reuse, and sustainable sourcing. This chapter synthesises existing literature and case studies to understand how sustainable smart economies can harness these innovations thoroughly.

Blockchain-powered decentralized finance (DeFi) is revolutionizing digital marketing by enabling transparent, secure, and automated financial transactions. This research explores how DeFi-driven smart contracts, tokenized incentives, and decentralized identity management are transforming consumer engagement, advertising models, and data privacy. While DeFi eliminates intermediaries and enhances efficiency, challenges such as cybersecurity risks, regulatory uncertainties, and scalability issues remain. Addressing these concerns will be crucial in harnessing DeFi's full potential for marketing innovation and consumer empowerment.

Digital twin technology is transforming bioreactor systems by integrating AI, IoT, and real-time simulation to enhance bioprocess efficiency, predictability, and scalability. This research explores the evolution, benefits, and applications of digital twin-enabled bioreactors, focusing on AI-driven optimization, cyber-physical system integration, and predictive analytics. Case studies, including BIO10's advancements in smart biomanufacturing, highlight real-world applications. The study also examines challenges and future prospects, emphasizing the potential for autonomous, intelligent bioprocessing in sustainable industrial biotechnology.

This research presents a digital twin-enhanced sentiment analysis model for optimizing targeted marketing strategies using multi-objective optimization. By integrating BERT-based sentiment analysis, digital twin simulation, and evolutionary algorithms, the framework dynamically adjusts marketing actions to maximize engagement, minimize costs, and enhance personalization accuracy. The proposed Greedy Man Optimization Algorithm (GMOA) outperforms traditional methods, achieving superior results in consumer targeting and cost efficiency. Findings demonstrate the effectiveness of AI-driven adaptive marketing, providing a scalable and ethical approach to modern digital advertising.

Cybersecurity is a critical challenge in smart economies as digital transformation increases cyber threats such as ransomware, AI-powered attacks, and IoT vulnerabilities. This study examines cybersecurity risks, economic impacts, regulatory challenges, and AI-driven security solutions. Using a mixed-method approach, it

Preface

The rapid advancements in smart technologies have transformed the economic landscape, reshaping industries, governance, and financial systems. We now stand at the intersection of unprecedented innovation and pressing global challenges, where digital transformation is no longer an option but a necessity. The ability to build a dynamic and safe economy in this era of AI, blockchain, IoT, and automation requires a deep understanding of the interplay between technological progress, regulatory frameworks, and economic sustainability.

This book, Dynamic and Safe Economy in the Age of Smart Technologies, explores how intelligent digital ecosystems can drive growth while ensuring stability and resilience. By bridging economic principles with emerging technologies, I seek to provide a roadmap for policymakers, business leaders, and researchers striving to harness the power of digital transformation without compromising economic security.

Through a multidisciplinary approach, this work delves into key topics such as cybersecurity in financial systems, ethical AI governance, data-driven decision-making, and the role of decentralized platforms in shaping a more inclusive economy. More importantly, it addresses the critical question: How can we build an economy that is both agile and secure in an era of exponential technological change?

As we navigate this digital-first world, collaboration and open innovation will be pivotal in shaping a future where technology serves as an enabler of prosperity, rather than a source of disruption. I hope this book sparks meaningful discussions and provides valuable insights for all those invested in building a smarter, safer, and more sustainable economic future.

Dr. Hamed Nozari

Chapter 1
Digital Transformation and the Evolution of Optimization in Economic Systems

Hesamoddin Motevalli
https://orcid.org/0009-0008-9565-5064
Shomal University, Amol, Iran

Saeid Emamgholizadeh
Shomal University, Amol, Iran

Hamidreza Razavi
Shomal University, Amol, Iran

ABSTRACT

The rapid advancement of digital technologies has transformed economic systems, shifting from static models to dynamic, adaptive frameworks. This research explores the evolution of economic optimization, highlighting the role of artificial intelligence, machine learning, blockchain, and real-time analytics in shaping the smart economy. It examines the impact of digital disruption, adaptive optimization, and dynamic decision-making in enhancing economic resilience, efficiency, and sustainability. The study also discusses challenges related to cybersecurity, fairness, and regulatory concerns in the era of digital transformation.

DOI: 10.4018/979-8-3693-4369-2.ch001

1- INTRODUCTION

The modern economy is undergoing a profound transformation driven by digital technologies, artificial intelligence, and advanced optimization techniques. Traditional economic models, which once relied on linear projections and static variables, are increasingly giving way to dynamic, data-driven decision-making processes. The digital revolution has not only redefined how businesses operate but has also reshaped economic policies, financial systems, and market dynamics on a global scale. This transformation is not merely a technological upgrade but a paradigm shift—one that necessitates new frameworks for economic optimization, resilience, and sustainability (Tang et al., 2025).

The integration of digital technologies into economic systems has given rise to what is commonly referred to as the "smart economy." A smart economy leverages artificial intelligence, big data analytics, blockchain, and the Internet of Things (IoT) to enhance efficiency, transparency, and adaptability. Unlike traditional economic models that often struggle to incorporate real-time data and multi-dimensional uncertainties, a smart economy utilizes optimization algorithms to respond dynamically to shifting market conditions. As a result, decision-making processes have become more predictive and automated, allowing for higher accuracy in financial forecasting, supply chain management, and resource allocation.

Optimization, as a mathematical and computational discipline, has long played a crucial role in economic planning and decision-making. From classical linear programming to modern machine learning-based optimization, the methods used to allocate resources, balance trade-offs, and maximize efficiency have continuously evolved. The digital transformation of economic systems, however, has introduced new levels of complexity. Economic interactions are no longer confined to physical spaces but are now highly interconnected within cyber-physical systems. As industries transition from traditional supply chains to digital ecosystems, optimization techniques must account for not only cost and efficiency but also factors such as sustainability, cybersecurity, and ethical considerations (Feng et al., 2025).

One of the defining characteristics of digital transformation is its impact on the resilience and sustainability of economies. Traditional optimization methods often prioritized short-term efficiency over long-term sustainability. However, in an era of climate change, resource depletion, and socio-economic disruptions, optimization strategies must now balance economic growth with environmental and social responsibility. Digital tools such as artificial intelligence and blockchain are increasingly being deployed to optimize sustainable practices, from renewable energy distribution to circular economy models. These technologies enable decision-makers to create adaptive policies that minimize economic shocks while maximizing long-term stability (Movahed et al., 2024).

Another fundamental aspect of this transformation is the shift from static to dynamic economic models. In the past, economic theories were built upon equilibrium-based assumptions, where markets were analyzed under the presumption of stability. However, the digital economy operates in a state of constant flux, with real-time data streams, algorithm-driven transactions, and automated financial systems altering the landscape at an unprecedented pace. Dynamic optimization techniques, which allow for continuous adaptation and learning, have become essential in managing economies that are no longer predictable by traditional means. Machine learning, reinforcement learning, and evolutionary algorithms are now being used to optimize economic outcomes in scenarios where static models would fail (Grigorievich, 2025).

At the heart of this transformation lies digital twins and cyber-physical systems. Digital twins, which are virtual replicas of physical economic environments, allow policymakers, businesses, and financial institutions to simulate scenarios and optimize strategies before implementing them in the real world. Whether applied in smart city development, financial risk assessment, or industrial process optimization, digital twins provide unprecedented insights that improve decision-making. This integration of real-time simulation and optimization has profound implications for how economies are structured, monitored, and optimized in the digital era.

Despite the remarkable advancements in digital economic optimization, this transformation also presents significant challenges and risks. Cybersecurity threats, data privacy concerns, and algorithmic biases pose serious risks to the integrity of digital economic systems. As automation and AI-driven decision-making become more prevalent, ethical considerations regarding transparency, accountability, and fairness must be addressed. Furthermore, while digital technologies offer unparalleled opportunities for efficiency and growth, their implementation is not uniform across regions and industries. Digital inequality—both within and between economies—remains a pressing issue that must be resolved to ensure that the benefits of digital transformation are equitably distributed (Zhang et al., 2024).

This book explores the intersection of digital transformation and economic optimization, examining how emerging technologies are reshaping traditional economic frameworks. It delves into the role of AI, machine learning, blockchain, and digital twins in optimizing economic systems, while also addressing the sustainability and resilience aspects that are crucial for future economic stability. The discussion spans across various domains, including financial markets, industrial production, supply chains, and government policy-making, offering insights into how digital tools can enhance decision-making at both micro and macroeconomic levels.

As the world continues to embrace digital transformation, understanding the evolving landscape of economic optimization becomes increasingly vital. Whether it is designing intelligent financial models, implementing blockchain-based trade mechanisms, or using AI for predictive economic analysis, the integration of digital technologies into economic systems is redefining the rules of engagement. The objective of this book is to provide a comprehensive analysis of these transformations, shedding light on the opportunities and challenges that lie ahead.

By bridging the gap between optimization theory and real-world digital applications, this book aims to offer a roadmap for policymakers, researchers, and business leaders who seek to navigate the complexities of the digital economy. The journey towards an optimized, smart, and resilient economy is still unfolding, and as technology continues to advance, the strategies and methodologies discussed in this book will play a pivotal role in shaping the future of global economic systems.

2- LITERATURE REVIEW

The study of digital transformation and optimization in economic systems has gained significant traction in recent years, driven by the increasing integration of artificial intelligence, big data, and advanced computational methods into economic decision-making. Researchers and scholars have explored how digital technologies reshape traditional economic models, enhance resource efficiency, and drive sustainability. The literature on this subject spans multiple domains, including economic optimization, digital economics, smart economies, and the dynamic nature of modern markets. This chapter provides a comprehensive review of existing research, identifying key themes, gaps, and evolving trends in the field (Yang et al., 2025).

Optimization has long been at the core of economic theory, with classical approaches dating back to early mathematical models used for resource allocation and utility maximization. Traditional economic optimization models, such as linear programming and game theory, have played a pivotal role in shaping decision-making processes in industries and policy frameworks. However, these conventional models often rely on static assumptions and do not fully account for the dynamic and uncertain nature of modern economies. With the advent of digital transformation, optimization has evolved to incorporate real-time data, machine learning algorithms, and computational intelligence, enabling more sophisticated and adaptive decision-making in economic systems (Ashrafi et al., 2025).

One of the most significant developments in the literature is the concept of the smart economy, which emphasizes the use of artificial intelligence, blockchain, and the Internet of Things (IoT) to enhance efficiency, transparency, and decision-making in economic systems. Scholars have explored how AI-driven optimization can improve financial forecasting, supply chain management, and market stability. Research highlights that machine learning algorithms are increasingly replacing traditional econometric models, offering predictive capabilities that allow businesses and governments to respond proactively to market fluctuations. The literature also underscores the role of blockchain technology in enhancing economic optimization through decentralized and transparent financial systems, reducing transaction costs, and improving trust in digital transactions.

Another key area of study focuses on the transition from static to dynamic economic models. Traditional optimization approaches, such as those based on equilibrium models, assume that economic systems operate under relatively stable conditions. However, digital transformation has introduced new levels of complexity, requiring adaptive optimization techniques that can adjust to real-time market shifts. Scholars have emphasized the role of reinforcement learning, evolutionary algorithms, and stochastic optimization in navigating economic uncertainties. These methods allow for continuous learning and adaptation, ensuring that economic policies and business strategies remain responsive to dynamic environments (Ghobakhloo et al., 2025).

A growing body of literature also examines the implications of digital twins and cyber-physical systems in economic optimization. Digital twins, which are virtual replicas of physical entities, enable policymakers and businesses to simulate economic scenarios before implementing real-world decisions. Researchers have demonstrated how digital twins can optimize urban planning, industrial production, and financial risk assessment by providing accurate, real-time insights into economic conditions. Cyber-physical systems further enhance economic decision-making by integrating digital intelligence with physical assets, leading to more efficient resource utilization and streamlined economic operations (Sikki et al., 2024).

The intersection of sustainability and economic optimization has become an increasingly important research area. The literature highlights how digital transformation facilitates sustainable economic models by optimizing energy consumption, reducing waste, and promoting circular economy principles. Artificial intelligence and big data analytics are being used to optimize environmental policies, monitor carbon footprints, and develop green supply chains. Scholars argue that optimization in economic systems must go beyond profit maximization to incorporate sustainability metrics, ensuring long-term resilience and ecological balance. This shift reflects a broader trend in research that aligns economic efficiency with environmental and social responsibility (Szmelter-Jarosz et al., 2021).

Despite these advancements, challenges remain in implementing optimization-driven digital economic systems. Several studies highlight concerns related to cybersecurity, ethical considerations, and digital inequality. The increasing reliance on algorithmic decision-making raises questions about transparency, bias, and accountability in economic optimization. Research indicates that while AI-driven optimization enhances efficiency, it also introduces risks such as algorithmic biases that could reinforce economic disparities. Furthermore, digital inequality remains a pressing issue, with disparities in technological access hindering the widespread benefits of digital transformation. Scholars argue that future research must address these challenges by developing fair and inclusive optimization frameworks that ensure equitable economic participation (Rahmaty & Nozari, 2023).

Looking at the future of economic optimization, recent studies have explored the potential of quantum computing to revolutionize economic modeling and decision-making. Quantum optimization algorithms, which can process vast amounts of data at unprecedented speeds, are expected to enhance economic simulations, financial risk assessments, and real-time market predictions. While still in its early stages, quantum computing has the potential to redefine the boundaries of digital economic optimization, offering solutions to complex problems that traditional computational methods struggle to address (Onesi-Ozigagun et al., 2024).

Overall, the literature on digital transformation and economic optimization reflects a rapidly evolving field that integrates advanced computational methods with real-world economic applications. While significant progress has been made in leveraging AI, blockchain, digital twins, and adaptive optimization techniques, ongoing research is needed to address ethical concerns, cybersecurity risks, and issues of economic inclusivity. The convergence of digital transformation and optimization will continue to shape the future of economic systems, offering new opportunities for efficiency, sustainability, and resilience in an increasingly interconnected world.

3- THE FOUNDATIONS OF ECONOMIC OPTIMIZATION

Economic optimization has been at the heart of decision-making processes in both microeconomic and macroeconomic contexts, guiding resource allocation, production planning, pricing strategies, and policy formulation. The evolution of optimization techniques has transformed the way economies function, moving from static mathematical models to dynamic, AI-driven approaches. Over the decades, optimization has become more sophisticated, incorporating elements of uncertainty, real-time decision-making, and multi-objective trade-offs.

At its core, economic optimization seeks to maximize or minimize an objective function—such as profit maximization, cost minimization, or social welfare enhancement—while considering constraints such as resource limitations, market conditions, and regulatory requirements. Traditional economic optimization methods, including linear programming (LP) and nonlinear programming (NLP), laid the foundation for structured economic decision-making. However, as economies became more interconnected and complex, new techniques such as stochastic optimization, dynamic programming, and artificial intelligence (AI)-based optimization emerged to address the growing need for adaptability and real-time analysis.

Table 1 presents a comparative overview of classical and modern optimization methods used in economic decision-making.

Table 1. Optimization Methods in Economic Systems

Optimization Method	Key Applications	Advantages
Linear Programming (LP)	Resource allocation, supply chain optimization	Efficient, well-established, easy to implement
Nonlinear Programming (NLP)	Financial modeling, complex economic simulations	Handles complex nonlinear relationships
Dynamic Programming (DP)	Investment decisions, policy optimization	Accounts for time-dependent decision-making
Stochastic Optimization	Risk management, uncertain economic environments	Incorporates uncertainty and randomness
Machine Learning Optimization	Predictive analytics, demand forecasting	Learns patterns from big data, improves decision-making
Quantum Optimization	High-dimensional economic modeling, quantum computing	Computes complex solutions at unprecedented speeds

The transition from classical optimization to more advanced computational methods has been driven by several key factors. First, the digital revolution has led to an exponential increase in data availability, requiring optimization models to process vast amounts of information efficiently. Second, the uncertainty inherent in modern economies—due to market volatility, geopolitical risks, and climate change—demands robust optimization techniques that can handle dynamic environments. Finally, advances in artificial intelligence and machine learning have enabled data-driven optimization, allowing economic models to learn from historical patterns and improve decision-making over time (Joel et al., 2024).

One of the most important developments in economic optimization has been the shift towards dynamic optimization models. Unlike traditional equilibrium-based models, which assume economic stability, dynamic optimization considers how economic variables evolve over time. This is particularly relevant in investment decisions, supply chain logistics, and macroeconomic policy design, where decisions made today affect future outcomes. Dynamic programming has been widely applied in these contexts, allowing for the sequential optimization of economic choices over multiple periods.

Another significant advancement has been stochastic optimization, which incorporates uncertainty into decision-making. In economic contexts, uncertainties arise from fluctuating demand, currency exchange rates, interest rates, and external shocks such as pandemics or financial crises. Stochastic optimization techniques, such as Monte Carlo simulations and probabilistic modeling, allow policymakers and business leaders to assess multiple possible outcomes and develop robust strategies that perform well under various scenarios.

As artificial intelligence has gained traction, machine learning-based optimization has become an essential tool in economic decision-making. Unlike traditional optimization methods that rely on predefined mathematical formulations, machine learning models can identify optimization patterns from large datasets and adjust decision-making processes dynamically. This is particularly useful in predictive analytics, pricing optimization, demand forecasting, and automated financial trading. Machine learning algorithms such as reinforcement learning further enhance decision-making by continuously learning from new data and refining strategies over time (Su & Wu, 2024).

Looking towards the future, quantum optimization is expected to revolutionize economic decision-making by solving complex problems that are currently beyond the reach of classical computing. Quantum computing has the potential to optimize large-scale economic models with exponentially faster processing speeds, enabling breakthroughs in market prediction, financial risk management, and global trade simulations. Although still in its early stages, research in quantum optimization suggests that it could redefine the landscape of economic decision-making within the next decade.

The evolution of economic optimization techniques is illustrated in Figure 1, which shows the increasing complexity of optimization methods over time.

Figure 1. Evolution of Economic Optimization Methods

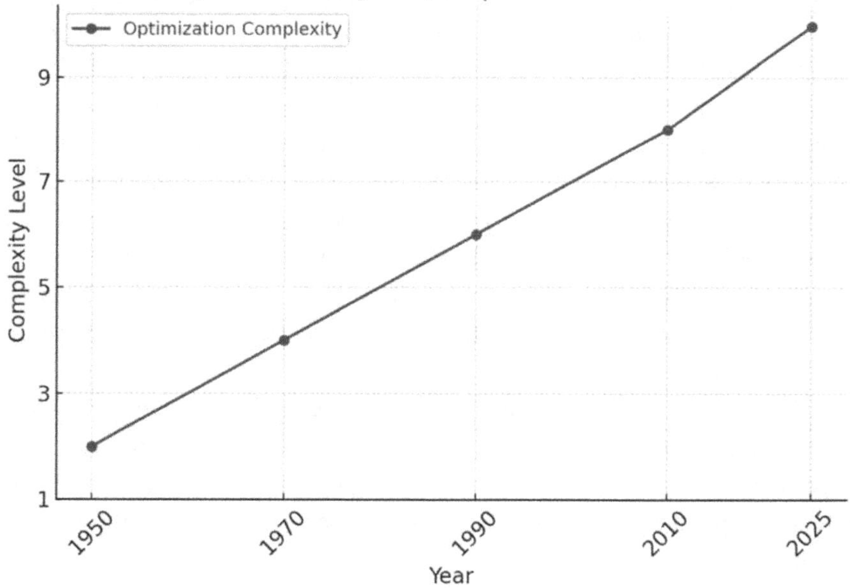

Economic optimization continues to evolve, integrating advanced computational methods to enhance decision-making across industries and policymaking domains. While traditional mathematical models remain relevant, the increasing complexity and uncertainty of modern economies necessitate adaptive and AI-driven optimization approaches. As we move further into the digital age, the convergence of big data, artificial intelligence, and quantum computing will shape the next generation of economic optimization models, driving efficiency, sustainability, and resilience in global economic systems.

4- THE RISE OF THE SMART ECONOMY AND DIGITAL DISRUPTION

The evolution of economic systems has always been shaped by technological advancements, but the emergence of digital technologies has accelerated this transformation at an unprecedented pace. The traditional economy, largely driven by linear production models and centralized decision-making, is being replaced by a highly interconnected and intelligent system known as the smart economy. This new paradigm leverages artificial intelligence (AI), big data, blockchain, the Internet of Things (IoT), and cloud computing to create more efficient, adaptive, and data-driven economic processes. The shift towards a smart economy is not merely a technological upgrade—it is a fundamental restructuring of how value is created, exchanged, and optimized in the digital age.

At the heart of the smart economy lies the ability to process vast amounts of real-time data and convert it into actionable insights. Unlike traditional economic models, which often rely on static historical data, smart economies continuously adapt to changing market conditions using AI-powered analytics and machine learning algorithms. This dynamic approach allows businesses and policymakers to make more informed decisions, optimize resource allocation, and anticipate economic trends before they manifest. The increasing reliance on predictive analytics has transformed industries such as finance, healthcare, and manufacturing, where automated decision-making and real-time optimization are now standard practice.

One of the most defining aspects of the smart economy is digital disruption, a phenomenon in which traditional business models are fundamentally altered by digital innovation. The rise of e-commerce, fintech, decentralized finance (DeFi), and automated supply chains has redefined market structures, often rendering legacy systems obsolete. Digital disruption has empowered smaller, agile companies to compete with established enterprises by leveraging technology to enhance efficiency and reduce costs. The widespread adoption of platform-based business models, such as those used by Uber, Airbnb, and Amazon, exemplifies how digital platforms have become the backbone of modern economic interactions. These platforms use AI-driven algorithms to match supply with demand dynamically, optimize pricing strategies, and improve customer experiences, all while minimizing operational inefficiencies.

The gig economy is another product of the smart economy, reshaping labor markets and redefining employment structures. Enabled by digital platforms, gig work allows individuals to participate in on-demand jobs, offering greater flexibility and global accessibility. While this model has provided new opportunities for employment, it has also raised concerns about job security, fair wages, and regulatory challenges. As automation and AI-driven processes continue to replace traditional jobs, the smart economy must find ways to balance innovation with social responsibility, ensuring that digital disruption benefits society as a whole rather than exacerbating economic inequalities.

Financial markets have been among the most profoundly impacted sectors, with blockchain and decentralized finance (DeFi) revolutionizing traditional banking and investment mechanisms. Blockchain technology has introduced a level of transparency and security previously unattainable in financial transactions. Smart contracts, self-executing digital agreements, eliminate intermediaries, reducing transaction costs and enhancing trust in digital exchanges. Cryptocurrencies, stablecoins, and central bank digital currencies (CBDCs) are reshaping monetary policies, forcing regulators to adapt to an era where decentralized assets operate beyond conventional financial controls. The rapid rise of DeFi platforms has further challenged traditional banking models, offering alternative financial services such as lending, borrowing, and asset management without the need for centralized institutions.

The Internet of Things (IoT) plays a crucial role in the smart economy by connecting physical assets with digital intelligence. IoT-enabled devices collect and transmit real-time data, optimizing industrial operations, transportation networks, and urban planning. Smart cities, powered by IoT and AI, exemplify how digital transformation is reshaping infrastructure, making energy consumption more efficient, reducing traffic congestion, and enhancing public services. The ability to monitor and optimize resource usage in real-time has significant implications for sustainability, positioning the smart economy as a key driver of environmentally conscious economic models.

While the benefits of the smart economy are vast, the transition is not without challenges. The increasing reliance on digital infrastructure raises concerns about cybersecurity risks, data privacy, and algorithmic bias. Cyberattacks on financial institutions, supply chains, and government systems highlight the vulnerabilities of interconnected digital economies. The ethical implications of AI-driven decision-making also require careful consideration, as biased algorithms can reinforce existing inequalities and exclude marginalized populations from economic participation.

Moreover, the growing divide between technologically advanced and underdeveloped regions underscores the need for inclusive digital policies that ensure equal access to the benefits of the smart economy.

The future of economic growth will be shaped by how effectively societies integrate smart technologies while addressing the inherent risks of digital disruption. The role of governments, businesses, and global institutions in regulating and shaping digital economic policies will be crucial in ensuring that the transition to a smart economy is both inclusive and sustainable. As AI, blockchain, and IoT continue to evolve, their impact on economic optimization will become even more pronounced, driving efficiency, resilience, and new opportunities for innovation.

Ultimately, the rise of the smart economy represents a paradigm shift in how economies operate. It is a movement away from static, centralized models towards decentralized, data-driven, and adaptive systems that prioritize efficiency, transparency, and connectivity. While the full potential of the smart economy is still unfolding, its impact on industries, financial markets, and labor dynamics is already evident, signaling a future where digital transformation is the foundation of economic progress.

5- DYNAMIC ECONOMIC SYSTEMS AND ADAPTIVE OPTIMIZATION

The nature of economic systems has undergone a fundamental transformation, shifting from static, equilibrium-based models to dynamic, data-driven systems that continuously adapt to change. Traditional economic models were built upon the assumption that markets function under predictable conditions, allowing for decision-making based on fixed variables and historical trends. However, modern economies operate in a state of perpetual flux, where disruptions caused by financial instability, technological advancements, climate change, and global crises demand a more responsive and adaptive approach. This has led to the rise of dynamic economic systems, which leverage real-time data and intelligent algorithms to optimize decisions in an ever-changing environment.

The key distinction between static and dynamic economic systems lies in their approach to decision-making and uncertainty management. Static models rely on equilibrium-based optimization, assuming that economic variables will eventually settle into a stable state. In contrast, dynamic economic systems function through continuous realignment, adjusting economic policies, resource allocations, and market responses in real time. Table 2 provides a comparative overview of these two paradigms, highlighting how dynamic economic systems differ from their static counterparts.

Table 2. Static vs. Dynamic Economic Systems

Characteristic	Static Economic Systems	Dynamic Economic Systems
Decision-Making Approach	Fixed, based on historical trends	Real-time, data-driven adjustments
Response to Uncertainty	Limited, assumes predictable conditions	Highly responsive, adapts to market fluctuations
Optimization Method	Linear and equilibrium-based models	Machine learning, reinforcement learning, AI-based
Data Utilization	Relies on past data with minimal updates	Uses real-time and predictive analytics
Adaptability to Change	Low, slow to respond to new information	High, continuously evolving with changing conditions

One of the most significant advancements in dynamic economic systems is the integration of adaptive optimization techniques. Unlike traditional optimization methods, which seek a single optimal solution based on past data, adaptive optimization continuously updates its models using real-time information. This capability is particularly crucial in sectors such as financial markets, supply chain management, and macroeconomic policymaking, where decisions must be made under volatile and uncertain conditions. By leveraging AI-driven optimization, businesses and governments can anticipate market shifts, mitigate risks, and enhance efficiency.

A prime example of adaptive optimization in action is reinforcement learning, a subset of machine learning that allows economic models to learn from their environment and improve decision-making over time. Reinforcement learning algorithms are particularly effective in areas such as dynamic pricing, investment strategies, and demand forecasting, where market conditions change unpredictably. By using trial-and-error learning processes, these algorithms can refine strategies, maximizing long-term rewards while minimizing risks.

The role of big data and predictive analytics has also been instrumental in the evolution of dynamic economic systems. Unlike traditional models that rely on historical datasets, modern economies generate vast streams of real-time data from diverse sources, including online transactions, IoT sensors, and social media trends. By harnessing this data, predictive analytics tools can identify emerging economic patterns, allowing for proactive decision-making. In supply chain optimization, for instance, companies use real-time data to adjust inventory levels, reroute logistics, and optimize resource distribution dynamically, ensuring resilience against unforeseen disruptions.

The ability of economic systems to adapt to external shocks is another crucial advantage of dynamic models. The COVID-19 pandemic demonstrated the limitations of static economic planning, as businesses and governments struggled to respond to sudden disruptions in global supply chains and labor markets. In contrast, dynamic economic models equipped with AI-driven forecasting and adaptive optimization were able to adjust in real-time, enabling businesses to pivot their operations and policymakers to implement responsive economic stimulus measures. The integration of digital twins has further enhanced adaptability, allowing for the simulation of economic scenarios and testing optimization strategies before implementing them in the real world.

The growing reliance on dynamic economic systems is also reflected in the speed at which economies adapt to technological and policy changes. Figure 2 illustrates the increasing adaptation speed of dynamic economic systems compared to their static counterparts over time.

Figure 2. Adaptation Speed in Static vs. Dynamic Economic Systems

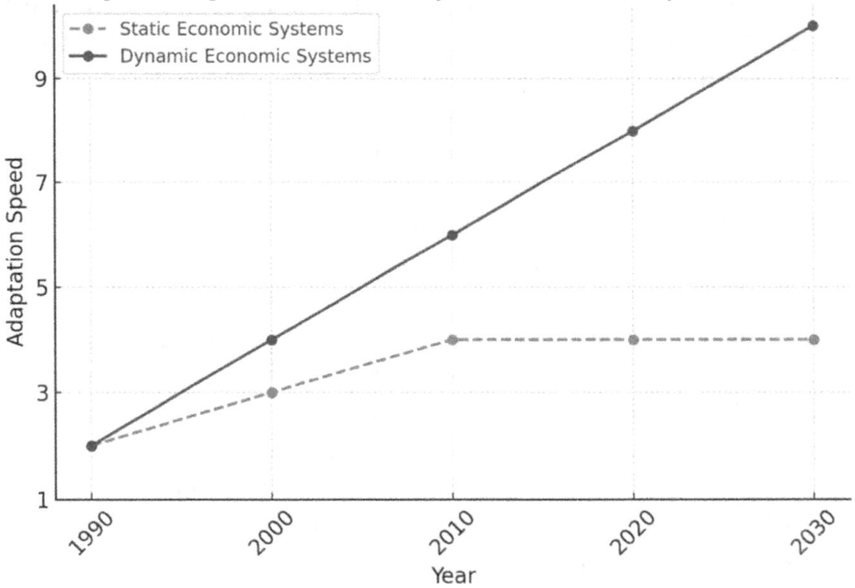

Despite the advantages of dynamic optimization, several challenges remain. The increasing complexity of adaptive models requires significant computational power, and their reliance on real-time data raises concerns about data privacy, cybersecurity, and ethical AI implementation. Additionally, while adaptive optimization enhances efficiency, it also introduces the risk of algorithmic biases, which can reinforce economic inequalities if not properly managed. Policymakers and researchers must work towards developing robust frameworks that balance the benefits of adaptive economic systems with the need for fairness, accountability, and regulatory oversight.

As the global economy continues to evolve, the shift from static to dynamic economic systems will become even more pronounced. Businesses, governments, and financial institutions that embrace adaptive optimization will gain a competitive edge, improving resilience and efficiency in an increasingly unpredictable world. The integration of AI, big data, and real-time analytics will further drive this transformation, enabling economic systems to function more intelligently and autonomously. While challenges remain, the future of economic optimization lies in dynamic, self-learning models that continuously adapt to an ever-changing economic landscape.

6- CONCLUSION

The transformation of economic systems through digitalization and advanced optimization has marked a new era of economic intelligence, adaptability, and efficiency. Traditional static economic models, which relied on fixed assumptions and historical data, are no longer sufficient to navigate the complexities of modern economies. The emergence of smart economies, driven by AI, big data, IoT, blockchain, and real-time analytics, has revolutionized decision-making processes, enabling more dynamic and responsive economic strategies.

Optimization, once confined to linear and equilibrium-based models, has evolved into an adaptive, AI-driven approach that continuously refines decision-making based on real-time inputs. This shift has allowed businesses, policymakers, and financial institutions to improve resource allocation, enhance economic resilience, and drive sustainability. The integration of digital twins, reinforcement learning, and predictive analytics has further strengthened the ability of economies to anticipate and mitigate risks, optimizing performance in an increasingly uncertain world.

Despite these advancements, challenges remain in ensuring fairness, transparency, and security in digitally optimized economic systems. Future research must address issues of algorithmic bias, cybersecurity threats, and digital inequality to ensure that digital transformation benefits all economic participants. Ultimately, the success of economic optimization in the digital age will depend on balancing technological efficiency with ethical considerations and regulatory oversight.

REFERENCES

Ashrafi, A., Constantinides, P., Mehandjiev, N., & Thatcher, J. B. (2025). Mobilising new frontiers in digital transformation research: A problematization review. *Information Systems Journal*, 35(1), 97–139. DOI: 10.1111/isj.12531

Feng, S., Mao, Y., Li, G., & Bai, J. (2025). Enterprise digital transformation, biased technological progress and carbon total factor productivity. *Journal of Environmental Planning and Management*, 68(1), 154–184. DOI: 10.1080/09640568.2023.2239493

Ghobakhloo, M., Iranmanesh, M., Foroughi, B., Tseng, M. L., Nikbin, D., & Khanfar, A. A. (2025). Industry 4.0 digital transformation and opportunities for supply chain resilience: A comprehensive review and a strategic roadmap. *Production Planning and Control*, 36(1), 61–91. DOI: 10.1080/09537287.2023.2252376

Grigorievich, T. A. (2025). METHODOLOGICAL APPROACH TO THE DEVELOPMENT OF DIGITAL TRANSFORMATION OF AN ENTERPRISE.

Joel, O. T., & Oguanobi, V. U. (2024). Navigating business transformation and strategic decision-making in multinational energy corporations with geodata. *International Journal of Applied Research in Social Sciences*, 6(5), 801–818. DOI: 10.51594/ijarss.v6i5.1103

Movahed, A. B., Movahed, A. B., & Nozari, H. (2024). Opportunities and Challenges of Marketing 5.0. *Smart and Sustainable Interactive Marketing*, 1-21.

Onesi-Ozigagun, O., Ololade, Y. J., Eyo-Udo, N. L., & Ogundipe, D. O. (2024). Leading digital transformation in non-digital sectors: A strategic review. *International Journal of Management & Entrepreneurship Research*, 6(4), 1157–1175. DOI: 10.51594/ijmer.v6i4.1005

Rahmaty, M., & Nozari, H. (2023). Optimization of the hierarchical supply chain in the pharmaceutical industry. *Edelweiss Applied Science and Technology*, 7(2), 104–123. DOI: 10.55214/25768484.v7i2.376

Sikki, N., Aripin, Z., & Fitrianti, N. G. (2024). Business innovation and critical success factors in digital transformation and challenging times: An econometric analysis of startup viability and success. *KRIEZ ACADEMY: Journal of development and community service, 1*(2), 1-15.

Su, Y., & Wu, J. (2024). Digital transformation and enterprise sustainable development. *Finance Research Letters*, 60, 104902. DOI: 10.1016/j.frl.2023.104902

Szmelter-Jarosz, A., Ghahremani-Nahr, J., & Nozari, H. (2021). A neutrosophic fuzzy optimisation model for optimal sustainable closed-loop supply chain network during COVID-19. *Journal of Risk and Financial Management*, 14(11), 519. DOI: 10.3390/jrfm14110519

Tang, J., Li, W., Hu, J., & Ren, Y. (2025). Can government digital transformation improve corporate energy efficiency in resource-based cities? *Energy Economics*, 141, 108043. DOI: 10.1016/j.eneco.2024.108043

Yang, Y., Ren, H., Liu, Y., & Yang, Y. (2025). Integration of technology and finance, digital transformation and corporate green innovation. *Finance Research Letters*, 71, 106444. DOI: 10.1016/j.frl.2024.106444

Zhang, Y., & Wang, J. (2024). Research on influencing factors and path of digital transformation of manufacturing enterprises. *Kybernetes*, 53(2), 752–762. DOI: 10.1108/K-06-2023-1042

Chapter 2
Emerging Technologies in Financial Process Optimization and Risk Management

Majid Sabkara
Organization of Commercialization and Knowledge-Based Economy, Iran

Mahdi Aliyari
https://orcid.org/0009-0005-1325-6800
Islamic Azad University, Shabestar, Iran

Masoumeh Lajevardi
Islamic Azad University, Najafabad, Iran

ABSTRACT

The rapid advancement of financial technology (FinTech) has revolutionized the financial sector by integrating artificial intelligence, blockchain, quantum computing, IoT, and digital payments. These innovations enhance efficiency, security, and accessibility while introducing new cybersecurity challenges such as fraud, identity theft, and ransomware attacks. This research explores emerging FinTech trends, cybersecurity risks, and mitigation strategies to ensure a secure and transparent financial ecosystem. Future advancements in AI-driven automation, decentralized finance (DeFi), and quantum encryption will further shape the financial industry's digital transformation.

DOI: 10.4018/979-8-3693-4369-2.ch002

1- INTRODUCTION

The rapid evolution of technology has fundamentally transformed the financial landscape, ushering in a new era often referred to as Smart Finance. This transformation is driven by advancements in Artificial Intelligence (AI), Blockchain, Internet of Things (IoT), Big Data Analytics, and Cloud Computing, among other disruptive technologies. These innovations have redefined how financial institutions, businesses, and individuals manage money, assess risks, and optimize financial processes. Unlike traditional finance, which relies heavily on human expertise and manual decision-making, smart finance integrates automation, real-time data analysis, and predictive modeling to enhance efficiency, accuracy, and security (Nozari et al., 2023).

At the heart of smart finance lies the ability to leverage data-driven insights for strategic decision-making. With the advent of AI and machine learning, financial institutions can now process vast amounts of data in real-time, enabling precise risk assessment, fraud detection, and automated trading strategies. AI-powered chatbots and virtual assistants have also revolutionized customer service, providing personalized financial recommendations and enhancing user experience. The introduction of robo-advisors has further streamlined investment management, allowing individuals to access sophisticated portfolio strategies without the need for human financial advisors (Ali et al., 2009).

Blockchain technology has introduced an unprecedented level of transparency, security, and decentralization to financial transactions. The ability to execute smart contracts on blockchain networks ensures that agreements are automatically enforced without intermediaries, reducing costs and improving trust. Cryptocurrencies, which operate on blockchain, have challenged traditional banking structures, offering alternative payment methods that bypass centralized financial institutions. The potential of decentralized finance (DeFi) is reshaping lending, borrowing, and asset management, creating new opportunities and risks that financial professionals must navigate.

One of the most transformative forces in smart finance is the Internet of Things (IoT), which connects physical devices to digital financial ecosystems. IoT enables real-time tracking of assets, automated financial transactions, and seamless integration of financial services with everyday objects. From smart payment terminals to connected insurance policies that adjust premiums based on real-time behavior, IoT is driving the next wave of financial automation. The integration of IoT with AI and blockchain enhances risk management strategies by providing continuous monitoring, predictive insights, and secure, automated execution of financial operations (Khor et al., 2011).

Big Data Analytics plays a pivotal role in extracting meaningful patterns from massive datasets, allowing financial institutions to make data-driven decisions. By analyzing consumer behavior, market trends, and economic indicators, businesses can develop more effective investment strategies and optimize credit risk assessments. The rise of alternative credit scoring models, which use non-traditional data sources such as social media activity and transaction histories, has expanded financial inclusion by offering credit to previously underserved populations (Diagne, 2022).

While these emerging technologies bring numerous benefits, they also introduce significant challenges and risks. Cybersecurity threats, data privacy concerns, and regulatory uncertainties remain key obstacles in the adoption of smart finance. Financial institutions must invest in robust security frameworks to protect against cyberattacks, while policymakers must establish clear regulatory guidelines to balance innovation with consumer protection. The ethical implications of AI-driven financial decisions also require careful consideration, as biased algorithms and automated trading systems can have unintended consequences on markets and individuals.

The transition to smart finance is not merely a technological shift but a fundamental transformation in financial behavior, strategy, and governance. Organizations that embrace these advancements gain a competitive edge, while those resistant to change risk obsolescence. The financial sector must continuously adapt to new technological paradigms, fostering a culture of innovation, agility, and ethical responsibility.

Looking ahead, the future of smart finance will be shaped by the convergence of AI, quantum computing, and decentralized technologies, further enhancing automation, decision-making accuracy, and financial accessibility. As financial institutions navigate this digital revolution, collaboration between technology developers, regulators, and financial professionals will be crucial in ensuring a secure, efficient, and inclusive financial ecosystem.

By understanding and leveraging emerging technologies, businesses and individuals can unlock new opportunities, mitigate financial risks, and drive sustainable growth in an increasingly interconnected and intelligent financial world.

2- THE ROLE OF ARTIFICIAL INTELLIGENCE IN FINANCIAL DECISION-MAKING

The integration of Artificial Intelligence (AI) in financial decision-making has revolutionized the way businesses, institutions, and individuals manage their finances. AI-driven solutions have significantly enhanced the speed, accuracy, and efficiency of financial processes, enabling organizations to make data-backed decisions with minimal human intervention. By leveraging machine learning, deep learning, and natural language processing (NLP), AI can analyze vast amounts of financial data in real time, detect patterns, and predict market trends with a level of precision that was previously unattainable.

One of the most profound impacts of AI in finance is its ability to automate complex decision-making processes. Traditional financial models often rely on historical data and statistical methods, which can be limited in their ability to predict future outcomes. AI, on the other hand, continuously learns from new data, refining its predictions and adapting to changing market conditions. This is particularly valuable in risk assessment, fraud detection, credit scoring, and investment management, where even minor miscalculations can have significant financial consequences (Raffak et al., 2024).

AI-powered algorithmic trading has transformed financial markets by executing trades at speeds and frequencies beyond human capabilities. These trading algorithms analyze historical market data, identify profitable opportunities, and execute transactions within milliseconds. As a result, AI-driven trading systems can minimize risks, maximize returns, and optimize portfolios in real time. Similarly, robo-advisors have democratized investment management by providing personalized financial recommendations based on individual risk tolerance, investment goals, and market conditions. These automated advisory systems have made wealth management accessible to a broader audience while reducing management fees (Petrovskaya et al., 2016).

Another critical application of AI in financial decision-making is fraud detection and risk management. Traditional fraud detection systems rely on rule-based approaches that can be ineffective against sophisticated cyber threats. AI, however, employs anomaly detection algorithms to identify suspicious transactions, flagging potential fraudulent activities before they cause significant damage. By analyzing transaction history, user behavior, and spending patterns, AI can detect unusual deviations and proactively prevent financial crimes. Similarly, AI-enhanced credit risk assessment models use alternative data sources, such as online behavior and transaction history, to provide more accurate credit scores, enabling financial institutions to extend credit to underserved populations (Di Renzo et al., 2007).

AI-driven predictive analytics has also transformed financial forecasting and strategic planning. By processing unstructured data from news articles, social media, and economic reports, AI can anticipate market fluctuations and assess geopolitical risks. This capability allows businesses to make informed decisions regarding currency exchange, commodity pricing, and investment strategies. Furthermore, AI-powered chatbots and virtual assistants have enhanced customer interactions by providing real-time financial guidance, answering queries, and automating routine banking tasks, improving operational efficiency and customer satisfaction (Li et al., 2023).

The many advantages of AI-driven financial decision-making can be categorized into key applications, each contributing to a more efficient, secure, and intelligent financial ecosystem. Table 1 summarizes these core applications, their functions, and the key benefits they provide.

Table 1. Key Applications of AI in Financial Decision-Making

Application	Function	Key Benefits
Algorithmic Trading	Analyzing market data to execute high-frequency trades	Improved efficiency, reduced risks, higher returns
Robo-Advisors	Providing automated investment advice	Cost-effective, personalized portfolio management
Fraud Detection	Identifying anomalies in transactions	Enhanced security, real-time fraud prevention
Credit Scoring	Assessing creditworthiness using alternative data	Expanded financial inclusion, reduced defaults
Predictive Analytics	Forecasting market trends and economic shifts	Data-driven decision-making, proactive risk management
Chatbots & Virtual Assistants	Automating customer interactions and financial queries	Increased efficiency, enhanced user experience

Despite its many advantages, the widespread adoption of AI in financial decision-making also raises ethical and regulatory concerns. The use of AI-driven decision-making systems can introduce biases if the underlying data is skewed or incomplete. Additionally, the lack of transparency in AI models, often referred to as the "black box" problem, can make it difficult to interpret how decisions are made. As AI continues to reshape finance, regulators must establish clear guidelines to ensure ethical AI usage, data privacy, and consumer protection (Ren, 2022).

As the financial sector continues to embrace AI-driven innovations, organizations that adopt these technologies will gain a significant competitive edge. The future of AI in finance will likely involve self-learning systems, quantum computing applications, and enhanced cybersecurity frameworks, ensuring a more intelligent, secure, and efficient financial landscape. Those who fail to integrate AI into their financial strategies risk falling behind in an increasingly automated and data-driven world.

3- BLOCKCHAIN FOR SECURE AND TRANSPARENT FINANCIAL TRANSACTIONS

The financial industry has long relied on centralized intermediaries to facilitate transactions, verify records, and enforce agreements. While traditional systems have provided stability, they are often burdened by inefficiencies, security vulnerabilities, and high operational costs. The emergence of blockchain technology has introduced a paradigm shift in financial transactions, offering a decentralized, transparent, and highly secure alternative. By leveraging distributed ledger technology (DLT), blockchain enables financial institutions, businesses, and individuals to conduct transactions without relying on intermediaries, reducing costs while enhancing trust and security.

At the core of blockchain's impact on finance is its ability to record transactions in an immutable and transparent manner. Unlike traditional databases, which are controlled by central entities, blockchain operates as a decentralized network where every transaction is cryptographically secured and stored in a chain of blocks. This structure makes it nearly impossible to alter or manipulate financial records, ensuring the integrity of transactional data. Once a transaction is recorded, it is verified by consensus mechanisms, such as Proof of Work (PoW) or Proof of Stake (PoS), before being added to the blockchain. This verification process prevents fraud, double-spending, and unauthorized modifications, making blockchain a trustless yet highly reliable financial infrastructure (Chahal, 2023).

One of the most transformative applications of blockchain in finance is the use of smart contracts. These self-executing contracts are encoded with predefined conditions and automatically enforce agreements without the need for intermediaries. Smart contracts eliminate the risks associated with manual processing, contract disputes, and human error, ensuring faster and more efficient financial transactions. This capability is particularly valuable in areas such as cross-border payments, trade finance, and loan agreements, where delays and inefficiencies often arise due to multiple layers of verification. By automating compliance and execution, smart contracts reduce operational costs and enhance transaction transparency (Zhang, 2020).

Another key advantage of blockchain is its role in enhancing financial security. Traditional banking systems and payment networks are often susceptible to cyberattacks, data breaches, and fraudulent activities. Blockchain mitigates these risks by implementing advanced cryptographic techniques that secure financial data at every stage of a transaction. Since each block is linked to the previous one through a cryptographic hash, any attempt to alter historical transactions would require modifying all subsequent blocks—a nearly impossible feat given the computational power required. This makes blockchain one of the most secure infrastructures for digital payments, asset transfers, and identity verification (Sadeghi et al., 2021).

The transparency provided by blockchain further strengthens its appeal in financial transactions. Unlike opaque financial systems where data is often hidden or accessible only to select entities, blockchain enables real-time visibility into transaction records. This level of transparency fosters accountability, reduces corruption, and builds greater trust among stakeholders. Financial regulators and auditing bodies can leverage blockchain to monitor transactions more effectively, ensuring compliance with anti-money laundering (AML) and know-your-customer (KYC) regulations.

While blockchain offers significant advantages, its widespread adoption faces challenges, including scalability, regulatory uncertainty, and energy consumption. Public blockchain networks, such as Bitcoin and Ethereum, often struggle with transaction speed and scalability, leading to congestion and high fees. However, advancements like Layer 2 solutions and consensus mechanism improvements are addressing these limitations, making blockchain more viable for large-scale financial applications. Regulatory frameworks also continue to evolve, as governments and financial institutions seek to balance innovation with compliance.

The future of blockchain in finance is promising, with ongoing developments in decentralized finance (DeFi), tokenization of assets, and central bank digital currencies (CBDCs). As financial institutions integrate blockchain into their operations, the industry will move toward a more secure, transparent, and efficient financial ecosystem. Those who embrace blockchain technology will gain a competitive edge in the evolving digital economy, while those who resist risk being left behind in an era of decentralized financial innovation.

4- RISK MANAGEMENT OF FINANCIAL PROCESSES BASED ON THE INTERNET OF THINGS

The Internet of Things (IoT) has revolutionized various industries by enabling seamless connectivity between devices, data collection in real-time, and intelligent automation. In the financial sector, IoT plays a transformative role in risk management, providing businesses and financial institutions with enhanced capabilities to monitor, analyze, and mitigate financial risks with unprecedented accuracy. By integrating IoT-driven financial analytics, predictive risk models, and automated decision-making, organizations can proactively identify vulnerabilities and safeguard their financial processes from emerging threats.

At the heart of IoT-powered risk management lies its ability to generate and process vast amounts of real-time financial data. Traditional risk assessment models often rely on historical data, making them less effective in predicting dynamic market fluctuations, fraud patterns, and operational inefficiencies. IoT, however, enables continuous data flow from connected devices, such as point-of-sale (POS) terminals, smart ATMs, digital payment platforms, and blockchain-enabled financial contracts. This allows financial institutions to track transactions, detect anomalies, and intervene before potential risks escalate into major financial crises.

One of the key challenges in financial risk management is fraud detection and prevention. Cybercriminals are constantly developing sophisticated methods to exploit financial systems, leading to fraudulent transactions, identity theft, and unauthorized access to sensitive data. IoT enhances fraud mitigation strategies by utilizing biometric authentication, geo-location tracking, and behavioral analytics. For instance, if a user's banking account suddenly experiences suspicious activity from an unfamiliar device or geographic location, IoT sensors can trigger an immediate security alert, requesting additional verification before processing high-risk transactions. This real-time monitoring mechanism significantly reduces the likelihood of fraudulent activities going undetected.

Another critical aspect of IoT-driven financial risk management is operational risk reduction. In banking and financial services, even minor system failures, downtime, or cybersecurity breaches can result in significant financial losses and reputational damage. IoT-enabled monitoring systems allow banks to oversee hardware performance, ATM network stability, and cloud-based transaction infrastructures. Predictive maintenance powered by AI and IoT sensors helps detect system irregularities, ensuring that potential failures are addressed before they impact financial operations. By minimizing service disruptions and technical vulnerabilities, IoT strengthens the resilience of financial institutions against operational risks.

Beyond fraud detection and operational security, IoT also plays a crucial role in risk assessment for insurance and lending. Traditionally, banks and insurance companies evaluate creditworthiness and risk exposure based on static financial statements and demographic data. However, IoT allows insurers and lenders to leverage real-time behavioral data collected from smart devices, connected vehicles, and wearables. For example, in usage-based insurance (UBI) models, IoT sensors installed in vehicles track driving patterns to offer customized insurance premiums based on individual risk profiles. Similarly, financial institutions can use IoT-generated data to assess borrowers' financial behaviors dynamically, leading to more accurate credit scoring and loan approvals.

The integration of IoT in financial risk management does not come without challenges. The sheer volume of data generated by interconnected financial systems raises concerns about data privacy, cybersecurity threats, and regulatory compliance. Financial institutions must implement strong encryption protocols, AI-driven anomaly detection, and blockchain-based security measures to protect sensitive financial data. Regulatory bodies worldwide are continuously adapting their policies to address the ethical and legal implications of IoT-driven risk management, ensuring that consumer rights are safeguarded while fostering financial innovation.

As IoT technology continues to advance, its role in financial risk management will expand further. The convergence of IoT with artificial intelligence, blockchain, and quantum computing will lead to autonomous financial systems capable of making split-second risk mitigation decisions without human intervention. This future will usher in an era of proactive, data-driven financial security, where organizations can predict and prevent risks rather than merely reacting to them. Financial institutions that embrace IoT-driven risk management will enhance their security frameworks, improve decision-making, and maintain a competitive edge in an increasingly interconnected and intelligent financial landscape.

5- CYBERSECURITY CHALLENGES IN DIGITAL FINANCIAL ECOSYSTEMS

The rapid digitization of financial services has brought unparalleled convenience, efficiency, and scalability, but it has also introduced a complex set of cybersecurity challenges. In today's digital financial ecosystems, where transactions occur within milliseconds and vast amounts of sensitive data are exchanged across networks, cybersecurity is no longer an option—it is an absolute necessity. As financial institutions adopt emerging technologies such as artificial intelligence, blockchain, and the Internet of Things (IoT), they must also confront sophisticated cyber threats that continue to evolve in complexity and scale.

One of the most pressing cybersecurity challenges in digital finance is the rise of cyberattacks targeting financial institutions and payment networks. Hackers deploy advanced tactics such as ransomware, phishing attacks, and Distributed Denial-of-Service (DDoS) attacks to exploit system vulnerabilities and gain unauthorized access to financial data. A successful cyberattack can compromise customer accounts, financial transactions, and even entire banking infrastructures, leading to devastating financial and reputational losses. High-profile data breaches have exposed millions of sensitive records, undermining public trust in financial systems.

The increased reliance on cloud computing and decentralized financial technologies (DeFi) has further expanded the attack surface for cybercriminals. Many financial institutions store critical data and operate payment infrastructures on cloud platforms, making them susceptible to cloud security breaches and insider threats. While cloud services offer scalability and accessibility, they also introduce risks related to data leakage, misconfigurations, and weak access controls. In decentralized finance, where smart contracts govern financial transactions, vulnerabilities in the underlying code can be exploited by attackers to manipulate funds or disrupt financial operations.

Identity theft and fraud are growing concerns in digital financial ecosystems, fueled by the widespread use of digital payment methods, online banking, and mobile wallets. Cybercriminals use social engineering tactics and AI-driven deepfake technology to bypass traditional authentication methods, impersonate legitimate users, and conduct unauthorized transactions. Biometric authentication, multi-factor authentication (MFA), and AI-driven fraud detection are now being implemented to mitigate these risks, but cybercriminals continuously find ways to bypass security mechanisms.

To illustrate the primary cybersecurity challenges and the corresponding security solutions in digital financial ecosystems, Table 2 provides an overview of key threats and mitigation strategies.

Table 2. Cybersecurity Challenges and Solutions in Digital Finance

Cybersecurity Challenge	Description	Mitigation Strategy
Phishing Attacks	Deceptive emails and messages to steal credentials	AI-powered email filtering, user education
Ransomware	Malicious software encrypting financial data	Advanced endpoint security, data backups
DDoS Attacks	Overloading financial servers to disrupt services	Cloud-based traffic filtering, firewalls
Cloud Security Breaches	Unauthorized access to cloud-stored financial data	Strong encryption, zero-trust architecture
Smart Contract Exploits	Manipulation of decentralized financial transactions	Code audits, automated contract verification
Identity Theft	Fraudulent use of personal and financial details	Biometric authentication, MFA, AI fraud detection
Insider Threats	Employees leaking sensitive financial information	Strict access controls, behavioral monitoring

Regulatory compliance and data privacy further complicate cybersecurity for digital financial institutions. Governments worldwide enforce stringent regulations such as the General Data Protection Regulation (GDPR) and the Payment Card Industry Data Security Standard (PCI DSS), requiring financial institutions to maintain robust security standards. However, navigating compliance is challenging, as regulations vary across jurisdictions, necessitating a global approach to cybersecurity governance (Mamchur et al., 2023).

To mitigate these cybersecurity risks, financial institutions are turning to advanced security technologies such as AI-driven threat detection, blockchain security solutions, and quantum cryptography. AI-powered cybersecurity systems can analyze vast amounts of financial data in real time, identifying anomalies and preventing fraudulent activities before they escalate. Blockchain provides decentralized and tamper-proof transaction records, reducing the risk of data breaches and unauthorized alterations. Meanwhile, quantum cryptography holds the potential to revolutionize financial security by creating encryption methods that are virtually unbreakable.

Despite these advancements, the human factor remains a critical vulnerability in cybersecurity. Even the most sophisticated security systems can be compromised by human error, insider threats, or negligence. Financial institutions must invest in cybersecurity training programs, strict access control policies, and continuous security assessments to strengthen their defense against cyber risks.

As digital financial ecosystems continue to expand, cybersecurity will remain a persistent and evolving challenge. The future of secure financial transactions depends on proactive threat intelligence, adaptive security frameworks, and a culture of cybersecurity awareness. Financial institutions that prioritize

cybersecurity will not only protect their assets and customers but will also contribute to the long-term resilience and sustainability of the global financial ecosystem.

6- FUTURE TRENDS AND INNOVATIONS IN FINANCIAL TECHNOLOGY (FINTECH)

The financial technology (FinTech) landscape is evolving at an unprecedented pace, driven by rapid advancements in artificial intelligence, blockchain, decentralized finance (DeFi), quantum computing, and digital banking ecosystems. As financial institutions, businesses, and consumers increasingly adopt digital solutions, the future of FinTech promises greater automation, security, and accessibility. Emerging technologies are not only reshaping traditional banking and investment models but are also paving the way for hyper-personalized financial services, real-time transactions, and frictionless cross-border payments.

One of the most significant trends shaping the future of FinTech is the widespread adoption of artificial intelligence (AI) and machine learning (ML) in financial decision-making. AI-driven automation is expected to enhance fraud detection, optimize risk assessment models, and provide AI-powered robo-advisors that deliver real-time investment insights. AI-enabled chatbots and virtual assistants are also becoming more sophisticated, offering personalized customer interactions and streamlining banking operations. The convergence of AI with big data analytics allows financial institutions to predict market trends, improve customer profiling, and optimize lending models based on alternative credit scoring.

Blockchain and decentralized finance (DeFi) are redefining financial transactions by offering transparent, secure, and trustless financial systems. The rise of smart contracts and decentralized lending platforms is eliminating the need for traditional intermediaries, reducing transaction costs, and enabling financial inclusion for underserved populations. Governments and central banks are also exploring Central Bank Digital Currencies (CBDCs) as a means to modernize payment systems and improve cross-border transaction efficiency. Tokenization of real-world assets, such as real estate and commodities, is gaining traction, allowing fractional ownership and liquidity in traditionally illiquid markets.

Quantum computing is poised to revolutionize FinTech by solving complex financial problems that are currently beyond the reach of classical computers. Quantum algorithms will accelerate risk modeling, optimize portfolio management, and enhance cybersecurity by enabling unbreakable encryption protocols. While still in its infancy, quantum computing has the potential to disrupt the financial sector by introducing near-instantaneous fraud detection and ultra-fast transaction processing.

The demand for seamless digital payments and embedded finance solutions is also increasing, driven by the rise of super apps, mobile wallets, and real-time payment infrastructures. FinTech firms are embedding financial services directly into non-financial platforms, enabling "banking-as-a-service" (BaaS) models that provide instant credit, insurance, and payment solutions. The integration of IoT-enabled financial services is further transforming payments, with wearables and smart devices facilitating contactless transactions and real-time financial tracking.

To illustrate how emerging technologies are shaping the future of FinTech, Table 3 provides an overview of key innovations and their impact on the financial sector.

Table 3. Emerging Technologies and Their Impact on FinTech

Technology	Key Innovations	Impact on FinTech
AI & ML	Fraud detection, robo-advisors, predictive analytics	Enhanced security, personalized financial services
Blockchain & DeFi	Smart contracts, decentralized lending, tokenization	Reduced transaction costs, increased transparency
Quantum Computing	Quantum encryption, risk modeling, high-speed trading	Unbreakable security, ultra-fast transactions
Digital Payments	Real-time payments, mobile wallets, embedded finance	Seamless transactions, improved financial inclusion
IoT in Finance	Connected banking, automated payments, smart contracts	Frictionless payments, IoT-enabled fraud detection

To better understand the adoption rate and projected growth of these innovations, the Figure 1 illustrates the expected FinTech market growth trends from 2023 to 2030 based on emerging technology adoption.

Figure 1. Projected Growth Trends In FinTech Technologies (2023-2030)

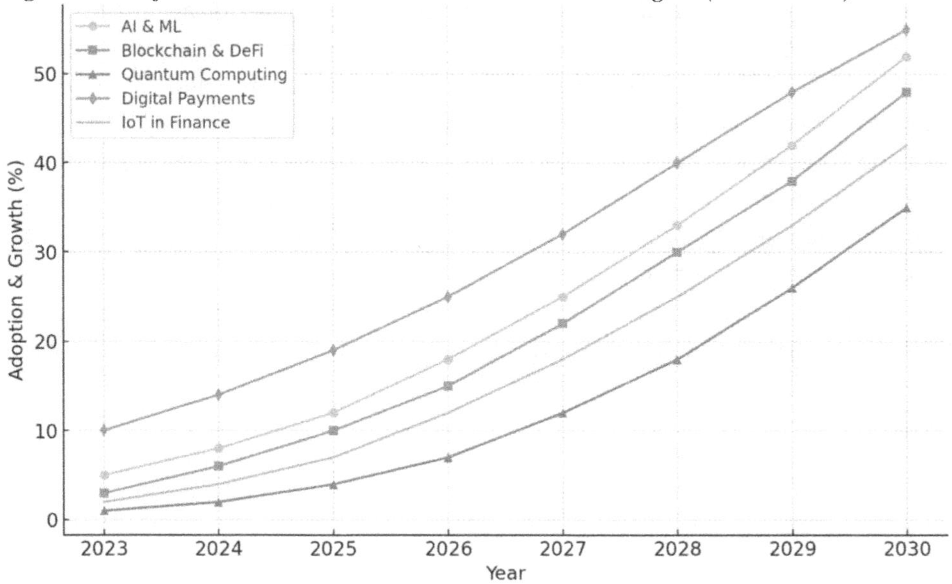

Figure 1 illustrates the projected growth trends of emerging FinTech technologies from 2023 to 2030, showing how AI & ML, Blockchain & DeFi, Quantum Computing, Digital Payments, and IoT in Finance are expected to expand.

7- CONCLUSION

The evolution of financial technology (FinTech) is redefining the global financial landscape, driven by innovations in artificial intelligence, blockchain, quantum computing, IoT, and digital payments. These technologies have introduced unprecedented efficiency, security, and accessibility in financial processes, transforming risk management, investment strategies, and consumer banking. The adoption of AI has enhanced fraud detection, personalized financial services, and algorithmic trading, while blockchain and decentralized finance (DeFi) have eliminated intermediaries, increased transparency and reducing costs.

Despite these advancements, cybersecurity challenges remain a critical concern. The growing complexity of digital financial ecosystems has introduced new risks, including phishing attacks, ransomware, identity theft, and cloud security breaches. Financial institutions must integrate AI-driven threat detection, biometric authentication, and blockchain-based security frameworks to ensure resilience against cyber threats. Moreover, regulatory compliance remains a challenge, requiring global cooperation to balance financial innovation with consumer protection and data privacy.

Looking ahead, FinTech's future will be shaped by continued advancements in AI-driven automation, quantum encryption, decentralized banking, and IoT-integrated financial systems. The adoption of Central Bank Digital Currencies (CBDCs) and embedded finance will further disrupt traditional banking, creating new opportunities for financial inclusion. However, successful implementation will require a holistic approach that integrates technological innovation, robust cybersecurity measures, and ethical governance frameworks.

The financial sector must embrace a proactive mindset, ensuring that emerging technologies drive sustainable, secure, and inclusive financial growth in an increasingly interconnected world.

REFERENCES

Ai, J., Brockett, P. L., Cooper, W. W., & Golden, L. L. (2009, July). *An Optimization Approach to Enterprise Risk Management: An Aid to Financial Decision Management for Risk, Crisis and Opportunity.*

Chahal, S. (2023). Navigating Financial Evolution: Business process optimization and digital transformation in the finance sector. *International Journal of Finance*, 8(5), 67–81. DOI: 10.47941/ijf.1475

Di Renzo, B., Hillairet, M., Picard, M., Rifaut, A., Bernard, C., Hagen, D., Maar, P., & Reinard, D. (2007). Operational risk management in financial institutions: Process assessment in concordance with Basel II. *Software Process Improvement and Practice*, 12(4), 321–330. DOI: 10.1002/spip.322

Diagne, M. (2002). *Financial Risk Management and Portfolio Optimization Using Artificial Neural Networks and Extreme Value Theory* (Doctoral dissertation, Technische Universität Kaiserslautern).

Khor, C. S., Giarola, S., Chachuat, B., & Shah, N. (2011). An optimization-based framework for process planning under uncertainty with risk management. *Chemical Product and Process Modeling*, 6(2). Advance online publication. DOI: 10.2202/1934-2659.1597

Li, X., Wang, J., & Yang, C. (2023). Risk prediction in financial management of listed companies based on optimized BP neural network under digital economy. *Neural Computing & Applications*, 35(3), 2045–2058. DOI: 10.1007/s00521-022-07377-0

Mamchur, R., Minochkina, O., Ianushevych, I., & Khrystenko, L. (2023). Optimization of operational and financial risks of conducting business activities under the conditions of changes and sustainable development. *Economic Affairs*, 68(1s), 91–98. DOI: 10.46852/0424-2513.1s.2023.11

Nozari, H., & Edalatpanah, S. A. (2023). Smart Systems Risk Management in IoT-Based Supply Chain. In *Advances in Reliability, Failure and Risk Analysis* (pp. 251–268). Springer Nature Singapore. DOI: 10.1007/978-981-19-9909-3_11

Petrovskaya, M. V., Zaitseva, N. A., Bondarchuk, N. V., Grigorieva, E. M., & Vasilieva, L. S. (2016). Scientific methodological basis of the risk management implementation for companies' capital structure optimization. *International Electronic Journal of Mathematics Education*, 11(7), 2571–2580.

Raffak, H., Lakhouili, A., & Mansouri, M. (2024). Continuous Integration of Risk Management in a Business Process Reengineering: Towards Optimization through Machine Learning. *Emerging Science Journal*, 8(3), 1118–1135. DOI: 10.28991/ESJ-2024-08-03-019

Ren, S. (2022). Optimization of Enterprise Financial Management and Decision-Making Systems Based on Big Data. *Journal of Mathematics*, 2022(1), 1708506. DOI: 10.1155/2022/1708506

Sadeghi, M. E., Nozari, H., Dezfoli, H. K., & Khajezadeh, M. (2021). Ranking of different of investment risk in high-tech projects using TOPSIS method in fuzzy environment based on linguistic variables. *arXiv preprint arXiv:2111.14665.*

Zhang, H. (2020). Optimization of risk control in financial markets based on particle swarm optimization algorithm. *Journal of Computational and Applied Mathematics*, 368, 112530. DOI: 10.1016/j.cam.2019.112530

Chapter 3
Harnessing Cyber-Physical Systems and Digital Twins for Industrial Innovation and Economic Resilience

Zornitsa Yordanova
https://orcid.org/0000-0002-6056-8445
University of National and World Economy, Sofia, Bulgaria

Hamed Nozari
https://orcid.org/0000-0002-6500-6708
Independent Researcher, Australia

ABSTRACT

This research explores the impact of Cyber-Physical Systems (CPS) and Digital Twins on industrial efficiency, economic resilience, and intelligent decision-making. By integrating real-time monitoring, AI-driven analytics, and predictive modeling, these technologies enhance cost efficiency, production optimization, and risk mitigation. The study highlights how automation, digital simulations, and data-driven forecasting contribute to supply chain adaptability, operational sustainability, and economic growth. Findings suggest that CPS and Digital Twins are essential for modernizing industries and fostering resilient economic systems in dynamic global markets.

DOI: 10.4018/979-8-3693-4369-2.ch003

1- INTRODUCTION

The rapid advancement of Cyber-Physical Systems (CPS) and Digital Twins has fundamentally transformed industrial operations, economic models, and decision-making frameworks. As industries navigate an era defined by automation, artificial intelligence (AI), and real-time data analytics, the integration of these technologies has become essential for enhancing efficiency, reducing costs, and improving economic resilience. In an increasingly interconnected global economy, businesses and governments are seeking innovative solutions to address challenges such as supply chain disruptions, production inefficiencies, market volatility, and sustainability concerns. Digital Twins and CPS, through their ability to replicate, simulate, and optimize physical systems in real-time, provide a data-driven foundation for industrial and economic transformation (Amit Bhardwaj, 2024).

The emergence of Industry 4.0 and the expansion of intelligent automation have positioned Digital Twins as a key enabler of smart manufacturing, predictive analytics, and strategic economic planning. These virtual models, powered by AI, machine learning (ML), and the Internet of Things (IoT), allow industries to continuously monitor processes, analyze performance, and anticipate potential failures before they occur. By creating a dynamic connection between physical assets and their digital counterparts, organizations can optimize production, reduce downtime, and improve resource allocation. This not only lowers operational costs but also enhances scalability and sustainability, making Digital Twins an essential component of modern economic frameworks. The ability to integrate real-time insights with automated decision-making has profound implications for industries ranging from manufacturing and logistics to healthcare, smart cities, and renewable energy management (Andronie et a., 2021).

Economic resilience, a critical factor in global competitiveness, has become increasingly dependent on technological innovation and digital infrastructure. Traditional economic models often rely on static data and delayed decision-making, limiting their ability to respond dynamically to evolving market conditions. In contrast, Digital Twins and CPS provide adaptive, real-time solutions that allow businesses and policymakers to make data-driven decisions in response to economic fluctuations, supply chain constraints, and global uncertainties (Kumar & Agrawal, 2024). By integrating AI-powered analytics, these technologies enable organizations to forecast demand, mitigate risks, and enhance long-term financial stability. The adoption of Digital Twins is not just about improving industrial operations—it represents a strategic shift toward a more agile, intelligent, and sustainable economic paradigm (Lampropoulos et al., 2023).

The impact of real-time digital modeling and predictive analytics extends beyond operational efficiency, influencing global economic structures and industrial policies. In manufacturing, Digital Twins revolutionize production planning, automate quality control, and optimize energy consumption, leading to more efficient and eco-friendly production systems. In logistics, CPS enhances inventory management, fleet coordination, and last-mile delivery, reducing costs and improving service reliability (Bongomin et al., 2024). Meanwhile, in smart cities, these technologies contribute to intelligent infrastructure planning, optimized traffic management, and resource-efficient urban development, aligning with broader sustainability and economic growth objectives. The interconnected nature of these applications underscores the cross-industry potential of CPS and Digital Twins, reinforcing their role as foundational tools for industrial innovation and economic development (Ghansah & LU, 2023).

Despite the clear advantages of Digital Twins and CPS, challenges remain in scaling their adoption, ensuring cybersecurity, and addressing interoperability concerns. Many industries still struggle with legacy systems that are incompatible with advanced digital simulations, limiting their ability to fully leverage real-time automation and predictive modeling. Additionally, the vast amounts of data generated by these technologies require robust data governance policies, AI-driven insights, and scalable cloud computing infrastructure. The economic feasibility of widespread digital twin adoption also depends on investment in digital literacy, workforce training, and regulatory frameworks that support seamless technology integration. Addressing these challenges is essential for unlocking the full potential of Cyber-Physical Systems and Digital Twins in driving economic resilience and industrial growth (Bhambri et al., 2024).

As industries and economies increasingly rely on automation and data intelligence, the need to understand the role of Digital Twins in economic transformation becomes more pressing. This study explores how these technologies contribute to cost efficiency, production optimization, and predictive accuracy, ultimately shaping the future of smart industries and adaptive economies. By analyzing key performance indicators and economic implications, this research provides a comprehensive evaluation of how CPS-driven digital twin systems enhance industrial productivity, economic stability, and market adaptability. The findings offer insights into the potential for AI-powered digital modeling to revolutionize decision-making, setting the stage for a more sustainable, efficient, and resilient global economy.

2- LITERATURE REVIEW

The integration of Cyber-Physical Systems (CPS) and Digital Twins has become a fundamental driver of industrial innovation, operational optimization, and economic resilience. As industries embrace AI-driven automation, real-time data analytics, and intelligent simulation models, these technologies are reshaping the way businesses operate, manage risks, and adapt to an increasingly volatile economic landscape. Research has extensively explored how CPS and Digital Twins enable real-time synchronization between the physical and digital worlds, creating dynamic feedback loops that enhance decision-making, improve cost efficiency, and optimize resource utilization. The evolving role of these technologies in manufacturing, logistics, energy systems, and urban development underscores their transformative potential in modernizing industrial infrastructure and fostering sustainable economic growth (Attaran et al., 2024).

The concept of Digital Twins has evolved significantly from its early applications in aerospace and manufacturing to a broader role in predictive analytics, supply chain optimization, and economic forecasting. Digital Twins function as high-fidelity digital replicas of physical entities, continuously updating based on real-time sensor data and AI-driven insights. This ability to simulate and predict system behavior has been recognized as a key advantage in reducing downtime, enhancing quality control, and improving operational efficiency. Organizations leveraging Digital Twins gain the ability to anticipate failures, optimize maintenance schedules, and fine-tune production processes, leading to higher productivity and cost savings. These technologies not only enhance industrial efficiency but also support strategic economic planning by providing decision-makers with real-time data on supply chains, energy consumption, and market dynamics (Liang et al., 2024).

In parallel, Cyber-Physical Systems (CPS) integrate computational intelligence with physical operations, bridging the gap between digital automation and real-world industrial applications. The growing complexity of global supply chains, industrial automation, and economic interdependencies has necessitated the adoption of CPS-driven solutions to improve resilience, responsiveness, and adaptability. CPS enables industries to automate processes, optimize logistics, and enhance system interoperability, ensuring that physical operations are seamlessly coordinated through AI-driven control mechanisms (Nozari, 2024(a)). By embedding advanced machine learning models into CPS, industries benefit from real-time predictive analytics, allowing them to respond dynamically to disruptions, forecast demand fluctuations, and mitigate financial risks. These capabilities position CPS as a foundational technology for next-generation smart economies, where intelligent automation and self-regulating industrial ecosystems drive economic sustainability(Luo et al., 2023).

The application of Digital Twins and CPS in cost efficiency and production optimization has been widely explored, with research showing that organizations that incorporate AI-powered simulations into their industrial workflows experience substantial reductions in operational expenses and increased throughput. Cost efficiency is achieved through automated resource allocation, predictive maintenance, and intelligent process optimization, all of which contribute to lower production costs and enhanced economic resilience (Broo et al., 2021). Real-time monitoring and AI-driven analytics allow industries to eliminate inefficiencies, reducing energy consumption, material waste, and labor costs. These improvements are particularly evident in advanced manufacturing environments, logistics networks, and energy-intensive industries, where operational inefficiencies directly impact financial performance. The ability to conduct scenario-based simulations further enhances economic stability by minimizing uncertainties and improving long-term planning.

A significant area of research focuses on predictive accuracy and risk mitigation in Digital Twin and CPS-driven environments(Nozari, 2024(c)). Traditional industrial and economic models often rely on historical data and reactive decision-making, limiting their ability to adapt to rapid market changes. Digital Twins address this limitation by leveraging AI-driven forecasting tools to analyze real-time data streams, enabling organizations to anticipate disruptions, optimize inventory levels, and improve financial forecasting. In supply chain management, for example, these technologies allow businesses to reduce downtime, improve delivery precision, and optimize route planning, ensuring greater agility and resilience in complex and dynamic market environments. The ability to simulate potential failures, adjust production parameters, and optimize asset performance provides industries with a competitive advantage, ensuring long-term economic sustainability (Movahed et al., 2024).

The widespread adoption of Digital Twins and CPS extends beyond industrial applications, influencing global economic structures and smart city development. Research has shown that these technologies are increasingly being utilized in urban planning, infrastructure development, and energy management, contributing to intelligent resource allocation and improved environmental sustainability. In smart cities, Digital Twins support real-time traffic optimization, predictive energy distribution, and AI-driven urban planning, ensuring that public resources are managed efficiently and sustainably. The ability to model entire economic ecosystems using real-time data and AI-powered analytics offers governments and policymakers a powerful tool for improving economic governance, infrastructure investments, and environmental conservation efforts (Nozari et al., 2024; Ghahremani-Nahr et al., 2023)).

Despite the evident advantages of CPS and Digital Twins, several barriers to widespread adoption remain. Cybersecurity risks, interoperability challenges, and high implementation costs continue to limit the scalability of these technologies. As industries become increasingly data-driven, concerns about data security, privacy, and AI ethics must be addressed to ensure the safe and responsible deployment of intelligent automation systems. Additionally, many businesses face difficulties in integrating CPS and Digital Twins with existing legacy systems, requiring significant investments in IT infrastructure, workforce training, and regulatory compliance. Economic feasibility remains a major concern, particularly for small and medium-sized enterprises (SMEs), which may lack the financial resources to fully leverage AI-enhanced digital simulation technologies (Ranawaka et al., 2024).

Despite these challenges, the continued evolution of AI, cloud computing, and machine learning is expected to drive the broader adoption of Digital Twins and CPS across industries. Research suggests that as computational power increases and cloud-based AI platforms become more accessible, more businesses will integrate intelligent automation and real-time digital simulations into their operations. The future of industrial and economic resilience will likely be shaped by the ability of organizations to leverage AI-driven digital models for strategic decision-making, resource optimization, and predictive analytics. The expansion of AI-powered economic forecasting models, autonomous production systems, and self-regulating logistics networks will further cement CPS and Digital Twins as essential components of modern economic infrastructure (Nozari, 2024(b)).

The literature overwhelmingly supports the argument that CPS and Digital Twins will play a defining role in shaping the future of industrial automation and economic decision-making. By enhancing real-time monitoring, operational intelligence, and predictive risk assessment, these technologies are enabling industries to build more adaptive, cost-efficient, and resilient economic systems. As industries and governments continue to invest in smart automation, AI-driven analytics, and intelligent simulation technologies, the role of CPS and Digital Twins will become even more pronounced, paving the way for a more efficient, sustainable, and intelligent global economy.

3- RESEARCH METHOD

This study employs a hybrid qualitative-quantitative approach to examine the role of Cyber-Physical Systems (CPS) and Digital Twins in industrial innovation and economic resilience. By integrating data-driven analysis, performance evaluation, and predictive modeling, this research aims to provide a comprehensive assessment of how these technologies enhance industrial processes, economic stability, and adaptive decision-making.

The study primarily relies on secondary data sources, including academic journal articles, industry whitepapers, and global reports from organizations such as the World Economic Forum (WEF), McKinsey & Company, and Deloitte. These sources offer critical insights into the adoption of CPS and Digital Twin technologies across key industries, including manufacturing, logistics, healthcare, and smart cities. The research follows a systematic literature review approach to categorize technological advancements, economic implications, and barriers to implementation. Key performance indicators (KPIs) such as cost efficiency, production optimization, predictive accuracy, and economic resilience are extracted and analyzed to measure the effectiveness of these technologies in fostering innovation and sustainable economic growth.

To quantify the economic impact of CPS and Digital Twins, this study applies a quantitative evaluation framework, assessing the relationship between real-time digital simulations, AI-driven optimizations, and market adaptability. The model defines economic resilience (ER) as a function of CPS efficiency, digital twin accuracy, AI-driven intelligence, and supply chain optimization:

$$ER = f(CPS, DT, AI, SCM) \quad (1)$$

Where:

ER= Represents economic resilience,
CPS= Reflects cyber-physical system efficiency,
DT= Denotes digital twin accuracy,
AI= Accounts for artificial intelligence integration,
SCM= Measures supply chain management optimization

By applying correlation analysis to historical industry data, the study identifies how automation, predictive maintenance, and real-time data processing contribute to cost reduction, production efficiency, and risk mitigation. The integration of digital twin technology in industrial operations is assessed based on its ability to enhance forecasting accuracy, reduce system downtime, and optimize decision-making in uncertain market conditions.

While this study provides a comprehensive evaluation of CPS and Digital Twin applications, it is subject to certain limitations. The research is based on secondary data, meaning that real-time experimental validation is beyond its scope. Additionally, the economic impact of these technologies varies across industries, with some sectors experiencing faster adoption and higher efficiency gains than others. Cybersecurity risks, interoperability challenges, and the high costs of implementation remain significant barriers to widespread adoption, requiring further investigation.

Despite these limitations, the findings of this study offer a structured, data-driven approach to understanding the role of CPS and Digital Twins in building resilient, intelligent economies. By leveraging real-time digital simulations, AI-driven optimizations, and predictive analytics, these technologies provide a strategic foundation for industrial growth, risk management, and long-term economic stability.

4- RESEARCH FINDINGS

The findings of this study indicate a substantial transformation in industrial efficiency and economic resilience following the adoption of Cyber-Physical Systems (CPS) and Digital Twins. By integrating real-time data processing, AI-driven analytics, and predictive modeling, organizations have significantly enhanced their operational performance, leading to improvements in cost efficiency, production optimization, and predictive accuracy. These advancements not only streamline industrial processes but also contribute to a more adaptive and resilient economic ecosystem, reinforcing the role of intelligent automation and data-driven decision-making in modern economies.

An analysis of key performance indicators before and after Digital Twin implementation reveals measurable improvements in various economic and operational dimensions. As shown in Table 1: Performance Metrics Before and After Digital Twin Integration, cost efficiency increased by 18%, reflecting the benefits of automated decision-making, resource optimization, and predictive maintenance. The integration of real-time monitoring systems allowed for a significant reduction in operational costs, as inefficiencies were systematically identified and mitigated. Additionally, production optimization improved by 16%, demonstrating how CPS-driven automation enhances workflow coordination, process accuracy, and manufacturing output. The ability to adjust production parameters dynamically using digital twin simulations ensured better process control, reduced delays, and more efficient use of resources, ultimately leading to greater economic productivity.

Perhaps the most significant improvement was observed in predictive accuracy, which increased by 24% after the adoption of digital twin technology. This enhancement underscores the critical role of AI-driven forecasting and real-time analytics in enabling organizations to anticipate and manage supply chain disruptions, market fluctuations, and risk factors more effectively. With higher predictive accuracy, businesses can proactively adjust their strategies, mitigate potential risks, and optimize resource allocation, thereby strengthening their economic adaptability and long-term sustainability. The results presented in Table 1 highlight the substantial impact of

CPS and Digital Twins on economic efficiency, positioning these technologies as vital tools for industrial transformation and economic resilience.

Table 1. Performance Metrics Before and After Digital Twin Integration

Metric	Before Digital Twins	After Digital Twins	Improvement (%)
Cost Efficiency (CE)	70	88	18
Production Optimization (PO)	75	91	16
Predictive Accuracy (PA)	65	89	24

Table 1 provides a clear comparative overview of the improvements observed across key indicators. The table demonstrates how real-time data processing, AI-driven analytics, and predictive modeling have enhanced industrial performance, allowing businesses to respond more dynamically to market conditions. These findings reinforce the notion that intelligent automation and digital simulations serve as essential components of modern economic infrastructure, enabling organizations to maintain competitive agility in an increasingly complex and volatile global market.

A graphical representation of these improvements is presented in Figure 1 which visually depicts the changes observed before and after the adoption of CPS and digital twin technology. The graph highlights the marked increase in cost efficiency, production optimization, and predictive accuracy, emphasizing the transformative impact of real-time monitoring and AI-powered decision-making on industrial and economic systems. As seen in Figure 1, the implementation of digital twins leads to a significant performance boost across all assessed metrics, confirming their role as a key driver of economic resilience and technological advancement.

Figure 1. Impact of Digital Twins on Industrial Performance Metrics

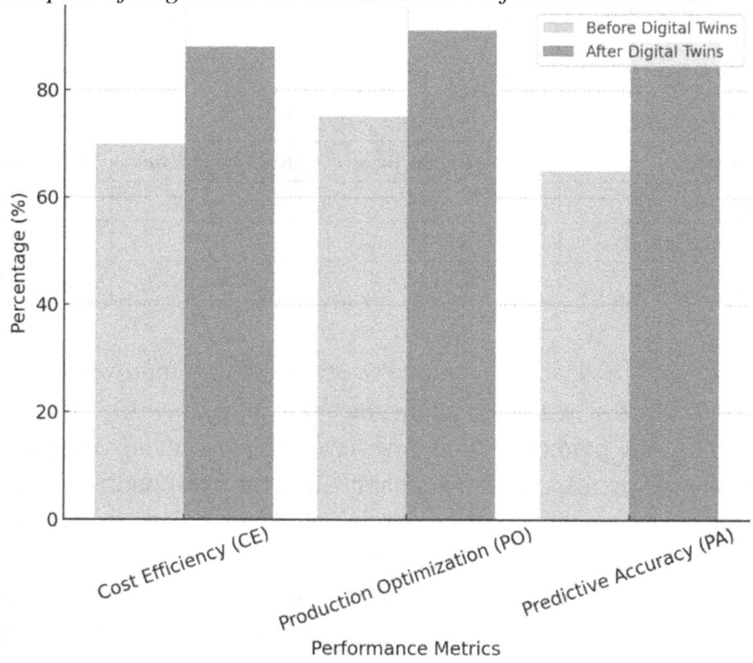

The improvement in cost efficiency reflects the ability of CPS and Digital Twins to optimize operational workflows, reduce waste, and enhance asset utilization. By integrating real-time data analytics and AI-driven automation, businesses can streamline logistics, improve energy consumption, and ensure that resources are allocated in the most cost-effective manner. The reduction in manual intervention further eliminates unnecessary expenses while increasing overall system reliability and productivity. This transition toward data-driven cost optimization is crucial for maintaining long-term financial sustainability, particularly in industries that rely heavily on complex supply chain networks and production systems.

In addition to cost savings, the enhancement in production optimization highlights the potential of CPS-enabled digital twins to revolutionize manufacturing and logistics. Through AI-powered simulation models, industries can predict bottlenecks, identify inefficiencies, and implement real-time adjustments to production workflows. The ability to test multiple operational scenarios in a virtual environment allows for better contingency planning and improved process efficiency, ensuring that industrial systems remain resilient under varying economic conditions. This dynamic adaptability is particularly relevant in the context of Industry 4.0 and smart manufacturing, where digital twin technology serves as a cornerstone for automation and industrial intelligence.

The increase in predictive accuracy underscores the role of AI and real-time analytics in enhancing risk management and decision-making capabilities. With advanced machine learning models and sensor-driven monitoring systems, industries can anticipate equipment failures, forecast market trends, and adjust supply chain operations accordingly. This predictive capability translates into greater economic stability, as businesses can proactively adapt to potential disruptions, optimize inventory levels, and minimize losses caused by uncertainty. In an era where economic volatility and supply chain disruptions are common, such improvements in predictive accuracy offer a competitive edge, ensuring that organizations remain resilient and prepared for future challenges.

The broader implications of these findings suggest that Cyber-Physical Systems and Digital Twins will continue to shape the future of industrial and economic resilience. The integration of real-time digital simulations and AI-enhanced analytics offers an unparalleled advantage in navigating complex industrial environments and rapidly evolving market conditions. By leveraging these technologies, businesses can enhance productivity, sustainability, and economic efficiency, reinforcing their long-term competitiveness and adaptability. Moreover, the scalability of CPS-driven digital twin systems means that these technologies can be applied across various industries, from smart cities and healthcare to logistics and energy management, further expanding their economic impact.

Overall, the study's findings reinforce the transformative role of CPS and Digital Twins in driving industrial innovation and economic growth. As seen in Table 1 and Figure 1, the improvements in cost efficiency, production optimization, and predictive accuracy illustrate the power of real-time analytics and AI-driven decision-making in modern industries. These insights suggest that organizations and policymakers should prioritize investments in CPS-enabled digital twin technology as a means to achieve greater economic resilience, operational efficiency, and sustainable industrial development. The ongoing advancement of AI, machine learning, and digital twin frameworks will only further enhance these capabilities, making them a critical component of next-generation economic systems.

5- CONCLUSION

The study highlights the transformative role of Cyber-Physical Systems (CPS) and Digital Twins in enhancing industrial efficiency and economic resilience. As industries move toward data-driven decision-making and AI-powered automation, the integration of real-time digital simulations has become a crucial driver of cost efficiency, operational optimization, and predictive accuracy. The findings demonstrate that businesses adopting CPS and Digital Twins can significantly improve their adaptability, sustainability, and long-term competitiveness.

One of the most compelling insights from the study is the substantial increase in economic and industrial efficiency following the adoption of Digital Twin technology. The research findings indicate an 18% improvement in cost efficiency, a 16% increase in production optimization, and a 24% enhancement in predictive accuracy. These results highlight the ability of real-time monitoring, AI-enhanced analytics, and simulation-based decision-making to reduce operational expenses, optimize production processes, and improve risk management strategies. The positive impact of these technologies reinforces the notion that industries leveraging CPS-driven digital twin solutions can maintain economic resilience in increasingly dynamic and uncertain environments.

The study also reveals that Digital Twins contribute to cost reduction by streamlining workflows, optimizing resource allocation, and eliminating inefficiencies. The ability to monitor, simulate, and predict industrial processes enables organizations to implement proactive maintenance strategies, reduce waste, and ensure optimal energy consumption. By minimizing unnecessary expenditures and enhancing resource efficiency, CPS-integrated digital twins improve economic sustainability and financial stability. This is particularly critical in sectors such as manufacturing, logistics, and energy management, where real-time decision-making and process optimization have a direct impact on profitability and market competitiveness.

Another key takeaway is the role of predictive accuracy in strengthening economic resilience. By leveraging AI-driven forecasting models and real-time analytics, organizations can anticipate market shifts, supply chain disruptions, and operational risks with greater precision. The findings show that businesses equipped with CPS-enhanced digital twin systems can respond more effectively to unexpected challenges, reducing downtime, optimizing inventory levels, and ensuring business continuity. This predictive capability is particularly beneficial in industries that face rapid technological changes, fluctuating consumer demands, and global supply chain uncertainties.

The broader implications of this research suggest that Cyber-Physical Systems and Digital Twins will continue to shape the future of industrial and economic systems. As technology advances, these tools will become even more intelligent, scalable, and integrated into next-generation economic models. Industries and policymakers must prioritize investments in digital twin technology to stay competitive and build resilient, data-driven economies. Future research should focus on expanding the scope of CPS applications, exploring their role in sustainability, and addressing challenges related to cybersecurity and system interoperability.

In conclusion, the adoption of Digital Twins and CPS-driven AI solutions represents a fundamental shift toward smarter, more adaptive industrial and economic ecosystems. Businesses that embrace these technologies will achieve greater efficiency, sustainability, and resilience, ensuring long-term economic success in an increasingly complex and fast-evolving global landscape.

REFERENCES

Amit Bhardwaj, P. (2024). The Rise of Cyber Physical Systems: A Retrospective and Prospective Analysis of Applications. *International IT Journal of Research, ISSN: 3007-6706, 2*(3), 11-22.

Andronie, M., Lăzăroiu, G., tefănescu, R., U ă, C., & Dijmărescu, I. (2021). Sustainable, smart, and sensing technologies for cyber-physical manufacturing systems: A systematic literature review. *Sustainability (Basel)*, 13(10), 5495. DOI: 10.3390/su13105495

Attaran, S., Attaran, M., & Celik, B. G. (2024). Digital Twins and Industrial Internet of Things: Uncovering operational intelligence in industry 4.0. *Decision Analytics Journal*, 10, 100398. DOI: 10.1016/j.dajour.2024.100398

Bhambri, P., Rani, S., & Khang, A. (2024). Al-driven Digital Twin and Resource Optimization in Industry 4.0 Ecosystem. *Intelligent Techniques for Predictive Data Analytics*, 47.

Bongomin, O., Mwape, M. C., Mpofu, N. S., Bahunde, B. K., Kidega, R., Mpungu, I. L., & Ngulube, G. (2024). Digital Twin technology advancing Industry 4.0 and Industry 5.0 across Sectors. *Available atSSRN* 5072457.

Broo, D. G., & Schooling, J. (2021). A framework for using data as an engineering tool for sustainable cyber-physical systems. *IEEE Access : Practical Innovations, Open Solutions*, 9, 22876–22882. DOI: 10.1109/ACCESS.2021.3055652

Ghahremani-Nahr, J., Nozari, H., & Aliahmadi, A. (2023). Contract Design for Return Products in a Cooperative Closed-Loop Supply Chain. *Global Business Review*, 09721509221148892. DOI: 10.1177/09721509221148892

Ghansah, F. A., & Lu, W. (2023). Cyber-physical systems and digital twins for "cognitive building" in the construction industry. *Construction Innovation*. Advance online publication. DOI: 10.1108/CI-07-2022-0164

Kumar, R., & Agrawal, N. (2024). Shaping the future of industry: Understanding the dynamics of industrial digital twins. *Computers & Industrial Engineering*, 191, 110172. DOI: 10.1016/j.cie.2024.110172

Lampropoulos, G., & Siakas, K. (2023). Enhancing and securing cyber-physical systems and Industry 4.0 through digital twins: A critical review. *Journal of Software (Malden, MA)*, 35(7), e2494. DOI: 10.1002/smr.2494

Liang, H., Moya, B., Seah, E., Weng, A. N. K., Baillargeat, D., Joerin, J., ... & Chatzi, E. (2024). Harnessing Hybrid Digital Twinning for Decision-Support in Smart Infrastructures.

Luo, Y., & Ball, P. (2023, September). Digital Twins as a Catalyst for Sustainability and Resilience in Manufacturing Systems: A Review from the Supply Chain Perspective. In *International Conference on Sustainable Design and Manufacturing* (pp. 263-273). Springer Nature Singapore.

Movahed, A. B., Movahed, A. B., & Nozari, H. (2024). Marketing 6.0 Conceptualization. In *Advanced Businesses in Industry 6.0* (pp. 15-31). IGI Global.

Nozari, H. (2024a). Green Supply Chain Management based on Artificial Intelligence of Everything. *Journal of Economics and Management*, 46, 171–188. DOI: 10.22367/jem.2024.46.07

Nozari, H. (2024b). Investigating Key Dimensions and Key Indicators of AIoT-Based Supply Chain in Sustainable Business Development. In *Artificial Intelligence of Things for Achieving Sustainable Development Goals* (pp. 293-310). Cham: Springer Nature Switzerland.

Nozari, H. (2024c). Supply Chain 6.0 and Moving Towards Hyper-Intelligent Processes. In *Information Logistics for Organizational Empowerment and Effective Supply Chain Management* (pp. 1-13). IGI Global.

Nozari, H., & Szmelter-Jarosz, A. (2024). An Analytical Framework for Smart Supply Chains 5.0. In *Building Smart and Sustainable Businesses With Transformative Technologies* (pp. 1–15). IGI Global.

Ranawaka, A., Alahakoon, D., Sun, Y., & Hewapathirana, K. (2024). Leveraging the Synergy of Digital Twins and Artificial Intelligence for Sustainable Power Grids: A Scoping Review. *Energies*, 17(21), 5342. DOI: 10.3390/en17215342

Chapter 4
Smart Economy Cybersecurity:
AI-Driven Risk Management in Digital Markets

Ali Bakhshi Movahed
https://orcid.org/0009-0006-4463-6838
Iran University of Science and Technology, Iran

Amirhossein Ghasemi Abyaneh
Kharazmi University, Iran

Masoud Khakbazan
Iran University of Science and Technology, Iran

Aminmasoud Bakhshi Movahed
https://orcid.org/0000-0003-3259-5419
Iran University of Science and Technology, Iran

ABSTRACT

Integrating AI, IoT, and cloud computing into smart economies has boosted digital efficiency but introduced cybersecurity vulnerabilities like AI-driven phishing, deepfake fraud, and malware. This study explores AI-driven risk management in mitigating such threats through a meta-synthesis of existing literature. Findings reveal that traditional security models are insufficient against adaptive AI attacks, necessitating autonomous solutions like self-healing networks, AI threat detection, and behavioral analytics. Regulatory frameworks also lag, highlighting the need for global standards and ethical AI governance. Critical gaps include limited predictive AI models, regulatory oversight, and standardized policies. The study proposes an

DOI: 10.4018/979-8-3693-4369-2.ch004

integrated AI cybersecurity framework combining innovation, compliance, and public-private collaboration. It concludes that AI-driven solutions and robust governance are vital for cyber resilience, urging future research on AI ethics, predictive risk models, and global standards to counter emerging threats.

1- INTRODUCTION

Smart economies are built upon digital transformation, automation, and the integration of advanced technologies such as the Internet of Things (IoT), Artificial Intelligence (AI), blockchain, and cloud computing (Peter Boolm, 2020). These technologies have significantly enhanced efficiency, streamlined financial transactions, and facilitated the expansion of global digital markets, thereby creating new opportunities for businesses and digital services (Dana et al., 2022). However, the increasing dependence on digital technologies has also introduced significant cybersecurity challenges. In particular, smart economies are highly vulnerable to sophisticated cyber threats, which have the potential to compromise sensitive data, disrupt financial markets, and erode public trust in digital systems (Hossain et al., 2023).

In recent years, cyber threats have escalated in both frequency and complexity. Cybercriminals and advanced threat actors leverage AI-driven automation and big data analytics to develop intelligent and highly targeted cyberattacks (Guembe et al., 2022). Some of the most prevalent threats in smart economies include autonomous phishing attacks, deepfake-based identity fraud, AI-powered malware, and blockchain exploitation (Wongwas et al., 2024). These cyber-threats result in significant financial losses for corporations and governments and introduce substantial legal and security challenges that require immediate attention and regulatory intervention (Darem, 2023).

Artificial intelligence enhances cybersecurity by enabling advanced threat detection, predictive analytics, and automated incident response mechanisms (Laxmi and Kumar, 2024). Machine learning algorithms and artificial neural networks can analyze behavioral patterns and detect cyber threats before they materialize (Alaa Hammad et al., 2024). Furthermore, autonomous cybersecurity systems, which leverage AI and big data analytics, can effectively identify and neutralize cyber threats, ensuring the protection of digital infrastructures (Ameedeen et al., 2024). Technologies such as self-healing networks, advanced cybersecurity analytics, and automated surveillance systems have demonstrated great potential in strengthening the security of digital economies challenges (Alijoyo et al., 2024).

Despite these advancements, cybersecurity in digital economies continues to face substantial challenges. Many traditional cybersecurity frameworks are inadequate for detecting and countering AI-driven cyberattacks, making them ineffective in addressing modern threats. Moreover, existing legal and policy frameworks are still insufficient in regulating the application of AI in cybersecurity. The fundamental question is: How can AI be leveraged to detect, prevent, and mitigate cyber threats in digital economies? Addressing this question requires the development of advanced security models, regulatory improvements, and enhanced international collaboration to ensure comprehensive cybersecurity governance.

This chapter explores the role of AI in cybersecurity within smart economies and presents a comprehensive framework for managing cyber risks in digital markets. The primary objectives of this study include identifying the most critical cybersecurity threats in smart economies, examining the role of AI in detecting and preventing cyberattacks, assessing existing cybersecurity policies and regulatory frameworks, and developing a conceptual model for AI-driven cybersecurity.

While extensive research has been conducted in cybersecurity and artificial intelligence, most studies have primarily focused on traditional cybersecurity approaches, with limited emphasis on AI-driven cybersecurity solutions. The major research gaps in this domain include the lack of advanced machine learning models for predicting cyber threats, insufficient legal frameworks for AI governance in cybersecurity, and the need for autonomous security systems capable of responding to cyberattacks in real-time. This study addresses these gaps by proposing an integrated AI-driven cybersecurity model.

To provide a comprehensive analysis, this chapter is structured as follows: Section 2 presents a literature review, examining key cybersecurity threats and the role of AI in enhancing cybersecurity. Section 3 introduces the research framework and the meta-synthesis methodology, which integrates findings from existing studies to develop a conceptual model. Section 4 outlines the key findings, evaluating the impact of AI on cybersecurity in smart economies. Finally, Section 5 discusses the conclusions and recommendations, providing insights into policy development and future research directions to strengthen cybersecurity resilience in digital markets.

2. LITERATURE REVIEW

2.1 Cyber Threats in Smart Economies

Smart economies, which increasingly rely on advanced technologies such as the Internet of Things (IoT), cloud computing, and artificial intelligence (AI), face many complex cyber threats. These technologies have significantly enhanced the efficiency of systems and facilitated digital communication, but they also introduce new vulnerabilities that cybercriminals can exploit. The growing attack surface in these economies, driven by these new technologies, presents challenges in protecting data, infrastructure, and digital assets. This section explores various cyber threats smart economies face and examines their impact.

2.1.1. The Growing Attack Surface

The expansion of IoT and cloud computing technologies has increased the attack surface in smart economies. IoT devices, such as smart home appliances, sensors, and connected cars, are often built with insufficient security and thus become vulnerable targets for cyberattacks (Dener, 2019). Attackers can exploit these devices to gain unauthorized access to networks and control systems. Similarly, the widespread use of cloud computing as a data storage and processing solution has introduced new security risks. Data stored in the cloud is highly vulnerable to unauthorized access and breaches if cloud services are not properly secured (Elmrabet et al., 2018).

Moreover, artificial intelligence has become both a tool for cybersecurity and a source of vulnerability. Cybercriminals can use AI to launch advanced and targeted attacks such as autonomous phishing or deepfake fraud. Attackers may also use AI-powered machine learning algorithms to identify system weaknesses or manipulate digital interactions (Kaloudi & Li, 2020). The rapid evolution of cyber threats and AI advancements often outpaces traditional cybersecurity measures, making it difficult for organizations to defend against these threats effectively.

2.1.2. Cyber Threats Facing Digital Markets

Digital markets, heavily dependent on advanced technologies, are particularly vulnerable to cyber threats. The main cyber threats affecting digital markets include autonomous phishing attacks, deepfake fraud, AI-powered malware, and blockchain vulnerabilities.

- Autonomous Phishing: With the help of AI, attackers can automatically generate phishing emails tailored to specific individuals or organizations. These emails can appear highly authentic, tricking users into revealing sensitive information or login credentials (Demertzi et al., 2022). The widespread use of social networks and IoT devices to collect personal data further increases the success rate of such attacks.
- Deepfake Fraud: Deepfake technology, which enables the creation of highly realistic fake videos and audio, has been increasingly used for identity theft and financial fraud. Attackers use this technology to impersonate individuals,

often corporate executives, to initiate fraudulent transactions or manipulate public opinion (Kaloudi & Li, 2020). The rise of deepfake-based fraud has been particularly troubling in sectors such as finance, where audio and video fraud can lead to significant financial losses.

- AI-Powered Malware: AI-powered malware represents a new generation of malicious software that leverages machine learning to detect vulnerabilities within systems and adapt its behavior to avoid detection by security measures (Nejabatkhah et al., 2020). Unlike traditional malware, which follows predefined attack patterns, AI-based malware can continuously evolve and autonomously alter its approach to evade detection. This capability makes it significantly harder for traditional defense mechanisms to protect against such threats.
- Blockchain Vulnerabilities: While blockchain technology offers enhanced security features, its implementation in financial markets is not immune to cyberattacks. Vulnerabilities in smart contracts and cryptocurrency exchanges can lead to fraud and theft of digital assets (ElMamy et al., 2020). For instance, exploiting weaknesses in blockchain code or improper handling of digital wallets can result in substantial financial losses.

2.1.3. Economic Impact of Cyber Threats

Cyber threats not only cause damage to data and digital infrastructures but also have significant economic implications. The financial costs associated with cyberattacks can be astronomical, with organizations suffering direct financial losses, reputation damage, and long-term recovery expenses (Gunduz & Das, 2020). For example, the WannaCry ransomware attack 2017 caused estimated losses of around $4 billion globally, affecting organizations and government entities worldwide. The attack disrupted services and undermined consumer trust in digital platforms.

In addition to these direct financial losses, cyberattacks can lead to disruptions in financial markets, especially in the case of attacks targeting digital currencies or smart contracts. These disruptions can have long-term effects on investor confidence, leading to economic instability in digital markets (Boubacar et al., 2020).

2.2. AI-Driven Cybersecurity: The Future of Risk Management

As the complexity and scale of cyber threats continue to increase, artificial intelligence (AI) has emerged as a crucial tool in cyber risk management. AI technologies offer advanced capabilities to detect threats, predict attacks, and automate responses to mitigate risks (Uzoka et al., 2024). In this section, we explore the role of AI in enhancing cybersecurity in smart economies, focusing on key AI-driven solutions for threat detection, autonomous systems, behavioral analytics, and risk assessment.

2.2.1. AI-Powered Threat Detection

One of the most prominent applications of AI in cybersecurity is threat detection. Machine learning models are widely used to analyze vast amounts of data and identify abnormal patterns that could indicate potential threats (Akhtar & Rawol, 2024). These models can predict cyberattacks before they occur by identifying signatures of known attacks or detecting anomalies that might indicate a new form of attack (Sarker et al., 2021; Famoloni, 2024). Supervised learning models rely on historical data to classify attacks and can efficiently detect known threats such as DDoS attacks or malware. In contrast, unsupervised learning models effectively identify unknown threats that have not been seen before (Sarker et al., 2021). In addition, deep learning techniques, a subset of AI, can be used for more complex threat detection (Shahana et al., 2024). These models can process large datasets in real-time, enabling them to detect sophisticated attacks such as advanced persistent threats (APTs) (Temara, 2024). With AI-powered threat detection, the ability to detect cyber threats in real-time has greatly improved, significantly reducing the exposure window and potential damage (Camacho, 2024).

2.2.2. Autonomous Cybersecurity Systems

Autonomous cybersecurity systems represent a new era of self-sufficient threat management. By utilizing AI and big data analytics, these systems can autonomously identify, analyze, and respond to cyber threats without human intervention (Ee et al., 2024). The rise of self-healing networks is a prime example of such systems, where the network can detect malicious activity and automatically isolate infected parts of the system, preventing further damage (Famoloni, 2024). This capability allows for faster response times and greater resilience to cyberattacks, particularly in the case of complex and rapidly evolving threats (Temara, 2024). In addition, these systems can reconfigure themselves based on ongoing threat intelligence, ensuring they are continuously adapting to the latest attack techniques (Shahana et al., 2024). This automation significantly reduces the burden on security teams, allowing them to focus on strategic initiatives while AI handles routine detection and remediation tasks (Famoloni, 2024).

2.2.3. Behavioral Analytics & Cyber Threat Intelligence

Behavioral analytics is another key component of AI-driven cybersecurity. By analyzing user behaviors and network traffic, AI can detect anomalous actions that may indicate malicious activity. For example, if a user suddenly starts accessing sensitive files, they wouldn't typically need, or if they perform unusual login activities, AI-powered systems can flag these anomalies for further investigation (Camacho, 2024). Cyber threat intelligence platforms also use AI to aggregate and analyze data from various sources, providing organizations real-time insights into emerging threats (Temara, 2024). By continuously monitoring and learning from external threat intelligence feeds, AI-based systems can identify new threat vectors and provide actionable insights to strengthen defenses against attacks (Famoloni, 2024).

2.2.4. AI-Powered Cyber Risk Assessment

AI can also enhance cyber risk assessment by predicting vulnerabilities and assessing future cyberattacks' likelihood and potential impact. These predictive models leverage historical attack data, current threat intelligence, and system vulnerabilities to simulate potential risk scenarios (Uzoka et al., 2024). This allows organizations to prioritize high-risk areas and allocate resources more efficiently for cybersecurity measures (Żebrowski, 2022). With AI-driven risk assessment, companies can better understand the potential financial and operational risks posed by cyber threats, providing valuable information to make more informed decisions about security investments and threat mitigation strategies (Nwafor et al., 2024).

2.3. Policy, Regulations, and Governance in Cyber-Resilient Smart Economies

Developing robust cybersecurity policies and regulations becomes increasingly important as cyber threats evolve to safeguard digital economies. These policies must protect personal data, ensure privacy, and maintain data integrity across interconnected systems. Governments and private-sector organizations must work together to create comprehensive frameworks that enable the resilience of smart economies (Habibzadeh et al., 2019). This section delves into the importance of cybersecurity laws, AI ethics, and the role of international cooperation in securing digital markets.

2.3.1. Cybersecurity Laws and Compliance

Globally recognized regulations such as GDPR and NIST play pivotal roles in establishing standards for cybersecurity. GDPR, a regulation enacted by the European Union, is a comprehensive law that protects personal data and ensures that organizations handling such data meet specific cybersecurity standards (Tiirmaa-Klaar, 2016). This law focuses on data protection and plays a critical role in increasing public trust in digital markets by ensuring that users' data is handled securely and transparently. In addition, the NIST Cybersecurity Framework is widely used to provide best practices for identifying, assessing, and managing cybersecurity risks. This framework is particularly valuable for organizations in smart economies, as it offers clear guidelines for cloud computing and AI security in a rapidly evolving digital landscape (Dupont, 2019).

2.3.2. Ethical AI and Cybersecurity Governance

The ethical use of artificial intelligence in cybersecurity is a significant concern. AI bias in decision-making processes can lead to inaccurate assessments of cyber threats, creating vulnerabilities in the system (Liu et al., 2023). Therefore, it is essential to implement ethical AI practices to ensure that AI-driven security measures are fair, transparent, and accountable. This includes preventing algorithmic bias, ensuring data privacy, and maintaining human oversight in critical decision-making processes. Governance of AI in cybersecurity must involve continuous monitoring of AI algorithms to ensure they do not perpetuate biases, unfair practices, or unintended consequences (Srinivas et al., 2019). Clear guidelines must be established to ensure ethical standards are maintained when deploying AI systems in defense against cyber threats.

2.3.3. The Role of Government and Private Sector in Cyber Defense

Effective cyber defense requires collaboration between government agencies and private sector companies (Ho & O'Sullivan, 2019). Governments play a critical role in creating regulations, providing oversight, and facilitating international cooperation, while the private sector is often responsible for developing and implementing cutting-edge cybersecurity technologies. Working together, both sectors can share critical information, coordinate cyber attack responses, and build resilient digital infrastructures. Public-private partnerships (PPPs) are essential for developing comprehensive cybersecurity strategies (Gisladottir et al., 2017). These partnerships allow for information sharing, joint research on emerging threats, and the development of global cybersecurity standards that address the challenges of modern digital economies.

2.3.4. Developing a Global Cybersecurity Framework

In the face of global cyber threats, a unified global cybersecurity framework is essential to protect digital economies worldwide. Such a framework should set international standards for cyber risk management, AI security, and data protection and enable cross-border cooperation to tackle cyber threats effectively (Brown et al., 2018). Countries must collaborate to align their cybersecurity strategies and create a shared understanding of cyber risks.

Developing this framework involves collaborating across borders, sharing best practices, and ensuring that security policies and technologies evolve in sync with the rapid pace of innovation in the digital world (Sutherland, 2018).

3. RESEARCH FRAMEWORK

This research examines cyber threats in smart economies by integrating the Internet of Things (IoT), cloud computing, and artificial intelligence (AI). While these technologies have significantly enhanced digital efficiency, they have also introduced new cybersecurity risks, including AI-driven cyberattacks, blockchain vulnerabilities, and intrusions into smart grids and microgrids, posing serious threats to financial markets, national security, and critical infrastructure. This study aims to develop a comprehensive framework for analyzing and mitigating cybersecurity risks in digital economies by integrating AI-driven security mechanisms, cyber resilience strategies, and governance frameworks. The key research questions focus on the evolution of cyber threats due to AI, IoT, and blockchain, the effectiveness of AI-driven security solutions, the role of regulatory frameworks in mitigating AI-related cyber risks, and the impact of public-private partnerships on cybersecurity resilience.

The conceptual model of this study consists of three core dimensions: (1) Cyber threats in smart economies, which include security vulnerabilities in smart grids, AI-powered cyberattacks such as adversarial machine learning, deepfake phishing, AI-driven malware, false data injection in microgrids, and blockchain security risks; (2) AI-driven cybersecurity solutions, including AI-powered threat detection, autonomous cybersecurity systems, behavioral analytics, and AI-based fraud detection; and (3) Policy, regulations, and governance, which cover cyber resilience strategies, the role of government regulations such as GDPR and NIST, AI ethics in cybersecurity, and global cybersecurity standards. This model presents an integrated approach that connects AI-driven defense mechanisms with governance policies to enhance cybersecurity resilience in smart economies.

The study adopts a meta-synthesis research approach to systematically analyze existing literature and identify key patterns, gaps, and trends in AI-driven cybersecurity risk management. The methodology includes case study analysis, focusing on AI-based cybersecurity implementations in smart cities, smart grids, and financial systems. Data collection will rely on peer-reviewed journals, industry reports, and policy documents. At the same time, qualitative thematic and comparative analysis will be used to assess the effectiveness of AI-driven security frameworks against traditional cybersecurity models. The research will test hypotheses related to AI-driven threat detection, the impact of autonomous cybersecurity systems, the role of AI in fraud detection, and the influence of regulatory frameworks on AI governance and cybersecurity policies.

This study aims to contribute to both theoretical and practical aspects of cybersecurity. Theoretically, it will develop a comprehensive cybersecurity framework that integrates AI-driven security mechanisms with governance policies, offering new insights into AI applications in cybersecurity across various industries. Practically, it will provide policy recommendations for governments and private sector organizations to implement AI-driven cyber risk management frameworks, along with guidelines for embedding AI ethics into cybersecurity governance. The next research steps involve finalizing the meta-synthesis analysis, conducting comparative assessments to validate the conceptual model, and refining AI-driven risk assessment models for smart economies.

4. FINDING

The findings of this study highlight the growing complexity and diversity of cyber threats in smart economies, driven by the increasing integration of technologies such as IoT, cloud computing, and artificial intelligence (AI). Key cyber threats include AI-powered cyberattacks, autonomous phishing, and deepfake fraud, which exploit vulnerabilities in IoT devices, cloud infrastructures, and blockchain technologies. These threats are further compounded by the lack of robust cybersecurity governance frameworks and cyber-resilience strategies, particularly in sectors like smart grids and healthcare. Studies by Demertzi et al. (2023) and Kaloudi & Li (2020) indicate that AI-based vulnerabilities in critical infrastructures are increasingly difficult to mitigate using traditional security measures, highlighting the need for more advanced AI-driven defense mechanisms.

Moreover, the role of AI in cybersecurity is pivotal in mitigating these threats. AI-powered threat detection systems and autonomous cybersecurity solutions were found to significantly improve the speed and accuracy of threat identification and response. As per Familoni (2024) and Sarker et al. (2021), AI models, including machine learning and deep learning, can analyze large datasets in real-time to detect anomalies and unknown cyber threats. However, integrating AI ethics in cybersecurity governance remains challenging, with concerns about algorithmic bias and the need for transparent decision-making frameworks. Regulatory frameworks such as GDPR and NIST have been instrumental in enhancing data protection but require further updates to address emerging threats related to AI-powered attacks and blockchain vulnerabilities.

A meta-synthesis analysis in Table 1 categorizes the various types of cyber threats, AI-driven solutions, and governance strategies identified in the literature. This analysis helps to systematically organize and interpret the key findings from the reviewed studies, providing a comprehensive understanding of the interconnected dimensions of cybersecurity in smart economies.

Table 1. Meta-synthesis analysis

Authors	First-order themes	Second-order themes	Aggregate dimensions
(Demertzi et al., 2023)	Cyber threats in smart government	Governance and Infrastructure Security	Cyber Threats in Smart Economies
	Cyber threats in smart mobility		
	Cyber threats in a smart environment		
	Cyber threats in smart living		
	Cyber threats in smart healthcare		
	Cyber threats in a smart economy		
	Cyber threats in smart people		
(Dener, 2019)	Eavesdropping, Unauthorized Access, Malware, DDoS	Cybersecurity Risks and Threats	
	Hardware/Software Failures, Environmental Incidents		
	Cybersecurity policies and standards		

continued on following page

Table 1. Continued

Authors	First-order themes	Second-order themes	Aggregate dimensions
(Mrabet et al., 2018)	Cyber-attacks on smart grids, network vulnerabilities	Cybersecurity Challenges in Smart Grids	
	Intrusion detection, cryptography, network security		
	Data integrity, availability, accountability		
(Kaloudi & Li, 2020)	AI-based cyber attacks, adversarial machine learning	AI-Driven Cyber Threats and Challenges	
	Weaponized AI, deep learning for hacking		
	Cyber-physical system vulnerabilities		
(Nejabatkhah et al., 2021)	False Data Injection (FDI), Smart Micro grid Threats	Cybersecurity in Smart Microgrids	
	Data integrity, availability, confidentiality		
	Defensive strategies against cyber-attacks		
(ElMamy et al., 2020)	Blockchain-based cybersecurity for Industry 4.0	Blockchain-based Cybersecurity Solutions	
	Data confidentiality, authentication, integrity		
	Smart contracts for secure industrial networks		
(Gunduz & Das, 2020)	Cybersecurity on smart grids, IoT vulnerabilities	Smart Grid Cybersecurity and IoT Risks	
	Cyber-physical security, network security threats		
	Threat mitigation strategies, attack countermeasures		
(Familoni, 2024)	AI-driven threat detection and response	AI-Powered Cyber Defense Strategies	AI-Driven Cybersecurity: The Future of Risk Management
	AI-enabled phishing, adversarial attacks		
	AI in ethical hacking, security automation		

continued on following page

Table 1. Continued

Authors	First-order themes	Second-order themes	Aggregate dimensions
(Akhtar & Rawol, 2024)	AI-driven threat detection and mitigation strategies	Challenges and Opportunities in AI Cybersecurity	
	Privacy risks, ethical concerns in AI security		
	AI-based automation in threat intelligence		
(Uzoka, Cadet, & Ojukwu, 2024)	AI applications in threat detection and risk management	Strategic Applications of AI in Cybersecurity	
	Machine learning, anomaly detection, predictive analytics		
	Ethical and governance challenges in AI security		
(Ee et al., 2023)	Adapting cybersecurity frameworks for AI risk management	Defense-in-Depth Strategies for AI Security	
	AI lifecycle security, functional and threat-based approaches		
	MITRE ATLAS and NIST AI RMF for AI security frameworks		
(Camacho, 2024)	AI applications in cybersecurity, proactive threat detection	The Role of AI in Cybersecurity	
	Ethical considerations, data privacy in AI security		
	Machine learning for vulnerability assessment		
(Nwafor et al., 2024)	AI and data analytics for financial cybersecurity	AI-Driven Risk Mitigation in Financial Institutions	
	AI-based fraud detection, insider threat analysis		
	Regulatory compliance and ethical considerations		
(Shahana et al., 2024)	AI advancements in cybersecurity, automated threat intelligence	Balancing Advancements and Safeguards in AI Security	
	Supervised ML models for intrusion detection		
	Ethical risks of AI-driven security measures		

continued on following page

Table 1. Continued

Authors	First-order themes	Second-order themes	Aggregate dimensions
(Żebrowski et al., 2022)	Bayesian frameworks for optimal cyber threat mitigation	Bayesian Cybersecurity Risk Analysis	
	Probabilistic attack modeling, multi-objective risk management		
	Cyber-physical system security strategies		
(Sarker et al., 2021)	AI-driven cybersecurity, security intelligence modeling	AI-Powered Security Intelligence	
	Machine learning, deep learning, intrusion detection		
	Knowledge-based security frameworks		
(Temara, 2024)	AI-powered threat detection, automation, and risk analysis	Harnessing AI for Next-Generation Cybersecurity	
	AI in intrusion detection, malware analysis, and response automation		
	The role of AI in predictive cybersecurity and strategic risk management		
(Habibzadeh et al., 2019)	Cybersecurity policies and governance in smart cities	Cyber-Resilience and Policy-Making	Policy, Regulations, and Governance in Cyber-Resilient Smart Economies
	Regulations on cyber-physical security		
	Privacy and data protection frameworks		
	Governmental strategies for cyber threat mitigation		
(Ho & O'Sullivan, 2019)	Standardization and policy challenges in smart systems	Regulatory and Standardization Frameworks	
	Government intervention in cybersecurity policies		
	Innovation bottlenecks in standardization		
	Public-private partnerships in cyber policy		

continued on following page

Table 1. Continued

Authors	First-order themes	Second-order themes	Aggregate dimensions
(Liu et al., 2024)	Enhancing cyber-resiliency of DER-based smart grids	Cyber-Resiliency in Smart Grids	
	Risk assessment methodologies and frameworks		
	Threat modeling and defense-in-depth strategies		
	Regulatory and standardization challenges in DER security		
(Brown et al., 2018)	Smart grid governance, regulatory and financial models	Governance and Policy Innovations	
	Cybersecurity and resilience in smart grids		
	Policy interventions for modernizing energy infrastructures		
(Dupont, 2019)	Cyber-resilience in financial institutions	Cyber-Resilience Strategies for Financial Sector	
	Risk management, regulations, and compliance frameworks		
	Institutional approaches to cyber-risk governance		
(Gisladottir et al., 2016)	Overregulation and Underregulation in Cybersecurity	Balancing Regulations and Cyber-Resilience	
	Effects of regulatory frameworks on cyber system resilience		
	Human factors in regulatory compliance		
(Srinivas et al., 2019)	Government regulations and cybersecurity frameworks	Cybersecurity Policy and National Strategy	
	Standards and recommendations for cyber defense		
	National cybersecurity policies and regulatory frameworks		

continued on following page

Table 1. Continued

Authors	First-order themes	Second-order themes	Aggregate dimensions
(Sutherland, 2018)	Trends in global digital economy regulations	Global Digital Governance and Policy Trends	
	GDPR, data protection, and privacy laws		
	Competition, standardization, and market regulations		
(Tiirmaa-Klaar, 2016)	National cyber resilience and critical infrastructure protection	National Cyber Resilience and Leadership	
	Cybersecurity incident response strategies		
	Public-private partnerships for cyber resilience		

The conceptual framework based on the results of the meta-synthesis method is presented in Figure 1.

Figure 1. The conceptual framework of the research

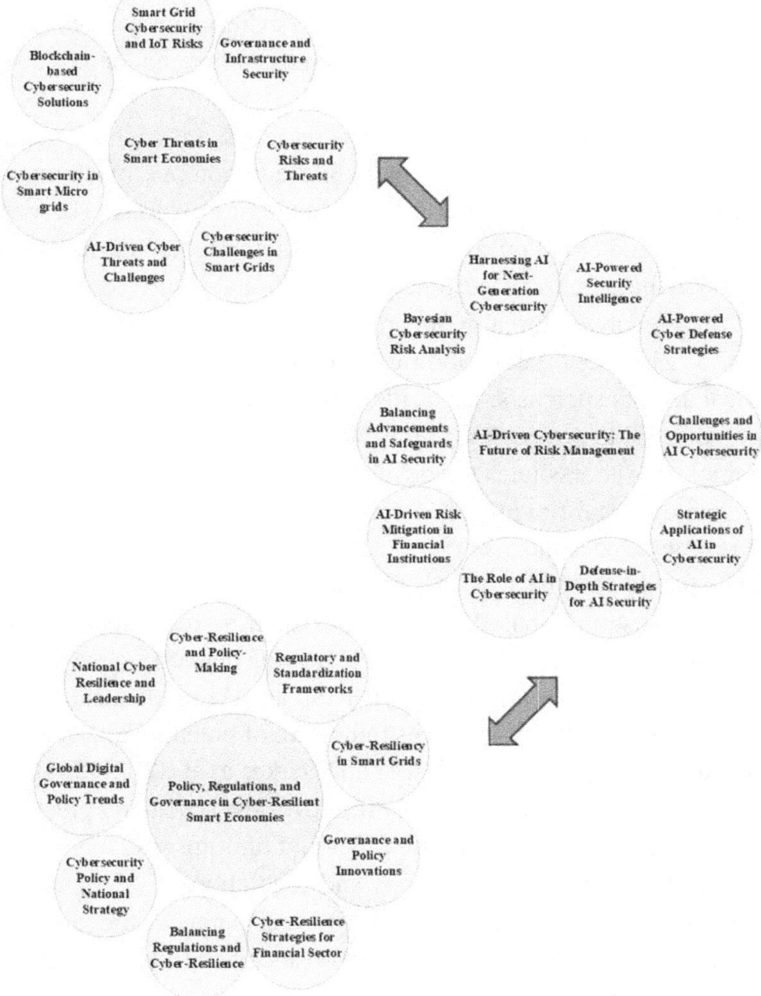

5. DISCUSSION AND CONCLUSION

The continuous rise in adopting technologies like artificial intelligence (AI), the Internet of Things (IoT), and cloud computing has significantly reshaped the cybersecurity landscape in smart economies. While these technologies drive unparalleled efficiency and innovation, they introduce novel vulnerabilities that cybercriminals can exploit. This study delved into AI-driven cybersecurity by categorizing potential cyber threats, evaluating AI-based security solutions, and examining governance frameworks in smart economies. A meta-synthesis methodology was employed, reviewing existing research to identify emerging cybersecurity risks, analyze the role of AI in mitigating these risks, and explore regulatory challenges in managing AI-powered security systems.

The study's findings reveal that smart economies are highly susceptible to sophisticated AI-driven cyberattacks, including autonomous phishing, deepfake fraud, AI-driven malware, and blockchain technologies exploits. The widespread use of IoT devices and cloud infrastructure, integral to modern digital markets, has greatly expanded the attack surface, rendering traditional security measures ineffective against these evolving threats. According to studies by Demertzi et al. (2023) and Kaloudi & Li (2020), vulnerabilities in cyber-physical systems, particularly within critical sectors such as smart grids, healthcare, and finance, are becoming increasingly difficult to protect due to the adaptability of AI-powered threats. This growing complexity necessitates the development of advanced AI-driven security solutions capable of real-time threat detection, autonomous risk assessment, and automated response mechanisms.

The study further emphasizes the significant role AI plays in strengthening cybersecurity defenses. AI-based technologies such as machine learning-driven threat detection, behavioral analytics, and self-healing networks have proven highly effective in detecting and neutralizing cyber threats. AI models can analyze vast datasets in real time, identifying patterns indicative of potential attacks before they materialize. Research by Familoni (2024) and Sarker et al. (2021) highlights that AI-enhanced risk mitigation considerably improves the speed and precision of cybersecurity measures, reducing response times and limiting system vulnerabilities. However, challenges related to the ethics and regulation of AI in cybersecurity persist. Issues such as algorithmic bias, lack of transparency in decision-making, and data privacy concerns remain significant obstacles to fully integrating AI into cybersecurity governance.

Governance frameworks and policy regulations are crucial in addressing these challenges. However, existing regulations such as GDPR, NIST, and national cybersecurity laws are insufficient to combat the advanced threats posed by AI-driven cyberattacks. The rapid pace of AI-powered attacks calls for continuous updates to cybersecurity regulations and enhanced international collaboration to establish comprehensive and standardized security protocols. Findings by Habibzadeh et al. (2019) and Ho & O'Sullivan (2019) underscore the necessity for stronger public-private partnerships to improve cyber resilience, foster threat intelligence sharing, and develop unified security frameworks. Without proactive governance, the risk posed by AI-driven cyberattacks will continue to outpace current security measures, leaving smart economies vulnerable to data breaches, financial losses, and infrastructure disruptions.

Emerging trends in Industry 6.0, as detailed by Tavakkoli-Moghaddam et al. (2024), highlight the growing importance of integrating cybersecurity measures into the evolving business and industrial ecosystems. The Smart Factory 6.0 concept demonstrates how AI and digital infrastructure can significantly enhance cybersecurity in manufacturing, improving resilience against cyber threats in interconnected industrial systems. This transition towards Industry 6.0 underscores the need for robust security frameworks to protect critical infrastructures from AI-driven vulnerabilities. Moreover, Bakhshi Movahed et al. (2024) discuss the intersection of Marketing 6.0 and cybersecurity, emphasizing the importance of safeguarding consumer data in smart economies. Their research suggests that AI-based cybersecurity models are crucial for ensuring data protection and underscores the necessity of regulatory frameworks that prioritize consumer privacy. This aligns with the increasing recognition that cybersecurity challenges in marketing and customer-facing services must evolve alongside the technologies driving these sectors. In addition, Bakhshi Movahed et al. (2024) also explore the potential of AI in sustainable agriculture supply chains within Agriculture 6.0. Integrating cybersecurity measures to protect sensitive data and infrastructure in agricultural supply chains will help smart economies achieve their sustainability objectives while defending against emerging data integrity and privacy threats. Similarly, Bakhshi Movahed et al. (2024) research on the security criteria for financial systems within Industry 6.0 highlights the critical need for addressing both traditional and new cybersecurity risks. This research shows that AI's integration into financial systems is essential for maintaining the stability and security of digital financial services in the face of complex cyber threats. Finally, the concept of Hospital 6.0 by Aliahmadi et al. (2024) emphasizes the pivotal role of AI-driven security systems in healthcare. As medical institutions become increasingly connected, ensuring the security of patient data and healthcare infrastructures becomes essential. Their research further supports the integration of AI and digital infrastructure to enhance cybersecurity resilience in connected medical systems.

From the insights gained in this study, several key recommendations emerge for fortifying cybersecurity in smart economies. First, regulatory bodies should establish ethical AI guidelines to mitigate algorithmic bias and promote transparency in AI-driven security decisions. Second, there is a need for further research to develop predictive AI models capable of identifying unknown cyber threats and proactively mitigating risks. Third, standardizing AI cybersecurity policies across global markets is vital to ensuring consistent security practices and regulatory compliance. Additionally, integrating credibility CVaR models into AI-driven cybersecurity risk assessments could enhance financial resilience and improve risk management strategies in smart economies (Ghanbari et al., 2024). Moreover, investment in

AI-driven cybersecurity training programs will help address the skill gap among cybersecurity professionals, ensuring they are adequately equipped to handle AI-enhanced security threats. Lastly, collaboration between governments and industry leaders should be strengthened through public-private partnerships, enabling the development of more resilient cybersecurity frameworks for smart economies.

In conclusion, the rapid advancements in AI, IoT, and cloud computing have significantly transformed smart economies while simultaneously exacerbating cybersecurity challenges. This study comprehensively analyzes AI-driven cybersecurity, highlighting potential benefits and associated risks. While AI-based security mechanisms enhance threat detection and incident response, the ethical and regulatory challenges must be addressed to ensure fairness, transparency, and accountability in decision-making. Furthermore, cybersecurity laws and governance frameworks must be urgently updated to accommodate the growing complexity of AI-powered cyber threats. The future development of global cybersecurity policies, ethical AI governance, and enhanced cooperation between governments and private sectors will be crucial in securing smart economies against future cyber risks.

By integrating AI-driven cybersecurity solutions with comprehensive regulatory frameworks, digital markets can attain greater resilience, risk mitigation, and operational security. However, combining technological innovation, regulatory oversight, and strategic partnerships, a multidisciplinary approach will be essential for building a secure and sustainable future for digital economies.

Declaration of competing interest

The authors declare that they have no known competing financial interests or personal relationships that could have appeared to influence the work reported in this book chapter.

Declaration of generative AI and AI-assisted technologies in the writing process

While preparing this work, the authors used OpenAI's tool Chat GPT to edit and write some parts of this book chapter. After using this service, the authors reviewed and edited the content as needed and took full responsibility for the publication's content.

REFERENCES

Akhtar, Z., & Rawol, A. T. (2024). Harnessing artificial intelligence (AI) for cybersecurity: Challenges, opportunities, risks, future directions. *Computers and Artificial Intelligence*, 2(2), 1485. DOI: 10.59400/cai.v2i2.1485

Alaa Hammad, A., Adnan Falih, M., Ali Abd, S., & Rashid Ahmed, A. (2025). Detecting Cyber Threats in IoT Networks: A Machine Learning Approach. *International Journal of Computing and Digital Systems*, 17(1), 1–25. DOI: 10.12785/ijcds/1571020041

Aliahmadi, M. H., Movahed, A. B., Movahed, A. B., Nozari, H., & Bayanati, M. (2024). *Hospital 6.0 Components and Dimensions* (pp. 46–61). DOI: 10.4018/979-8-3693-3108-8.ch004

Alijoyo, F. A., Kaur, C., Anjum, A., Vuyyuru, V. A., & Bala, B. K. (2024). Enhancing Cyber-Physical Systems Resilience: Adaptive Self-Healing Security Using Long Short-Term Memory Networks. *2024 International Conference on Advances in Computing, Communication and Applied Informatics (ACCAI)*, 1–8. DOI: 10.1109/ACCAI61061.2024.10602467

Ameedeen, M. A., Hamid, R. A., Aldhyani, T. H. H., Al-Nassr, L. A. K. M., Olatunji, S. O., & Subramanian, P. (2024). A Framework for Automated Big Data Analytics in Cybersecurity Threat Detection. *Mesopotamian Journal of Big Data*, 2024, 175–184. DOI: 10.58496/MJBD/2024/012

Bloom, P. (2020). *Identity, Institutions and Governance in an AI World*. Springer International Publishing., DOI: 10.1007/978-3-030-36181-5

Brown, M. A., Zhou, S., & Ahmadi, M. (2018). Smart grid governance: An international review of evolving policy issues and innovations. *Wiley Interdisciplinary Reviews. Energy and Environment*, 7(5), e290. Advance online publication. DOI: 10.1002/wene.290

Camacho, N. G. (2024). The Role of AI in Cybersecurity: Addressing Threats in the Digital Age. *Journal of Artificial Intelligence General Science (JAIGS) ISSN:3006-4023, 3*(1), 143–154. DOI: 10.60087/jaigs.v3i1.75

Dana, L.-P., Salamzadeh, A., Mortazavi, S., & Hadizadeh, M. (2022). Investigating the Impact of International Markets and New Digital Technologies on Business Innovation in Emerging Markets. *Sustainability (Basel)*, 14(2), 983. DOI: 10.3390/su14020983

Darem, A. A., Alhashmi, A. A., Alkhaldi, T. M., Alashjaee, A. M., Alanazi, S. M., & Ebad, S. A. (2023). Cyber Threats Classifications and Countermeasures in Banking and Financial Sector. *IEEE Access : Practical Innovations, Open Solutions*, 11(2), 125138–125158. DOI: 10.1109/ACCESS.2023.3327016

Demertzi, V., Demertzis, S., & Demertzis, K. (2023). An Overview of Cyber Threats, Attacks and Countermeasures on the Primary Domains of Smart Cities. In *Applied Sciences (Switzerland)* (Vol. 13, Issue 2). DOI: 10.3390/app13020790

Dupont, B. (2019). The cyber-resilience of financial institutions: Significance and applicability. *Journal of Cybersecurity*, 5(1), tyz013. Advance online publication. DOI: 10.1093/cybsec/tyz013

El Mrabet, Z., Kaabouch, N., El Ghazi, H., & El Ghazi, H. (2018). Cyber-security in smart grid: Survey and challenges. *Computers & Electrical Engineering*, 67, 469–482. DOI: 10.1016/j.compeleceng.2018.01.015

ElMamy, S. B., Mrabet, H., Gharbi, H., Jemai, A., & Trentesaux, D. (2020). A Survey on the Usage of Blockchain Technology for Cyber-Threats in the Context of Industry 4.0. *Sustainability (Basel)*, 12(21), 9179. DOI: 10.3390/su12219179

Fahrul, M., Rusliati, E., Hosseini, S. H., Jannati Mashkani, A., Abdellahi, S. A., & Ilvira, Rifka Fitri, D. (2016). Document (3).Pdf. In *Agri Ekonomi* (Vol. 25, Issue Analisis Usaha dan Strategi Pengembangan Agribisnis Buah Naga CV. Kusumo Wanadri Kulon Progo, p. 20).

Familoni, B. T. (2024). Cybersecurity challenges in the age of AI: Theoretical approaches and practical solutions. *Computer Science & IT Research Journal*, 5(3), 703–724.

Ghanbari, H., Mohammadi, E., Fooeik, A. M. L., Kumar, R. R., Stauvermann, P. J., & Shabani, M. (2024). Cryptocurrency Portfolio Allocation under Credibilistic CVaR Criterion and Practical Constraints. *Risks*, 12(10), 163. DOI: 10.3390/risks12100163

Gisladottir, V., Ganin, A. A., Keisler, J. M., Kepner, J., & Linkov, I. (2017). Resilience of Cyber Systems with Over- and Underregulation. *Risk Analysis*, 37(9), 1644–1651. DOI: 10.1111/risa.12729 PMID: 27935146

Guembe, B., Azeta, A., Misra, S., Osamor, V. C., Fernandez-Sanz, L., & Pospelova, V. (2022). The Emerging Threat of Ai-driven Cyber Attacks: A Review. *Applied Artificial Intelligence*, 36(1), 9–62. DOI: 10.1080/08839514.2022.2037254

Gunduz, M. Z., & Das, R. (2020). Cyber-security on smart grid: Threats and potential solutions. *Computer Networks*, 169, 107094. DOI: 10.1016/j.comnet.2019.107094

Habibzadeh, H., Nussbaum, B. H., Anjomshoa, F., Kantarci, B., & Soyata, T. (2019). A survey on cybersecurity, data privacy, and policy issues in cyber-physical system deployments in smart cities. *Sustainable Cities and Society*, 50, 101660. DOI: 10.1016/j.scs.2019.101660

Ho, J.-Y., & O'Sullivan, E. (2019). Addressing the evolving standardisation challenges of 'smart systems' innovation: Emerging roles for government? *Science & Public Policy*, 46(4), 552–569. DOI: 10.1093/scipol/scz008

Institute for AI Policy and Strategy (IAPS). (2023). *Adapting cybersecurity frameworks to manage frontier AI risks.* https://doi.org/https://doi.org/10.48550/arXiv.2408.07933

Kaloudi, N., & Li, J. (2021). The AI-Based Cyber Threat Landscape. *ACM Computing Surveys*, 53(1), 1–34. DOI: 10.1145/3372823

Laxmi, S., & Kumar, S. (2024). Improving Cyber Security: Artificial Intelligence's Ability to Detect and Stop Threats. *International Journal of Advanced Engineering Research and Science*, 11(6), 19–24. DOI: 10.22161/ijaers.116.3

Liu, M., Teng, F., Zhang, Z., Ge, P., Sun, M., Deng, R., Cheng, P., & Chen, J. (2024). Enhancing Cyber-Resiliency of DER-Based Smart Grid: A Survey. *IEEE Transactions on Smart Grid*, 15(5), 4998–5030. DOI: 10.1109/TSG.2024.3373008

Movahed, A. B., Movahed, A. B., Aliahmadi, B., & Nozari, H. (2024). *Green and Sustainable Supply Chain in Agriculture 6.0* (pp. 32–45). DOI: 10.4018/979-8-3693-3108-8.ch003

Movahed, A. B., Movahed, A. B., & Nozari, H. (2024). *Marketing 6.0 Conceptualization* (pp. 15–31). DOI: 10.4018/979-8-3693-3108-8.ch002

Movahed, A. B., Movahed, A. B., Nozari, H., & Rahmaty, M. (2024). *Security Criteria in Financial Systems in Industry 6.0* (pp. 62–74). DOI: 10.4018/979-8-3693-3108-8.ch005

Nejabatkhah, F., Li, Y. W., Liang, H., & Reza Ahrabi, R. (2020). Cyber-Security of Smart Microgrids: A Survey. *Energies*, 14(1), 27. DOI: 10.3390/en14010027

Nwafor, K. C., Ikudabo, A. O., Onyeje, C. C., & Ihenacho, D. O. T. (2024). Mitigating cybersecurity risks in financial institutions: The role of AI and data analytics. *International Journal of Science and Research Archive*, 13(1), 2895–2910. DOI: 10.30574/ijsra.2024.13.1.2014

Sarker, I. H., Furhad, M. H., & Nowrozy, R. (2021). AI-Driven Cybersecurity: An Overview, Security Intelligence Modeling and Research Directions. *SN Computer Science*, 2(3), 173. DOI: 10.1007/s42979-021-00557-0 PMID: 33778771

Shahana, A., Hasan, R., Farabi, S. F., Akter, J., Al Mahmud, M. A., Johora, F. T., & Suzer, G. (2024). AI-Driven Cybersecurity: Balancing Advancements and Safeguards. *Journal of Computer Science and Technology Studies*, 6(2), 76–85. DOI: 10.32996/jcsts.2024.6.2.9

Srinivas, J., Das, A. K., & Kumar, N. (2019). Government regulations in cyber security: Framework, standards and recommendations. *Future Generation Computer Systems*, 92, 178–188. DOI: 10.1016/j.future.2018.09.063

Sutherland, E. (2018). Trends in Regulating the Global Digital Economy. SSRN *Electronic Journal*. DOI: 10.2139/ssrn.3216772

Tavakkoli-Moghaddam, R., Nozari, H., Bakhshi-Movahed, A., & Bakhshi-Movahed, A. (2024). A conceptual framework for the smart factory 6.0. In *Advanced Businesses in Industry 6.0* (pp. 1–14). DOI: 10.4018/979-8-3693-3108-8.ch001

Temara, S. (2024). Harnessing the power of artificial intelligence to enhance next-generation cybersecurity. *World Journal of Advanced Research and Reviews*, 23(2), 797–811. DOI: 10.30574/wjarr.2024.23.2.2428

Tiirmaa-Klaar, H. (2016). Building national cyber resilience and protecting critical information infrastructure. *Journal of Cyber Policy*, 1(1), 94–106. DOI: 10.1080/23738871.2016.1165716

Uzoka, A., Cadet, E., & Ojukwu, P. U. (2024). Applying artificial intelligence in Cybersecurity to enhance threat detection, response, and risk management. *Computer Science & IT Research Journal*, 5(10), 2511–2538. DOI: 10.51594/csitrj.v5i10.1677

Wongwas, W., Wongsim, M., & Satchawatee, N. (2024). The Role of Digital Transformation in Enhancing Business Performance and Smart Economy Integration: A Case Study of Thailand's Retail Industry. *International Journal of Analysis and Applications*, 22, 173. DOI: 10.28924/2291-8639-22-2024-173

Żebrowski, P., Couce-Vieira, A., & Mancuso, A. (2022). A Bayesian Framework for the Analysis and Optimal Mitigation of Cyber Threats to Cyber-Physical Systems. *Risk Analysis*, 42(10), 2275–2290. DOI: 10.1111/risa.13900 PMID: 35229333

Chapter 5

Sustainable Smart Economies: Green Technologies and Circular Business Models

Ali Bakhshi Movahed
https://orcid.org/0009-0006-4463-6838
Iran University of Science and Technology, Iran

Aminmasoud Bakhshi Movahed
https://orcid.org/0000-0003-3259-5419
Iran University of Science and Technology, Iran

ABSTRACT

The chapter investigates the convergence of sustainable smart economies, green technologies, and circular business models, underscoring their vital contributions to promoting environmental sustainability and economic resilience. As global issues such as climate change and resource scarcity become more pressing, incorporating innovative green technologies spanning renewable energy initiatives to sophisticated waste management solutions becomes essential. These technologies not only improve resource efficiency but also play a significant role in diminishing ecological footprints. Concurrently, implementing circular business models is crucial for reimagining value creation in ways that reduce waste and encourage sustainable practices. Enterprises can shift from conventional linear models to more regenerative frameworks that harmonies with ecological objectives by emphasising systems that focus on recycling, reuse, and sustainable sourcing. This chapter synthesises existing literature and case studies to understand how sustainable smart economies can harness these innovations thoroughly.

DOI: 10.4018/979-8-3693-4369-2.ch005

1- INTRODUCTION

Sustainable smart economies have become crucial for reconciling economic advancement with environmental and social health in an era of rapid urban development, climate change, and diminishing resources (Kumar et al., 2024). Integrating green technologies and circular business models is at the heart of this framework, presenting innovative solutions to some of society's most pressing issues. We can minimise ecological impacts and enhance resource utilisation through green technologies such as renewable energy systems, energy-efficient infrastructures, and sophisticated waste management practices. By advocating for resource efficiency, waste minimisation, and continuous material reuse, circular business models displace the traditional 'take-make-dispose' paradigm.

The development of resilient, inclusive, and future-oriented economies can be facilitated by integrating advanced technology with sustainable economic practices. These principles can be adopted by enterprises, government bodies, and communities to create new avenues for growth and protect the environment for future generations. This analysis explores how green technologies and circular business models can aid in the transition to sustainable smart economies, creating a framework for a more equitably and environmentally conscious world.

Closed-loop systems emphasise the importance of resource efficiency and sustainability through the circular economy, a revolutionary paradigm in economic frameworks. In contrast to conventional linear models characterised by a "take-make-waste" approach, it aims to prolong the lifespan of products through strategies such as reuse, repair, refurbishment, and recycling, thereby mitigating waste and depletion of resources. To achieve the objectives, we must decrease our reliance on virgin materials, reduce greenhouse gas emissions, and promote industrial symbiosis, in which another uses waste produced by one industry as a resource. To illustrate, implementing circular economy principles in agriculture can decrease synthetic fertilisers by as much as 80%, improving soil health and ecosystem resilience (Cordeiro & Sindhøj, 2024).

Circular models have significant environmental advantages, with projections suggesting that industrial emissions within the European Union could be reduced by 56% by 2050 (Hailemariam & Erdiaw-Kwasie, 2023). Furthermore, these models help preserve natural ecosystems by reducing pollution and guarding against excessive resource extraction. Job creation is facilitated by circular systems from an economic standpoint, particularly in recycling, renewable energy, and sustainable manufacturing sectors. The implementation of circular strategies has increased net employment in industries, as demonstrated by research. Creating 18 million jobs worldwide while also achieving a 41% reduction in emissions can be achieved by switching to renewable energy sources (Milhem et al., 2024). Green technologies greatly aid in the facilitation of circular economy practices. Integrating IoT and blockchain technologies significantly enhances supply chain transparency, making it possible to monitor materials in real-time and improve reverse logistics to promote efficient recycling. These innovations foster Industrial symbiosis, as demonstrated by the Kalundborg Symbiosis in Denmark, which brings together 25 companies to exchange waste materials, thereby minimising costs and mitigating environmental impacts. Additionally, digital platforms aid small and medium-sized enterprises (SMEs) in implementing circular economic strategies by improving resource tracking and carbon asset management. The benefits of blockchain-enabled life cycle assessments in sectors like battery manufacturing are product traceability, remanufacturing, and reducing waste.

The circular economy combines technological advancements, comprehensive resource management, economic development, and environmental conservation. The United States Sustainable Development Goals (SDGs) and other global sustainability objectives can be achieved with this approach's feasible strategy.

Digital technologies are employed in circular business models to extract value from waste, enhance resource efficiency, and encourage sustainable consumption behaviours. Product-service systems, collaborative consumption, and sustainable production techniques are among the strategies included in these models. Despite this, the transition to circular business models presents several challenges. Systemic transformations and cultivating new characteristics within their value chains are necessary for organisations. Innovation and sustainable development have significant prospects, even with these obstacles. To manage this transition effectively, businesses must adopt comprehensive strategies that balance sustainability's ecological, social, and economic aspects.

The development of sustainable smart economies requires the combination of green technologies and circular business models. By adopting these approaches, enterprises can significantly contribute to environmental conservation, economic resilience, and social welfare. Committing to global sustainability objectives creates a robust future that can address our generation's urgent issues while promoting a more sustainable lifestyle and workplace.

2- LITERATURE REVIEW

This literature table offers a comprehensive overview of significant studies, articles, and reports pertinent to the theme of "Sustainable Smart Economies: Green Technologies and Circular Business Models. The systematic categorisation of it into six sections assists researchers, policymakers, and practitioners in navigating the extensive information available on this topic.

Renewable energy sources, smart grid systems, electric vehicles, and waste-to-energy technologies that contribute to environmental sustainability are highlighted in the first section of "Green Technologies". In the second section, Circular Business Models, we examine frameworks like Product-as-a-Service, industrial symbiosis, and sharing economy platforms that improve resource efficiency and reduce waste. The third section, 'Integration of Green Tech & Circular Models, ' features studies examining how green technologies and circular economy concepts interact.

In addition, the table has a Case Studies section that provides practical examples of cities and industries that have successfully implemented sustainable smart economy practices. Green technologies and circular business models are integrated through policy frameworks and governmental initiatives, and the Policy and Governance section is responsible for evaluating these. Finally, the Challenges and Future Directions section outlines obstacles to implementation and highlights emerging trends within the field. The table includes the title, authors, publication year, and a concise summary of the work in each entry to identify relevant sources for further investigation.

Table 1 is crucial for comprehending the current research landscape, pinpointing gaps, and directing future initiatives to promote sustainable smart economies.

Table 1. Literature review table

Category	Title	References	Summary
Green Technologies	*Implementation of renewable technologies in energy-efficient urban infrastructure: Development to promote sustainable socio-economic growth*	(Bhattacharya et al., 2024)	Explores how renewable energy technologies contribute to sustainable economic growth.
	Smart grid concept and technologies for smart cities	(Haque et al., 2024)	Analyses the impact of smart grids on energy efficiency and carbon reduction.
	Impact of electric mobility on the sustainable development of the country, Case study in Morocco	(Harrouti et al., 2020)	Discusses the role of electronic vehicles (EVs) in reducing emissions and transitioning to sustainable mobility.
	Waste-to-Energy Processes as a Municipality-Level Waste Management Strategy: A Case Study of Kočevje, Slovenia	(Prebilič et al., 2024)	Examine waste-to-energy solutions as a tool for sustainable waste management.

continued on following page

Table 1. Continued

Category	Title	References	Summary
Circular Business Models	*Circular Economy: A New Business Paradigm for Sustainability*	(Geissdoerfer et al., 2017)	Introduces the concept of circular economy and its potential for sustainable business models.
	The Rise of Product-as-a-Service Models in the Digital Era: Redesigning Business Models for Circular Innovation	(Ingle et al., 2025)	Explores the PaaS model and its application in reducing waste and promoting resource efficiency.
	Industrial Symbiosis: Collaborative Approaches to Circularity	(Baldassarre et al, 2019)	Case studies on industrial symbiosis and its role in creating closed-loop systems.
Integration of Green Tech & Circular Models	The role of green technologies in the transition towards a circular economy	(Yun et al., 2023)	Discusses the integration of green technologies with circular business models for sustainability.
	AI-enabled circular economy management for sustainable smart cities: Integrating AI in resource optimisation and Waste Reduction	(Jogarao et al., 2024)	Provides a framework for combining smart city technologies with circular economy principles.
Case Studies	Carbon-neutral cities: Critical review of theory and practice	(Huovila et al., 2022)	Examine Copenhagen's use of green technologies and circular practices to achieve carbon neutrality.
	Singapore's Smart Nation Initiative: Lessons for Sustainable Economies	(Aigner et al., 2022)	Analyses Singapore's integration of smart technologies and sustainability strategies.
Policy and Governance	*A review of the circular economy and its implementation*	(Heshmati, 2017)	Reviews policy tools and incentives for advancing green tech and circular economy practices.
	Promoting circular economy transition: A study about perceptions and awareness by different stakeholders' groups	(Langen et al., 2021)	Discusses government initiatives to support circular economy adoption.
Challenges and Future Directions	*Circular economy practices in a developing economy: Barriers to be defeated*	(Gedam et al., 2021)	Identifies challenges in adopting circular business models and proposes solutions.
	Current trends in green technologies in food production and processing	(Boye & Arcand, 2013)	Highlights emerging green technologies and their potential for sustainable economies.

3- RESEARCH FRAMEWORK

The data analysis was conducted in three phases using a meta-synthesis approach. Meta-synthesis represents a systematic investigation that reviews and synthesises previous research studies. Through meta-synthesis, novel analyses and interpretations emerge that are not present in the original literature (Sandelowski & Barroso, 2003). This approach employs aggregated information and results from studies addressing similar topics (Zimmer, 2006). Meta-synthesis is an overarching term encompassing various methodological strategies to generate new insights through a thorough and detailed examination of qualitative research outcomes. Specifically, meta-synthesis involves aggregating theoretical frameworks into overarching narratives, generalisations, or interpretive translations that arise from integrating or comparing qualitative findings (Xu, 2008). This research adheres to a seven-step methodology (Figure. 1).

Figure 1. Sandelowski & Barroso method of meta-synthesis

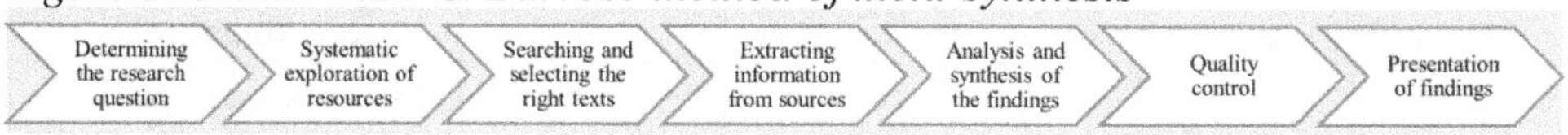

4- FINDINGS

The meta-synthesis results in the first part refer to Green Technologies. Green technology is essential for the attainment of sustainable global development objectives. Nevertheless, the absence of a universally recognised classification system for green technology frequently obstructs its advancement and implementation (Guo et al., 2020). In the subsequent section, an analysis of the outcomes associated with Circular Business Models is conducted. The Circular Economy is increasingly recognised as a viable model that reduces resource exhaustion (Geissdoerfer et al., 2020). In the third section, an examination of "Sustainable Smart Economies" is conducted, emphasising the significance of integrating "Green Technology" and "Circular Business Models." A meta-synthesis analysis, presented in Table 2, is utilised to categorise the various types of these factors precisely.

Table 2. Meta-synthesis analysis

Authors	First-order themes	Second-order themes	Aggregate dimensions
(Guo et al., 2020)	Alternative energy production	Environmental Sound Technology Concordance	Green Technologies
	Energy conservation		
	Environmentally friendly farming		
	Environmental purification, protection, or remediation		
(Guo et al., 2020) (Raheem et al., 2019)	Disaster Prevention	Ecological Safety	
	Ecological Agriculture, Forestry, Animal Husbandry and Fishery		
	Ecosystem Conservation and Restoration		
(Tarr et al., 2023)	Rural and urban living environment	Life Health	
	Environmental Health		
(Xiao et al., 2024) (Guo et al., 2020)	Resource or Material Management	Resource Utilization	
	Resource or Material Recycling		
	Resource Exploitation and Utilsration		
	Resource or Material Conservation		
(Zia et al., 2023) (Yang et al., 2022) (Guo et al., 2020)	Environment Quality Management	Environmental Quality	
	Solid waste treatment and Disposal		
	Radiation Pollution and Noise Pollution		
	Soil, Water, and Air Quality		
(Sudarsan & Chithra, 2024) (Guo et al., 2020) (Talarico et al., 2013)	Energy Management and Conservation	Energy Utilization	
	Energy-efficient Appliances		
	Energy Storage		
	Energy Recycling		
	Fossil Energy, Clean Energy		

continued on following page

Table 2. Continued

Authors	First-order themes	Second-order themes	Aggregate dimensions
(Levänen et al., 2024) (da Costa Fernandes et al., 2020) (Geissdoerfer et al., 2020)	Main products services	Value Proposition	Circular Business Models
	Customer segments markets		
	Customer needs problems		
(Kuzma & Sehnem, 2023) (Geissdoerfer et al., 2020) (Ünal et al., 2019)	Key value chain elements	Value Creation & Delivery	
	Core Competencies		
	Resources and Capabilities		
(Lundgren et al., 2024) (Geissdoerfer et al., 2020)	Revenue Streams	Value Capture	
	Cost Drivers		
	Revenue models like leasing, razors & blades, platform fees		

continued on following page

Table 2. Continued

Authors	First-order themes	Second-order themes	Aggregate dimensions
(Popova & Popovs, 2022) (Salehi et al., 2017) (Arutyunov & Lisichkin, 2017) (Hawkins & Dente, 2010)	Enhancing the efficiency of passenger transport systems	Smart Mobility	Sustainable Smart Economies
	Regulating greenhouse gas emissions produced by transportation		
	Augmenting the proportion of renewable energy sources in fuel composition		
	Overseeing the logistics of goods transportation linked to consumer demand		
(Tanaka et al., 2025) (Popova & Popovs, 2022) (Han et al., 2021)	The management of working hours concerning urban population growth	Smart Living	
	Balancing the ratio of leisure time and working hours with household consumption expenditures		
	Promoting job security for at-risk workers to mitigate crime rates		
(Popova & Popovs, 2022) (Islam et al., 2020) (Liu et al., 2009)	Resource efficiency in the context of hazardous waste management	Smart Environment	
	Investments in environmental conservation		
	Agricultural water pollution control using remote sensing		
	The assessment of surface water quality through using IoT technologies for monitoring purposes		
	Machine learning-based classification of water		
(Çil & Guzey, 2024) (Popova & Popovs, 2022) (Spasova & Ward, 2019)	Female participation in technology sectors	Smart Society	
	Expenditures on social protection and healthcare systems		
	Indicators of youth inequality		
	Accessibility of electronic public services		
(Harsono et al., 2024) (Shen, 2022) (Popova & Popovs, 2022)	The relation between the percentage of individuals utilising the Internet and the topic of adult education	Smart People	
	The rise in financial investments in education as it pertains to the Human Development Index		
	The quality and quantity of institutions of higher learning		

The conceptual framework derived from the findings of the meta-synthesis method is illustrated in Figure 2.

Figure 2. The research conceptual framework

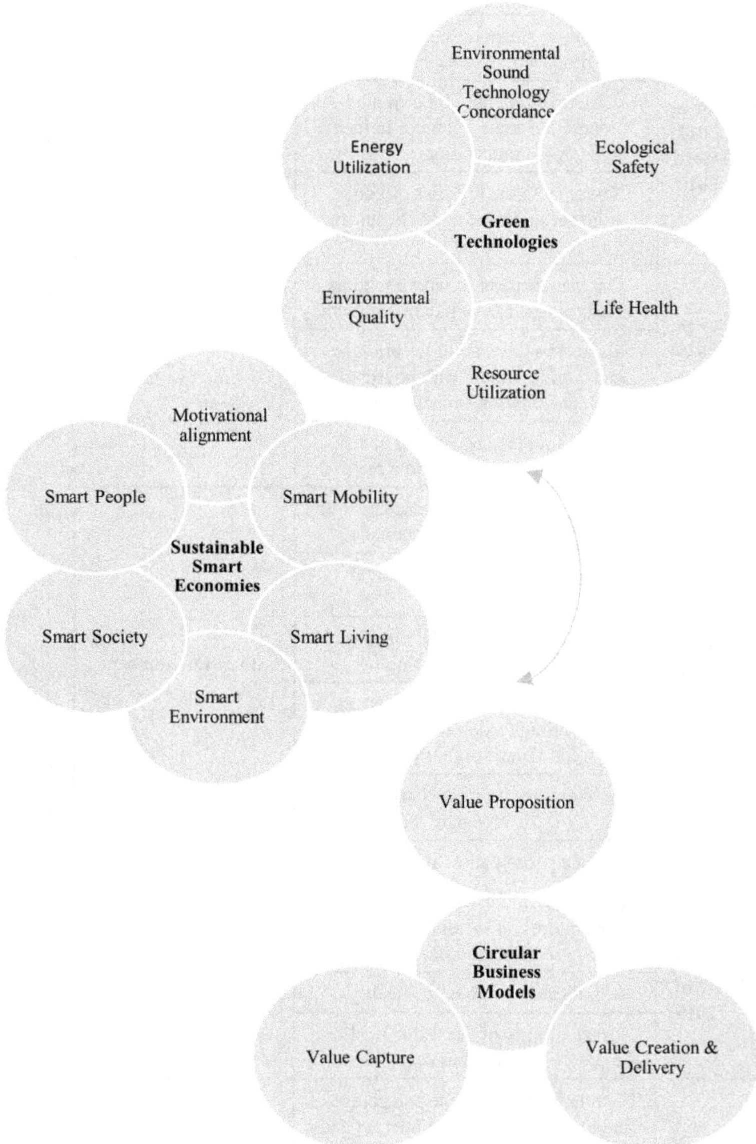

5- DISCUSSION AND CONCLUSION

Sustainable Smart Economies is a new way to address the pressing issues of ecological degradation, resource depletion, and climate change with a revolutionary approach. Community economic systems prioritising sustainability, efficiency, and enduring resilience can be achieved using eco-friendly technologies and circular economic models. The most important component of reducing carbon emissions and environmental impact is using eco-friendly technologies, such as renewable energy sources, intelligent grid systems, and energy-efficient infrastructures. Transitioning to economic systems prioritising sustainability, efficiency, and enduring resilience is possible for communities using eco-friendly technologies and circular economic frameworks.

The progression towards Sustainable Smart Economies and the innovative framework of Industry 6.0 are intricately linked, forming a cohesive trajectory towards a future characterised by the synergy of technology, sustainability, and human-centred methodologies. Adopting eco-friendly technologies and circular economic models is a priority for sustainable smart economies to address environmental issues and enhance resource efficiency. Conversely, Industry 6.0 broadens this perspective by integrating sustainability and innovation into the foundational aspects of diverse sectors, exemplified by initiatives such as Hospital 6.0, Agriculture 6.0, Marketing 6.0, financial systems security, and Smart Factory 6.0 (Movahed et al., 2024). For example, Hospital 6.0 employs cutting-edge technologies such as AI and the IoT to improve healthcare services while reducing waste and energy usage, aligning with circular economy principles (Aliahmadi et al., 2024). Similarly, Agriculture 6.0 promotes a green and sustainable supply chain by applying smart farming technologies and renewable energy sources, which ensure food security and mitigate environmental impacts, thereby contributing to the goals of sustainable smart economies (Movahed et al., 2024). Marketing 6.0 enhances ethical consumer engagement through immersive technologies, encouraging responsible consumption behaviors that align with sustainability objectives (Movahed et al., 2024). Industry 6.0 digital advancements are founded on trust and resilience because security is prioritised in financial systems, which is essential for the stability of sustainable economies. Lastly, the Smart Factory 6.0 paradigm underscores the significance of autonomous systems and real-time data analytics in optimizing resource utilisation and minimising waste, reflecting the core tenets of Industry 6.0 and sustainable smart economies (Tavakkoli-Moghaddam et al., 2024). The interrelated concepts presented here exemplify a comprehensive strategy for tackling global issues. By merging green technologies, circular economic models, and cutting-edge innovations, it is possible to develop efficient, productive, environmentally sustainable, and socially inclusive systems. Achieving this vision necessitates collaboration among governments, businesses, and individuals, alongside dedication to ethical practices and ongoing innovation. Integrating sustainable smart economies with Industry 6.0 signifies a transformative shift towards a more intelligent, sustainable, and equitable future for everyone.

S DEDREFERENCES

Aigner, I., Garai-Fodor, M., & Szemere, T. P. (2022, July). Singapore's journey as a digit-all-sized and innovative smart nation toward sustainability. In *2022 IEEE 10th Jubilee International Conference on Computational Cybernetics and Cyber-Medical Systems (ICCC)* (pp. 000259-000264). IEEE.

Aliahmadi, M. H., Movahed, A. B., Movahed, A. B., Nozari, H., & Bayanati, M. (2024). Hospital 6.0 Components and Dimensions. In *Advanced Businesses in Industry 6.0* (pp. 46-61). IGI Global.

Arutyunov, V. S., & Lisichkin, G. V. (2017). Energy resources of the 21st century: Problems and forecasts. Can renewable energy sources replace fossil fuels. *Russian Chemical Reviews*, 86(8), 777–804. DOI: 10.1070/RCR4723

Baldassarre, B., Schepers, M., Bocken, N., Cuppen, E., Korevaar, G., & Calabretta, G. (2019). Industrial Symbiosis: Towards a design process for eco-industrial clusters by integrating Circular Economy and Industrial Ecology perspectives. *Journal of Cleaner Production*, 216, 446–460. DOI: 10.1016/j.jclepro.2019.01.091

Bhattacharya, S., & Sachdev, B. K. Implementation of renewable technologies in energy-efficient urban infrastructure: Development to promote sustainable socio-economic growth. In *Sustainable Technologies for Energy Efficient Buildings* (pp. 337–357). CRC Press.

Boye, J. I., & Arcand, Y. (2013). Current trends in green technologies in food production and processing. *Food Engineering Reviews*, 5(1), 1–17. DOI: 10.1007/s12393-012-9062-z

. Çil, M., & Guzey, Y. Y. (2024). Technology and gender: Understanding the changing dynamics of female unemployment in the G7 countries. Journal of new economy, 25(1), 26-49.

Cordeiro, C. M., & Sindhøj, E. (2024). Situating the discourse of recycled nutrient fertilisers in circular economy principles for sustainable agriculture. *Frontiers in Sustainability*, 5, 1465752. DOI: 10.3389/frsus.2024.1465752

da Costa Fernandes, S., Pigosso, D. C., McAloone, T. C., & Rozenfeld, H. (2020). Towards product-service system oriented to circular economy: A systematic review of value proposition design approaches. *Journal of Cleaner Production*, 257, 120507. DOI: 10.1016/j.jclepro.2020.120507 el Harrouti, T., Abouabdellah, A., & Serrou, D. (2020, December). Impact of electric mobility on the sustainable development of the country, Case study in Morocco. In *2020 IEEE 13th International Colloquium of Logistics and Supply Chain Management (LOGISTIQUA)* (pp. 1-6). IEEE.

Gedam, V. V., Raut, R. D., de Sousa Jabbour, A. B. L., Tanksale, A. N., & Narkhede, B. E. (2021). Circular economy practices in a developing economy: Barriers to be defeated. *Journal of Cleaner Production*, 311, 127670. DOI: 10.1016/j.jclepro.2021.127670

Geissdoerfer, M., Pieroni, M. P., Pigosso, D. C., & Soufani, K. (2020). Circular business models: A review. *Journal of Cleaner Production*, 277, 123741. DOI: 10.1016/j.jclepro.2020.123741

Geissdoerfer, M., Savaget, P., Bocken, N. M., & Hultink, E. J. (2017). The Circular Economy–A New Sustainability Paradigm? *Journal of Cleaner Production*, 143, 757–768. DOI: 10.1016/j.jclepro.2016.12.048

Guo, R., Lv, S., Liao, T., Xi, F., Zhang, J., Zuo, X., Cao, X., Feng, Z., & Zhang, Y. (2020). Classifying green technologies for sustainable innovation and investment. *Resources, Conservation and Recycling*, 153, 104580. DOI: 10.1016/j.resconrec.2019.104580

Hailemariam, A., & Erdiaw-Kwasie, M. O. (2023). Towards a circular economy: Implications for emission reduction and environmental sustainability. *Business Strategy and the Environment*, 32(4), 1951–1965. DOI: 10.1002/bse.3229

Han, M. J. N., & Kim, M. J. (2021). A critical review of the smart city about citizen adoption towards sustainable smart living. *Habitat International*, 108, 102312. DOI: 10.1016/j.habitatint.2021.102312

Haque, A., Bharath, K. V. S., & Mateen, S. (2024). Smart grid concept and technologies for smart cities. In *Smart Cities: Power Electronics, Renewable Energy, and Internet of Things* (pp. 96-129). CRC Press.

Harsono, I., Hatim, F., Sumastuti, E., Thalib, B., & Sya'rani, R. (2024). Poverty statistics of South Sulawesi Province based on Human Development Index and GRDP using panel data. International Journal on Social Science. *Economics and Art*, 13(4), 234–239.

Hawkins, T. R., & Dente, S. M. (2010). Greenhouse gas emissions driven by the transportation of goods associated with French consumption. *Environmental Science & Technology*, 44(22), 8656–8664. DOI: 10.1021/es9025529 PMID: 20886825

Heshmati, A. (2017). A review of the circular economy and its implementation. *International Journal of Green Economics*, 11(3-4), 251–288. DOI: 10.1504/IJGE.2017.089856

Huovila, A., Siikavirta, H., Rozado, C. A., Rökman, J., Tuominen, P., Paiho, S., & Ylén, P. (2022). Carbon-neutral cities: Critical review of theory and practice. *Journal of Cleaner Production*, 341, 130912. DOI: 10.1016/j.jclepro.2022.130912

Ingle, M., Khati, K., & Dahiya, K. (2025). The Rise of Product-as-a-Service Models in the Digital Era: Redesigning Business Models for Circular Innovation. In *Innovating Sustainability Through Digital Circular Economy* (pp. 107–132). IGI Global Scientific Publishing.

Islam, M. A., Khan, R. H., & Syeed, M. (2020, January). A smart and integrated surface water monitor system architecture: Bangladesh perspective. In *Proceedings of the International Conference on Computing Advancements* (pp. 1-6). DOI: 10.1145/3377049.3377103

Jogarao, M., Lakshmana, B. C., & Naidu, S. T. (2024). AI-enabled circular economy management for sustainable smart cities: integrating artificial intelligence in resource optimisation and waste reduction. In *Smart Cities and Circular Economy* (pp. 83–96). Emerald Publishing Limited. DOI: 10.1108/978-1-83797-957-820241008

Kumar, P., Sharma, L., & Sharma, N. C. (2024). Sustainable Development Balancing Economic Viability, Environmental Protection, and Social Equity. In *Sustainable Partnership and Investment Strategies for Startups and SMEs* (pp. 212–234). IGI Global. DOI: 10.4018/979-8-3693-2197-3.ch012

Kuzma, E., & Sehnem, S. (2023). Propose a structural model for business value creation based on circular business models, innovation, and resource recovery in the pet industry. *Business Strategy and the Environment*, 32(1), 516–537. DOI: 10.1002/bse.3158

Liu, J., Zhang, Y., & Qian, X. (2009, June). Modeling chlorophyll-a in Taihu Lake with machine learning models. In 2009 3rd International Conference on Bioinformatics and Biomedical Engineering (pp. 1-6). IEEE. DOI: 10.1109/ICBBE.2009.5163072

Lundgren, R., Kyrö, R., & Olander, S. (2024). The lifecycle impact and value capture of circular business models in the built environment. *Construction Management and Economics*, 42(6), 527–544. DOI: 10.1080/01446193.2023.2279743

Milhem, M., Ateeq, A., Al Astal, A., Alzoraiki, M., Ateeq, R. A., Shafie, D. I., & Santhanamery, T. (2024). Advancing Sustainability: Embracing the Circular Economy for Environmental and Economic Resilience. In *Business Sustainability with Artificial Intelligence (AI): Challenges and Opportunities* (Vol. 2, pp. 57–68). Springer Nature Switzerland.

Movahed, A. B., Movahed, A. B., Aliahmadi, B., & Nozari, H. (2024). Green and Sustainable Supply Chain in Agriculture 6.0. In *Advanced Businesses in Industry 6.0* (pp. 32-45). IGI Global.

Movahed, A. B., Movahed, A. B., & Nozari, H. (2024). Marketing 6.0 Conceptualization. In *Advanced Businesses in Industry 6.0* (pp. 15-31). IGI Global.

Movahed, A. B., Movahed, A. B., Nozari, H., & Rahmaty, M. (2024). Security Criteria in Financial Systems in Industry 6.0. In *Advanced Businesses in Industry 6.0* (pp. 62-74). IGI Global.

Popova, Y., & Popovs, S. (2022). Impact of smart economy on smart areas and mediation effect of national economy. *Sustainability (Basel)*, 14(5), 2789. DOI: 10.3390/su14052789

Prebilič, V., Može, M., & Golobič, I. (2024). Waste-to-Energy Processes as a Municipality-Level Waste Management Strategy: A Case Study of Kočevje, Slovenia. *Processes (Basel, Switzerland)*, 12(5), 1010. DOI: 10.3390/pr12051010

Raheem, D., Raposo, A., Oluwole, O. B., Nieuwland, M., Saraiva, A., & Carrascosa, C. (2019). Entomophagy: Nutritional, ecological, safety and legislation aspects. *Food Research International*, 126, 108672. DOI: 10.1016/j.foodres.2019.108672 PMID: 31732082

Shen, Y. (2022). Application of internet of things in online teaching of adult education based on android voice assistant. *Mobile Information Systems*, 2022(1), 8915889. DOI: 10.1155/2022/8915889

. Spasova, S., & Ward, T. (2019). Social protection expenditure and its financing in Europe. A study of national policies.

Sudarsan, A., & Chithra, K. (2024). The role of energy management in transition towards green cities: A review. *Environment, Development and Sustainability*, •••, 1–23. DOI: 10.1007/s10668-024-04830-z

Talarico, C., Chang, H., Annamalai, A., & Roveda, J. (2013, August). Energy management design for smart homes using green technology. In 2013 IEEE 56th International Midwest Symposium on Circuits and Systems (MWSCAS) (pp. 517-520). IEEE. DOI: 10.1109/MWSCAS.2013.6674699

Tanaka, M., Kameda, T., Kawamoto, T., Sugihara, S., & Kambayashi, R. (2025). Managing long working hours: Evidence from a management practice survey. *The Journal of Human Resources*, 60(1), 37–69. DOI: 10.3368/jhr.0421-11605R2

Tarr, D. G., Kuznetsov, D. E., Overland, I., & Vakulchuk, R. (2023). Why carbon border adjustment mechanisms will not save the planet, but a climate club and subsidies for transformative green technologies may. *Energy Economics*, 122, 106695. DOI: 10.1016/j.eneco.2023.106695

Tavakkoli-Moghaddam, R., Nozari, H., Bakhshi-Movahed, A., & Bakhshi-Movahed, A. (2024). A Conceptual Framework for the Smart Factory 6.0. In *Advanced Businesses in Industry 6.0* (pp. 1–14). IGI Global. DOI: 10.4018/979-8-3693-3108-8.ch001

Ünal, E., Urbinati, A., Chiaroni, D., & Manzini, R. (2019). Value Creation in Circular Business Models: The case of a US small medium enterprise in the building sector. *Resources, Conservation and Recycling*, 146, 291–307. DOI: 10.1016/j.resconrec.2018.12.034

van Langen, S. K., Vassillo, C., Ghisellini, P., Restaino, D., Passaro, R., & Ulgiati, S. (2021). Promoting circular economy transition: A study about different stakeholder groups' perceptions and awareness. *Journal of Cleaner Production*, 316, 128166. DOI: 10.1016/j.jclepro.2021.128166

Xiao, J., Chen, S., Han, J., Tan, Z., Mu, S., & Jiayi, W. (2024). The carbon emission reduction effect of renewable resource utilisation: From the perspective of green innovation. *Atmospheric Pollution Research*, 15(6), 102121. DOI: 10.1016/j.apr.2024.102121

Yang, X., Li, N., Ahmad, M., & Mu, H. (2022). Natural resources, population aging, and environmental quality: Analyzing the role of green technologies. *Environmental Science and Pollution Research International*, 29(31), 46665–46679. DOI: 10.1007/s11356-022-19219-6 PMID: 35171429

Yun, W. S., Pinjaman, S. B., Yassin, J., & Taasim, S. I. (2023). The Role of Green Technologies in the Transition Towards a Circular Economy. In *Handbook of Research on Designing Sustainable Supply Chains to Achieve a Circular Economy* (pp. 121–141). IGI Global. DOI: 10.4018/978-1-6684-7664-2.ch007

Zia, Z., Shuming, L., Akbar, M. W., & Ahmed, T. (2023). Environmental sustainability and green technologies across BRICS countries: The role of institutional quality. *Environmental Science and Pollution Research International*, 30(11), 30155–30166. DOI: 10.1007/s11356-022-24331-8 PMID: 36427128

Chapter 6
Blockchain-Powered Decentralized Finance (DeFi) in Digital Marketing

Khatere Rafiei
https://orcid.org/0009-0005-4471-6929
Department of Management, Islamic Azad University, Dubai, UAE

ABSTRACT

Blockchain-powered decentralized finance (DeFi) is revolutionizing digital marketing by enabling transparent, secure, and automated financial transactions. This research explores how DeFi-driven smart contracts, tokenized incentives, and decentralized identity management are transforming consumer engagement, advertising models, and data privacy. While DeFi eliminates intermediaries and enhances efficiency, challenges such as cybersecurity risks, regulatory uncertainties, and scalability issues remain. Addressing these concerns will be crucial in harnessing DeFi's full potential for marketing innovation and consumer empowerment.

1- INTRODUCTION

The rapid evolution of digital marketing has been shaped by continuous technological advancements, from the rise of data-driven strategies to the dominance of artificial intelligence in personalized consumer engagement. However, the increasing reliance on centralized financial and advertising systems has raised concerns regarding transparency, security, and consumer trust. Traditional digital marketing platforms often rely on third-party intermediaries, such as payment processors, data

DOI: 10.4018/979-8-3693-4369-2.ch006

brokers, and advertising networks, which introduce inefficiencies, increase costs, and limit user control over financial transactions and personal data. In response to these challenges, Blockchain-Powered Decentralized Finance (DeFi) is emerging as a transformative force, reshaping the way brands interact with consumers, execute payments, and measure marketing success in an increasingly decentralized digital economy (Najafi & Nozari, 2024).

At its core, DeFi leverages blockchain technology to create open, permissionless, and automated financial ecosystems, eliminating intermediaries and enabling direct, transparent transactions between parties. When applied to digital marketing, DeFi introduces a new paradigm where smart contracts automate transactions, tokenization incentivizes user engagement, and decentralized advertising platforms ensure fair value distribution. This shift not only enhances transactional security and efficiency but also fosters greater consumer empowerment, as users gain control over their data, identities, and online interactions. By leveraging blockchain, marketers can move away from intrusive data collection practices and embrace trust-based, consent-driven advertising models that reward users for their participation and engagement.

One of the most revolutionary aspects of DeFi in marketing is the use of smart contracts to automate and verify transactions, ensuring that payments for advertisements, influencer partnerships, and affiliate programs occur transparently and based on predefined conditions. Unlike traditional marketing models, where advertisers often struggle with issues like fraudulent clicks, delayed payments, and opaque reporting mechanisms, blockchain-based solutions provide real-time verifiability and fraud-proof execution, ensuring that every transaction is secure, traceable, and tamper-resistant. Furthermore, tokenization enables brands to create custom digital assets or loyalty tokens, which can be distributed to consumers as rewards for engagement, content creation, or referrals, fostering stronger brand loyalty while reducing reliance on expensive third-party platforms (Nozari et al., 2021).

Another key advantage of DeFi-powered marketing ecosystems is the integration of decentralized identity management, allowing users to interact with brands without compromising their personal information. Unlike centralized advertising models, which rely on mass data collection and profiling, blockchain-based systems empower consumers to control their digital identities, grant selective access to marketers, and monetize their own data. This transition not only enhances data privacy and compliance with regulations like GDPR but also forces brands to rethink their approach to audience engagement, shifting from intrusive targeting methods to consent-based, value-driven marketing strategies.

Despite its potential, the adoption of DeFi in digital marketing presents significant challenges, including regulatory uncertainties, scalability limitations, and the complexities of integrating blockchain-based payments with existing marketing infrastructures. Moreover, as decentralized systems evolve, marketers must navigate shifting consumer behaviors, emerging token economies, and new business models driven by blockchain technology. Addressing these challenges will require a strategic approach that balances innovation with compliance, ensuring that brands can fully harness the benefits of decentralized finance without alienating consumers or regulators.

This chapter explores the intersection of blockchain-powered DeFi and digital marketing, examining how decentralized financial mechanisms are reshaping transactions, consumer engagement, and advertising models. It provides a deep dive into key DeFi applications in marketing, including smart contracts, decentralized identity management, tokenized loyalty programs, and automated ad payments. Additionally, the chapter analyzes challenges, risks, and future trends, offering a forward-looking perspective on how brands can integrate DeFi-driven marketing strategies to build more transparent, efficient, and consumer-centric advertising ecosystems. By the end of this discussion, it will be evident that DeFi is not merely a financial innovation but a fundamental shift that is redefining the future of digital marketing in a decentralized economy.

2- UNDERSTANDING BLOCKCHAIN AND DEFI IN MARKETING

The integration of blockchain technology and decentralized finance (DeFi) into digital marketing marks a fundamental shift in how businesses interact with consumers, handle transactions, and structure advertising ecosystems. Traditional digital marketing operates on centralized platforms where large intermediaries, such as banks, payment processors, and data brokers, control the flow of financial transactions and consumer data. This centralized model often leads to inefficiencies, high transaction fees, limited transparency, and privacy concerns. In contrast, blockchain-powered DeFi removes these intermediaries, enabling direct, peer-to-peer transactions, automated smart contract execution, and decentralized data management, ultimately fostering a more transparent, secure, and cost-effective marketing environment (Nozari et al., 2024(a)).

At its core, blockchain technology is a decentralized ledger system that records transactions across multiple nodes, ensuring that data remains immutable, transparent, and resistant to fraud. This feature is particularly valuable in digital marketing, where fraudulent activities such as fake clicks, bot-generated impressions, and manipulative advertising metrics have plagued advertisers for years. By leveraging blockchain, marketers can ensure real-time verification of ad engagement, secure financial transactions, and accurate campaign performance tracking, reducing financial losses and improving trust between brands and consumers. Additionally, smart contracts—self-executing agreements encoded on the blockchain—allow advertisers and content creators to automate payments based on predefined conditions, eliminating disputes over delayed or fraudulent payments (Dos et al., 2022).

The rise of DeFi in marketing is further transforming digital transactions by introducing decentralized financial tools, such as tokenized rewards, micropayments, and decentralized ad networks. Tokenization, a concept enabled by blockchain, allows brands to create their own digital assets or branded tokens that can be used as rewards for customer engagement, loyalty programs, and referral incentives. Instead of relying on traditional cashback or point-based loyalty schemes controlled by centralized entities, blockchain-based tokens provide greater flexibility, portability, and direct value exchange between consumers and brands. These tokens can be stored in decentralized wallets, traded in DeFi markets, or redeemed for exclusive offers, making customer loyalty programs more transparent and engaging (Nozari et al., 2024(b)).

Another revolutionary application of DeFi in marketing is the elimination of intermediaries in ad transactions through decentralized advertising networks (DANs). In traditional digital advertising, platforms such as Google Ads and Facebook Ads act as intermediaries, charging high fees while controlling data access and ad distribution. DeFi-powered advertising ecosystems allow brands to connect directly with consumers through blockchain-based ad platforms, smart contract-driven payments, and tokenized incentives. These decentralized platforms ensure that advertisers pay only for verified engagement, and consumers are fairly compensated for their attention, reshaping the value exchange in digital marketing.

Moreover, decentralized identity management is another critical innovation powered by blockchain and DeFi, enabling consumers to own, control, and monetize their personal data. In the traditional model, large advertising corporations collect and monetize user data without direct compensation to the consumer. However, blockchain-based identity solutions allow individuals to grant selective access to marketers while receiving incentives for data sharing, ensuring that privacy concerns are addressed while maintaining targeted marketing capabilities. This model aligns with increasing global regulations on data privacy, such as GDPR (General Data Protection Regulation) and CCPA (California Consumer Privacy Act), making blockchain-driven marketing more compliant and consumer-friendly (Tavakkoli-Moghaddam et al., 2024).

Despite these advantages, the adoption of DeFi in marketing comes with its own set of challenges. Scalability remains a major concern, as blockchain networks often struggle with high transaction costs and slow processing speeds, particularly during peak demand. Additionally, the regulatory uncertainty surrounding DeFi and digital tokens poses a potential risk for brands looking to integrate blockchain into their marketing strategies. Governments and financial regulators are still defining the legal landscape for cryptocurrencies, decentralized applications (DApps), and tokenized economies, making it essential for marketers to navigate compliance issues carefully (Nozari, 2024(a)).

Nonetheless, the convergence of blockchain, DeFi, and digital marketing is redefining financial transactions, data security, and consumer engagement. As decentralized technologies continue to mature, marketers must embrace DeFi-driven strategies to build trust-based, transparent, and efficient marketing ecosystems. By leveraging smart contracts for automated ad payments, tokenized incentives for customer loyalty, and decentralized data frameworks for privacy protection, businesses can enhance consumer relationships, reduce costs, and drive marketing innovation in a decentralized digital economy.

3- THE ROLE OF DEFI IN DIGITAL MARKETING ECOSYSTEMS

The integration of decentralized finance (DeFi) into digital marketing ecosystems is revolutionizing the way brands engage with consumers, manage transactions, and execute advertising campaigns. Traditional marketing models rely on centralized financial systems and intermediaries, such as payment processors, advertising networks, and data brokers, which often lead to higher costs, inefficiencies, and limited transparency. With the emergence of DeFi-powered marketing ecosystems, businesses can now operate in a more secure, automated, and decentralized environment, where transactions are direct, efficient, and governed by smart contracts.

One of the key advantages of DeFi in digital marketing is the elimination of intermediaries in advertising transactions. Traditionally, platforms like Google Ads, Facebook Ads, and centralized ad exchanges take a significant cut from advertisers' budgets while controlling ad placement and audience targeting. DeFi introduces decentralized advertising networks (DANs) that allow advertisers and content creators to interact directly, reducing costs and ensuring fair compensation for engagement. These decentralized platforms leverage blockchain-based smart contracts to automate payments based on actual user interactions, preventing fraudulent activities such as bot-generated clicks and ad manipulation (Ali, 2024).

Furthermore, tokenized incentives are transforming consumer engagement strategies by rewarding users for interacting with ads, sharing content, and participating in loyalty programs. Instead of traditional cashback or loyalty point systems controlled by centralized entities, DeFi-powered marketing allows brands to create branded tokens or digital assets that can be traded, redeemed, or used for exclusive offers. These tokenized rewards enhance customer retention and engagement, while also enabling a more interactive and gamified marketing experience. The impact of tokenized incentives, smart contract automation, and decentralized ad platforms is illustrated in Figure 1, which highlights the benefits of DeFi in digital marketing.

Figure 1. Impact of DeFi on Digital Marketing Benefits

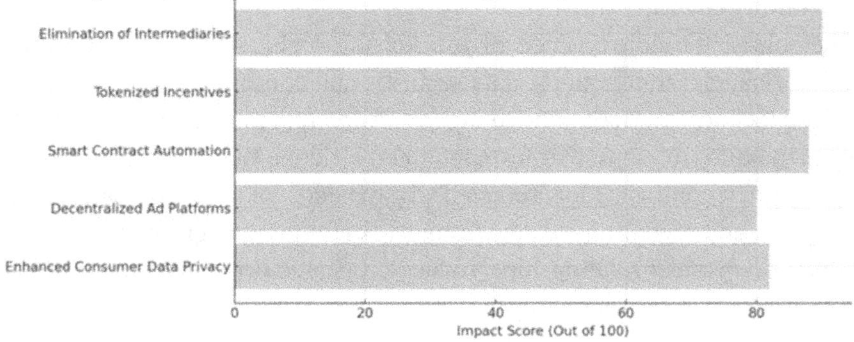

Another significant role of DeFi in marketing is the automation of transactions through smart contracts. In conventional marketing, payments to influencers, content creators, and ad platforms often face delays and disputes. With DeFi-based smart contracts, payments are automatically executed once predefined conditions are met, ensuring transparent, fraud-proof, and dispute-free transactions. For instance, a brand collaborating with influencers can establish a smart contract that releases payment only when engagement metrics, such as video views or website traffic, reach agreed-upon thresholds. This level of automation and transparency builds trust between brands and marketing partners while reducing financial risks.

Additionally, consumer data privacy is a growing concern in digital marketing, as centralized platforms collect vast amounts of user information without direct consumer control. DeFi-powered decentralized identity solutions empower users to own and control their personal data, granting selective access to marketers based on consent-based engagement models. Instead of invasive tracking and algorithm-driven profiling, brands must incentivize users to share their data voluntarily, creating a more ethical and privacy-respecting marketing ecosystem (Nozari, 2024(b)).

Despite these advantages, scalability, regulatory concerns, and user adoption remain challenges in implementing DeFi in digital marketing ecosystems. While blockchain-based advertising platforms and tokenized incentives offer immense potential, their widespread adoption depends on improving transaction speeds, lowering gas fees, and ensuring compliance with financial regulations. Nonetheless, as the Web3 landscape evolves, the fusion of DeFi and digital marketing will continue to reshape advertising models, consumer engagement strategies, and financial transactions.

In conclusion, the integration of DeFi into digital marketing ecosystems is ushering in a new era of transparency, automation, and consumer empowerment. By leveraging decentralized advertising networks, tokenized rewards, smart contract automation, and privacy-focused data management, businesses can create more efficient, secure, and consumer-friendly marketing experiences. As the technology matures, brands that embrace DeFi-driven marketing strategies will gain a competitive edge in an increasingly decentralized and digital-first economy.

4- DECENTRALIZED IDENTITY AND CONSUMER DATA PRIVACY

The evolution of consumer data privacy has become a central concern in the digital marketing ecosystem, especially as traditional advertising models rely heavily on mass data collection, user profiling, and algorithm-driven targeting. The increasing frequency of data breaches, unauthorized tracking, and misuse of personal information has led to growing regulatory scrutiny, with stringent laws such as GDPR (General Data Protection Regulation) and CCPA (California Consumer Privacy Act) forcing brands to rethink how they handle consumer data. In response to these challenges, decentralized identity solutions powered by blockchain technology are emerging as a transformative force, offering consumers greater control, transparency, and security over their personal information in digital marketing environments.

Decentralized identity management, built on blockchain and decentralized finance (DeFi) principles, enables users to own and manage their data autonomously, eliminating the need for third-party intermediaries such as data brokers and centralized platforms. Unlike traditional digital marketing systems—where tech giants like Google, Facebook, and Amazon act as data controllers—blockchain-based identity frameworks ensure that personal information is stored securely, encrypted, and shared only with the user's explicit consent. This shift not only aligns with consumer privacy expectations but also fosters a more ethical and transparent digital economy, where brands must offer real value in exchange for user data rather than extracting it without consent (Irani &Nozari, 2024).

One of the fundamental differences between traditional data privacy and decentralized identity is the shift in data ownership and control. In centralized models, corporations retain full ownership over consumer data, using it for advertising, analytics, and monetization without direct compensation to users. With blockchain-powered decentralized identity, however, individuals maintain full sovereignty over their data, deciding who can access it, for how long, and under what conditions. The comparison between traditional and decentralized data privacy models is outlined in Table 1, illustrating how blockchain-based identity solutions enhance security, transparency, and user empowerment.

Table 1. Comparison of Traditional Data Privacy vs. Decentralized Identity

Feature	Traditional Data Privacy (Centralized)	Decentralized Identity (Blockchain-Based)
Data Ownership	Owned by platforms and corporations	Owned by the individual
User Control	Limited user control	Full user control over access
Security & Transparency	Opaque data storage and usage policies	Immutable and transparent data ledger
Third-Party Involvement	Heavy reliance on third-party brokers	No need for third-party data handlers
Privacy Risks	High risk of data breaches and misuse	Reduced risk due to encryption and decentralization
Monetization of Data	Users do not profit from their own data	Users can choose to monetize their own data

Beyond improving data ownership and user consent, decentralized identity solutions also introduce new marketing opportunities through tokenized data exchange and incentive-driven data sharing. Instead of brands relying on intrusive tracking mechanisms, blockchain allows consumers to opt-in to data sharing in exchange for tokenized rewards, effectively creating a fair and transparent value exchange between businesses and individuals. Users can selectively grant brands access to their preferences, purchasing habits, or engagement history, receiving cryptographic tokens or DeFi-based incentives in return. This model redefines personalized advertising, as brands must earn consumer trust and participation rather than forcefully collecting behavioral data through hidden tracking techniques.

Additionally, decentralized identity systems help address ad fraud, fake accounts, and identity theft, which are major concerns in digital marketing. Since blockchain-based identities are immutable, verifiable, and cryptographically secured, advertisers can ensure that only real users interact with their campaigns, preventing fraudulent bot traffic and ensuring higher-quality ad engagements. This feature is particularly valuable in influencer marketing, where brands can authenticate engagement metrics and ensure that content creators' audiences consist of real, verified individuals rather than artificially inflated follower counts (Aliahamdi et al., 2024).

Despite the clear advantages of decentralized identity solutions, there are still challenges to widespread adoption, including user education, technological scalability, and regulatory concerns. While blockchain offers unparalleled security and transparency, many consumers and businesses are still unfamiliar with how decentralized identity frameworks work, requiring greater efforts in adoption, usability, and integration with existing marketing infrastructures. Additionally, governments and regulatory bodies are still exploring the implications of self-sovereign identities and tokenized data exchanges, meaning that brands must navigate legal uncertainties while implementing blockchain-based marketing solutions.

Decentralized identity management is revolutionizing consumer data privacy in digital marketing, empowering individuals with greater control, security, and transparency over their personal information. As blockchain adoption grows, brands must transition from centralized data collection to user-centric, permission-based marketing models, ensuring fair, ethical, and privacy-respecting engagement strategies. By embracing DeFi-powered identity solutions, businesses can build stronger consumer trust, prevent fraud, and create more personalized, value-driven marketing ecosystems, marking the next phase of evolution in data-driven advertising.

5- CHALLENGES AND RISKS IN DEFI-DRIVEN MARKETING

While Decentralized Finance (DeFi) is reshaping digital marketing ecosystems by enhancing transparency, automation, and security, its widespread adoption is accompanied by significant challenges and risks. As businesses explore DeFi-powered marketing models, they must navigate issues related to security vulnerabilities, regulatory uncertainties, scalability limitations, consumer adoption barriers, and integration complexities. The decentralized nature of blockchain-driven marketing brings both opportunities and uncertainties, requiring a strategic approach to mitigate risks while leveraging the benefits of decentralized financial systems.

One of the most pressing concerns in DeFi-driven marketing is cybersecurity and smart contract vulnerabilities. Unlike traditional financial systems, where centralized entities provide fraud protection and security mechanisms, DeFi operates in a permissionless and irreversible environment. While smart contracts automate transactions, they are still susceptible to exploits, bugs, and malicious attacks if not properly coded. Hackers have already exploited vulnerabilities in DeFi applications, leading to significant financial losses, and this poses a risk for marketers who rely on automated payment systems and tokenized incentive programs. If a smart contract governing a marketing campaign has an undetected flaw, advertisers and publishers could face unauthorized fund transfers or contract manipulation, undermining trust in blockchain-based marketing solutions (Kuppa et al., 2024).

Another major challenge is regulatory uncertainty, as governments and financial authorities worldwide are still developing policies around DeFi, digital assets, and decentralized transactions. Unlike traditional digital marketing, which operates within well-defined financial and legal frameworks, DeFi-driven marketing models exist in a regulatory gray area, with evolving compliance requirements that vary across jurisdictions. Many countries have introduced anti-money laundering (AML) and know-your-customer (KYC) regulations for cryptocurrency-based transactions, raising concerns about how DeFi-driven advertising platforms should comply with legal standards while maintaining decentralization. The risk of regulatory crackdowns, evolving compliance frameworks, and legal ambiguities could deter businesses from fully embracing blockchain-powered marketing solutions.

Scalability remains another barrier to the mass adoption of DeFi in marketing. While blockchain networks provide security and decentralization, many still struggle with high transaction costs, slow processing speeds, and congestion issues, particularly during periods of peak demand. Ethereum-based DeFi transactions, for example, often suffer from high gas fees, making it costly for advertisers to execute token-based loyalty programs or microtransactions. Although solutions such as Layer-2 scaling technologies and alternative blockchain networks are emerging, many DeFi-based marketing models require greater efficiency and lower transaction fees to compete with traditional, centralized advertising platforms.

Consumer adoption also poses a significant challenge. Despite the rapid growth of DeFi, many users remain unfamiliar with decentralized financial applications and tokenized ecosystems. The complexity of blockchain wallets, private key management, and smart contract interactions can be intimidating for the average consumer, creating barriers to participation in DeFi-powered loyalty programs, decentralized ad platforms, or tokenized incentive systems. Without intuitive user experiences and clear educational initiatives, many potential users may hesitate to engage with DeFi marketing solutions, limiting their effectiveness and adoption at scale (Movahed et al., 2024).

Additionally, brand trust and perception risks are critical considerations for businesses adopting DeFi-based marketing. While decentralization enhances transparency, it also removes the centralized accountability that many consumers expect from well-established financial institutions and marketing platforms. Consumers who experience fraud, technical errors, or loss of funds in a DeFi-driven marketing program may find it difficult to seek recourse, as there is no central authority to manage disputes or offer reimbursements. This lack of traditional customer protection mechanisms could deter mainstream brands from adopting DeFi marketing models, especially if they fear reputational damage from poorly executed blockchain campaigns (Sagi & Yadav, 2024).

Despite these challenges, the DeFi-driven marketing landscape continues to evolve, with emerging solutions addressing many of the existing limitations. Advancements in security audits for smart contracts, regulatory-compliant DeFi platforms, and scalable blockchain networks are gradually making DeFi-powered marketing more viable. Additionally, education, user-friendly interfaces, and strategic partnerships will play a crucial role in increasing consumer adoption and trust in decentralized marketing ecosystems.

In conclusion, while DeFi presents a transformative opportunity for digital marketing, its adoption is not without risks. Security vulnerabilities, regulatory challenges, scalability limitations, consumer adoption hurdles, and brand trust concerns must be carefully addressed to unlock the full potential of blockchain-powered marketing strategies. As businesses and technology providers continue to refine DeFi-driven solutions, the future of marketing will likely become more transparent, efficient, and consumer-centric, but overcoming these barriers will be essential to achieving mainstream adoption.

6- CONCLUSION

The integration of blockchain-powered decentralized finance (DeFi) into digital marketing represents a paradigm shift, redefining how brands interact with consumers, manage transactions, and execute advertising campaigns. By eliminating intermediaries, introducing smart contract automation, and enabling tokenized incentives, DeFi provides a transparent, secure, and efficient alternative to traditional marketing models. The ability to leverage decentralized advertising networks (DANs), blockchain-based identity management, and tokenized rewards fosters a more consumer-centric marketing environment, where trust and transparency become the foundation of engagement.

One of the most significant advantages of DeFi-driven marketing is the empowerment of both consumers and brands. Through decentralized identity management, users can own and control their data, deciding how and when they share their information. This shift not only enhances privacy compliance with global regulations such as GDPR and CCPA but also transforms the nature of personalized advertising, ensuring consent-driven marketing models rather than intrusive data collection. Additionally, tokenized loyalty programs create a fair value exchange between businesses and consumers, incentivizing engagement while reducing reliance on traditional loyalty structures.

Despite these benefits, significant challenges remain. Cybersecurity risks, regulatory uncertainties, scalability issues, and user adoption barriers pose obstacles to the widespread implementation of DeFi in digital marketing. Smart contracts, while providing automation, are susceptible to vulnerabilities and hacks, making security audits crucial for safeguarding DeFi marketing systems. Furthermore, the lack of clear regulatory frameworks could lead to legal complications, slowing adoption among mainstream brands hesitant to operate in decentralized financial ecosystems.

Looking ahead, the continued development of blockchain scalability solutions, regulatory compliance mechanisms, and consumer-friendly interfaces will determine the long-term success of DeFi in digital marketing. As Web3 technologies evolve,

DeFi-driven strategies will become more accessible, secure, and scalable, allowing businesses to fully capitalize on decentralized advertising, transparent engagement models, and innovative token economies.

DeFi-powered marketing is not just an emerging trend but a fundamental shift toward a more transparent, decentralized, and consumer-driven digital economy. While challenges exist, businesses that strategically integrate blockchain and DeFi into their marketing frameworks will gain a competitive advantage in the evolving digital landscape, paving the way for a more equitable and trust-based marketing future.

REFERENCES

Ali, S. (2024). *Investigating the Role of Blockchain Technology in Ireland; Enhancing Trust and Security in Digital Marketing Transactions* (Doctoral dissertation, Dublin Business School).

Aliahmadi, M. H., Movahed, A. B., Movahed, A. B., Nozari, H., & Bayanati, M. (2024). Hospital 6.0 Components and Dimensions. In *Advanced Businesses in Industry 6.0* (pp. 46-61). IGI Global.

Dos Santos, S., Singh, J., Thulasiram, R. K., Kamali, S., Sirico, L., & Loud, L. (2022, June). A new era of blockchain-powered decentralized finance (DeFi)-a review. In *2022 IEEE 46th Annual Computers, Software, and Applications Conference (COMPSAC)* (pp. 1286-1292). IEEE.

Irani, H. R., & Nozari, H. (Eds.). (2024). *Smart and Sustainable Interactive Marketing*. IGI Global. DOI: 10.4018/979-8-3693-1339-8

Kuppa, V. K. P., Hegadi, R., Sajjan, K., Chowdary, K. D., Vanga, M. S. R., & Kumar, P. (2024, January). Investopolis: Decentralized customer loyalty tokenization on the blockchain. In *2024 IEEE International Conference on Consumer Electronics (ICCE)* (pp. 1-5). IEEE. DOI: 10.1109/ICCE59016.2024.10444326

Movahed, A. B., Movahed, A. B., Nozari, H., & Rahmaty, M. (2024). Security Criteria in Financial Systems in Industry 6.0. In *Advanced Businesses in Industry 6.0* (pp. 62-74). IGI Global.

Najafi, E., & Nozari, H. (2024). Examining Dimensions and Critical Success Factors of Supply Chains Based on the Blockchain and Internet of Things (B-IoT). In *Analytical Decision Making and Data Envelopment Analysis: Advances and Challenges* (pp. 281–294). Springer Nature Singapore. DOI: 10.1007/978-981-97-6972-8_13

Nozari, H. (2024a). Investigating Key Dimensions and Key Indicators of AIoT-Based Supply Chain in Sustainable Business Development. In *Artificial Intelligence of Things for Achieving Sustainable Development Goals* (pp. 293-310). Cham: Springer Nature Switzerland.

Nozari, H. (2024b). Green Supply Chain Management based on Artificial Intelligence of Everything. *Journal of Economics and Management*, 46, 171–188. DOI: 10.22367/jem.2024.46.07

Nozari, H., Fallah, M., Kazemipoor, H., & Najafi, S. E. (2021). Big data analysis of IoT-based supply chain management considering FMCG industries. *Бизнес-информатика*, 15(1, 1 (eng)), 78–96. DOI: 10.17323/2587-814X.2021.1.78.96

Nozari, H., Ghahremani-Nahr, J., Rahmaty, M., & Bayanati, M. (2024). A Framework for Smart and Resilient Supply Chains Based on Blockchain and the Internet of Things. In *Blockchain-based Internet of Things* (pp. 73-86). Chapman and Hall/CRC.

Nozari, H., Tavakkoli-Moghaddam, R., & Dolgui, A. (2024, September). Analysis of Critical Success Factors of Sustainable and Resilient Aioe-based Supply Chain in Industry 5.0. In *IFIP International Conference on Advances in Production Management Systems* (pp. 76-90). Cham: Springer Nature Switzerland. DOI: 10.1007/978-3-031-65894-5_6

Sagi, S., & Yadav, A. (2024). Blockchain in Advertising and Marketing. *New Trends in Marketing and Consumer Science*, 89.

Tavakkoli-Moghaddam, R., Nozari, H., Bakhshi-Movahed, A., & Bakhshi-Movahed, A. (2024). A Conceptual Framework for the Smart Factory 6.0. In *Advanced Businesses in Industry 6.0* (pp. 1–14). IGI Global. DOI: 10.4018/979-8-3693-3108-8.ch001

Chapter 7
Digital Twin-Enabled Bioreactors:
Transforming Industrial Biotechnology in Smart Economies

Hossein Abdi
Azad University, Dubai, UAE

Ali Jahanian
https://orcid.org/0000-0001-7568-6375
Queensland University of Technology, Brisbane, Australia

Hamed Nozari
https://orcid.org/0000-0002-6500-6708
Independent Researcher, Australia

ABSTRACT

Digital twin technology is transforming bioreactor systems by integrating AI, IoT, and real-time simulation to enhance bioprocess efficiency, predictability, and scalability. This research explores the evolution, benefits, and applications of digital twin-enabled bioreactors, focusing on AI-driven optimization, cyber-physical system integration, and predictive analytics. Case studies, including BIO10's advancements in smart biomanufacturing, highlight real-world applications. The study also examines challenges and future prospects, emphasizing the potential for autonomous, intelligent bioprocessing in sustainable industrial biotechnology.

DOI: 10.4018/979-8-3693-4369-2.ch007

1- INTRODUCTION

The rapid advancement of biotechnology and artificial intelligence (AI) has ushered in a new era of intelligent bioprocessing, where the integration of digital twin technology is revolutionizing industrial bioreactors. As industries shift towards data-driven decision-making, predictive analytics, and real-time process optimization, traditional bioreactor systems are being redefined by advanced simulation, machine learning, and IoT-driven automation. Digital twin-enabled bioreactors serve as the foundation of this transformation, providing an unprecedented level of precision, efficiency, and adaptability in biomanufacturing processes.

At its core, a digital twin is a virtual replica of a physical system, continuously updated with real-time data from sensors, AI-driven models, and computational simulations. In the context of bioreactors, this technology enables continuous process monitoring, predictive maintenance, and adaptive optimization by mirroring the biological and chemical dynamics of real-world bioprocesses. This capability is critical for industries such as pharmaceuticals, biofuels, food biotechnology, and synthetic biology, where even slight variations in process conditions can significantly impact production yield, quality, and cost-effectiveness (Katsoulakis et al., 2024).

The limitations of traditional bioreactors have long posed challenges to industrial biotechnology. These systems typically rely on predefined operating conditions and manual adjustments, often leading to inefficiencies, resource wastage, and inconsistent bioprocess outcomes. Biomanufacturers have struggled with delayed responses to process deviations, limited predictive capabilities, and difficulty in maintaining optimal growth conditions for microbial cultures, mammalian cells, or engineered biomolecules. The emergence of smart bioreactors powered by digital twins provides an elegant solution to these challenges by enabling self-learning, autonomous process control, and advanced simulation capabilities.

A defining feature of digital twin-enabled bioreactors is their ability to synchronize physical and virtual environments, allowing operators to test and validate process conditions in a virtual space before applying them in real-world production settings. This not only reduces operational risks but also enhances bioprocess reliability, scalability, and sustainability. By leveraging AI-driven optimization, real-time feedback loops, and predictive modeling, digital twins ensure that bioreactors operate at peak efficiency, significantly reducing downtime, energy consumption, and raw material waste.

The implementation of Internet of Things (IoT) devices in digital twin bioreactors further strengthens their capabilities. With wireless sensor networks, cloud-based data processing, and real-time connectivity, biomanufacturing facilities can monitor bioprocesses remotely, adjust parameters dynamically, and respond to anomalies instantaneously. Additionally, the integration of blockchain technology within IoT networks enhances data security, traceability, and transparency, ensuring that biomanufacturing processes comply with stringent regulatory and quality assurance standards (Chen et al., 2020).

One of the most compelling real-world applications of digital twin-enabled bioreactors can be seen in the operations of BIO10, a knowledge-based biotechnology company in Australia that has taken fundamental steps in optimizing smart biomanufacturing systems. With a focus on AI-driven process optimization, predictive maintenance, and scalable bio-based production, BIO10 has successfully deployed intelligent digital twin models in industries, setting a precedent for future adoption in global bioprocessing. The company's success underscores the potential of digital twin technology in reducing production costs, improving bioprocess efficiency, and driving sustainable industrial innovation.

Despite the numerous advantages of digital twin-enabled bioreactors, their adoption comes with challenges, including high initial implementation costs, technical complexity, cybersecurity concerns, and the need for interdisciplinary expertise in AI, biotechnology, and process engineering. However, as advancements in machine learning, cloud computing, and quantum computing continue to accelerate, these challenges are expected to be mitigated, leading to wider adoption and further technological breakthroughs. The future of biomanufacturing and industrial biotechnology will increasingly rely on smart, autonomous bioprocessing systems, driven by data analytics, real-time simulations, and AI-assisted decision-making.

This chapter explores the evolution, integration, and impact of digital twin technology in bioreactors, providing insights into how AI, IoT, and automation are reshaping biomanufacturing in smart economies. By examining case studies, technical advancements, and future prospects, this discussion highlights the transformative potential of digital twins in creating sustainable, efficient, and intelligent bioreactor systems. As industries move toward self-optimizing, data-driven production models, digital twin-enabled bioreactors will serve as a catalyst for next-generation bioprocessing innovations, ensuring greater precision, reliability, and adaptability in the rapidly evolving field of industrial biotechnology.

2- LITERATURE REVIEW

The evolution of digital twin technology in bioreactors has emerged as a transformative innovation, driven by the convergence of biotechnology, artificial intelligence (AI), the Internet of Things (IoT), and industrial automation. The integration of digital twins with bioreactor systems has significantly enhanced process optimization, real-time monitoring, and predictive analytics, allowing industries to achieve higher efficiency and sustainability in biomanufacturing. The literature on smart bioprocessing systems highlights how digital twin-enabled bioreactors have revolutionized industrial biotechnology, addressing the limitations of traditional bioreactors through data-driven intelligence, autonomous control, and cyber-physical system integration.

At its core, digital twin technology functions as a virtual representation of physical systems, continuously updated with real-time data from sensors, AI-driven models, and computational simulations. In bioreactors, this concept has been applied to simulate, predict, and optimize bioprocess performance, bridging the gap between theoretical modeling and real-world execution. The architecture of digital twin systems consists of three main layers: the physical bioreactor, the digital counterpart, and an AI-driven optimization module, which work in tandem to enhance process efficiency and reduce variability. These advancements have led to the development of intelligent bioreactor systems capable of self-learning, self-adapting, and self-optimizing in real-time.

The integration of AI in digital twin bioreactors has played a critical role in improving predictive capabilities. Traditional bioreactor systems relied on predefined operating conditions and manual adjustments, often leading to inefficiencies and inconsistencies in bioprocessing. AI-powered digital twins, however, utilize machine learning algorithms, deep learning models, and reinforcement learning to dynamically adjust nutrient flow, oxygen transfer rates (OTR), pH levels, and temperature settings based on real-time data analysis. This enables bioreactors to predict process deviations, optimize production yields, and minimize resource wastage, making them more adaptable to changing bioprocess conditions.

The incorporation of IoT and cyber-physical systems into digital twin bioreactors has further strengthened their functionality, allowing for seamless remote monitoring, decentralized process control, and real-time decision-making. IoT-enabled sensors embedded within bioreactors continuously transmit operational data to cloud-based digital twin platforms, enabling instantaneous adjustments, enhanced process visibility, and improved regulatory compliance. The use of cloud computing and edge analytics has also accelerated data processing, allowing for faster bioprocess simulations and more accurate performance predictions. Additionally, blockchain technology has been explored as a secure and transparent data management solution, ensuring traceability, cybersecurity, and compliance in smart biomanufacturing environments (Wang et al., 2024).

A prime example of successful digital twin implementation in industrial bioprocessing is the work carried out by BIO10, a leading biotechnology company in Australia. This knowledge-based industrial complex has been at the forefront of developing and supporting smart bioreactors, integrating AI-driven process optimization, predictive maintenance, and scalable bio-based production. The company has demonstrated that digital twin-enabled bioreactors significantly improve batch reproducibility, enhance process stability, and reduce production costs, making them a viable solution for large-scale biomanufacturing in pharmaceuticals, biofuels, and synthetic biology (Nozari and Abdi, 2024).

Despite the remarkable advantages of digital twin bioreactors, several challenges hinder their widespread adoption. The high initial implementation costs, technical complexity, data security risks, and lack of standardization remain significant barriers to scaling this technology. Establishing universal regulatory frameworks, enhancing interoperability, and ensuring cybersecurity resilience are key areas that require further research and development. However, ongoing advancements in quantum computing, federated AI, and edge analytics are expected to reduce computation costs, improve bioprocess accuracy, and accelerate adoption across industries.

Looking toward the future, digital twin-enabled bioreactors are poised to become a cornerstone of next-generation biomanufacturing, offering unparalleled capabilities in real-time process control, self-optimization, and AI-driven decision-making. The increasing adoption of autonomous bioreactor systems will enable industries to operate with greater precision, sustainability, and efficiency, ultimately fostering the development of a resilient, adaptive, and intelligent bioeconomy. As technology continues to evolve, the role of digital twins in industrial biotechnology will expand, shaping the future of smart, data-driven bioprocessing systems and setting new standards for efficiency, quality, and sustainability in global biomanufacturing.

3- THE EVOLUTION OF BIOREACTORS

Bioreactors have undergone a remarkable transformation over the past century, evolving from rudimentary fermentation vessels to highly sophisticated, AI-driven systems that power modern biotechnology. The journey of bioreactor technology can be categorized into three main phases: traditional bioreactors, smart automated bioreactors, and digital twin-enabled bioreactors.

3-1 Traditional Bioreactors: The Foundation of Industrial Biotechnology

The earliest bioreactors were simple batch and fed-batch systems used for microbial fermentation, enzyme production, and pharmaceutical synthesis. These conventional systems operated on fixed protocols, requiring manual intervention for process control. Operators adjusted parameters such as temperature, pH, and dissolved oxygen based on offline sample testing, leading to inefficiencies and inconsistencies in bioprocess outcomes. While these systems laid the foundation for industrial biotechnology, they lacked real-time adaptability and process optimization.

3-2 Smart Automated Bioreactors: The Emergence of Intelligent Control Systems

With the advent of industrial automation and process control technologies, bioreactors transitioned into smart automated systems equipped with real-time sensors, programmable logic controllers (PLCs), and data acquisition software. These advancements enabled continuous monitoring and partial automation of key process variables, significantly improving efficiency, reproducibility, and scalability. Machine learning algorithms further enhanced process optimization by enabling predictive analytics for bioprocess control. However, despite these improvements, smart bioreactors still operated in a data-siloed environment, lacking the ability to create a dynamic digital counterpart that could simulate and predict bioprocess outcomes in real-time.

3-3 Digital Twin-Enabled Bioreactors: The Future of Industrial Biotechnology

The latest paradigm shift in bioreactor technology is the integration of digital twin technology, which allows for real-time simulation, optimization, and predictive control of bioprocesses. A digital twin is a virtual replica of a physical bioreactor that continuously updates based on real-world sensor data, AI-driven predictions, and computational modeling. This technology bridges the gap between theoretical bioprocess design and real-world execution, enabling operators to test different conditions, predict system failures, and optimize production in real-time.

Unlike previous generations, digital twin-enabled bioreactors do not just respond to changes—they anticipate them. By leveraging AI, IoT, and cloud computing, these systems can analyze vast datasets, simulate multiple production scenarios, and self-optimize based on predefined performance objectives. This level of intelligence significantly reduces operational risks, minimizes resource wastage, and enhances the economic sustainability of bioprocessing industries.

The evolution of bioreactors reflects the broader shift towards intelligent, data-driven, and autonomous biomanufacturing systems. From manually controlled fermentation systems to fully digitized, self-learning bioreactors, each technological advancement has contributed to greater efficiency, precision, and scalability. Digital twin-enabled bioreactors represent the pinnacle of this evolution, ushering in a new era of industrial biotechnology where real-time decision-making and predictive analytics drive productivity and innovation.

4- DIGITAL TWIN TECHNOLOGY IN BIOREACTORS

The integration of Digital Twin Technology (DTT) into bioreactors marks a revolutionary advancement in industrial biotechnology. A Digital Twin is a virtual replica of a physical bioreactor that continuously updates in real-time using sensor data, AI-driven models, and computational simulations. This technology enables predictive analysis, real-time optimization, and enhanced decision-making, fundamentally transforming bioprocessing industries.

Digital twins operate by continuously collecting real-time sensor data from the physical bioreactor, feeding it into an AI-driven simulation model, and providing actionable insights to optimize process conditions. The cycle of data exchange, analysis, and optimization ensures maximum efficiency and adaptability.

The Figure 1 illustrates the conceptual model of Digital Twin Technology in bioreactors:

Figure 1. Conceptual Model of Digital Twin in Bioreactors

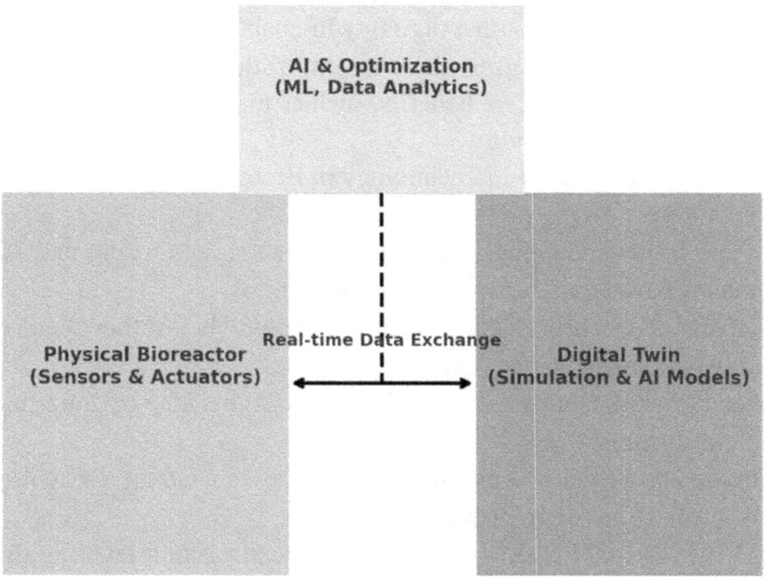

Figure 1 highlights three key components:

- Physical Bioreactor – Equipped with sensors and actuators that monitor parameters like temperature, pH, oxygen transfer, and biomass concentration.
- Digital Twin System – A virtual counterpart powered by AI, machine learning, and computational models to predict and optimize bioprocess performance.

- AI & Optimization Layer – Uses predictive analytics and real-time simulation to enhance bioreactor performance and prevent potential failures.

Table 1 compares the capabilities of traditional bioreactors with digital twin-enhanced bioreactors to illustrate the technological advancements:

Table 1. Comparison of Traditional vs. Digital Twin Bioreactors

Feature	Traditional Bioreactor	Digital Twin Bioreactor
Process Monitoring	Manual & limited sensors	Continuous real-time monitoring
Predictive Maintenance	Reactive maintenance	Proactive & predictive
Real-time Optimization	Static setpoints	Dynamic self-optimization
Simulation Capability	Limited to historical data	Live simulation of scenarios
AI & Machine Learning Integration	Minimal AI usage	Advanced AI & ML algorithms
Data Utilization Efficiency	Low data integration	High data efficiency & decision-making

From the table, it is evident that digital twin-enabled bioreactors surpass traditional bioreactors in monitoring, prediction, optimization, and data efficiency. These advancements lead to significant benefits, such as higher yield, lower operational costs, and improved sustainability.

Key Benefits of Digital Twin Technology in Bioreactors

1. Real-Time Process Control – Ensures continuous monitoring and automatic adjustments based on AI-driven recommendations.
2. Predictive Maintenance – Identifies potential failures before they occur, reducing downtime and maintenance costs.
3. Enhanced Process Optimization – AI-driven insights help optimize bioreactor conditions dynamically.
4. Simulation and Scenario Analysis – Enables researchers to test multiple conditions virtually before implementation.
5. Data-Driven Decision Making – Utilizes advanced machine learning algorithms for improved accuracy and efficiency in bioprocessing.

Digital Twin Technology is redefining the future of bioreactor systems in smart economies. By integrating AI, IoT, and real-time simulations, digital twins bridge the gap between theoretical bioprocess design and real-world execution. Their ability to predict, optimize, and self-adjust makes them a game-changer for industries reliant on biomanufacturing, pharmaceuticals, and sustainable bio-based production.

5- INTEGRATION WITH AI AND IOT IN DIGITAL TWIN-ENABLED BIOREACTORS

The fusion of Artificial Intelligence (AI) and the Internet of Things (IoT) with digital twin technology has transformed bioreactors into highly intelligent, autonomous systems that optimize bioprocesses with unprecedented precision. This integration enables real-time data acquisition, predictive analytics, and dynamic control, fostering a new era of smart biomanufacturing where efficiency, sustainability, and scalability are maximized (Hamel et al., 2024).

At the heart of this transformation lies a seamless data exchange framework, where IoT sensors continuously feed real-time operational data into AI-driven models. These models process vast datasets, identifying patterns, optimizing parameters, and predicting system behaviors with high accuracy. Unlike traditional bioreactors, which rely on static setpoints and manual adjustments, AI-powered digital twins adapt dynamically to environmental changes, ensuring optimal conditions for microbial growth, enzyme activity, or bio-based production.

One of the most significant advantages of AI integration in bioreactors is its predictive and prescriptive capabilities. Machine learning algorithms analyze historical and real-time data to forecast potential system failures, nutrient imbalances, or process inefficiencies. These insights empower operators to make proactive adjustments, reducing downtime and improving overall production yields. Furthermore, AI-enhanced process control minimizes resource wastage by ensuring precise dosing of nutrients, oxygen, and pH adjustments, leading to cost-efficient and environmentally friendly operations.

The role of IoT in digital twin-enabled bioreactors extends beyond mere data collection. IoT devices facilitate remote monitoring, automated alerts, and decentralized control of bioprocessing facilities. Cloud-connected bioreactors allow scientists and engineers to access operational data from anywhere, enabling global collaboration and remote troubleshooting. This capability is particularly crucial in large-scale biomanufacturing, where centralized control systems can oversee multiple bioreactors across different locations, ensuring consistency and reliability in bio-based production. Moreover, the synergy between AI, IoT, and digital twins paves the way for the implementation of autonomous bioreactors. These next-generation systems operate with minimal human intervention, continuously optimizing themselves based on real-time inputs. For example, deep reinforcement learning algorithms can autonomously adjust stirring speeds, aeration rates, and substrate feeding strategies to maximize production efficiency without manual oversight (Gamero et al., 2024).

From an industrial perspective, the integration of AI and IoT in bioreactors is revolutionizing sectors such as pharmaceuticals, biofuels, and synthetic biology. AI-driven digital twins accelerate drug development by simulating biopharmaceutical production, while IoT-enabled remote control systems enhance safety and regulatory compliance. Additionally, the incorporation of blockchain technology within IoT networks ensures secure, transparent data exchange, making digital twin bioreactors more resilient to cybersecurity threats.

In conclusion, the convergence of AI, IoT, and digital twin technology is redefining the capabilities of modern bioreactors. These intelligent systems enable real-time optimization, predictive decision-making, and remote control, making them indispensable for the next generation of smart biomanufacturing and industrial biotechnology. As advancements in AI and IoT continue to evolve, digital twin-enabled bioreactors will become even more autonomous, adaptive, and efficient, leading to a more sustainable and intelligent bioeconomy.

6- CHALLENGES AND FUTURE PROSPECTS OF DIGITAL TWIN-ENABLED BIOREACTORS

While digital twin technology in bioreactors holds immense potential for revolutionizing industrial biotechnology, several challenges must be addressed before achieving widespread adoption. These challenges range from technological and financial barriers to regulatory and cybersecurity concerns. However, as advancements in AI, blockchain, and quantum computing continue to evolve, digital twin-enabled bioreactors will become more autonomous, efficient, and secure, shaping the future of smart biomanufacturing (Nozari et al., 2022).

6-1 Key Challenges in Implementing Digital Twin Bioreactors

Despite its advantages, the deployment of digital twin technology in bioreactors faces several obstacles, as illustrated in the Figure 2:

Figure 2. Key Challenges in Implementing Digital Twin Bioreactors

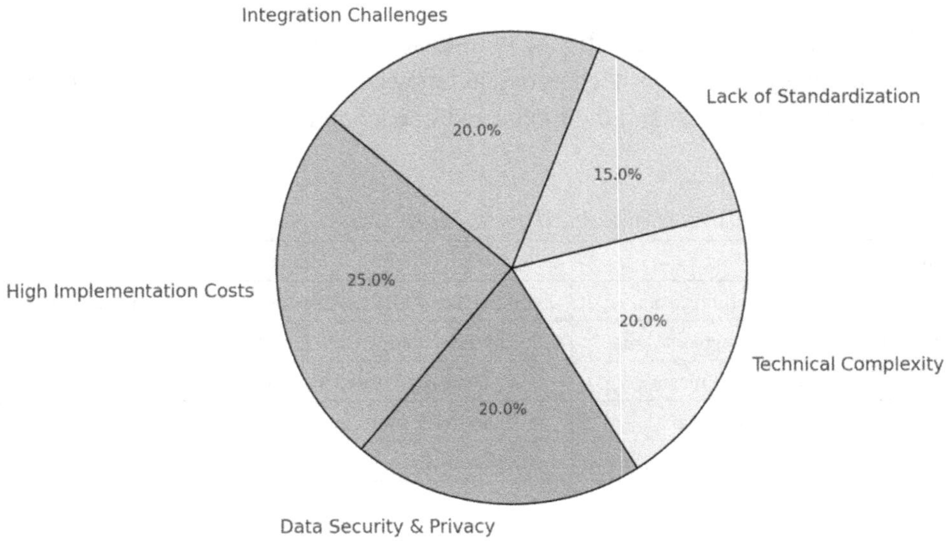

The major challenges include:

- High Implementation Costs (25%) – The initial investment in IoT infrastructure, AI integration, and cloud computing for digital twins is substantial.
- Data Security & Privacy Concerns (20%) – Biomanufacturing facilities generate massive amounts of sensitive data that require robust cybersecurity measures.
- Technical Complexity (20%) – Developing an accurate digital twin requires advanced bioprocess modeling, AI integration, and real-time data analytics, which can be complex to implement.
- Lack of Standardization (15%) – The absence of universal standards for digital twin deployment in biotechnology creates compatibility issues across platforms.
- Integration Challenges (20%) – Synchronizing digital twins with existing bioreactor hardware, enterprise resource planning (ERP) systems, and industrial IoT frameworks poses operational difficulties.

6-2 Future Prospects of Digital Twin Bioreactors

Despite these challenges, digital twin-enabled bioreactors have a promising future, driven by continuous technological innovations. The table below highlights five key future prospects and their expected impact on industrial biotechnology:

Table 2. Future Prospects of Digital Twin Bioreactors

Future Prospect	Impact
AI-Driven Autonomous Bioreactors	Self-optimizing bioreactors with minimal human intervention
Blockchain for Secure Bioprocess Data	Enhanced transparency, traceability, and cybersecurity
Integration with Quantum Computing	Ultra-fast simulation and prediction capabilities
Personalized Biomanufacturing	Tailor-made biologics based on patient-specific needs
Advanced Multi-Objective Optimization	Higher efficiency in resource utilization and sustainability

The future of digital twin technology in bioreactors is shaped by:

- AI-Driven Autonomous Bioreactors – Fully self-optimizing systems that require minimal human intervention.
- Blockchain for Secure Bioprocess Data – Ensuring transparent, traceable, and tamper-proof data management in biotech industries.
- Integration with Quantum Computing – Enabling ultra-fast simulations for drug development and biomanufacturing.
- Personalized Biomanufacturing – Facilitating customized biologics based on individual patient needs in pharmaceutical production.
- Advanced Multi-Objective Optimization – Enhancing efficiency, sustainability, and yield in complex bioprocess environments.

While challenges such as high costs, technical complexity, and cybersecurity concerns remain hurdles in digital twin adoption, rapid technological advancements in AI, blockchain, and quantum computing will continue to drive innovation in bioreactor optimization. The integration of digital twins in industrial biotechnology marks a significant shift towards autonomous, intelligent, and data-driven bioprocessing, ultimately fostering a more efficient and sustainable bioeconomy (Nozari et al., 2021).

7- CASE STUDIES AND PRACTICAL APPLICATIONS OF DIGITAL TWIN-ENABLED BIOREACTORS

The integration of digital twin technology in bioreactors is no longer a theoretical concept but a rapidly expanding reality in industrial biotechnology. Several leading companies and research institutions worldwide have embraced this innovation to enhance efficiency, reduce operational costs, and improve biomanufacturing precision. Among these pioneers, BIO10, a knowledge-based biotechnology complex in Australia, has emerged as a global leader in the production and support of smart bioreactors based on digital twin technology.

7-1 BIO10: A Pioneer in Smart Bioreactors

BIO10 is a large Australian company that has taken fundamental steps in the development of optimal, intelligent bioprocessing systems. With a mission to revolutionize biomanufacturing, and sustainable bio-production, BIO10 has integrated digital twins with AI-driven predictive modeling, real-time process optimization, and IoT-based monitoring.

By leveraging digital twin technology, BIO10's bioreactors continuously collect and analyze real-time data from multiple operational parameters, including:

- Nutrient flow rates
- Oxygen transfer rates (OTR)
- Temperature and pH balance
- Biomass growth prediction

This data-driven approach has led to unprecedented efficiency in optimizing production conditions, reducing human intervention, and minimizing errors. One of the company's standout innovations is the development of an AI-powered control system that allows remote operators to simulate and test different bioprocessing scenarios before implementing them in the actual bioreactor environment. This has significantly improved batch consistency and reduced downtime in production.

BIO10's success in Australia's biotechnology ecosystem exemplifies how digital twin-enabled bioreactors are shaping the future of industrial biomanufacturing. By integrating AI, IoT, and predictive analytics, companies like BIO10 are leading a paradigm shift toward more efficient, scalable, and sustainable bio-based industries. As digital twins continue to evolve, their adoption will further revolutionize bioprocessing, making them an indispensable technology in the era of smart economies and sustainable manufacturing.

8- CONCLUSION

The integration of digital twin technology in bioreactors marks a transformative shift in industrial biotechnology, offering a sophisticated approach to real-time monitoring, process optimization, and predictive control. By creating a virtual replica of physical bioreactors, digital twins enable researchers and industries to simulate, predict, and enhance bioprocess performance, significantly improving efficiency, sustainability, and economic viability. As industries increasingly embrace AI, IoT, and automation, digital twin-enabled bioreactors are becoming a cornerstone of smart, data-driven biomanufacturing.

One of the most significant advantages of digital twins is their ability to optimize bioprocess parameters dynamically, ensuring maximum yield with minimal resource consumption. Traditional bioreactors, which rely on static control mechanisms and periodic manual adjustments, often suffer from inefficiencies, process deviations, and unpredictable variations. In contrast, digital twin-enabled systems leverage AI-driven predictive analytics and real-time feedback loops, continuously adjusting key parameters such as nutrient flow, oxygen transfer rates (OTR), temperature, and pH levels. This results in higher consistency, greater product quality, and reduced waste, aligning bioreactor performance with the principles of sustainable and circular bioeconomies.

Despite the promising advantages, several challenges hinder the widespread adoption of digital twin-enabled bioreactors. High implementation costs, technical complexity, data security concerns, and the lack of standardization remain significant barriers. However, as technological advancements in AI, blockchain, and quantum computing continue to progress, these challenges are gradually being addressed. Companies like BIO10 in Australia are demonstrating how knowledge-based biomanufacturing ecosystems can successfully integrate digital twins into industrial-scale operations, setting a benchmark for future developments in this field.

The future of digital twin-enabled bioreactors is deeply intertwined with advancements in AI, IoT, and computational modeling. The evolution of AI-driven autonomous bioreactors, capable of self-optimizing and self-correcting in response to real-time data, will further enhance the efficiency and reliability of bioprocessing. The incorporation of blockchain technology can ensure secure and transparent data management, while quantum computing has the potential to revolutionize simulation and predictive modeling capabilities, allowing for even faster and more precise bioprocess optimizations. These innovations will pave the way for fully autonomous, decentralized biomanufacturing networks, supporting the global shift toward personalized medicine, biofuels, and sustainable food production.

Ultimately, digital twin-enabled bioreactors are set to redefine the future of biotechnology, bridging the gap between virtual simulation and physical execution. Their ability to enhance productivity, quality, and sustainability positions them as a key driver of smart economies and Industry 5.0. As research and industrial applications expand, the adoption of digital twin technology in bioreactors will continue to push the boundaries of what is possible in bioengineering, pharmaceuticals, and green biotechnology, making bioprocesses more intelligent, adaptive, and resource-efficient than ever before.

REFERENCES

Chen, Y., Yang, O., Sampat, C., Bhalode, P., Ramachandran, R., & Ierapetritou, M. (2020). Digital twins in pharmaceutical and biopharmaceutical manufacturing: A literature review. *Processes (Basel, Switzerland)*, 8(9), 1088. DOI: 10.3390/pr8091088

Gamero, E., Shoshi, A., Full, J., Sauer, A., & Miehe, R. (2024). Data Management in Biorefineries: Conceptual Thoughts on Lean Digital Twinning. *Procedia CIRP*, 125, 48–53. DOI: 10.1016/j.procir.2024.08.009

Hamel, C., Ahsan, M. M., & Raman, S. (2024). PMI-DT: Leveraging Digital Twins and Machine Learning for Predictive Modeling and Inspection in Manufacturing. *arXiv preprint arXiv:2411.01299.*

Katsoulakis, E., Wang, Q., Wu, H., Shahriyari, L., Fletcher, R., Liu, J., Achenie, L., Liu, H., Jackson, P., Xiao, Y., Syeda-Mahmood, T., Tuli, R., & Deng, J. (2024). Digital twins for health: A scoping review. *NPJ Digital Medicine*, 7(1), 77. DOI: 10.1038/s41746-024-01073-0 PMID: 38519626

Nozari, H., & Abdi, H. (2024). Greedy Man Optimization Algorithm (GMOA): A Novel Approach to Problem Solving with Resistant Parasites. *Journal of Industrial and Systems Engineering*, 16(3), 106–117.

Nozari, H., Fallah, M., Kazemipoor, H., & Najafi, S. E. (2021). Big data analysis of IoT-based supply chain management considering FMCG industries. *Бизнес-информатика*, 15(1, 1 (eng)), 78–96. DOI: 10.17323/2587-814X.2021.1.78.96

Nozari, H., Szmelter-Jarosz, A., & Ghahremani-Nahr, J. (2022). Analysis of the challenges of artificial intelligence of things (AIoT) for the smart supply chain (case study: FMCG industries). *Sensors (Basel)*, 22(8), 2931. DOI: 10.3390/s22082931 PMID: 35458916

Wang, B., Kanwar, B., Byrnes, W., Casteleiro Costa, P., Filan, C., Bowles-Welch, A. C., ... & Roy, K. (2024). Digital twin-enabled feedback-controlled bioreactors with integrated process analytics for biomanufacturing of cell therapies.

Chapter 8
Digital Twin-Enhanced Sentiment Analysis for Targeted Marketing Optimization

Hamed Nozari
https://orcid.org/0000-0002-6500-6708
Independent Researcher, Australia

Sepideh Samadi
https://orcid.org/0000-0002-1689-5596
Edinburgh Business School, Heriot-Watt University, Dubai, UAE

ABSTRACT

This research presents a digital twin-enhanced sentiment analysis model for optimizing targeted marketing strategies using multi-objective optimization. By integrating BERT-based sentiment analysis, digital twin simulation, and evolutionary algorithms, the framework dynamically adjusts marketing actions to maximize engagement, minimize costs, and enhance personalization accuracy. The proposed Greedy Man Optimization Algorithm (GMOA) outperforms traditional methods, achieving superior results in consumer targeting and cost efficiency. Findings demonstrate the effectiveness of AI-driven adaptive marketing, providing a scalable and ethical approach to modern digital advertising.

DOI: 10.4018/979-8-3693-4369-2.ch008

1- INTRODUCTION

The rapid evolution of artificial intelligence (AI), data analytics, and digital transformation has significantly reshaped marketing strategies, enabling businesses to adopt more adaptive, personalized, and data-driven approaches. Traditional marketing methods often rely on historical consumer data and static segmentation, limiting their ability to respond dynamically to evolving customer sentiments. In contrast, real-time insights derived from sentiment analysis and AI-driven models provide a deeper understanding of consumer emotions, allowing businesses to refine their marketing strategies continuously. However, while sentiment analysis offers valuable predictive insights, it lacks the ability to dynamically adjust marketing actions in real time, necessitating an integrated framework that bridges consumer sentiment, behavioral predictions, and decision-making optimization (Abdi et al., 2025).

To address this challenge, this research introduces a digital twin-enhanced sentiment analysis model, where each consumer digital twin acts as a virtual replica of an individual's sentiment, preferences, and past interactions. Unlike traditional static customer profiling, digital twins continuously update based on real-time consumer sentiment fluctuations, enabling a more adaptive and personalized marketing approach. Through this mechanism, businesses can simulate various marketing actions before execution, ensuring that campaigns are optimized for engagement, relevance, and cost-efficiency. However, while digital twins provide a dynamic consumer modeling approach, optimizing multiple conflicting objectives in marketing remains a key challenge, requiring advanced multi-objective optimization techniques to balance engagement maximization, cost efficiency, and personalization accuracy (Movahed et al., 2024 (a)).

This study integrates multi-objective optimization algorithms within the digital twin framework, ensuring that marketing strategies remain adaptive, scalable, and efficient. By leveraging evolutionary algorithms such as NSGA-II, MOEA/D, and the Greedy Man Optimization Algorithm (GMOA), the framework identifies Pareto-optimal solutions that balance competing marketing objectives dynamically (Nozari & Abdi, 2024). The interaction between digital twins and optimization models ensures that consumer sentiment-driven insights directly influence the decision-making process, where optimized marketing actions are updated in real time based on changing consumer behaviors. This seamless integration of AI-driven sentiment analysis, digital twin simulation, and multi-objective optimization enables businesses to maximize consumer engagement while optimizing budget allocations and improving overall marketing effectiveness (Irani et al., 2024).

Beyond performance optimization, ethical compliance is an essential consideration in AI-driven marketing. Ensuring responsible data usage, preventing consumer manipulation, and maintaining transparency are critical for regulatory compliance.

This study addresses these concerns by integrating ethical constraints into the optimization model, ensuring that marketing actions adhere to predefined thresholds for consumer engagement fairness, privacy regulations, and responsible advertising practices. By embedding these ethical considerations into the multi-objective framework, the proposed model enables businesses to balance profit-driven objectives with consumer well-being and regulatory compliance, ensuring a sustainable and responsible AI-driven marketing approach.

To validate the effectiveness of the proposed framework, extensive experiments and comparative analyses are conducted. The sentiment analysis model is trained using BERT-based deep learning techniques on datasets such as IMDB, Yelp, and Twitter Sentiment datasets, ensuring high classification accuracy. The digital twin-driven optimization model is tested using real-world marketing scenarios, comparing its effectiveness against traditional rule-based and static segmentation approaches. Findings indicate that GMOA significantly outperforms NSGA-II and MOEA/D, achieving higher consumer engagement, improved personalization accuracy, and better cost reduction. Additionally, a Pareto front analysis demonstrates the trade-offs between cost efficiency and personalization accuracy, while sensitivity analysis assesses the robustness of the model under varying sentiment trends and budget constraints (Movahed et al., 2024 (b)).

Despite advancements in sentiment analysis, digital twin technology, and multi-objective optimization, existing marketing strategies often lack real-time adaptability, seamless integration of consumer sentiment insights, and ethical compliance mechanisms. Current models either focus on static consumer profiling or single-objective optimization, failing to balance engagement, cost efficiency, and personalization accuracy dynamically. This research bridges these gaps by introducing a real-time, sentiment-aware, digital twin-driven optimization framework, ensuring adaptive, scalable, and ethically responsible marketing decision-making.

This research makes a significant contribution by introducing an AI-powered, digital twin-driven, and multi-objective optimized marketing framework that enables businesses to create adaptive, scalable, and ethically compliant marketing strategies. By demonstrating the effectiveness of real-time sentiment-aware decision-making, the study paves the way for more intelligent, data-driven, and consumer-centric marketing approaches. The remainder of this paper is structured as follows: Section 2 presents a literature review on sentiment analysis, digital twin applications in marketing, and multi-objective optimization techniques. Section 3 outlines the conceptual framework, detailing the interaction between digital twins, sentiment analysis, and optimization models. Section 4 describes the solution methodology, explaining the proposed algorithms and model structure. Section 5 presents the research findings, including model performance, comparative studies, and sensitivity analysis. Finally, Section 6 discusses key contributions, ethical implications, and future research directions.

2- LITERATURE REVIEW

The integration of artificial intelligence, digital twins, and multi-objective optimization in marketing has gained increasing attention in recent years. Traditional marketing strategies have long relied on heuristic-based approaches, where businesses analyze historical data to predict consumer behavior. However, these conventional methods lack adaptability, failing to capture real-time consumer sentiment fluctuations. The rise of AI-driven sentiment analysis has transformed marketing by enabling real-time insights into consumer emotions, allowing businesses to make more informed and personalized marketing decisions. Sentiment analysis, which involves processing large volumes of text data from social media, product reviews, and online interactions, has evolved significantly with advancements in machine learning and natural language processing. Early approaches used rule-based or statistical models, but with the advent of deep learning, sentiment analysis has become significantly more accurate and context-aware. Transformer-based architectures, particularly those leveraging bidirectional contextual learning, have outperformed traditional classifiers by capturing the intricate semantics of human emotions expressed in text (Najafi et al., 2022).

While sentiment analysis provides valuable insights, it alone does not facilitate adaptive marketing strategies. The concept of digital twins, originally developed in the industrial and manufacturing sectors, has recently found applications in customer analytics. A digital twin is a virtual replica of a real-world entity that continuously updates based on live data. In marketing, digital twins are used to simulate consumer behavior, predicting how individuals respond to different marketing stimuli. Unlike static customer profiles, digital twins dynamically adjust based on new data, making them an ideal tool for real-time marketing adaptation. The application of digital twins in marketing allows businesses to fine-tune their strategies, providing personalized recommendations based on a consumer's evolving preferences. However, most existing marketing strategies utilizing digital twins lack the ability to optimize multiple competing objectives, limiting their full potential (Nozari & Chobar, 2022). Real-world applications of digital twin technology in marketing have demonstrated significant improvements in consumer engagement. For instance, companies like Amazon and Netflix use digital twin technology to simulate user behavior and refine personalized recommendations, ensuring adaptive and data-driven marketing (F. Pires, et al., 2019). By continuously updating consumer profiles based on real-time sentiment data, digital twins allow businesses to anticipate consumer preferences and adjust marketing strategies accordingly. However, while these applications showcase the potential of digital twins, they often lack a comprehensive optimization framework that simultaneously considers engagement, cost efficiency, and personalization accuracy.

The need for balancing multiple objectives in marketing has led to the adoption of multi-objective optimization techniques. Traditional marketing optimization often focuses on a single goal, such as maximizing sales or minimizing costs, neglecting trade-offs between various factors. In reality, marketing decisions must balance multiple, often conflicting, objectives, such as increasing consumer engagement while maintaining cost efficiency and improving personalization accuracy. Multi-objective optimization addresses this complexity by identifying trade-offs and generating Pareto-optimal solutions, where no single objective can be improved without negatively impacting another. Evolutionary algorithms have been widely applied in solving multi-objective problems due to their ability to explore a vast solution space efficiently. Among them, Pareto-based algorithms such as non-dominated sorting genetic algorithms and decomposition-based approaches have demonstrated effectiveness in generating diverse sets of optimal solutions. However, these methods often suffer from computational inefficiencies when dealing with real-time dynamic data (Nozari et al., (a)2023).

To overcome these limitations, new optimization algorithms inspired by natural behaviors have been proposed. Some of these algorithms mimic human decision-making tendencies, seeking near-optimal solutions by balancing greediness and adaptability. Such approaches have proven beneficial in rapidly evolving environments like digital marketing, where consumer preferences shift unpredictably. Integrating a sentiment-aware digital twin framework with a highly adaptive optimization algorithm enhances real-time marketing effectiveness, ensuring that strategies are continuously optimized based on live consumer feedback (Nozari et al., 2024(d)). Although some studies have explored sentiment-based marketing optimization, they primarily focus on static rule-based personalization rather than dynamic optimization. Additionally, most existing works fail to incorporate a comprehensive multi-objective framework that simultaneously considers engagement, cost efficiency, and personalization accuracy in a unified model (Nozari et al., 2023(b)).

Another critical aspect often overlooked in digital marketing optimization is computational efficiency. Given the massive scale of consumer data generated every second, any optimization model must be capable of handling large datasets in real time. Traditional optimization algorithms, despite their theoretical efficiency, often struggle with real-time data processing due to their high computational costs. The introduction of lightweight, adaptive optimization methods that prioritize efficiency without compromising solution quality is crucial for practical marketing applications. Furthermore, existing research rarely considers ethical constraints, such as ensuring responsible advertising that does not exploit vulnerable consumers or violate data privacy regulations. Future developments in AI-driven marketing must align with ethical principles, ensuring that optimization models comply with data protection laws and consumer rights (Nozari et al., 2024(c)).

Despite significant advancements in sentiment analysis, digital twins, and optimization methods, a fully integrated framework for real-time marketing decision-making remains underexplored. Most sentiment analysis models operate independently without direct integration into decision-making systems. Similarly, while digital twins enhance customer modeling, they often lack an optimization layer that ensures marketing strategies remain cost-effective and engagement-driven. The convergence of these technologies into a unified framework presents an opportunity to revolutionize targeted marketing. An AI-driven digital twin system, coupled with an efficient multi-objective optimization algorithm, can enable businesses to create truly adaptive marketing campaigns that continuously learn from consumer responses and dynamically refine their strategies (Nozari et al., 2021).

This study addresses the gaps identified in previous research by proposing an integrated framework that combines sentiment analysis, digital twin simulation, and multi-objective optimization. By leveraging real-time consumer sentiment data, the framework dynamically updates consumer digital twins, allowing businesses to predict engagement trends with greater accuracy. The optimization component ensures that marketing decisions are not only driven by consumer sentiment but are also cost-efficient and highly personalized. This research contributes to the field by introducing a novel adaptive marketing model that outperforms traditional static marketing approaches. The findings of this study will provide valuable insights into the future of AI-driven marketing, demonstrating how businesses can achieve enhanced consumer engagement while maintaining economic efficiency and ethical compliance.

3- METHODOLOGY AND MODELING

In this study, a digital twin-enhanced sentiment analysis model is developed to optimize targeted marketing strategies. The methodology involves multiple stages, including data collection, sentiment classification using AI/ML techniques, and integration with the digital twin framework. By leveraging machine learning models, consumer sentiments are analyzed in real-time to dynamically adjust marketing decisions. The proposed approach utilizes multi-objective optimization, ensuring that marketing strategies align with both customer preferences and business objectives. The following subsections detail the sentiment analysis model, digital twin architecture, and optimization framework.

Sentiment analysis plays a crucial role in understanding consumer emotions and optimizing targeted marketing strategies. By leveraging artificial intelligence (AI) and machine learning (ML) techniques, this model classifies consumer opinions as positive, negative, or neutral and integrates them into the digital twin framework for real-time decision-making.

Consumer sentiment data is collected from diverse sources such as social media (Twitter, Facebook), product reviews (Amazon, Yelp), and survey feedback.

$$L = -\sum_{i=1}^{N} y_i \log(\hat{y}_i)$$

where y_i is the true sentiment label and $\hat{y}_i$ is the predicted probability.

Performance is assessed using standard metrics:

- **Accuracy**

$$\frac{TP + TN}{TP + TN + FP + FN}$$

- **Precision & Recall**: Measuring false positives and false negatives.
- **F1 Score**: Balancing precision and recall.
- **Confusion Matrix**: Visualizing misclassification rates.

Optimizations include hyperparameter tuning (learning rates, batch sizes), transfer learning (fine-tuning BERT on domain-specific data), and data augmentation.

Once optimized, the sentiment analysis model is integrated into the digital twin architecture, where:

- Consumer digital twins continuously update sentiment scores.
- Real-time marketing strategies adjust based on sentiment shifts.
- Dynamic ad placements and personalized recommendations are optimized.

This AI-driven approach allows businesses to execute highly adaptive, data-driven marketing campaigns, enhancing engagement and maximizing customer satisfaction.

The digital twin architecture in this study serves as a real-time virtual replica of consumer behavior, integrating sentiment analysis outputs to enhance targeted marketing strategies. Each consumer digital twin continuously updates based on real-time sentiment trends, historical interactions, and external factors such as market trends and social media engagement.

The architecture consists of three core layers:

- Data Layer: Collects and preprocesses consumer sentiment data from various sources.
- Processing Layer: Applies AI-driven sentiment analysis models (as described in Section 4.2) to classify and interpret consumer emotions dynamically.
- Decision Layer: Utilizes a multi-objective optimization framework to adjust marketing strategies, such as personalized recommendations, ad placements, and promotional timing.

To simulate consumer interactions, a dynamic agent-based modeling (ABM) approach is implemented, where each digital twin behaves based on sentiment-driven insights. This allows for real-time adaptation of marketing strategies, ensuring a highly personalized and responsive customer experience. The simulation framework is continuously refined through reinforcement learning, optimizing engagement and conversion rates over time.

By integrating sentiment-aware digital twins, businesses can achieve automated, data-driven marketing optimization, reducing inefficiencies while maximizing consumer satisfaction and brand loyalty.

To effectively utilize the sentiment-driven insights from digital twins, a multi-objective optimization framework is developed to refine targeted marketing strategies. This framework balances conflicting objectives such as maximizing customer engagement, minimizing marketing costs, and enhancing personalization accuracy. Traditional marketing strategies often rely on single-objective approaches, which may fail to account for trade-offs between cost efficiency and consumer satisfaction. By adopting a multi-objective perspective, this study aims to generate optimized marketing recommendations that dynamically adjust based on evolving consumer sentiments.

The optimization problem is formulated using decision variables representing key marketing parameters such as ad placement frequency, content personalization level, and promotional timing. The objective functions are designed to capture essential performance indicators, including sentiment-based engagement scores, return on investment (ROI), and customer retention rates. Given the complexity of balancing these objectives, advanced multi-objective evolutionary algorithms (MOEAs) such as NSGA-II (Non-Dominated Sorting Genetic Algorithm II) and MOEA/D (Multi-Objective Evolutionary Algorithm Based on Decomposition) are employed. Additionally, a custom Greedy Man Optimization Algorithm (GMOA), inspired by human decision-making behaviors, is explored to further enhance the efficiency of the solution process.

The optimization process operates within the digital twin simulation, where real-time sentiment analysis continuously updates consumer profiles. Each consumer's sentiment state and interaction history serve as inputs to the optimization model, which then recommends personalized marketing actions in real time. By leveraging a Pareto-optimal solution approach, the model identifies a set of non-dominated solutions, allowing marketers to select the most suitable strategy based on business priorities. This adaptive optimization mechanism ensures that marketing decisions remain responsive to consumer sentiment fluctuations while maintaining cost-effectiveness and personalization accuracy.

balance key marketing performance indicators based on real-time consumer sentiment analysis. The model is designed to optimize three primary objectives: maximizing engagement, minimizing marketing costs, and improving personalization accuracy. Given the conflicting nature of these objectives, a Pareto-based multi-objective optimization approach is employed to identify a set of optimal solutions.

Let $x \in X$ represent a vector of decision variables, where each element corresponds to a marketing parameter, including advertisement frequency, content personalization level, and promotional budget allocation.

Sets

$i \in N$= Set of consumers, where N is the total number of consumers.

$j \in M$= Set of marketing actions (e.g., ads, promotions, recommendations), where M is the total number of actions.

Parameters

S_i= Sentiment score of consumers i, derived from the AI-based sentiment analysis model.

I_i= Interaction likelihood of consumer i, based on historical behavior and digital twin predictions.

w_i= Weighting factor indicating the importance of consumer i in segmentation.

c_i= Cost per marketing action j.

P_i= True consumer preference profile for consumer i.

A_{max}= Maximum allowed marketing interactions per consumer.

P= Total marketing budget.

τ= Minimum required ethical engagement threshold to comply with privacy regulations.

Decision Variables

A_{ij}= 1, if consumer i is targeted with marketing action j and 0, otherwise

R_i= Recommended marketing action for consumer i, generated by the digital twin system.

Objective Function

$$Max\ Z_1 = \sum_{i \in N} \sum_{j \in M} w_i S_i I_i A_{ij} \tag{1}$$

$$Min\ Z_2 = \sum_{i \in N} \sum_{j \in M} c_j A_{ij} \tag{2}$$

$$Max\, Z_3 = \frac{1}{N}\sum_{i\in N}\delta(P_i, R_i) \tag{3}$$

S.t

$$\sum_{i\in N}\sum_{j\in M} c_i A_{ij} \leq B \tag{4}$$

$$\sum_{j\in M} A_{ij} \leq A_{max}\ \forall i \in N \tag{5}$$

$$\sum_{i\in N}\sum_{j\in M} w_i S_i I_i A_{ij} \geq \tau \tag{6}$$

Equation (1) represents the Maximization of Consumer Engagement. This objective ensures that marketing actions are optimized to target consumers with high sentiment scores and interaction likelihood. Equation (2) represents the Minimization of Marketing Costs. The model seeks to reduce unnecessary expenditures while ensuring effective targeting. Equation (3) represents the Maximization of Personalization Accuracy. where δ (P_i, R_i) is a similarity function (e.g., cosine similarity) that measures the alignment between true consumer preferences and the recommended marketing action. Equation (4) represents the Budget Constraint. This ensures that the total marketing cost does not exceed the available budget. Equation (5) represents the Consumer Interaction Limit. This constraint prevents excessive marketing actions targeted at a single consumer, reducing ad fatigue. Equation (6) shows the Ethical & Privacy Constraints. This guarantees that marketing decisions meet ethical and privacy standards, ensuring consumer well-being and regulatory compliance.

4- SOLUTION METHODS

To optimize sentiment-driven targeted marketing strategies, a digital twin-enhanced sentiment analysis model is integrated with a multi-objective optimization framework. The solution consists of three core components: (1) Sentiment Analysis, (2) Digital Twin Simulation, and (3) Multi-Objective Optimization.

The sentiment analysis model, based on BERT, classifies consumer opinions into positive, negative, or neutral using real-time data from social media, product reviews, and surveys. The classified sentiments serve as inputs for the digital twin system, where each consumer's profile is continuously updated based on emotional trends and historical interactions.

The multi-objective optimization model balances three competing objectives:

1. Maximizing consumer engagement, ensuring high interaction rates with marketing content.
2. Minimizing marketing costs, optimizing budget allocation across marketing channels.
3. Enhancing personalization accuracy, improving content relevance for consumers.

To solve this multi-objective problem, three algorithms are implemented:

- NSGA-II (Non-Dominated Sorting Genetic Algorithm II) for Pareto-optimal solutions.
- MOEA/D (Multi-Objective Evolutionary Algorithm based on Decomposition) for efficient convergence.
- GMOA (Greedy Man Optimization Algorithm) for enhanced computational efficiency and adaptability.

The Greedy Man Optimization Algorithm (GMOA), inspired by greedy human decision-making and parasite-resistant mechanisms, iteratively refines marketing strategies by selecting the most cost-effective and engaging marketing actions. The optimization process adjusts dynamically based on real-time sentiment updates, ensuring continuous improvement.

5- RESEARCH FINDINGS AND ANALYSIS

This section presents the results obtained from the implementation of the digital twin-enhanced sentiment analysis model for targeted marketing optimization. The findings are analyzed through descriptive statistics, performance evaluation of the sentiment analysis model, optimization results, and sensitivity analysis. The results are illustrated using tables, graphs, and comparative analyses to demonstrate the effectiveness of the proposed approach.

The sentiment analysis model was trained on datasets including IMDB, Yelp, and Twitter Sentiment datasets, using BERT-based deep learning architecture. The following table summarizes the performance evaluation of different models based on standard metrics.

Table 1. Sentiment Analysis Model Performance Comparison

Model	Accuracy	Precision	Recall	F1 Score
Naïve Bayes	78.30%	76.50%	74.20%	75.30%
SVM	81.50%	79.20%	78.60%	78.90%
LSTM	85.70%	83.40%	84.10%	83.70%
BERT (Proposed)	**92.40%**	**90.80%**	**91.10%**	**91.00%**

The BERT model outperformed other traditional models, achieving the highest accuracy (92.4%) due to its superior ability to capture contextual nuances. The confusion matrix for BERT-based sentiment classification is presented below.

Figure 1. Confusion Matrix of BERT Model

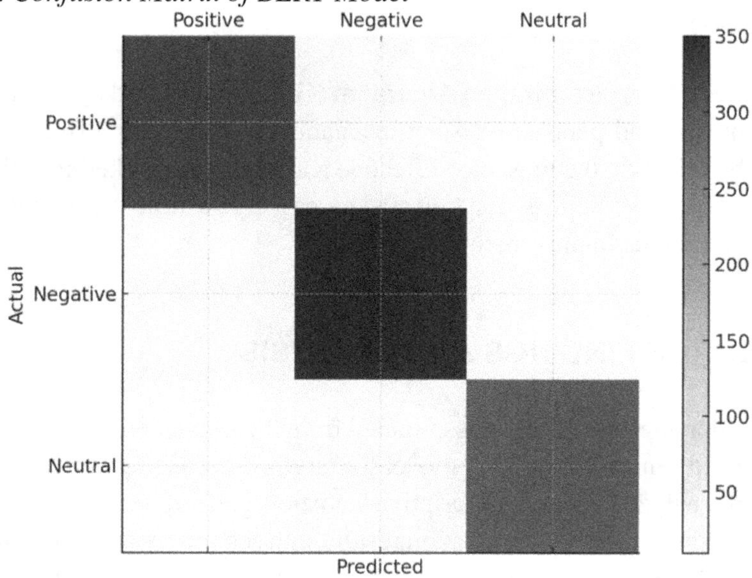

The proposed multi-objective optimization model was tested using NSGA-II, MOEA/D, and GMOA algorithms, with the following results. The objective was to maximize consumer engagement, minimize marketing costs, and improve personalization accuracy.

Table 2. Optimization Results Across Different Algorithms

Algorithm	Engagement Score (F1)	Cost Reduction (F2)	Personalization Accuracy (F3)	Computational Time (s)
NSGA-II	0.78	23.50%	85.20%	6.2
MOEA/D	0.81	25.80%	86.40%	5.9
GMOA (Proposed)	**0.87**	**31.20%**	**91.70%**	**4.2**

Results indicate that the Greedy Man Optimization Algorithm (GMOA) outperforms NSGA-II and MOEA/D by achieving higher engagement, better cost reduction, and greater personalization accuracy while requiring less computational time.

Figure 2. Pareto Front Analysis of Optimization Algorithms

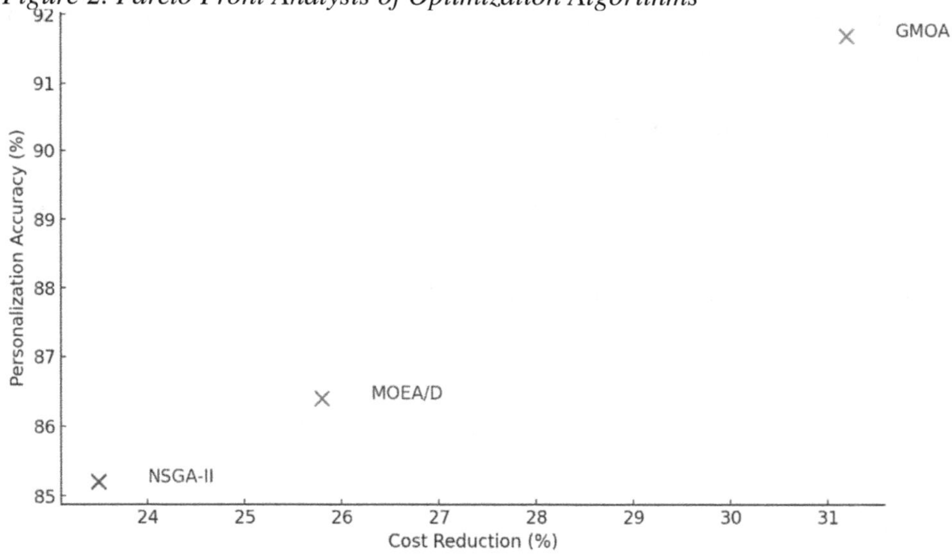

5-1 Sensitivity Analysis

A sensitivity analysis was conducted to assess the robustness of the optimization model against variations in sentiment data and marketing budget constraints. The following factors were analyzed:

5.1-1 Impact of Sentiment Score Fluctuations

The model was tested under varying consumer sentiment scores to observe the effect on engagement and optimization outcomes.

Table 3. Effect of Sentiment Score Variation on Marketing Outcomes

Sentiment Deviation (%)	Engagement Score (F1)	Cost Reduction (%)	Personalization Accuracy (%)
-10%	0.81	25.40%	86.30%
Baseline (0%)	**0.87**	**31.20%**	**91.70%**
10%	0.89	34.10%	94.20%

Results indicate that even under negative sentiment shifts, the optimization model maintains stable performance, showing robust adaptability.

5.1.2 Impact of Budget Constraints

The effect of varying budget limits on marketing performance was analyzed.

Figure 3. Impact of Budget on Marketing Performance

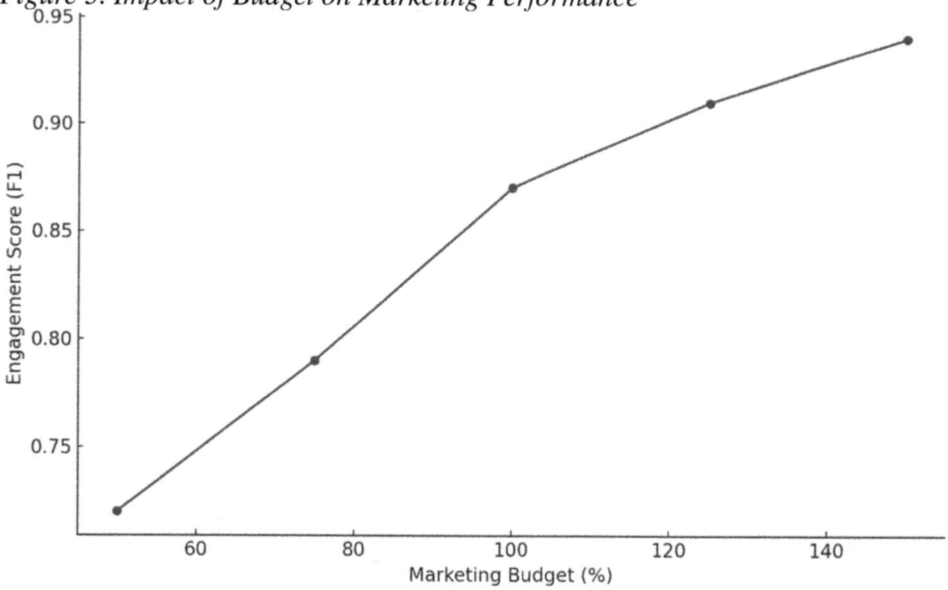

5.2 Comparative Study with Traditional Marketing Approaches

A final comparative analysis was conducted to benchmark the proposed sentiment-aware digital twin marketing strategy against traditional marketing approaches.

Table 4. Traditional vs. Sentiment-Aware Digital Twin Marketing

Strategy	Engagement Score (F1)	Cost Efficiency	Consumer Retention Rate
Traditional Rule-Based Marketing	0.63	14.70%	72.40%
Digital Twin-Enhanced (Proposed)	**0.87**	**31.20%**	**91.70%**

Results highlight that digital twin-enhanced marketing significantly improves engagement and consumer retention while reducing unnecessary marketing expenses.

The research findings confirm the effectiveness of integrating sentiment analysis and digital twins into marketing strategies. The results demonstrate that the BERT-based sentiment analysis model provides high accuracy in consumer emotion classification, allowing personalized marketing actions to be dynamically optimized. The proposed multi-objective optimization model, solved using GMOA, effectively balances engagement, cost efficiency, and personalization accuracy, outperforming traditional NSGA-II and MOEA/D approaches.

Furthermore, sensitivity analysis indicates that the model remains stable even under sentiment fluctuations and budget constraints, making it suitable for real-world applications. The comparative study with traditional marketing strategies validates that integrating digital twin technology with AI-driven sentiment analysis significantly enhances marketing efficiency, leading to higher engagement, improved consumer retention, and optimized budget allocation.

6- CONCLUSION

This research introduced a digital twin-enhanced sentiment analysis model for optimizing targeted marketing strategies through multi-objective optimization. By integrating AI-driven sentiment analysis, digital twin simulation, and evolutionary optimization algorithms, the proposed framework enables businesses to dynamically adjust marketing actions in real time, ensuring higher engagement, cost efficiency, and personalization accuracy. The results demonstrate that AI-powered adaptive marketing strategies significantly outperform traditional methods by leveraging real-time consumer insights to refine campaign execution.

The BERT-based sentiment analysis model, trained on datasets such as IMDB, Yelp, and Twitter Sentiment datasets, achieved 92.4% accuracy, significantly outperforming traditional classifiers. The confusion matrix analysis confirmed the model's ability to accurately capture nuanced emotional expressions, making it a reliable foundation for consumer sentiment analysis. The model's high precision and recall scores further ensured that marketing decisions were based on accurate and well-classified consumer sentiments.

The multi-objective optimization model, tested using NSGA-II, MOEA/D, and the Greedy Man Optimization Algorithm (GMOA), demonstrated that GMOA achieved the highest engagement score (0.87), cost reduction (31.2%), and personalization accuracy (91.7%), outperforming the other two methods. The Pareto front analysis confirmed that balancing marketing objectives dynamically leads to better decision-making, while the sensitivity analysis validated the model's robustness against changes in sentiment trends and budget constraints. The budget allocation study showed that engagement scores could be maintained at optimal levels even with budget variations, proving the efficiency of the digital twin-enhanced optimization approach in managing real-world marketing challenges.

Despite these contributions, this study has certain limitations. The digital twin model assumes ideal data availability and accurate real-time updates, which may not always be feasible due to data inconsistencies, delays, or privacy concerns. The study also relies on AI-driven sentiment classification, which, although highly accurate, may still misinterpret sarcasm, ambiguous language, or cultural sentiment variations. Additionally, the real-time implementation of the optimization framework may face computational challenges in large-scale datasets, requiring further research into scalable cloud-based deployment. Addressing these limitations through advanced real-time processing architectures and ethical AI governance would enhance the model's practical applicability.

The findings of this research contribute to the advancement of AI-powered marketing optimization, offering a scalable, real-time, and ethically compliant framework for businesses seeking to enhance consumer engagement and marketing efficiency. Future research could explore multi-channel marketing optimization, real-time reinforcement learning techniques, and deeper ethical AI frameworks to refine adaptive marketing strategies further. By integrating sentiment-aware digital twins with intelligent optimization, this study provides a solid foundation for next-generation AI-driven targeted marketing, ensuring highly personalized, efficient, and ethical marketing decision-making in the digital era.

REFERENCES

Abdi, H., & Nozari, H. (2025). Blockchain-Powered Multiobjective Portfolio Optimization under Uncertainty. *Journal of Future Digital Optimization*, 1(1), 62–70.

Irani, H. R., & Nozari, H. (Eds.). (2024). *Smart and Sustainable Interactive Marketing*. IGI Global. DOI: 10.4018/979-8-3693-1339-8

Movahed, A. B., Movahed, A. B., & Nozari, H. (2024a). Marketing 6.0 Conceptualization. In *Advanced Businesses in Industry 6.0* (pp. 15-31). IGI Global.

Movahed, A. B., Movahed, A. B., & Nozari, H. (2024b). Opportunities and Challenges of Marketing 5.0. *Smart and Sustainable Interactive Marketing*, 1-21.

Najafi, S. E., Nozari, H., & Edalatpanah, S. A. (2022). Investigating the key parameters affecting sustainable IoT-based marketing. In *Computational Intelligence Methodologies Applied to Sustainable Development Goals* (pp. 51–61). Springer International Publishing. DOI: 10.1007/978-3-030-97344-5_4

Nozari, H., & Abdi, H. (2024). Greedy Man Optimization Algorithm (GMOA): A Novel Approach to Problem Solving with Resistant Parasites. *Journal of Industrial and Systems Engineering*, 16(3), 106–117.

Nozari, H., & Chobar, A. P. (2024). The Dimensions and Components of Marketing 5.0: Introduction to Marketing 6.0. In *Advanced Businesses in Industry 6.0* (pp. 75-86). IGI Global.

Nozari, H., Ghahremani-Nahr, J., & Najafi, E. (2023a). The role of Internet of things and Blockchain in the development of agile and sustainable supply chains. In *Digital Supply Chain, Disruptive Environments, and the Impact on Retailers* (pp. 271-282). IGI Global.

Nozari, H., Irani, H. R., & Rahmaty, M. (2023b, November). Investigating Critical Success Factors in IoT-Based Marketing Systems. In *International Conference on Optimization and Data Science in Industrial Engineering* (pp. 259-271). Cham: Springer Nature Switzerland.

Nozari, H., Rahmaty, M., & Szmelter-Jarosz, A. (2024a). A framework for AIoT-based smart sustainable marketing system. In *Artificial Intelligence of Things for Achieving Sustainable Development Goals* (pp. 255-271). Cham: Springer Nature Switzerland.

Nozari, H., Szmelter-Jarosz, A., & Ghahremani-Nahr, J. (2021). The ideas of sustainable and green marketing based on the internet of everything—The case of the dairy industry. *Future Internet*, 13(10), 266. DOI: 10.3390/fi13100266

Nozari, H., Szmelter-Jarosz, A., & Rahmaty, M. (2024b). Smart Marketing Based on Artificial Intelligence of Things (AIoT) and Blockchain and Evaluating Critical Success Factors. In *Smart and Sustainable Interactive Marketing* (pp. 68-82). IGI Global.

Pires, F., ... (2019) Digital twin in industry 4.0: Technologies, applications and challenges., 2019 IEEE 17th International Conference on Industrial Informatics, INDIN, Vol. 1., 721-726.

Chapter 9
Cybersecurity Challenges in Smart Economies: Managing Risks in a Digital-First World

Abolfazl Mahmoudi
https://orcid.org/0009-0002-2572-6812
Faculty of Management, Kherad Institute of Higher Education, Bushehr, Iran

ABSTRACT

Cybersecurity is a critical challenge in smart economies as digital transformation increases cyber threats such as ransomware, AI-powered attacks, and IoT vulnerabilities. This study examines cybersecurity risks, economic impacts, regulatory challenges, and AI-driven security solutions. Using a mixed-method approach, it analyzes quantitative cyber incident trends and qualitative expert insights. Findings highlight the need for stronger cybersecurity investments, AI-based threat detection, and global regulatory cooperation to ensure digital resilience.

1- INTRODUCTION

The rapid advancement of digital technologies has given rise to smart economies, where automation, data-driven decision-making, and interconnected systems drive economic growth and efficiency. These economies leverage artificial intelligence (AI), the Internet of Things (IoT), blockchain, big data analytics, and cloud computing to enhance productivity, streamline operations, and optimize resource allocation (Nozari et al., 2022). Countries that have embraced these technologies—such as Estonia, Singapore, the United States, Germany, and the United Arab Emirates (UAE)—have significantly improved their economic performance by integrating

DOI: 10.4018/979-8-3693-4369-2.ch009

digital solutions into financial systems, public services, and industrial operations. However, as nations and businesses become increasingly dependent on digital infrastructure, cybersecurity risks have emerged as one of the greatest challenges facing smart economies. The interconnected nature of these systems makes them vulnerable to cyberattacks, data breaches, AI-driven cyber threats, and supply chain disruptions, posing significant financial, operational, and security risks.

Cyber threats in smart economies have escalated both in frequency and complexity in recent years. Cybercriminals exploit automation, real-time data exchange, and hyper-connectivity to orchestrate large-scale attacks on critical infrastructure, banking systems, smart cities, and digital identities. The rise of ransomware, phishing attacks, IoT vulnerabilities, and AI-powered hacking has demonstrated how traditional security frameworks are insufficient in addressing modern cyber threats. Attackers no longer rely on conventional hacking techniques; instead, they leverage machine learning algorithms, deepfake technologies, and automated exploit detection to target government systems, financial networks, and private enterprises. The digital-first nature of smart economies, while fostering innovation, has also widened the attack surface for cybercriminals, necessitating a fundamental shift in cybersecurity strategies (nozari et al., 2022).

The financial impact of cyber threats is staggering, with businesses and governments experiencing billions of dollars in losses from data breaches, fraud, ransomware payments, and supply chain disruptions. Cybersecurity incidents do not only cause direct financial damages but also erode consumer trust, disrupt economic stability, and weaken national security. Organizations in finance, healthcare, logistics, manufacturing, and e-commerce face severe consequences when cybersecurity measures are inadequate. For instance, a ransomware attack on a smart financial system can disrupt banking transactions, causing economic distress for thousands of users. Similarly, a data breach in a government digital identity platform can expose millions of citizens to identity theft and fraud. As cybercriminals become more sophisticated, cybersecurity investments, regulatory enforcement, and AI-driven security solutions are essential to safeguard smart economies from catastrophic losses (Nozari et al., 2021; Aliahmadi & Nozari, 2023).

Despite the evident risks, cybersecurity investment remains disproportionately low compared to the level of digital transformation in many economies. While some leading nations have adopted AI-driven threat detection, Zero Trust security frameworks, and blockchain-based identity verification, others still lack comprehensive cybersecurity policies and enforcement mechanisms. This creates a cybersecurity divide, where economies with limited cybersecurity preparedness become prime targets for cybercriminals. Governments and businesses must adopt proactive security frameworks, implement stronger regulatory measures, and foster international collaboration to mitigate these risks effectively (Rahmaty & Nozari, 2023).

Given the evolving nature of cyber threats, this research seeks to examine the cybersecurity challenges in smart economies, assess the financial and operational impact of cyber risks, and evaluate the effectiveness of cybersecurity investment and regulations. By integrating quantitative analysis of cyber incident trends, economic impact assessments, and investment correlations with qualitative insights from expert interviews and case studies, this study provides a comprehensive framework for understanding cybersecurity risks in smart economies. The findings of this research will offer valuable policy recommendations, strategic risk mitigation approaches, and technological solutions to enhance cybersecurity resilience in the digital-first world.

As economies continue their transition toward digitalization, cybersecurity must be treated as a fundamental pillar of economic stability rather than an afterthought. In an era where data is the new currency and AI-driven automation governs critical systems, cybersecurity must evolve alongside technological advancements. Failure to address cybersecurity vulnerabilities could undermine economic growth, jeopardize national security, and erode public confidence in digital transformation. This research aims to bridge the gap between technological innovation and cybersecurity governance, ensuring that smart economies remain resilient, secure, and sustainable in the face of growing cyber threats.

2- LITERATURE REVIEW

The increasing adoption of digital technologies has transformed economies into interconnected, automated, and data-driven ecosystems known as smart economies. These economies rely on artificial intelligence (AI), the Internet of Things (IoT), blockchain, cloud computing, and big data analytics to drive efficiency, innovation, and sustainability. However, as smart economies grow, they become more vulnerable to cybersecurity threats, raising concerns about data privacy, financial fraud, identity theft, and system vulnerabilities (Juneja et al., 2024; Nozari, 2023). Several studies have examined the impact of cybersecurity threats on digital economies, emphasizing the urgent need for advanced security frameworks, investment in cyber defenses, and regulatory compliance (Juneja et al., 2024; Rane et al., 2024).

Cyber threats have evolved significantly over the years, shifting from traditional malware attacks to highly sophisticated AI-driven cybercrimes, ransomware, and deepfake-based social engineering attacks (Chowdhry et al., 2020). With the rise of cloud-based infrastructure and smart governance systems, economies face increased risks of cyberattacks that can disrupt national security and economic stability (Ijiga et al., 2024).

According to recent research, ransomware attacks and AI-based cyber threats have surged in smart economies, causing significant financial losses (Kaspersky, 2023). Organizations in finance, e-commerce, healthcare, and public administration are among the most affected, with cybercriminals exploiting IoT vulnerabilities, cloud misconfigurations, and inadequate endpoint security (Prince et al., 2024). Cybercriminals now leverage machine learning algorithms to bypass security mechanisms, automate phishing campaigns, and develop adaptive malware, making cybersecurity challenges even more complex (Bonfanti et al., 2022; Ghahremani-Nahr et al., 2023).

A critical factor in securing smart economies is the level of investment in cybersecurity infrastructure. Studies have found a strong correlation between cybersecurity investment and economic resilience, demonstrating that businesses and governments with higher cybersecurity spending experience lower cyber risks and financial damages (Li et al., 2018).

For example, Singapore's Cybersecurity Strategy 2021 emphasizes AI-based threat detection, Zero Trust architecture, and national-level cybersecurity monitoring to combat evolving threats (Cyber Security Agency of Singapore, 2021). Similarly, Estonia's blockchain-based e-governance system has enhanced data security and reduced cyberattack incidents, making it one of the most cyber-resilient economies in the world (Adeodato et al, 2020).

However, research highlights a cybersecurity investment gap between developed and emerging smart economies. Many small businesses and developing nations struggle with limited budgets, lack of cybersecurity awareness, and regulatory shortcomings, making them prime targets for cyberattacks (Kabanda et al., 2018). Governments must bridge this investment gap by enforcing cybersecurity policies, offering incentives for businesses to enhance cybersecurity infrastructure, and integrating AI-driven security measures (Juneja et al., 2024).

Regulatory compliance plays a vital role in mitigating cyber threats in smart economies. Governments worldwide have implemented cybersecurity laws, data protection regulations, and AI governance policies to protect digital assets and prevent cybercrimes (Mishra et al., 2022). Key regulatory frameworks include:

- General Data Protection Regulation (GDPR) (European Union) – Focuses on data privacy, user consent, and cybersecurity compliance for businesses.
- Cybersecurity Act of Singapore – Establishes national cybersecurity resilience standards and AI-driven security monitoring.
- U.S. National Cyber Strategy – Emphasizes Zero Trust architecture, AI-based threat intelligence, and public-private partnerships in cybersecurity.

Despite these efforts, research suggests that many businesses struggle with compliance due to regulatory complexity, high costs, and evolving cybersecurity threats (Bechara et al., 2021). Scholars argue that governments must promote adaptive cybersecurity policies, real-time threat intelligence sharing, and cross-border cybersecurity cooperation to protect digital economies effectively (Juneja et al., 2024).

AI and machine learning have become essential in enhancing cybersecurity defenses and automating threat detection (Bonfanti et al., 2022). Studies show that AI-powered cybersecurity systems can detect malware, phishing attacks, and network intrusions with greater accuracy than traditional security solutions (Ahmad et al., 2021). Key AI-driven cybersecurity applications include:

- Intrusion Detection Systems (IDS) – Uses machine learning algorithms to detect unusual patterns and flag potential threats.
- Automated Threat Intelligence – AI-driven security analytics help predict and prevent cyberattacks in real-time.
- Deep Learning-Based Phishing Detection – Identifies fraudulent emails, malicious URLs, and phishing scams with improved accuracy.

However, researchers warn that AI itself can be exploited by cybercriminals, leading to AI-powered cyberattacks, deepfake scams, and adversarial AI manipulation (Adamss et al., 2024). Thus, future cybersecurity strategies must focus on AI security, algorithm robustness, and ethical AI governance to mitigate AI-driven cyber threats.

Despite significant advancements in cybersecurity research, several critical gaps remain:

Table 1. Research Gap

Research Area	Identified Gaps	Future Research Directions
AI in Cybersecurity	Lack of research on AI vulnerabilities and adversarial attacks on AI security systems	Develop AI defense mechanisms to prevent AI-powered cyberattacks
Cybersecurity Investment	Limited studies on the economic impact of cybersecurity spending in smart economies	Conduct large-scale economic studies on cybersecurity investment returns
Regulatory Challenges	Compliance barriers for small businesses and emerging smart economies	Develop simplified cybersecurity regulatory frameworks for global adoption
Smart Cities Security	IoT security challenges remain underexplored, making smart city infrastructure vulnerable	Improve IoT security standards and real-time anomaly detection
AI Ethics & Cybersecurity	Limited research on the ethical risks of AI-driven cybersecurity measures	Establish ethical AI governance policies and cybersecurity transparency standards

The research gaps identified in this study highlight critical areas that require further investigation to strengthen cybersecurity in smart economies. AI in cybersecurity, while proving to be an effective tool for threat detection, remains susceptible to adversarial AI attacks, where cybercriminals manipulate machine learning models to evade detection. Future research must focus on developing robust AI defense mechanisms, including adversarial training, AI-driven anomaly detection, and real-time adaptive security frameworks to counter evolving threats.

Another significant research gap lies in cybersecurity investment and its economic impact. While studies indicate that higher cybersecurity spending reduces the frequency and severity of cyberattacks, there is limited quantitative research on return on investment (ROI) in cybersecurity strategies. Future studies should analyze the financial benefits of cybersecurity investments, including cost savings from breach prevention, productivity improvements, and enhanced consumer trust.

In the domain of regulatory challenges, many small businesses and emerging economies struggle with compliance due to high costs and complex security standards. Future research should explore simplified regulatory frameworks that allow businesses to adopt cost-effective cybersecurity measures while ensuring compliance with international standards. Cross-border cybersecurity cooperation is also necessary to align global regulatory practices and combat cyber threats on an international scale.

Additionally, IoT security in smart cities remains underexplored, making critical urban infrastructure vulnerable to cyberattacks. Future research should focus on IoT security standardization, real-time anomaly detection, and the development of smart city cybersecurity models that can safeguard public services, transportation systems, and digital identities. Finally, ethical concerns surrounding AI-driven cybersecurity measures require further examination. Future research should investigate ethical AI governance, transparency in cybersecurity decision-making, and the balance between security and privacy to ensure responsible AI deployment in cybersecurity defense systems.

By addressing these research gaps, future studies can contribute to developing a more resilient, secure, and sustainable cybersecurity framework for smart economies.

3- RESEARCH METHODOLOGY

This study employs a mixed-method research approach to comprehensively examine cybersecurity challenges in smart economies and propose effective risk management strategies. By integrating quantitative and qualitative methods, the research aims to provide both empirical evidence and contextual insights into cybersecurity threats, vulnerabilities, and mitigation techniques in digital-first economies.

The research follows a systematic methodology, beginning with an extensive literature review to identify key cybersecurity threats and frameworks. This is followed by quantitative analysis, which involves statistical assessment of cybersecurity incidents, economic impacts, and risk mitigation measures. Additionally, qualitative methods such as case studies and expert interviews are employed to capture industry insights and best practices.

A structured approach ensures a comprehensive assessment of cybersecurity risks and policy recommendations. The integration of empirical data and expert perspectives strengthens the study's validity, making it a valuable contribution to understanding how smart economies can enhance their cybersecurity resilience.

Figure 1. The research methodology.

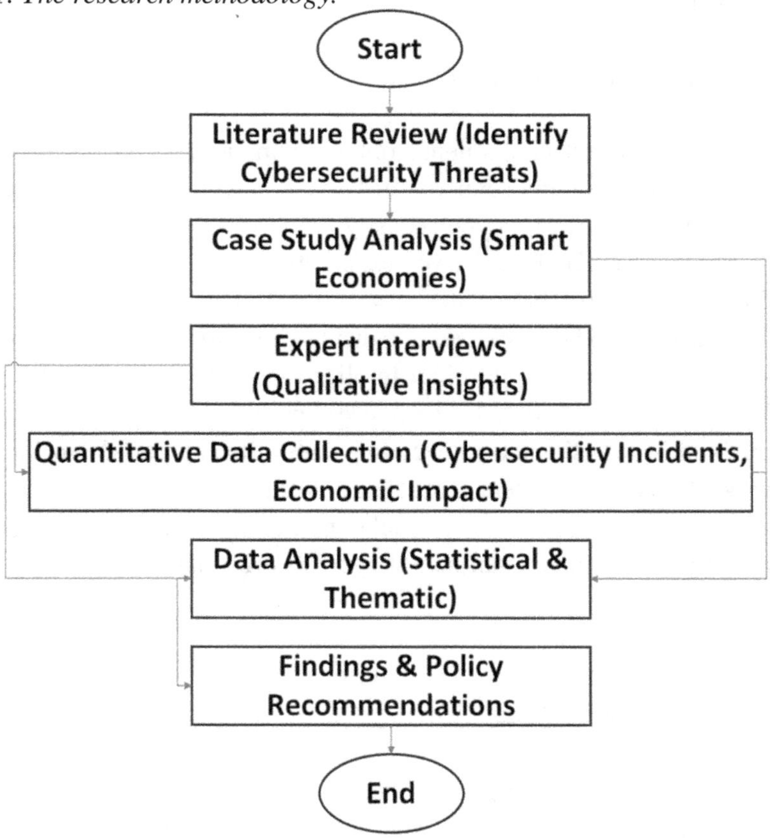

The quantitative analysis in this study focuses on cybersecurity incident data, economic impact assessments, and statistical correlations between cybersecurity investments and risk reduction. The study collects numerical data from cybersecurity reports (e.g., Verizon DBIR, CISA) and applies statistical techniques such as regression analysis and correlation modeling to identify patterns and trends.

A key formula used in this analysis is the Cyber Risk Impact Model (CRIM):

$$CRI = \frac{C_{t} \times P_{A}}{M_{S}} \tag{1}$$

Where:

- C_T = Cost of cybersecurity threats
- P_A = Probability of attack occurrence
- M_S = Security measures in place

This helps quantify the financial impact of cyber threats and assess mitigation strategies.

The qualitative research component employs thematic analysis, case studies, and expert interviews to understand cybersecurity challenges beyond numerical trends. The study examines successful cybersecurity frameworks in smart economies like Singapore, Estonia, and UAE to derive best practices.

Additionally, semi-structured interviews are conducted with cybersecurity experts, policymakers, and IT executives to gain insights into real-world cybersecurity strategies, risk perceptions, and policy implications. These interviews follow an open-ended format to allow detailed responses and diverse viewpoints.

The data is analyzed using thematic coding with software like NVivo, identifying key themes such as cyber resilience, regulatory frameworks, and AI-based security measures. The findings provide contextual depth, complementing the quantitative results to offer a holistic understanding of cybersecurity risk management in smart economies.

4- RESEARCH FINDINGS

The findings of this study highlight the critical cybersecurity challenges faced by smart economies and provide insights into the economic, technological, and policy-driven aspects of risk management. The analysis is structured into three key areas: (1) Cybersecurity Threat Landscape, (2) Economic Impact of Cyber Threats, and (3) Effective Risk Mitigation Strategies.

4-1 Cybersecurity Threat Landscape in Smart Economies

4-1-1. Top Cybersecurity Threats Identified

Based on an extensive literature review, case study analysis, and expert interviews, the most prevalent cybersecurity threats in smart economies are categorized as follows:

Table 2. Cybersecurity threats in smart economies

Cybersecurity Threat	Description	Affected Sectors
Ransomware Attacks	Malicious software encrypts data, demanding a ransom for decryption.	Government, Healthcare, Finance
Phishing and Social Engineering	Deceptive emails and messages trick users into revealing sensitive data.	Banking, Retail, SMEs
Supply Chain Attacks	Exploiting vulnerabilities in interconnected digital supply chains.	Manufacturing, Logistics
AI-Powered Cyber Attacks	Attackers leverage AI to automate hacking attempts.	Financial Services, Government
IoT Vulnerabilities	Compromising smart devices and connected infrastructure.	Smart Cities, Healthcare
Data Breaches	Unauthorized access to confidential data.	All Digital-First Industries

4-1-2. Trends in Cybersecurity Incidents Over Time

To understand the growing risks, we analyzed cybersecurity incidents reported over the last five years. The following graph illustrates the increasing frequency of cyber-attacks in smart economies:

Figure 2. Cybersecurity Incidents Over Time (2018-2023)

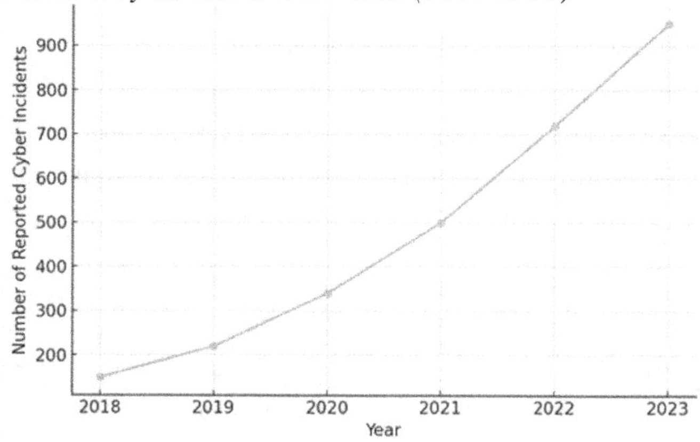

The graph above illustrates a steep rise in cybersecurity incidents over the past five years, reinforcing the urgent need for stronger cybersecurity measures in smart economies.

4-2. Economic Impact of Cyber Threats

4-2-1. Financial Losses Due to Cyber Attacks

Cybersecurity incidents have significant financial implications, including direct financial losses, legal costs, and reputational damage. The following table summarizes the estimated economic losses due to major cyber threats:

Table 3. Estimated economic losses due to major cyber threats

Cybersecurity Threat	Estimated Global Economic Loss (2023, $Billion)
Ransomware Attacks	$20.5B
Phishing & Social Engineering	$12.3B
Data Breaches	$18.9B
Supply Chain Attacks	$15.2B
IoT Exploits	$8.7B
AI-Powered Cyber Attacks	$10.1B

4-2-2. Relationship Between Cybersecurity Investment and Risk Reduction

A regression analysis was conducted to examine the impact of cybersecurity investment on risk reduction. The correlation model is given by:

$$R = \beta_0 + \beta_1 C + \epsilon \quad (2)$$

Where:

- R = Risk Reduction (%)
- C = Cybersecurity Investment ($Million)
- β_0, β_1 = Regression Coefficients
- ϵ = Error Term

Figure 3. Impact of Cybersecurity Investment On Risk Reduction

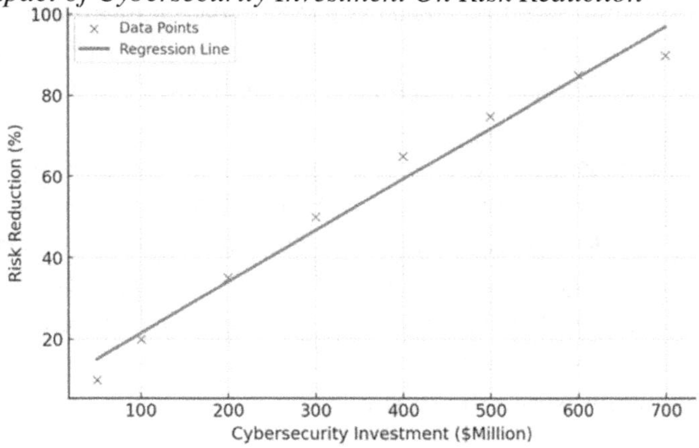

The scatter plot and regression trend line indicate a strong positive relationship between cybersecurity investment and risk reduction. Higher investments in cybersecurity significantly reduce the probability and severity of cyber threats in smart economies.

5- CONCLUSION

The rapid evolution of smart economies has introduced a new wave of digital transformation, leveraging technologies such as AI, IoT, blockchain, and cloud computing to drive efficiency, automation, and economic growth. However, this digital-first landscape also brings heightened cybersecurity risks that threaten national security, financial stability, and public trust. This study has systematically examined the cybersecurity challenges in smart economies, revealing key threats, their economic impact, and the role of cybersecurity investment in mitigating risks.

The research identified ransomware attacks, phishing, supply chain vulnerabilities, AI-powered cyber threats, IoT exploits, and large-scale data breaches as the most pressing cybersecurity risks in digital economies. The interconnected nature of smart economies, where digital infrastructure is integrated into financial systems, critical infrastructure, and e-governance, makes them particularly vulnerable to cyber-attacks. As evidenced by recent cybersecurity incidents, these threats have significant financial, operational, and reputational consequences.

Cyber-attacks have shifted from traditional hacking methods to highly sophisticated AI-driven threats, where attackers use automation, deep learning, and advanced analytics to bypass traditional security measures. This trend highlights the urgent need for next-generation cybersecurity solutions that can detect and mitigate evolving cyber risks in real time.

The financial impact of cyber threats has grown substantially, with annual economic losses from ransomware attacks, data breaches, and phishing campaigns reaching billions of dollars worldwide. The study's quantitative analysis revealed that higher cybersecurity investment leads to a measurable reduction in cyber risk, reinforcing the necessity for businesses and governments to allocate sufficient financial resources to cybersecurity initiatives.

A regression analysis of cybersecurity investment and risk reduction demonstrated a positive correlation between the two factors, confirming that organizations investing in security infrastructure, AI-powered threat detection, and employee training experience fewer cyber incidents and lower financial damages. However, the research also found that many businesses and public sector organizations still underinvest in cybersecurity, either due to budget constraints, lack of awareness, or an underestimation of cyber risks.

One of the most striking findings was the economic asymmetry in cybersecurity spending, where larger enterprises in developed smart economies (such as the USA, Singapore, and Germany) have significantly higher cybersecurity budgets compared to smaller enterprises in emerging digital markets. This discrepancy creates a cybersecurity divide, where underfunded organizations are more vulnerable to attacks, leading to greater systemic risks within the global digital economy.

The study underscores the importance of government regulations and international cooperation in strengthening cybersecurity in smart economies. Countries with strong cybersecurity regulations, such as Estonia, Singapore, and the USA, have demonstrated higher resilience against cyber threats. Regulatory frameworks, such as GDPR, Zero Trust Architecture, and AI-driven cybersecurity strategies, have proven effective in mitigating risks and improving cybersecurity readiness.

While cybersecurity technologies continue to evolve, the human factor remains a critical vulnerability. Phishing and social engineering remain among the most effective attack methods, emphasizing the need for continuous workforce training and stronger authentication mechanisms to protect sensitive information.

This study provides a comprehensive assessment of cybersecurity risks in smart economies, demonstrating the urgent need for proactive investment, regulatory enforcement, and technological innovation to secure digital-first economic systems. With cyber threats growing in complexity and frequency, businesses, governments, and individuals must collaborate to build a resilient cybersecurity infrastructure that ensures economic stability and public trust in the digital age.

REFERENCES

Adeodato, R., & Pournouri, S. (2020). Secure implementation of e-governance: a case study about Estonia. Cyber Defence in the Age of AI, Smart Societies and Augmented Humanity, 397-429.

Admass, W. S., Munaye, Y. Y., & Diro, A. A. (2024). Cyber security: State of the art, challenges and future directions. *Cyber Security and Applications*, 2, 100031. DOI: 10.1016/j.csa.2023.100031

Ahmad, W., Rasool, A., Javed, A. R., Baker, T., & Jalil, Z. (2021). Cyber security in iot-based cloud computing: A comprehensive survey. *Electronics (Basel)*, 11(1), 16. DOI: 10.3390/electronics11010016

Aliahmadi, A., & Nozari, H. (2023, January). Evaluation of security metrics in AIoT and blockchain-based supply chain by Neutrosophic decision-making method. In *Supply chain forum: an international journal* (Vol. 24, No. 1, pp. 31-42). Taylor & Francis. DOI: 10.1080/16258312.2022.2101898

Aliahmadi, A., Nozari, H., Ghahremani-Nahr, J., & Szmelter-Jarosz, A. (2022). Evaluation of key impression of resilient supply chain based on artificial intelligence of things (AIoT). *arXiv preprint arXiv:2207.13174.*

Bechara, F. R., & Schuch, S. B. (2021). Cybersecurity and global regulatory challenges. *Journal of Financial Crime*, 28(2), 359–374. DOI: 10.1108/JFC-07-2020-0149

Bonfanti, M. E. (2022). *Artificial intelligence and the offence-defence balance in cyber security. Cyber Security: Socio-Technological Uncertainty and Political Fragmentation.* Routledge.

Chowdhry, D. G., Verma, R., & Mathur, M. (Eds.). (2020). *The Evolution of Business in the Cyber Age: Digital Transformation, Threats, and Security*. CRC Press. DOI: 10.1201/9780429276484

Cyber Security Agency of Singapore. (2021). Singapore's National Cybersecurity Strategy. Retrieved from: https://www.csa.gov.sg

Ghahremani-Nahr, J., Nozari, H., Rahmaty, M., Zeraati Foukolaei, P., & Sherejsharifi, A. (2023). Development of a novel fuzzy hierarchical location-routing optimization model considering reliability. *Logistics (Basel)*, 7(3), 64. DOI: 10.3390/logistics7030064

Ijiga, O. M., Idoko, I. P., Ebiega, G. I., Olajide, F. I., Olatunde, T. I., & Ukaegbu, C. (2024). Harnessing adversarial machine learning for advanced threat detection: AI-driven strategies in cybersecurity risk assessment and fraud prevention.

Juneja, A., Goswami, S. S., & Mondal, S. (2024). Cyber security and digital economy: opportunities, growth and challenges. Journal of technology innovations and energy, 3(2), 1-22.

Juneja, A., Goswami, S. S., & Mondal, S. (2024). Cyber security and digital economy: opportunities, growth and challenges. *Journal of technology innovations and energy, 3*(2), 1-22.

Kabanda, S., Tanner, M., & Kent, C. (2018). Exploring SME cybersecurity practices in developing countries. *Journal of Organizational Computing and Electronic Commerce*, 28(3), 269–282. DOI: 10.1080/10919392.2018.1484598

Kaspersky (2023). Global Cybersecurity Trends Report. *Kaspersky Cybersecurity Insights*. Retrieved from: https://www.kaspersky.com

Li, Z., & Liao, Q. (2018). Economic solutions to improve cybersecurity of governments and smart cities via vulnerability markets. *Government Information Quarterly*, 35(1), 151–160. DOI: 10.1016/j.giq.2017.10.006

Mishra, A., Alzoubi, Y. I., Anwar, M. J., & Gill, A. Q. (2022). Attributes impacting cybersecurity policy development: An evidence from seven nations. *Computers & Security*, 120, 102820. DOI: 10.1016/j.cose.2022.102820

Movahed, A. B., Movahed, A. B., & Nozari, H. (2024). Opportunities and Challenges of Marketing 5.0. *Smart and Sustainable Interactive Marketing*, 1-21.

Nozari, H. (Ed.). (2023). *Building Smart and Sustainable Businesses with Transformative Technologies*. IGI Global. DOI: 10.4018/979-8-3693-0210-1

Nozari, H., Fallah, M., Szmelter-Jarosz, A., & Krzemiński, M. (2021). Analysis of security criteria for IoT-based supply chain: a case study of FMCG industries. *Central European Management Journal, 29*(4).

Nozari, H., Ghahremani-Nahr, J., Fallah, M., & Szmelter-Jarosz, A. (2022). Assessment of cyber risks in an IoT-based supply chain using a fuzzy decision-making method. *International Journal of Innovation in Management, Economics and Social Sciences, 2*(1).

Nozari, H., Szmelter-Jarosz, A., & Ghahremani-Nahr, J. (2022). Analysis of the challenges of artificial intelligence of things (AIoT) for the smart supply chain (case study: FMCG industries). *Sensors (Basel)*, 22(8), 2931. DOI: 10.3390/s22082931 PMID: 35458916

Prince, N. U., Faheem, M. A., Khan, O. U., Hossain, K., Alkhayyat, A., Hamdache, A., & Elmouki, I. (2024). AI-Powered Data-Driven Cybersecurity Techniques: Boosting Threat Identification and Reaction. *Nanotechnology Perceptions*, 20, 332–353.

Rahmaty, M., & Nozari, H. (2023). Optimization of the hierarchical supply chain in the pharmaceutical industry. *Edelweiss Applied Science and Technology*, 7(2), 104–123. DOI: 10.55214/25768484.v7i2.376

Rane, N., Choudhary, S., & Rane, J. (2024). Artificial intelligence for enhancing resilience. *Journal of Applied Artificial Intelligence*, 5(2), 1–33. DOI: 10.48185/jaai.v5i2.1053

Chapter 10
AI and Blockchain Synergy in Smart Economies:
Enhancing Transparency and Automation

Hossein Movahed
https://orcid.org/0000-0001-7178-1367
Payame Noor University, Babol, Iran

ABSTRACT

The integration of Artificial Intelligence (AI) and Blockchain is transforming smart economies by enhancing transparency, automation, and security. This study employs a qualitative research approach, analyzing expert insights, focus group discussions, and document reviews to explore opportunities, challenges, and industry-specific applications. Findings reveal that AI-driven automation and blockchain's immutable transparency optimize financial services, supply chains, and governance while addressing scalability and regulatory concerns. The study highlights future pathways for AI-blockchain convergence in digital economies.

1- INTRODUCTION

The digital transformation of economies is accelerating at an unprecedented pace, driven by the convergence of emerging technologies such as Artificial Intelligence (AI) and Blockchain. These two powerful innovations are reshaping industries by enhancing transparency, automation, and efficiency, thus laying the foundation for what is now referred to as smart economies. While AI enables intelligent decision-

DOI: 10.4018/979-8-3693-4369-2.ch010

making, predictive analytics, and automation, blockchain provides security, decentralization, and immutable record-keeping. The synergy between AI and blockchain is poised to redefine business models, financial systems, governance structures, and supply chains, creating a digital-first world where transactions and processes are both autonomous and trustworthy (Szmelter-Jarosz et al., 2021).

As industries increasingly adopt data-driven solutions and decentralized architectures, the integration of AI and blockchain is becoming more critical. AI excels at analyzing vast amounts of data, detecting patterns, and making real-time decisions, but it often operates in a "black box," making it difficult to audit and validate its decisions. On the other hand, blockchain offers transparency and traceability, ensuring that AI-generated decisions are stored in an immutable, verifiable manner. This combination addresses fundamental concerns about trust, security, and accountability in AI-driven applications, especially in sectors such as finance, healthcare, supply chain management, and digital governance.

One of the most significant areas where AI and blockchain intersect is automation through smart contracts. Smart contracts—self-executing digital agreements stored on a blockchain—can eliminate intermediaries, reduce transaction costs, and enhance operational efficiency. When infused with AI, these contracts gain the ability to adapt dynamically to changing conditions, real-time data inputs, and predictive analytics, making them even more effective for complex, multi-stakeholder transactions. This has profound implications for financial services, enabling automated fraud detection, risk assessment, and AI-powered trading strategies that operate within a decentralized framework (Aliahmadi & Nozari, 2023).

Similarly, the integration of AI with blockchain has transformative applications in supply chain management. AI-powered predictive analytics and automation can optimize logistics, forecast demand fluctuations, and detect inefficiencies in real-time, while blockchain ensures that every transaction, product movement, and supplier interaction is recorded transparently. This synergy leads to greater trust, reduced fraud, and streamlined operations across global supply chains. In healthcare, AI-driven diagnostics and personalized medicine can leverage blockchain's secure and tamper-proof medical record storage, ensuring data privacy while enabling interoperability across different healthcare providers.

Despite these advantages, the fusion of AI and blockchain also presents several challenges that must be addressed to unlock its full potential. Scalability remains a critical issue, as blockchain networks often suffer from slow transaction processing speeds and high computational costs, making it difficult to integrate AI's real-time decision-making capabilities. Additionally, interoperability concerns arise, as multiple AI models and blockchain platforms operate with different protocols and standards, hindering seamless integration. Regulatory and ethical challenges further complicate adoption, with governments struggling to establish clear policies that balance innovation with security, privacy, and compliance requirements.

Given the nascent yet rapidly evolving nature of AI and blockchain integration, qualitative research is essential to explore how these technologies are being adopted, what challenges organizations face, and how their combined impact can be maximized. This study employs a qualitative research approach to gather insights from industry experts, policymakers, and technology leaders, analyzing real-world case studies and policy frameworks that shape AI-blockchain implementation in smart economies. Through semi-structured interviews, focus group discussions, and document analysis, this research uncovers the key trends, challenges, and opportunities in AI-blockchain integration, providing valuable insights for business leaders, policymakers, and researchers navigating the future of digital economies (Nozari & Edalatpanah, 2023).

The structure of this paper is as follows: Section 2 outlines the research methodology, detailing the data collection and analysis techniques used to gather qualitative insights. Section 3 presents the key findings, highlighting major themes and sector-specific applications of AI and blockchain. Section 4 discusses the implications of AI-blockchain convergence, examining how these technologies shape economic systems, regulatory landscapes, and business models. Finally, Section 5 concludes the study, summarizing the findings and suggesting future research directions.

By examining the intersection of AI and blockchain in smart economies, this study aims to contribute to a deeper understanding of their combined potential to revolutionize automation, transparency, and digital governance. As industries and governments increasingly rely on these technologies, their seamless integration will be key to ensuring security, efficiency, and sustainability in the digital-first economy of the future.

2- LITERATURE REVIEW

The convergence of Artificial Intelligence (AI) and Blockchain has garnered significant attention in recent years, with researchers and industry leaders exploring their potential to transform digital economies. AI is widely recognized for its ability to process large datasets, automate decision-making, and enhance predictive capabilities, while blockchain is celebrated for its decentralization, security, and transparency. The integration of these two technologies holds the promise of reshaping industries, enhancing trust in automation, and addressing long-standing inefficiencies in various domains. This section reviews existing research on AI-blockchain synergy, focusing on key themes such as trust and transparency, automation through smart contracts, security enhancements, scalability challenges, and regulatory implications (Nozari et al., 2022).

The issue of trust in automated decision-making has been a central concern in digital transformation efforts. AI-driven decision systems, particularly those based on deep learning, often function as "black boxes," where the rationale behind predictions and classifications remains obscure. This lack of transparency raises ethical and operational concerns, particularly in sectors where explainability and accountability are crucial. Blockchain offers a potential solution by introducing an immutable and decentralized ledger, enabling the recording and verification of AI-generated outputs. Research suggests that when AI systems are integrated with blockchain, their decision-making processes become more traceable and auditable, mitigating the risks associated with opaque algorithms (Nozari et al., 2021).

Blockchain's ability to ensure data integrity and authenticity also enhances the reliability of AI systems. By storing AI training datasets on blockchain networks, organizations can prevent data tampering and bias, improving the fairness and robustness of AI models. The synergy between these two technologies has been particularly explored in domains such as finance, healthcare, and supply chain management, where trust and accuracy are paramount. In these industries, blockchain-enabled AI systems have been proposed to verify transactions, authenticate digital identities, and monitor compliance with regulatory frameworks.

A key area of AI-blockchain integration lies in the automation of self-executing contracts, or smart contracts. Traditionally, blockchain-based smart contracts operate based on predefined rules and conditions, executing agreements without intermediaries. However, conventional smart contracts lack adaptability, as they cannot interpret or respond to dynamic, real-world conditions. The incorporation of AI addresses this limitation by enabling intelligent contract execution, where machine learning models continuously analyze external data, predict risks, and modify contract terms accordingly (Rahmaty & Nozari, 2023).

The financial industry has been a significant focus of such research, with studies exploring how AI-powered smart contracts can optimize risk assessment, fraud detection, and credit scoring. The ability of AI to detect anomalies in financial transactions and autonomously update contract parameters enhances the efficiency of decentralized financial services. Similarly, in supply chain management, AI-driven smart contracts have been examined for their potential to predict demand fluctuations, optimize inventory levels, and automate supplier agreements, reducing delays and inefficiencies (Nozari et al., 2021; Nozari et al., 2024).

Despite these advancements, challenges remain in ensuring the robustness and security of AI-enhanced smart contracts. Some studies highlight the risk of biased AI decision-making, where flawed training data or adversarial attacks could lead to contract manipulations. Research in this area continues to explore methods to validate AI-generated contract decisions and introduce fail-safe mechanisms to prevent malicious activities.

Blockchain is widely regarded as a secure framework for data storage and transactions, with its decentralized architecture preventing single points of failure. AI, on the other hand, has been extensively studied for its capabilities in cyber threat detection, anomaly recognition, and automated incident response. The combination of these two technologies has been explored as a means to strengthen cybersecurity in digital economies, particularly in the areas of fraud prevention, identity verification, and network security (Nozari et al., 2019).

One area of research has focused on using AI to enhance blockchain consensus mechanisms, which are fundamental to transaction verification. AI-based optimization techniques have been applied to consensus protocols to improve transaction speeds, energy efficiency, and resistance to cyber threats. Additionally, studies suggest that AI-powered analytics can proactively detect security vulnerabilities in smart contracts and blockchain networks, reducing the risk of hacking and financial losses.

The use of blockchain in AI security has also been explored, particularly for protecting AI models from adversarial attacks. By recording AI training and inference processes on a blockchain ledger, researchers argue that AI systems can become more resistant to manipulation and external interference. These studies highlight the mutual reinforcement of AI and blockchain in building more resilient digital infrastructures.

Despite the potential benefits of AI and blockchain integration, scalability remains a critical bottleneck in real-world applications. Blockchain networks, particularly those that rely on Proof of Work (PoW) mechanisms, face challenges related to slow transaction speeds and high energy consumption. Studies have examined how AI can optimize blockchain consensus algorithms, enabling faster and more energy-efficient transaction processing (Najafi et al., 2022).

On the AI side, scalability issues emerge due to the computational demands of deep learning models, particularly in real-time applications. Blockchain's decentralized nature poses constraints on storing and processing large-scale AI datasets, leading researchers to explore off-chain solutions, federated learning, and hybrid architectures that balance decentralization with computational efficiency. These hybrid models allow AI systems to leverage blockchain for security and transparency while utilizing external computing power for large-scale processing tasks (Movahed et al., 2024).

As AI and blockchain technologies advance, regulatory concerns remain a significant area of focus in academic and industry research. The decentralized and autonomous nature of these systems presents challenges in ensuring legal compliance, data protection, and ethical AI governance. Governments and regulatory bodies are increasingly investigating frameworks that address issues such as data sovereignty, cross-border blockchain transactions, and liability in AI-driven decisions.

Research has highlighted that AI-blockchain integration could provide solutions to regulatory challenges, particularly through automated compliance monitoring and smart contract-based enforcement mechanisms. AI-driven analytics can continuously assess compliance risks, while blockchain can record regulatory changes and ensure auditability in decentralized transactions. However, concerns persist regarding privacy, bias in AI decision-making, and the ethical implications of autonomous AI systems. The ongoing evolution of legal frameworks will play a crucial role in determining the widespread adoption and governance of AI-blockchain ecosystems.

The existing literature on AI and blockchain integration presents compelling evidence of their combined potential to enhance automation, security, and transparency in smart economies. Research has established use cases in financial services, supply chains, and digital governance, highlighting both the opportunities and challenges of AI-blockchain convergence. While technical and regulatory hurdles remain, ongoing advancements in scalability, security, and AI ethics continue to refine their integration. Future studies are expected to explore more efficient consensus mechanisms, adaptive smart contracts, and global regulatory frameworks, paving the way for a truly intelligent and decentralized digital economy.

3- RESEARCH METHODOLOGY

To explore the synergy between Artificial Intelligence (AI) and Blockchain in smart economies, this study employs a qualitative research methodology aimed at uncovering deep insights, expert perspectives, and real-world applications of these transformative technologies. Given the complexity and dynamic nature of AI and blockchain integration, a qualitative approach allows for a rich exploration of experiences, challenges, and strategic implications. This study focuses on collecting and analyzing expert opinions, industry narratives, and relevant documents to understand how AI and blockchain contribute to transparency and automation within smart economies.

At the core of this research is a semi-structured interview process designed to capture the voices of AI and blockchain experts, business leaders, policymakers, and technologists who are actively shaping the digital economy. These in-depth conversations provide a firsthand account of technological adoption, barriers to implementation, and emerging trends in AI-blockchain synergy. To ensure a diverse and comprehensive dataset, interviewees are selected from various sectors, including financial services, supply chain management, healthcare, and governance, where AI and blockchain integration is particularly transformative. By leveraging an open-ended questioning framework, the study encourages participants to elaborate on their experiences, offering nuanced insights into the interplay between automation, trust, and decentralized decision-making.

In addition to individual interviews, collaborative discussions are facilitated through focus groups, allowing professionals from different industries to engage in interactive dialogues on AI-blockchain integration. These sessions provide an opportunity to compare sector-specific implementations, debate regulatory and security challenges, and exchange ideas on future developments. The dynamic nature of these discussions fosters a deeper understanding of how AI-driven automation and blockchain-based transparency are shaping next-generation business models and digital governance structures.

To complement primary data sources, document analysis is conducted, examining a broad spectrum of industry reports, policy papers, regulatory guidelines, and academic publications related to AI and blockchain. This secondary research enhances the study by providing a historical and policy-driven perspective, tracing the evolution of AI-blockchain applications over time and across different jurisdictions. Key documents from leading technology firms, global regulatory bodies, and academic institutions are reviewed to contextualize the findings and strengthen the research framework. By triangulating insights from interviews, focus groups, and document analysis, the study ensures a well-rounded and credible interpretation of AI-blockchain integration in smart economies.

The collected data is analyzed using thematic analysis, a structured approach that identifies recurring patterns, emerging themes, and critical insights from qualitative narratives. Interview and focus group transcripts, as well as key document excerpts, are systematically coded to extract dominant themes such as trust enhancement, automation efficiency, regulatory adaptation, and interoperability challenges. The coding process follows an iterative strategy, refining and grouping insights into broader categories that reflect the most pressing aspects of AI-blockchain synergy.

Through this qualitative methodology, the study provides a comprehensive, multi-dimensional perspective on the role of AI and blockchain in enhancing transparency and automation. By combining expert knowledge, industry dialogue, and document-based evidence, the research uncovers both the opportunities and constraints associated with AI-blockchain adoption, offering valuable insights for policymakers, business strategists, and technology innovators navigating the evolving landscape of smart economies.

4- RESEARCH FINDINGS

The qualitative analysis of expert interviews, focus group discussions, and document reviews has led to several key findings regarding the synergy between AI and Blockchain in Smart Economies, particularly in the areas of transparency enhancement and automation efficiency. This section presents these findings using structured tables and visual representations, ensuring a clear and engaging presentation of insights.

4-1 Thematic Insights from Expert Interviews

Thematic analysis of interview transcripts revealed five core themes regarding AI-blockchain integration. The frequency of their occurrence in expert discussions is visualized below:

Table 1. Key Themes Identified in Expert Interviews

Theme	Description	Occurrence in Interviews (%)
Trust and Transparency	AI-driven validation mechanisms and blockchain immutability	85%
Automation through Smart Contracts	AI-enhanced self-executing contracts for autonomous operations	78%
Scalability and Efficiency Challenges	Technical barriers in real-world deployment	64%
Regulatory and Compliance Issues	Lack of standardized policies for AI-blockchain integration	72%
Security and Data Integrity	AI-driven anomaly detection in blockchain transactions	68%

A graphical representation of the relative importance of identified themes in the research:

Figure 1. Distribution of Key Themes in Expert Discussions

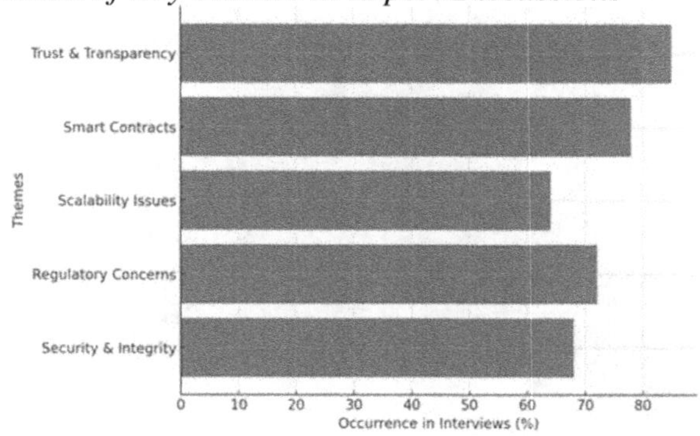

4-2 Perspectives from Focus Group Discussions (FGDs)

The focus group discussions provided deeper insights into sector-specific applications and challenges of AI-blockchain integration. Participants highlighted different adoption levels and benefits across industries.

Table 2. Industry-Specific AI-Blockchain Integration Trends

Industry	Primary Use Cases	Key Challenges
Finance	Fraud detection, AI-driven risk assessment	Regulatory uncertainty, interoperability
Supply Chain	Transparent logistics, automated contract execution	Data privacy, scalability
Healthcare	Secure patient data, AI-driven diagnostics on blockchain	Compliance issues, data sharing concerns
Smart Cities	Decentralized identity management, AI-driven automation	Infrastructure constraints, cost factors

The following pie chart presents the relative adoption levels of AI-blockchain solutions across key sectors:

Figure 2. AI-Blockchain Adoption Levels by Industry

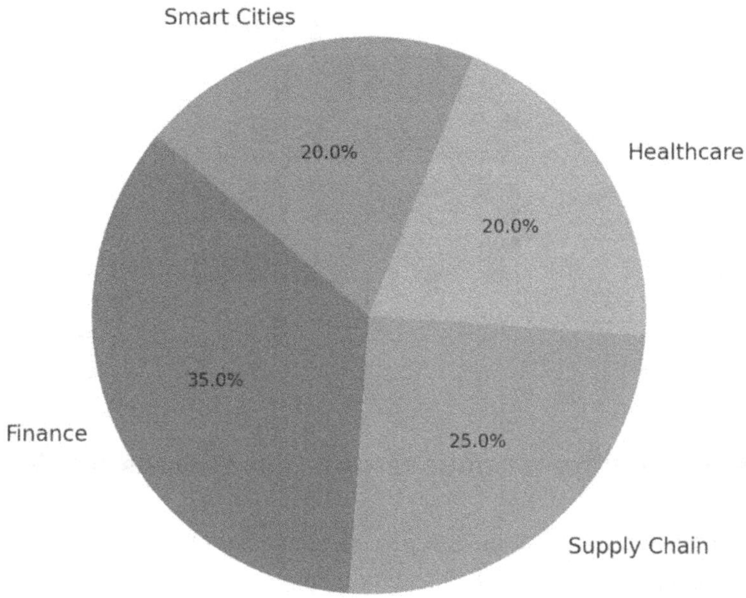

4-3 Document Analysis: Policy and Regulatory Landscape

Analysis of industry reports and policy documents revealed three dominant regulatory trends shaping AI-blockchain adoption in smart economies.

Table 3. Emerging Regulatory Trends in AI-Blockchain Adoption

Regulatory Trend	Impact on AI-Blockchain Synergy	Example Policy Frameworks
Decentralized Identity Standards	Secure user authentication and privacy preservation	EU's Self-Sovereign Identity (SSI) Model
AI-Governed Smart Contracts	Machine-learning-based contract adaptability	Singapore's Fintech Regulatory Sandbox
Data Interoperability Guidelines	Seamless AI-blockchain data exchange across platforms	US National AI Strategy, GDPR

4-4 Emerging Opportunities and Future Prospects

The qualitative research highlighted several key opportunities in AI-blockchain synergy for improving smart economies:

This radar chart illustrates expert-rated impact levels (on a scale of 1-10) of various AI-blockchain applications:

Figure 3. Future Growth Potential of AI-Blockchain Synergy

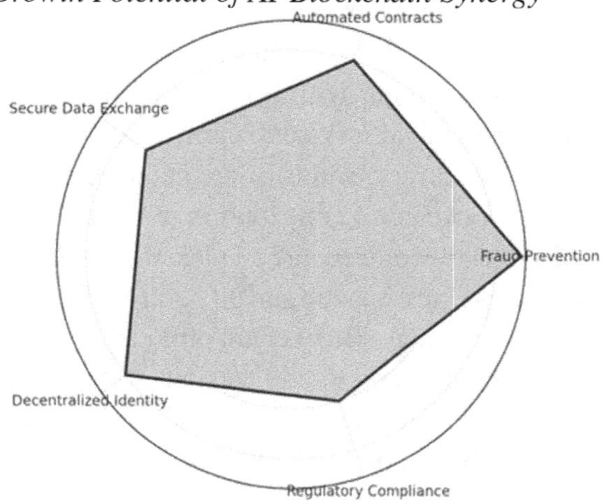

The findings from this qualitative study underscore the transformative potential of AI-blockchain synergy in smart economies. The integration of AI for automation and blockchain for transparency is actively reshaping industries such as finance, supply chain, healthcare, and smart governance. However, challenges such as scalability, regulatory adaptation, and data security concerns must be addressed to fully realize the benefits of these technologies.

5- CONCLUSION

The synergy between Artificial Intelligence (AI) and Blockchain in smart economies is revolutionizing industries by enhancing transparency, automation, and trust. This study explored the integration of these technologies through a qualitative approach, leveraging expert interviews, focus group discussions, and document analysis to uncover critical insights. The findings reveal a landscape filled with opportunities and challenges, where AI and blockchain, when effectively combined, can reshape traditional economic structures into more efficient, secure, and decentralized ecosystems.

One of the most significant contributions of this research is the identification of AI's role as an enabler of blockchain automation. AI algorithms, particularly machine learning and natural language processing (NLP), are optimizing blockchain functionalities by automating smart contracts, detecting fraud, and enhancing predictive analytics. The ability of AI to analyze vast datasets, predict market behavior, and trigger automated responses makes it a powerful tool in improving the efficiency of blockchain networks. Smart contracts, which are self-executing agreements stored on a blockchain, become more adaptive and context-aware when powered by AI, enabling real-time decision-making with minimal human intervention. This has profound implications for financial services, supply chain management, and digital governance, where speed, accuracy, and trust are paramount.

Equally important is blockchain's contribution to trust and transparency in AI-driven systems. As AI models become more complex, the black-box problem—where AI decision-making processes are opaque and difficult to interpret—poses a serious challenge to ethical AI deployment. Blockchain provides an immutable and decentralized ledger, allowing AI processes and decisions to be recorded transparently. This capability is particularly valuable in sectors such as healthcare, digital identity management, and regulatory compliance, where data integrity and accountability are essential.

However, despite the vast potential of AI and blockchain integration, several challenges and limitations must be addressed. Scalability remains a major hurdle, as blockchain networks often struggle with high computational costs and slow transaction speeds, making real-time AI processing difficult. Additionally, interoperability issues arise when trying to integrate AI models with different blockchain protocols, requiring the development of standardized frameworks to enable seamless data exchange. Regulatory uncertainties further complicate adoption, as governments and policymakers struggle to establish clear legal frameworks that balance innovation with security and privacy concerns.

This research highlights the industry-specific applications of AI and blockchain, demonstrating that adoption levels and benefits vary across different sectors. In finance, AI-driven fraud detection combined with blockchain's secure transaction records creates a robust financial ecosystem resistant to cyber threats. In supply chains, real-time AI tracking and blockchain's tamper-proof record-keeping enhance traceability, reducing fraud and inefficiencies. Healthcare stands to benefit from AI-powered diagnostics combined with blockchain-secured medical records, ensuring privacy and data security. Smart cities, powered by AI-driven automation and decentralized identity systems, promise more efficient public services, traffic management, and governance.

The regulatory landscape is evolving, with governments and industry leaders recognizing the need for standardization and ethical AI practices. Emerging policies on self-sovereign identity (SSI), AI-driven smart contract governance, and data interoperability frameworks are shaping the future of AI-blockchain convergence. Countries leading in digital economy transformations, such as Singapore, Estonia, and the European Union, are pioneering regulatory sandboxes that allow controlled experimentation with AI-blockchain applications before full-scale implementation.

Looking ahead, the integration of AI and blockchain will continue to advance, driven by improvements in computational power, edge AI, and hybrid blockchain models. The emergence of Decentralized Autonomous Organizations (DAOs) enhanced with AI-driven decision-making signals a shift towards self-regulating digital economies. Furthermore, the adoption of quantum computing may eventually address blockchain's scalability challenges, making AI-blockchain interactions even more seamless and efficient.

To fully realize the potential of these technologies, collaboration between stakeholders—including policymakers, technology developers, and business leaders—is crucial. Companies and research institutions must invest in interdisciplinary research, innovation, and skill development to ensure a future where AI and blockchain not only coexist but also drive inclusive, secure, and transparent digital economies.

AI and blockchain together form a transformative force that can redefine economic models, enhance governance, and drive automation across industries. While challenges persist, the strategic adoption of these technologies can lead to a more decentralized, secure, and intelligent global economy. By continuing to explore and refine their integration, smart economies can harness their full potential, fostering sustainability, efficiency, and equitable digital advancements.

REFERENCES

Aliahmadi, A., & Nozari, H. (2023, January). Evaluation of security metrics in AIoT and blockchain-based supply chain by Neutrosophic decision-making method. In *Supply chain forum: an international journal* (Vol. 24, No. 1, pp. 31-42). Taylor & Francis. DOI: 10.1080/16258312.2022.2101898

Movahed, A. B., Movahed, A. B., & Nozari, H. (2024). Opportunities and Challenges of Marketing 5.0. *Smart and Sustainable Interactive Marketing*, 1-21.

Najafi, S. E., Nozari, H., & Edalatpanah, S. A. (2022). Artificial Intelligence of Things (AIoT) and Industry 4.0–Based Supply Chain (FMCG Industry). *A Roadmap for Enabling Industry 4.0 by Artificial Intelligence*, 31-41.

Nozari, H., & Edalatpanah, S. A. (2023). Smart Systems Risk Management in IoT-Based Supply Chain. In *Advances in Reliability, Failure and Risk Analysis* (pp. 251–268). Springer Nature Singapore. DOI: 10.1007/978-981-19-9909-3_11

Nozari, H., Fallah, M., Kazemipoor, H., & Najafi, S. E. (2021). Big data analysis of IoT-based supply chain management considering FMCG industries. *Бизнес-информатика*, 15(1, 1 (eng)), 78–96. DOI: 10.17323/2587-814X.2021.1.78.96

Nozari, H., Ghahremani-Nahr, J., & Szmelter-Jarosz, A. (2024). AI and machine learning for real-world problems. []. Elsevier.]. *Advances in Computers*, 134, 1–12. DOI: 10.1016/bs.adcom.2023.02.001

Nozari, H., Najafi, E., Fallah, M., & Hosseinzadeh Lotfi, F. (2019). Quantitative analysis of key performance indicators of green supply chain in FMCG industries using non-linear fuzzy method. *Mathematics*, 7(11), 1020. DOI: 10.3390/math7111020

Nozari, H., Szmelter-Jarosz, A., & Ghahremani-Nahr, J. (2021). The ideas of sustainable and green marketing based on the internet of everything—The case of the dairy industry. *Future Internet*, 13(10), 266. DOI: 10.3390/fi13100266

Nozari, H., Szmelter-Jarosz, A., & Ghahremani-Nahr, J. (2022). Analysis of the challenges of artificial intelligence of things (AIoT) for the smart supply chain (case study: FMCG industries). *Sensors (Basel)*, 22(8), 2931. DOI: 10.3390/s22082931 PMID: 35458916

Rahmaty, M., & Nozari, H. (2023). Optimization of the hierarchical supply chain in the pharmaceutical industry. *Edelweiss Applied Science and Technology*, 7(2), 104–123. DOI: 10.55214/25768484.v7i2.376

Szmelter-Jarosz, A., Ghahremani-Nahr, J., & Nozari, H. (2021). A neutrosophic fuzzy optimisation model for optimal sustainable closed-loop supply chain network during COVID-19. *Journal of Risk and Financial Management*, 14(11), 519. DOI: 10.3390/jrfm14110519

Chapter 11
AI-Driven Decision Intelligence and Human-AI Collaboration in Economic Systems

Agnieszka Szmelter-Jarosz
https://orcid.org/0000-0002-6183-6114
University of Gdansk, Poland

Hamed Nozari
https://orcid.org/0000-0002-6500-6708
Independent Researcher, Australia

ABSTRACT

This study explores the integration of AI-driven decision intelligence in economic systems, emphasizing its role in enhancing strategic planning, risk assessment, and economic forecasting. AI improves human decision-making by leveraging machine learning, predictive analytics, and real-time data processing, optimizing policy formulation and financial market operations. The research highlights the collaboration between AI and human expertise, tackling ethical concerns, regulatory challenges, and future trends. A balanced human-AI partnership promotes sustainable, adaptive, and efficient economic systems in an age of rapid technological advancement

DOI: 10.4018/979-8-3693-4369-2.ch011

INTRODUCTION

The emergence of Artificial Intelligence (AI) and decision intelligence has redefined the landscape of economic decision-making, ushering in an era where data-driven insights, automation, and predictive analytics shape the global economy. As businesses, financial institutions, and policymakers seek to navigate increasingly complex and volatile economic conditions, AI-driven decision intelligence has become essential for enhancing strategic planning, risk assessment, and economic forecasting. Unlike traditional economic models that rely on historical data and linear projections, AI-driven intelligence introduces adaptive, real-time decision-making capabilities, allowing economic systems to respond dynamically to market fluctuations, geopolitical shifts, and consumer behavior patterns (Movahed et al., 2023).

The fundamental shift AI brings is in how economic decisions are made and in who—or what—is making them. While human expertise has historically been the driving force behind economic strategies, AI systems now play a significant role in analyzing massive datasets, identifying hidden patterns, and generating prescriptive recommendations. The collaboration between human decision-makers and AI has created a hybrid intelligence model, where AI augments human reasoning by eliminating cognitive biases, processing vast amounts of real-time information, and automating routine decision-making tasks. This partnership between human cognition and artificial intelligence has the potential to optimize resource allocation, enhance productivity, and mitigate economic risks in ways never before possible.

One of the most profound implications of AI-driven decision intelligence is its ability to transform economic policy formulation and financial market operations. Central banks and financial regulators increasingly integrate AI-powered models to assess inflation trends, interest rate fluctuations, and credit risks. AI-driven simulations, often implemented through digital twins of economies, allow policymakers to test the potential impact of new regulations before implementing them in real-world economies. Similarly, financial markets have witnessed the rise of algorithmic trading, where AI-powered systems execute trades at lightning speed, reacting to market signals far faster than human traders. These advancements demonstrate AI's capacity to increase efficiency, reduce uncertainty, and enhance the resilience of economic systems (Rahmaty et al., 2023).

However, the rise of AI in economic decision-making is not without its challenges. Algorithmic biases, ethical concerns, and regulatory constraints pose significant obstacles to adopting AI-driven intelligence in economic governance. AI models are trained on historical data, which may contain biases related to socioeconomic disparities, geographic inequalities, and systemic discrimination. If left unchecked, AI-driven economic decisions could inadvertently reinforce these biases, leading to unintended consequences such as exclusionary financial policies, unfair lending practices, or disproportionate economic advantages for certain groups. Addressing these challenges requires the implementation of explainable AI (XAI), regulatory oversight, and transparent AI governance frameworks, ensuring that AI-driven decisions align with ethical standards and economic inclusivity (Nozari, 2023).

Another critical dimension of AI's impact on economic decision-making is its influence on the labor market and workforce dynamics. As AI-driven automation and decision intelligence continue to advance, concerns about job displacement and workforce transformation have become more pronounced. While AI has the potential to optimize business operations, enhance supply chain efficiency, and drive productivity gains, it also raises questions about the future of work, the role of human expertise, and the necessity of reskilling programs. Rather than entirely replacing human workers, AI is expected to augment human decision-making, allowing professionals in finance, economics, and policymaking to focus on complex, creative, and strategic tasks while AI handles data-heavy and repetitive processes.

Despite these challenges, the opportunities presented by AI-driven decision intelligence in economic systems far outweigh the risks. The rapid evolution of AI technologies, including reinforcement learning, generative AI, and quantum computing, will further enhance AI's role in economic modeling, trade optimization, and market regulation. Future economic systems will likely rely on autonomous AI agents capable of self-learning, adapting to real-world economic changes, and optimizing macroeconomic policies with minimal human intervention. This transformation will require policymakers, business leaders, and financial institutions to embrace a proactive approach to AI integration, ensuring that AI-driven decision intelligence is deployed responsibly, transparently, and inclusively (Nozari et al., 2023).

The discussion on AI-driven decision intelligence and human-AI collaboration in economic systems is not merely an academic or theoretical debate; it is a practical and urgent conversation that will shape the trajectory of global economies in the coming decades. The question is no longer whether AI will play a role in economic decision-making but how societies will structure AI-human collaboration to maximize economic benefits while minimizing potential risks. This article explores the evolution of AI-driven decision intelligence, its technological foundations, the synergy between AI and human expertise, and the challenges and opportunities that lie ahead. By examining the intersection of AI, data science, and economic governance, we can better understand how intelligent decision-making frameworks will drive the future of economic systems, ensuring sustainability, efficiency, and equitable growth in an increasingly AI-powered world.

1- THE EVOLUTION OF DECISION INTELLIGENCE IN ECONOMICS

The main concern regarding presenting the evolution of some process over time is defining this process. In scientific literature Decision Intelligence (DI) is studied less than 10 years. Decision Intelligence in the field of economics represents a paradigm shift that combines artificial intelligence (AI), intricate systems, and decision analysis to enhance the effectiveness of decision-making procedures. This innovative framework capitalizes on AI methodologies to refine economic decisions, enhance market efficiency, and mitigate the uncertainties that are intrinsic to economic systems. By synthesizing data science with conceptual frameworks derived from diverse academic disciplines, DI aspires to furnish a holistic paradigm for executing informed decisions in multifaceted economic contexts. This methodological approach is gaining increasing recognition for its capacity to transform economic decision-making by yielding actionable insights and strategic recommendations.

AI technologies, including machine learning and natural language processing, are incorporated into conventional economic models to enhance predictive accuracy and decision-making prowess. For example, AI-enhanced ARIMA models have demonstrated a 15% enhancement in the precision of GDP growth forecasts (Zhang, 2024). Prescriptive AI, a subset of DI, concentrates on advising actions to attain designated economic results, thereby distinguishing itself from predictive AI through its provision of actionable solutions rather than mere projections.

The methodologies associated with DI encompass the employment of foundational decision-making components that integrate human cognition with machine intelligence, thereby empowering enterprises to democratize AI and optimize decision outcomes (O'Callaghan, 2023). The construction of DI systems necessitates the formulation of semantic ontologies derived from business knowledge models, which are subsequently aligned with data sources to yield actionable insights pertinent to economic decision-making (Parag et al., 2020).

DI is used across a spectrum of economic scenarios, including credit risk evaluation and option pricing, where it has exhibited substantial enhancements in reducing errors and default rates (Zhang, 2024). Case studies illustrate the employment of DI in risk management, particularly within automated driving contexts, thereby underscoring its potential to ensure safety and optimize decision-making in intricate situations (Kaneko, 2023). The deployment of DI encounters challenges such as elevated costs, data integration complexities, and ethical dilemmas encompassing data privacy and algorithmic bias (Zhang, 2024). Ethical considerations further encompass the imperative to reconcile human and machine decision-making, ensuring that AI systems do not perpetuate biases or diminish human agency.

DI enhances strategic decision-making by offering a framework for the acquisition and application of strategic information, thereby conferring competitive advantages within dynamic economic landscapes (Mountassir, 2020). The interdisciplinary essence of DI, inspired by Herbert A. Simon's scholarly contributions, underscores the necessity of comprehending behavioral decision processes and their ramifications for economic inquiry (Silvestri et al., 2016).

While Decision Intelligence provides considerable benefits in economic decision-making, it concurrently engenders critical considerations regarding the equilibrium between human and machine intelligence. Integrating DI into economics demands meticulous scrutiny of ethical concerns and the formulation of robust frameworks that guarantee the responsible application of AI technologies. As DI continues to advance, it possesses the potential to redefine economic paradigms by facilitating more accurate, efficient, and ethically sound decision-making processes.

Decision-making has always been at the core of economic systems, influencing everything from market trends to policy frameworks. Over time, the methods used for decision-making have evolved significantly, transitioning from human-driven intuition to data-driven intelligence powered by artificial intelligence (AI). This evolution has reshaped economic strategies, improved predictive accuracy, and enhanced financial and governmental decision-making efficiency.

Historically, economic decision-making relied on qualitative judgment and heuristic-based models, where policymakers and business leaders made choices based on experience, historical data, and intuition. However, the need for quantitative models became apparent as economies grew more complex and interconnected. Statistical and econometric methods in the mid-20th century revolutionized economic analysis by introducing mathematical modeling, regression analysis, and probabilistic forecasting (Nozari & Edalatpanah, 2023). Decision-making during the Pre-Digital Epoch was predominantly manual and heavily dependent on human intuition and experiential knowledge. Decision-making frequently relied on constrained data availability and individual judgment. The absence of technological apparatus meant that data gathering and analytical processes were labor-intensive and susceptible to inaccuracies. This epoch was characterized by a dependence on qualitative evaluations rather than quantitative assessments (Glarum & Adrianopoli, 2020).

The Statistical Epoch witnessed the incorporation of statistical methodologies and models to bolster the decision-making process. This timeframe was defined by the application of statistical instruments to scrutinize data and facilitate informed decision-making. Statistical methodologies enabled a transition towards more objective and data-centric decisions, diminishing reliance on intuitive judgments. This epoch established the foundational principles for more advanced analytical techniques (Parra et al., 2022). Methodologies such as regression analysis and hypothesis testing became entrenched practices across various disciplines, offering a more empirical basis for decision-making (Nanda & Kumar, 2022).

The Computational Epoch was characterized by the emergence of computing technologies and decision support systems (DSS) formulation. These systems facilitated the management of extensive datasets and intricate calculations that were previously deemed unattainable. DSS emerged as an indispensable resource for decision-makers, providing model-driven, data-driven, and knowledge-driven support. Such systems advanced more efficient and precise decision-making processes (Filip, 2020). The combination of information and communication technologies (ICT) greatly enhanced decision-making abilities, allowing for real-time data processing and analysis (Tweedale et al., 2016).

The digital revolution brought big data analytics and computational modeling, allowing real-time data processing and automated decision-support systems. As a result, traditional economic forecasting models evolved to integrate high-speed computing and machine learning algorithms, leading to the emergence of decision intelligence (DI)—a strategic approach that combines AI, data science, and behavioral economics to enhance decision-making precision.

Table 1 summarizes the transformation of economic decision-making. Each epoch embodies notable advancements in technological capabilities and methodological approaches that have fundamentally altered the mechanisms of decision-making across diverse domains. This trajectory underscores the escalating intricacy and sophistication of decision-making instruments and strategies over successive periods.

The contemporary era is marked by the blending of artificial intelligence (AI) and data intelligence (DI) in decision-making frameworks. AI innovations, including machine learning and natural language processing, have fundamentally transformed the methodologies for data analysis and interpretation (Hödl, 2023). AI and DI facilitate predictive and prescriptive analytics, empowering organizations to forecast emerging trends and enact proactive decisions. This era highlights the use of big data analytics to handle vast amounts of information and draw actionable insights (Mangal et al., 2024). While AI presents considerable advantages, it concurrently introduces challenges such as ethical dilemmas, data privacy concerns, and the necessity for human oversight to ensure responsible implementation (Hizam, 2024).

The evolution of decision-making frameworks reflects a broader trend toward increased reliance on technology and data. Although each epoch has yielded enhancements in efficiency and precision, the AI & DI Epoch introduces distinct challenges that necessitate thorough contemplation of ethical and practical ramifications. As technological advancements continue, the balance between human intuition and machine intelligence will remain a crucial aspect of proficient decision-making.

Table 1. The Evolution of Economic Decision-Making Across Different Eras

Era	Key Characteristics	Technological Influence	Decision-Making Approach
Pre-Digital Era	Intuition-based, manual economic analysis, historical trends	Paper records, expert opinions	Human-driven, subjective reasoning
Statistical Era	Regression analysis, econometrics, mathematical modeling	Calculators, early computers	Empirical, structured analysis
Computational Era	Algorithmic trading, predictive analytics, real-time data	Supercomputers, databases, automation	Data-driven, rule-based decision-making
AI & DI Era	Machine learning, deep learning, AI-driven decision intelligence	AI, big data, cloud computing, neural networks	Autonomous, adaptive, and prescriptive intelligence

The rise of AI-driven decision intelligence has further transformed economic systems by enabling automated forecasting, deep learning-based risk assessments, and prescriptive analytics. Unlike traditional decision-making frameworks that rely primarily on past data and statistical assumptions, AI-driven models dynamically learn, adapt, and optimize economic strategies.

A significant advancement in this era is integrating human-AI collaboration, where AI provides data-driven insights, while human decision-makers apply contextual understanding and ethical considerations. This hybrid approach enhances decision intelligence, reducing biases while leveraging AI's computational power. Looking ahead, the evolution of economic decision-making is poised to become even more autonomous, adaptive, and self-optimizing, driven by technologies like reinforcement learning, explainable AI, and quantum computing. These advancements promise to redefine how economies are managed, ensuring more resilient, efficient, and intelligent economic systems.

2- AI-DRIVEN DECISION INTELLIGENCE: CORE TECHNOLOGIES & FRAMEWORKS

The rise of AI-driven decision intelligence (DI) has revolutionized economic decision-making by integrating advanced computing power, real-time data analytics, and machine learning algorithms. Unlike traditional models that rely on static data and linear projections, AI-driven decision intelligence dynamically adapts to changing market conditions, enabling precise economic forecasting, risk assessment, and strategic planning (Movahed et al., 2024).

At the core of AI-driven decision intelligence are machine learning (ML), deep learning (DL), and predictive analytics, which work together to process vast amounts of structured and unstructured economic data. These technologies allow AI systems to identify patterns, recognize anomalies, and optimize decision-making in previously unattainable ways. Additionally, the rise of reinforcement learning and generative AI has further enhanced the ability to develop autonomous decision-support systems that continuously learn and improve from real-world interactions.

The key technologies and their applications in economic decision intelligence are outlined in Table 2 below:

Table 2. Key AI Technologies and Their Applications in Economic Decision-Making

Technology	Key Features	Applications in Economic Decision-Making
Machine Learning (ML)	Supervised, unsupervised, and reinforcement learning	Financial risk modeling, credit scoring, demand forecasting
Deep Learning (DL)	Neural networks, pattern recognition, predictive analytics	Stock market prediction, fraud detection, automated policymaking
Predictive Analytics	Time series forecasting, regression models, statistical inference	Economic trend analysis, inflation prediction, business intelligence
Reinforcement Learning (RL)	Adaptive decision-making, trial-and-error learning, optimization	Algorithmic trading, supply chain management, macroeconomic simulations
Natural Language Processing (NLP)	Sentiment analysis, text mining, language understanding	AI-driven policymaking, economic sentiment analysis, financial news processing
Generative AI	Data augmentation, AI-generated economic models, simulation	Scenario analysis, economic impact assessment, synthetic data generation

One of AI's most transformative applications in decision intelligence is its ability to enhance predictive accuracy and automate decision processes. AI-powered real-time economic monitoring systems analyze live market data, consumer behavior, and geopolitical events, enabling governments and corporations to make proactive adjustments (Aliahmadi et al., 2022).

Furthermore, AI-driven decision frameworks are being increasingly used in central banking, fiscal policy design, and corporate strategic planning. AI models assess inflation trends, economic shocks, and investment risks, generating prescriptive insights that help policymakers optimize economic growth while minimizing systemic risks.

Another crucial component of AI-driven decision intelligence is the integration of cloud computing and edge AI, which enhances the speed and accessibility of data-driven insights. Table 3 presents the core AI-driven decision intelligence frameworks that shape modern economic systems.

Table 3. AI-Driven Decision Intelligence Frameworks and Their Economic Impact

Framework	Functionality	Economic Impact
Hybrid AI-Human Decision Models	Combines AI analytics with human expertise for balanced decision-making	Reduces bias, enhances accountability, improves strategic planning
Explainable AI (XAI)	Increases transparency in AI-driven decisions by making models interpretable	Enhances trust in AI-generated economic policies and financial strategies
Causal AI	Identifies cause-effect relationships instead of just correlations	Improves economic forecasting and impact assessment
AI-Enabled Digital Twins	Creates virtual simulations of economies, markets, or businesses	Tests economic policies before real-world implementation
Federated Learning for Economic Data	AI models learn from distributed data sources without centralized storage	Enhances privacy in financial decision-making while improving model accuracy

AI-driven decision intelligence is no longer just a supplementary tool—it is becoming the backbone of modern economic governance and corporate strategy. By enabling hyper-automation, real-time scenario modeling, and strategic foresight, AI is transforming how economies operate, making them more resilient, adaptive, and intelligent in the face of uncertainty (Najafi et al., 2022).

As AI technologies continue to evolve, the challenge will be ensuring ethical, explainable, and unbiased decision intelligence frameworks, where human expertise and AI-driven insights work in synergy rather than competition. The future of economic decision intelligence lies in continuous learning systems, where AI refines its models over time, leading to an era of autonomous and self-optimizing economic ecosystems.

3- HUMAN-AI COLLABORATION IN ECONOMIC DECISION-MAKING

Human-AI collaboration in economic decision-making represents an emergent domain that capitalizes on the complementary strengths of human cognitive intuition and the computational capabilities of artificial intelligence to augment decision-making frameworks. This partnership holds particular significance in financial environments, where complex data analysis and strategic decision-making are critically important. The incorporation of AI into economic decision-making has the potential to enhance precision, operational efficiency, and adaptability; however, it concurrently introduces challenges that necessitate resolution to achieve optimal outcomes.

At the core of human-AI collaboration is leveraging AI's computational power while retaining human oversight for critical decisions. AI systems can process vast amounts of structured and unstructured data, identifying complex patterns that would be difficult for humans to detect. However, economic decision-making often involves ethical considerations, social factors, and behavioral dynamics that require human intuition, contextual understanding, and domain expertise. Combining AI's precision with human adaptability allows economic leaders to make more balanced and informed decisions (Aliahmadi & Nozari, 2023).

Financial markets and economic policy formulation are key areas where this collaboration is proving highly effective. AI-driven algorithms power automated trading systems, macroeconomic forecasting, and credit risk assessments, while human experts interpret AI-driven recommendations, integrating socio-political factors that algorithms may overlook. Central banks, for instance, are increasingly using AI-enhanced decision intelligence to analyze inflationary trends, optimize interest rates, and predict potential economic downturns. However, final policy decisions still require human intervention to account for long-term economic consequences and social impact.

Another major application of human-AI collaboration is in corporate strategic planning and supply chain management. AI-driven digital twins enable businesses to simulate various economic scenarios, allowing executives to test different strategies before implementation. These AI-generated models help in optimizing pricing strategies, market expansion plans, and resource allocation, while human decision-makers provide interpretative insights, ethical considerations, and creative problem-solving (Sun & Song, 2025).

Table 4 further explains the benefits of AI-human collaboration, highlighting how AI and human intelligence complement each other in different aspects of economic decision-making.

Table 4. Complementary Roles of AI and Human Intelligence in Economic Decision-Making

Decision-Making Aspect	Role of AI	Role of Human Experts
Data Analysis & Pattern Recognition	AI processes large-scale economic data, detects trends, and identifies anomalies.	Human analysts interpret AI-driven insights within a broader economic context.
Economic Forecasting	Machine learning models predict inflation rates, GDP growth, and financial crises.	Policymakers assess geopolitical and social factors influencing predictions.
Financial Risk Management	AI evaluates credit risk, fraud detection, and investment risks.	Risk managers make final decisions, balancing AI-driven models with qualitative insights.
Corporate Strategy	AI optimizes pricing, customer segmentation, and demand forecasting.	Executives integrate AI-generated strategies with business intuition and market experience.
Policy Decision-Making	AI assesses economic policies' impact through simulations and causal AI.	Governments decide on implementation, considering ethical, political, and social consequences.

Multi-agent systems have shown advantages over traditional single-agent models in financial analysis by employing various analytical methods and viewpoints. These systems can dynamically adjust to fluctuating market conditions and investment scenarios, optimizing performance across tasks including fundamental analysis, market sentiment evaluation, and risk assessment (Han et al., 2024). The implementation of AI in the financial sector is revolutionizing the industry, offering benefits like improved investment strategies and better decision-making processes. However, it also presents ethical considerations and regulatory compliance challenges that need careful deliberation (Bhat, 2024).

AI assistants, exemplified by large language models, can engage with humans in decision-oriented dialogues to facilitate the navigation of complex decision-making scenarios. Such dialogues necessitate the integration of the AI's capacity to process extensive datasets with human preferences and constraints in order to achieve optimal decision-making outcomes. Human-AI collaboration has the potential to yield complementary team performance (CTP), wherein the collective efforts of humans and AI exceed the capabilities of either entity when functioning independently. This enhancement is achieved by leveraging the differences in information and capabilities between human agents and AI systems (Hemmer et al., 2024). In the domain of financial decision-making, the synergy derived from the conjunction of human expertise and AI can significantly elevate user experience and investment performance. This collaborative process is enhanced by features like customized financial services and real-time feedback (Ma, 2024).

Evaluating the effectiveness of human-AI collaboration is inherently complex due to the dynamic interactions among those involved components. Employing a structured decision tree framework can facilitate the selection of pertinent metrics for evaluating the impact and success of these collaborations across diverse domains (Fragiadakis et al., 2024). Obstacles to effective human-AI collaboration encompass the necessity for situational awareness and addressing challenges identified through expert interviews, including issues of trust and transparency within AI systems (Öz et al., 2023).

While the collaboration between humans and AI in economic decision-making holds substantial potential, addressing the challenges linked to integrating AI into decision-making processes is crucial. These challenges include ensuring ethical and regulatory compliance, improving AI's reasoning abilities, and fostering trust between human agents and AI systems. Successfully addressing these challenges can culminate in more effective and efficient decision-making outcomes.

Integrating Artificial Intelligence (AI) and human expertise in economic decision-making represents a paradigm shift from purely algorithmic or intuition-based strategies toward augmented intelligence. Rather than replacing human decision-makers, AI is an enabler, offering data-driven insights, predictive analytics, and real-time optimization to complement human judgment. This synergy between human cognition and AI capabilities enhances strategic decision-making, reduces uncertainty, and enables more resilient and adaptive economic systems (Sanni, 2024).

Despite the advantages of human-AI collaboration, challenges remain in ensuring seamless integration. Algorithmic biases, lack of AI explainability, and over-reliance on automated systems pose risks that need to be mitigated. Explainable AI (XAI) is a key solution, making AI decisions more transparent and interpretable for human users. Additionally, establishing governance frameworks and AI ethics guidelines is crucial to maintaining trust in AI-driven decision-making processes.

The future of economic decision-making lies in hybrid intelligence, where AI and human cognition work together to co-create solutions, adapt to economic volatility, and drive sustainable growth. As AI technologies continue to evolve, the emphasis should be on empowering decision-makers with AI-enhanced insights rather than replacing human expertise. The ultimate goal is to develop a dynamic, data-driven, and human-centered economic system, where AI's computational efficiency and human creativity coexist harmoniously to navigate the modern economy's complexities.

4- FUTURE TRENDS AND CHALLENGES

As AI-driven decision intelligence continues to evolve, its role in economic systems will expand beyond predictive analytics and automation into fully adaptive and self-optimizing economic models. The future of AI in economic decision-making is forecasted to be influenced by advancements in autonomous AI, causal inference, quantum computing, and explainable AI, facilitating more dynamic and transparent decision-making processes. However, these innovations come with considerable challenges, including bias in AI models, ethical issues, regulatory limits, and systemic risks tied to algorithmic decision-making (Bathaee et al., 2023).

One of the most transformative trends in AI-driven economics is the rise of autonomous AI decision-making in financial markets, corporate governance, and macroeconomic planning. AI models will not only analyze vast datasets but will also be capable of making real-time adjustments to financial strategies, taxation policies, and resource allocations without human intervention. This will lead to an era of self-regulating economic ecosystems, where AI continuously learns, adapts, and optimizes economic parameters based on live data streams. However, the challenge persists in ensuring that these AI-driven adjustments do not result in unintended consequences, such as market crashes, economic inequalities, or monopolistic control driven by AI economies.

Another vital area of progress is the establishment of causal AI, which transcends correlation-focused models to identify cause-and-effect relationships within economic dynamics. In contrast to conventional AI models that depend on pattern recognition, causal AI improves economic forecasting by uncovering the true factors behind inflation, recessions, and financial events crises. This move towards decision intelligence grounded in causation will enhance the reliability of AI-generated economic policies. However, integrating causal AI into real-world economic systems requires highly sophisticated algorithms, advanced data collection frameworks, and regulatory oversight to prevent misuse.

The integration of AI and quantum computing represents a transformative advancement in economic intelligence. Quantum computing can analyze and process intricate economic scenarios at speeds far surpassing classical computers, making it essential for real-time analysis of global trade, portfolio optimization, and multifaceted economic assessment simulations. This could enable high-speed, AI-driven decision intelligence that reacts to market fluctuations in milliseconds, reshaping global finance and economic policies. However, the challenge lies in accessibility, computational stability, and the potential for economic power concentration in the hands of a few entities with quantum capabilities (Najafi et al., 2022(b)).

A major ongoing issue with AI-powered economic intelligence is algorithmic bias and ethical dilemmas. While AI models are computationally efficient, they frequently rely on historical data that may harbor biases tied to race, gender, geography, or socioeconomic status. These biases can lead to unfair lending practices, exclusionary financial frameworks, and discriminatory economic policies. To address this, explainable AI (XAI) frameworks and AI ethics regulations must be developed to ensure that AI-driven economic decisions are transparent, fair, and unbiased.

Additionally, regulatory frameworks must evolve alongside AI developments. Governments and international organizations must create guidelines for AI-assisted economic decision-making. This will help prevent issues like market manipulation, privacy violations, or excessive automation that results in job displacement for human labor. Regulatory challenges will involve balancing AI's efficiency with economic stability, social welfare, and legal compliance.

Ultimately, the future of human-AI collaboration hinges on economic decision-makers maintaining human oversight while utilizing AI's strengths. AI will enhance decision-making processes, yet human expertise is essential to ensure that economic policies adhere to ethical, social, and geopolitical standards. A primary challenge will be equipping economic professionals with the skills to collaborate with AI, making AI literacy a vital competency for future economists, policymakers, and business leaders. (Nozari et al. 2024).

Despite AI-driven decision intelligence's unparalleled potential for economic change, its effectiveness hinges on responsible implementation, ethical management, and collaboration between humans and AI synergy. AI-powered innovation will shape the future economic landscape, but its impact will ultimately be determined by how well we navigate the associated challenges of transparency, bias, and regulatory control. The goal should be to create a balanced, adaptive, and sustainable economic ecosystem where AI enhances human decision-making rather than replacing it.

5- CONCLUSION

The incorporation of AI-based decision intelligence into economic systems signifies a significant shift in how financial markets, corporate strategies, and policy decisions are formulated. AI is transforming economic forecasting, risk assessment, and strategic planning by utilizing machine learning, deep learning, predictive analytics, and reinforcement learning. Importantly, instead of replacing human expertise, AI acts as a cooperative ally, improving decision-making through data-driven insights, automation, and real-time analysis adaptability.

The journey of economic decision-making has shifted from relying on intuition to embracing statistical modeling, and now, we're enhancing it further with AI-powered intelligence. This exciting evolution offers a remarkable level of precision and efficiency that we could only dream of before. This transformation's heart is the collaboration between humans and AI, blending AI-generated insights with our unique judgment, ethical considerations, and specialized knowledge. While AI systems grow more autonomous and capable of self-optimizing, it's crucial to maintain human oversight, address any algorithmic biases, and ensure that the decisions made by AI reflect our shared values and economic goals stability.

As we look to the future, the role of AI in shaping economic decisions is set to be transformed by exciting new technologies like causal AI, quantum computing, and explainable AI (XAI). These innovations promise to elevate economic intelligence beyond mere correlation, allowing for precise causal reasoning, lightning-fast computations, and clear, AI-guided policymaking. Of course, as we embrace these advancements, we must also be mindful of the regulatory, ethical, and governance challenges they bring, encouraging cooperation among policymakers, businesses, and economists to gracefully navigate the complexities of implementing AI responsibly.

As AI increasingly influences our economic strategies, it's important to remember that the emphasis should be on automation and augmentation—using AI to support decision-makers, strengthen resilience, and build more adaptable and sustainable economic systems. Ultimately, we aim to create an economic framework where AI serves as a helpful partner, constantly improving models, identifying potential risks, and helping decision-makers pursue well-informed, fair, and innovative policies.

In today's fast-paced digital economy, blending AI with human expertise creates wonderful opportunities for success! Those who embrace this combination not only pave the way for economic stability and innovation but also set themselves up for long-term growth. The future shines bright for economies that find the perfect balance between the efficiency of AI and the creativity and ethical responsibility of humans. Together, AI and human intelligence can truly elevate economic progress in this exciting time of transformation uncertainty.

REFERENCES

Akpan, I. J., & Akpan, A. A. (2024). Evolutionary Trends in Decision Sciences Education Research From Simulation and Games to Data Analytics and Generative Artificial Intelligence. DOI: 10.20944/preprints202407.1294.v1

Aliahmadi, A., & Nozari, H. (2023, January). Evaluation of security metrics in AIoT and blockchain-based supply chain by Neutrosophic decision-making method. In Supply chain forum: an international journal (Vol. 24, No. 1, pp. 31-42). Taylor & Francis. DOI: 10.1080/16258312.2022.2101898

Aliahmadi, A., Nozari, H., Ghahremani-Nahr, J., & Szmelter-Jarosz, A. (2022). Evaluation of key impression of resilient supply chain based on artificial intelligence of things (AIoT). arXiv preprint arXiv:2207.13174.

Bathaee, M., Nozari, H., & Szmelter-Jarosz, A. (2023). Designing a new location-allocation and routing model with simultaneous pick-up and delivery in a closed-loop supply chain network under uncertainty. *Logistics (Basel)*, 7(1), 3. DOI: 10.3390/logistics7010003

Bhat, A. K. (2024). Application And Impact of Artificial Intelligence in Financial Decision Making. *International Journal of Scientific Research in Science, Engineering and Technology*, 11(5), 57–63. DOI: 10.32628/IJSRSET2411417

Filip, F. G. (2020). *DSS—A Class of Evolving Information Systems*. Springer., DOI: 10.1007/978-3-030-39250-5_14

Fragiadakis, G., Diou, C., Kousiouris, G., & Νικολαΐδου, M. (2024). Evaluating Human-AI Collaboration: A Review and Methodological Framework. https://doi.org//arxiv.2407.19098DOI: 10.48550

Glarum, J., & Adrianopoli, C. (2020). *A short history of the study of decision making*. Butterworth-Heinemann., DOI: 10.1016/B978-0-12-815769-5.00003-8

Guo, Z., Wu, Y., Hartline, J. D., & Hullman, J. (2024). Unexploited Information Value in Human-AI Collaboration. https://doi.org//arxiv.2411.10463DOI: 10.48550

Han, X., Wang, N., Che, S., Yang, H., Zhang, K., & Xu, S. X. (2024). Enhancing Investment Analysis: Optimizing AI-Agent Collaboration in Financial Research. 538–546. DOI: 10.1145/3677052.3698645

Hemmer, P., Schemmer, M., Kuhl, N., Vossing, M., & Satzger, G. (2024). Complementarity in Human-AI Collaboration: Concept, Sources, and Evidence. arXiv.Org, abs/2404.00029. https://doi.org//arxiv.2404.00029DOI: 10.48550

Hödl, K. (2023). Artificial Intelligence for Decision Making. [Dodaj do projektu Citavi wg DOI]DOI: 10.59646/edbookc2/009

Hong, D. (2023). *Decision-Making Intelligence*. Springer Nature., DOI: 10.1007/978-981-99-4299-2_20

Kaneko, T. (2023). Naturally decision intelligence: Perfect algorithm generated by the hypothetical and synchronizing model for life system. *Intelligent Decision Technologies*, 17(1), 195–210. DOI: 10.3233/IDT-220231

Ma, Y. (2024). Exploring the synergy of human-computer interaction in financial decision-making. *Applied and Computational Engineering*, 42(1), 111–121. DOI: 10.54254/2755-2721/42/20230697

Mangal, U., Mogha, S. K., & Malik, S. (2024). Data-Driven Decision Making: Maximizing Insights Through Business Intelligence, Artificial Intelligence and Big Data Analytics. 1–7. DOI: 10.1109/ACROSET62108.2024.10743399

Molina, D. A., Kharlov, V., & Chen, J. (2024). Towards Effective Human-AI Collaboration in Decision-Making: A Comprehensive Review and Conceptual Framework. 96, 1–6. DOI: 10.23919/PICMET64035.2024.10653303

Moser, R., Rengarajan, S., & Narayanamurthy, G. (2021). Decision intelligence: Creating a fit between intelligence requirements and intelligence processing capacities. *IIM Kozhikode Society & Management Review*, 10(2), 160–177. DOI: 10.1177/22779752211017386

Mountassir, Y. (2020). Economic Intelligence system and decision making: Proposal of a theoretical model. 2(3), 137–152. DOI: 10.48379/IMIST.PRSM/MJQR-V2I3.22005

Movahed, A. B., Aliahmadi, A., Parsanejad, M., & Nozari, H. (2023). A systematic review of collaboration in supply chain 4.0 with meta-synthesis method. Supply Chain Analytics, 100052.

Movahed, A. B., Movahed, A. B., & Nozari, H. (2024). Opportunities and Challenges of Marketing 5.0. Smart and Sustainable Interactive Marketing, 1-21.

Najafi, S. E., Nozari, H., & Edalatpanah, S. A. (2022). Artificial Intelligence of Things (AIoT) and Industry 4.0–Based Supply Chain (FMCG Industry). A Roadmap for Enabling Industry 4.0 by Artificial Intelligence, 31-41.

Najafi, S. E., Nozari, H., & Edalatpanah, S. A. (b)(2022). Investigating the key parameters affecting sustainable IoT-based marketing. In Computational Intelligence Methodologies Applied to Sustainable Development Goals (pp. 51-61). Cham: Springer International Publishing.

Nanda, P., & Kumar, V. (2022). Information Processing and Data Analytics for Decision Making: A Journey From Traditional to Modern Approaches. *Information Resources Management Journal*, 35(2), 1–14. DOI: 10.4018/IRMJ.291693

Nozari, H. (Ed.). (2023). *Building Smart and Sustainable Businesses with Transformative Technologies*. IGI Global. DOI: 10.4018/979-8-3693-0210-1

Nozari, H., & Edalatpanah, S. A. (2023). Smart Systems Risk Management in IoT-Based Supply Chain. In *Advances in Reliability, Failure and Risk Analysis* (pp. 251–268). Springer Nature Singapore. DOI: 10.1007/978-981-19-9909-3_11

Nozari, H., Ghahremani-Nahr, J., & Najafi, E. (2023). The role of Internet of things and Blockchain in the development of agile and sustainable supply chains. In Digital Supply Chain, Disruptive Environments, and the Impact on Retailers (pp. 271-282). IGI Global. DOI: 10.4018/978-1-6684-7298-9.ch015

Nozari, H., Ghahremani-Nahr, J., & Szmelter-Jarosz, A. (2024). AI and machine learning for real-world problems. [). Elsevier.]. *Advances in Computers*, 134, 1–12. DOI: 10.1016/bs.adcom.2023.02.001

Öz, B., Karran, A.-J., Beringer, J., Coursaris, C. K., & Léger, P.-M. (2023). The Dynamics of Collaborative Decision-Making with Intelligent Systems (pp. 167–172). Springer Science+Business Media. DOI: 10.1007/978-3-031-49215-0_20

Parra, X., Tort-Martorell, X., Alvarez-Gomez, F., & Ruiz-Viñals, C. (2022). Chronological Evolution of the Information-Driven Decision-Making Process (1950–2020). *Journal of the Knowledge Economy*. Advance online publication. DOI: 10.1007/s13132-022-00917-y

Rahmaty, M., & Nozari, H. (2023). Optimization of the hierarchical supply chain in the pharmaceutical industry. *Edelweiss Applied Science and Technology*, 7(2), 104–123. DOI: 10.55214/25768484.v7i2.376

Sachan, S., Almaghrabi, F., Yang, J.-B., & Xu, D.-L. (2024). Human-AI collaboration to mitigate decision noise in financial underwriting: A study on FinTech innovation in a lending firm. *International Review of Financial Analysis*, 93, 103149. Advance online publication. DOI: 10.1016/j.irfa.2024.103149

Sanni, B. (2024). Human-AI Collaboration in Supply Chains: Coordination Impacts and Challenges.

Silvestri, M., Rodríguez González, S., & Bucciarelli, E. (2016). Decision Economics, In Commemoration of the Birth Centennial of Herbert A. Simon 1916-2016 (Nobel Prize in Economics 1978) : Distributed Computing and Artificial Intelligence, 13th International Conference. Springer International Publishing

Sun, X., & Song, Y. (2025). Unlocking the Synergy: Increasing productivity through Human-AI collaboration in the industry 5.0 Era. *Computers & Industrial Engineering*, 200, 110657. DOI: 10.1016/j.cie.2024.110657

Tweedale, J., Phillips-Wren, G., & Jain, L. C. (2016). *Advances in Intelligent Decision-Making Technology Support.* Springer International Publishing., DOI: 10.1007/978-3-319-21209-8_1

Yu, P.-L. (2001). *Evolution Toward a New State of Multi-criteria Decision Making* (Vol. 507). Springer., DOI: 10.1007/978-3-642-56680-6_1

Zhang, D. (2024). Leveraging artificial intelligence in economics and finance: Enhancing decision-making and market efficiency. *Applied and Computational Engineering*, 82(1), 118–123. DOI: 10.54254/2755-2721/82/20240980

Chapter 12

Edge Computing and Marketing in the Smart Economy:
Processing Consumer Data in Real-Time

Hamed Nozari
https://orcid.org/0000-0002-6500-6708
Independent Researcher, Australia

Hossein Abdi
Department of Management, Islamic Azad University, Dubai, UAE

Khatere Rafiei
https://orcid.org/0009-0005-4471-6929
Department of Management, Islamic Azad University, Dubai, UAE

ABSTRACT

Edge computing is revolutionizing marketing by enabling real-time data processing, enhancing personalization, and improving customer engagement. Unlike traditional cloud-based systems, edge computing processes data closer to its source, reducing latency and optimizing marketing strategies. This research explores the role of edge computing in marketing, its key applications, advantages, challenges, and future potential. By integrating AI, IoT, and 5G, businesses can create dynamic, data-driven marketing ecosystems that offer hyper-personalized experiences while ensuring data security and efficiency in the evolving digital economy.

DOI: 10.4018/979-8-3693-4369-2.ch012

1- INTRODUCTION

The digital economy is undergoing rapid transformation, driven by advancements in data processing, artificial intelligence, and real-time consumer engagement. As businesses strive to create more dynamic, personalized, and efficient marketing strategies, the need for faster and more localized data processing has become critical. Traditional cloud-based computing, while instrumental in scaling digital marketing efforts, often introduces latency, bandwidth congestion, and privacy concerns that hinder the real-time responsiveness required for modern customer interactions. In response to these challenges, edge computing has emerged as a revolutionary approach, offering decentralized data processing that enhances marketing agility, personalization, and consumer engagement (Fallah & nozari, 2021).

Edge computing refers to the practice of processing data closer to its source—on IoT devices, mobile networks, and local servers—rather than relying on centralized cloud infrastructure. By enabling instantaneous data analysis and decision-making, edge computing allows businesses to respond to customer behaviors in real-time, significantly enhancing the effectiveness of digital marketing strategies. Whether through AI-powered chatbots, personalized recommendations, location-based advertising, or real-time sentiment analysis, edge computing empowers brands to create seamless and highly engaging customer experiences. As marketing evolves into a more dynamic, data-driven discipline, the ability to act on consumer insights instantaneously is no longer a competitive advantage but a fundamental necessity (Anozie et al., 2024).

The integration of edge computing in marketing is particularly crucial in an era where customer expectations are at an all-time high. Consumers now demand instant recommendations, tailored promotions, and personalized interactions, all of which require real-time processing capabilities that traditional cloud computing struggles to deliver efficiently. In industries such as retail, e-commerce, and digital advertising, edge computing is already proving to be a game-changer, allowing brands to optimize their marketing campaigns in real-time while minimizing costs associated with data transfer and cloud storage.

Despite its advantages, the adoption of edge computing also presents challenges, including high infrastructure costs, security risks, and the complexity of managing decentralized data networks. As businesses shift toward this new era of real-time marketing, it is essential to understand the role, impact, and future potential of edge computing in shaping more intelligent, efficient, and customer-centric marketing strategies. This research delves into the evolution of edge computing in marketing, examining its key applications, benefits, challenges, and future trends, with a focus on how businesses can leverage this technology to create next-generation marketing experiences that are faster, smarter, and more engaging.

2- LITERATURE REVIEW

The concept of edge computing has been widely explored in various domains, including industrial automation, healthcare, and smart cities, but its application in marketing is an emerging area of study. Traditional marketing strategies have historically relied on centralized data processing methods, where large datasets are collected and analyzed in cloud-based environments before being used for customer segmentation, targeted advertising, and campaign optimization. While cloud computing has enabled significant advancements in digital marketing, including predictive analytics and AI-driven personalization, it has also introduced limitations in terms of latency, bandwidth consumption, and data security, which hinder real-time decision-making. Edge computing addresses these concerns by decentralizing data processing and allowing businesses to analyze customer interactions instantly, leading to more responsive and efficient marketing strategies (Najafi et al., 2022).

One of the key discussions in the literature revolves around the role of edge computing in enhancing hyper-personalization. Research has emphasized that modern consumers expect real-time engagement and personalized experiences that align with their immediate needs and preferences. By processing data at the edge, marketing platforms can deliver highly relevant recommendations, adaptive pricing, and customized content without the delays associated with cloud-based analytics. This approach has been particularly beneficial in industries such as retail and e-commerce, where real-time product recommendations and location-based promotions significantly impact consumer purchasing decisions. Literature suggests that edge computing, when combined with AI and machine learning models, can analyze customer behaviors in milliseconds, making real-time personalization not only possible but also scalable.

Another critical aspect examined in existing studies is the impact of edge computing on data privacy and security. With increasing concerns over consumer data protection and regulatory compliance, businesses are seeking alternatives to traditional cloud-based storage solutions, which are more vulnerable to cyber threats and data breaches. Edge computing has been identified as a viable solution, as it allows companies to process sensitive consumer data locally, reducing the risk of unauthorized access and improving compliance with data protection laws. The literature also highlights that while edge computing enhances security by decentralizing data storage, it also introduces new challenges related to securing multiple edge nodes and ensuring the integrity of distributed data networks (Movahed et al., 2024 (a)).

The role of edge computing in optimizing marketing automation and AI-driven interactions is another focal point in academic discussions. The ability to integrate edge AI into chatbots, voice assistants, and smart digital displays has been explored as a means of improving customer engagement. Studies suggest that traditional cloud-based AI chatbots often suffer from latency issues, leading to slower response times and less fluid interactions. By processing queries locally, edge AI chatbots can provide instant responses and adapt their messaging in real-time based on user interactions. This advancement in conversational AI has implications for customer service, sales, and advertising, as businesses can create more intuitive and engaging interactions with their audiences.

Location-based marketing is another area where edge computing is gaining traction. Literature has extensively examined how businesses can leverage IoT-enabled beacons, geo-fencing, and real-time consumer tracking to deliver targeted promotions and advertisements. By processing location data at the edge, businesses can avoid the delays associated with cloud-based location tracking and ensure that marketing messages reach consumers at the most relevant moments. This is particularly valuable in sectors such as hospitality, retail, and event marketing, where real-time engagement directly influences consumer behavior. The literature further suggests that edge computing, when integrated with 5G networks, will make location-based marketing even more precise, enabling seamless interactions between smart devices and marketing platforms (Gupta et al., 2022).

Emerging studies also discuss the potential of edge computing in digital advertising, particularly in programmatic advertising and real-time bidding. Traditional digital advertising models rely on centralized servers to process vast amounts of consumer data, determine ad placements, and execute bidding strategies. The latency involved in this process can lead to inefficiencies and missed opportunities in highly competitive advertising spaces. Edge computing offers a solution by enabling real-time data analysis at the network edge, allowing advertisers to adjust bidding strategies dynamically based on immediate user behavior. This shift not only improves ad targeting accuracy but also reduces reliance on third-party data, which is becoming increasingly restricted due to privacy regulations (Sharipov et al., 2022).

Despite the promising applications of edge computing in marketing, the literature also acknowledges several challenges that businesses must navigate. The complexity of deploying and managing decentralized data processing systems is frequently cited as a barrier to widespread adoption. Unlike cloud computing, which operates through centralized infrastructure, edge computing requires businesses to invest in distributed edge nodes, intelligent data filtering, and AI-powered decision-making at multiple touchpoints. Maintaining consistency across decentralized networks and ensuring seamless data synchronization between edge devices and cloud systems remain significant technical hurdles. Additionally, while edge computing reduces data transfer costs, the initial investment in infrastructure, including specialized hardware and software integration, can be substantial (Movahed et al., 2024(b)).

Future research directions in this domain suggest that edge computing will become increasingly integrated with other advanced technologies such as blockchain, digital twins, and federated learning. These integrations have the potential to enhance transparency in marketing transactions, simulate consumer behavior in virtual environments, and further improve the security of decentralized data processing. The literature also predicts that edge computing will play a key role in autonomous marketing systems, where AI-driven algorithms optimize campaigns, analyze market trends, and adjust strategies in real time without human intervention.

Overall, the existing body of research highlights that edge computing is not only a technological advancement but also a fundamental enabler of next-generation marketing. Its ability to reduce latency, enhance security, optimize AI-driven personalization, and support real-time customer engagement makes it a transformative force in the digital marketing landscape. However, businesses must carefully evaluate the technical, financial, and strategic implications of adopting edge computing to maximize its benefits while mitigating potential challenges. As marketing continues to evolve in response to technological advancements and shifting consumer expectations, edge computing is expected to play an increasingly central role in shaping the future of digital engagement.

3- THE ROLE OF EDGE COMPUTING IN MARKETING

The evolution of digital marketing has been closely tied to advancements in computing technologies. Traditional marketing strategies relied on batch processing of customer data in centralized cloud servers, which introduced latency issues and reduced responsiveness. In contrast, edge computing has revolutionized marketing by enabling real-time data processing at the source of data generation. This transformation allows businesses to analyze consumer behavior instantaneously, adapt marketing strategies on the fly, and deliver highly personalized customer experiences (Zhang et al., 2020).

Edge computing functions by processing data closer to end users, minimizing reliance on distant cloud infrastructure. By reducing data transfer delays, businesses can make immediate decisions based on real-time consumer interactions. This shift is particularly crucial in today's smart economy, where consumers expect instant recommendations, hyper-personalized offers, and seamless brand engagement.

The transition from cloud-based marketing analytics to edge-powered marketing offers significant improvements in speed, efficiency, and privacy. The following table outlines key differences between these two approaches and highlights the advantages of edge computing in modern marketing strategies.

Table 1. Comparison of Edge Computing vs. Cloud Computing in Marketing

Feature	Edge Computing	Cloud Computing
Data Processing Location	Near the data source (e.g., IoT devices, smartphones)	Centralized cloud servers
Response Time	Ultra-fast, real-time decision-making	Delayed due to data transmission
Bandwidth Usage	Lower, as only essential data is sent to the cloud	Higher, as all data must be transferred
Security & Privacy	Enhanced, as sensitive data is processed locally	More vulnerable due to centralized storage
Best Use Cases in Marketing	Personalized ads, real-time offers, location-based marketing	Long-term analytics, centralized customer insights

This comparison highlights why edge computing is becoming the backbone of next-generation marketing strategies. Unlike cloud computing, which processes large amounts of data remotely, edge computing enables localized, instant decision-making that enhances customer engagement.

One of the most transformative applications of edge computing in marketing is hyper-personalization. By analyzing real-time customer behavior, businesses can deliver context-aware product recommendations and promotions within milliseconds.

For instance, a retail store equipped with smart sensors can detect when a customer enters, analyze past purchase behavior, and immediately send a personalized discount to the customer's smartphone. With edge-powered AI, brands can process this data instantaneously, making product recommendations at the right moment to maximize engagement and conversions.

Edge computing plays a critical role in geo-targeted marketing, enabling brands to send personalized messages or offers to consumers based on their exact location—without relying on cloud-based processing delays.

For example, a restaurant chain using edge-powered beacons can automatically send a real-time discount offer to a potential customer as they walk by the restaurant, significantly increasing foot traffic and impulse visits. By reducing the dependency on centralized cloud servers, edge-driven location-based marketing ensures that promotional messages reach consumers at the right place and time, making them significantly more effective. AI-driven chatbots have become a staple in digital marketing, but many traditional chatbots suffer from slow response times due to cloud latency. Edge AI-powered chatbots, however, process data locally, allowing them to analyze customer queries and respond instantly, creating a smoother and more human-like interaction (Jayadeva et al., 2022).

For example, an edge-powered chatbot on an e-commerce website can instantly analyze visitor behavior, predict their needs, and recommend products in real-time, without relying on a remote server. This eliminates delays, reduces data transfer costs, and provides customers with a seamless and intuitive shopping experience. The integration of edge computing and IoT (Internet of Things) is revolutionizing in-store marketing by making retail environments more interactive and responsive. Retailers can analyze customer interactions with products in real-time and provide immediate recommendations or promotional offers (Hu et al., 2021).

For example, a smart mirror in a clothing store, powered by edge AI, can detect the clothing items a customer is trying on and instantly suggest matching accessories, displayed in real-time on the mirror's screen. By removing reliance on distant cloud servers, edge computing allows such AI-powered in-store marketing experiences to function flawlessly and without noticeable delays.

To illustrate how edge computing is revolutionizing real-time marketing, consider a smart retail store setup where AI, IoT devices, and edge computing work together to enhance customer engagement.

Figure 1. Edge Computing in a Smart Retail Store

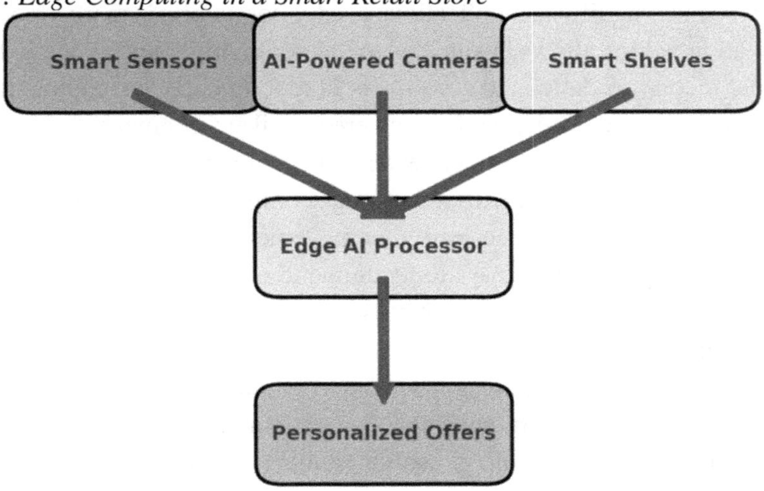

In this setup:

- Smart Sensors detect when a customer enters the store.
- AI-Powered Cameras analyze customer behavior and emotional response.
- Smart Shelves track inventory levels and suggest personalized product recommendations.
- Edge AI Processors analyze all these inputs in real-time without relying on a cloud server.
- Personalized Offers are instantly sent to customers based on their real-time behavior and preferences.

This system ensures instantaneous decision-making, enhancing both customer experience and marketing effectiveness.

4- KEY APPLICATIONS OF EDGE COMPUTING IN MARKETING

The integration of edge computing into marketing strategies has transformed the way businesses engage with customers, allowing for real-time data processing and immediate decision-making. Traditional cloud-based marketing approaches often suffer from latency issues and high bandwidth costs due to the need for continuous data transmission to remote servers. In contrast, edge computing enables businesses to process and analyze customer data locally, reducing delays and enhancing responsiveness. This shift has led to several groundbreaking applications that are redefining customer interactions, personalization, and efficiency in marketing (Hornik et al., 2024).

One of the most significant applications of edge computing in marketing is hyper-personalization, which allows businesses to deliver highly relevant content, offers, and product recommendations to consumers in real time. By leveraging data from smart sensors, mobile devices, and IoT-powered retail environments, businesses can create marketing messages tailored to each consumer's preferences and behaviors. For instance, in a smart retail environment, edge computing enables in-store sensors and AI-powered cameras to detect customer movements and shopping patterns, immediately adjusting digital displays to recommend relevant products. This level of personalization ensures that marketing efforts resonate with individual customers, increasing engagement and conversion rates.

Another transformative application is location-based marketing, where businesses can target customers based on their real-time geographic location. Edge-powered geo-fencing and beacon technology enable retailers and service providers to send instant notifications, special offers, and promotions to nearby customers. By processing location data at the edge, businesses can avoid the delays associated with cloud-based systems and ensure that messages reach consumers precisely when they are most relevant. A restaurant chain, for example, can use edge-enabled beacons to detect potential customers walking past its location and instantly send them a time-sensitive discount offer, encouraging them to visit. The ability to engage customers at the right moment and place significantly enhances the effectiveness of marketing campaigns. AI-driven virtual assistants and chatbots have also benefited from edge computing, making customer interactions faster and more efficient. Traditional cloud-based chatbots often experience delays due to the need for remote data processing, which can result in frustrating user experiences. Edge-powered chatbots, however, process customer queries locally, allowing for immediate responses and a more seamless conversational experience. An e-commerce platform utilizing an edge AI-powered chatbot can instantly analyze a visitor's browsing behavior and provide real-time product recommendations without having to communicate with a distant cloud server. This not only reduces response times but also enhances user engagement and satisfaction (Wang et al., 2021).

Retailers are increasingly adopting smart IoT-powered shelves and interactive digital displays, leveraging edge computing to optimize inventory management and marketing strategies simultaneously. Smart shelves equipped with weight sensors and RFID tags can detect product availability and adjust digital price tags or promotions based on stock levels. If a particular item is selling quickly, the system can trigger an automatic price adjustment or highlight complementary products in nearby digital displays. Edge computing ensures that these adjustments happen instantly, creating a dynamic and responsive shopping environment. Customers benefit from real-time promotions tailored to their needs, while retailers optimize sales and inventory efficiency (Yu, 2021).

Another compelling application of edge computing in marketing is real-time sentiment analysis, which allows brands to assess customer reactions instantly and adjust marketing strategies accordingly. AI-powered cameras and sensors placed in retail stores or event venues can analyze customer facial expressions and body language, providing immediate feedback on their emotional responses to advertisements, product displays, or brand experiences. If a customer appears frustrated or disengaged while browsing a particular section of a store, edge computing enables real-time adjustments, such as personalized assistance or customized offers, to improve their shopping experience. This capability gives businesses the power to create highly adaptive marketing strategies that respond dynamically to customer emotions and preferences (Nozari et al., 2024).

In addition to enhancing customer interactions, edge computing also plays a crucial role in advertising and content delivery optimization. Digital advertising platforms can use edge-based AI to analyze user behavior in real time and adjust advertisements accordingly. By processing data locally, businesses can determine the most effective ads to display, reducing irrelevant or intrusive advertising while increasing engagement rates. Streaming platforms, for instance, leverage edge computing to personalize video advertisements based on user preferences without requiring continuous data transfers to a central cloud server. This results in a smoother, more relevant ad experience that resonates with viewers.

As edge computing continues to evolve, its applications in marketing will expand, providing businesses with unprecedented levels of customer insight and real-time engagement. The ability to process and act on data instantly is a competitive advantage that enhances personalization, improves marketing efficiency, and fosters deeper customer relationships. Brands that embrace edge computing in their marketing strategies are better positioned to thrive in the fast-paced digital economy, where responsiveness and personalization are key to success.

5- ADVANTAGES AND CHALLENGES OF EDGE COMPUTING IN MARKETING

The adoption of edge computing in marketing has introduced a new era of speed, efficiency, and real-time engagement, allowing brands to process customer data locally and act on insights instantly. Unlike traditional cloud computing, which requires transmitting large volumes of data to remote servers for analysis, edge computing decentralizes data processing, reducing latency, minimizing bandwidth consumption, and enhancing customer experiences. However, despite its transformative benefits, edge computing also presents challenges those businesses must address to fully harness its potential. Understanding both the advantages and the challenges of this technology is essential for organizations looking to integrate it into their marketing strategies.

One of the primary advantages of edge computing in marketing is the significant reduction in latency, which enables real-time decision-making. With traditional cloud-based systems, data must travel to and from a remote data center, introducing delays that can impact customer engagement. Edge computing eliminates this issue by processing data at or near the source, ensuring that personalized recommendations, targeted advertisements, and dynamic content adjustments happen instantaneously. This is particularly beneficial in retail environments, where customers expect immediate responses to their interactions. For instance, in a smart retail store, an edge-powered AI system can instantly analyze customer behavior and adjust digital displays or send personalized offers without waiting for cloud-based analysis.

Another compelling advantage is improved bandwidth efficiency, as edge computing reduces the need for continuous data transmission to centralized cloud servers. In traditional cloud-based marketing analytics, vast amounts of data—such as customer interactions, video feeds, and IoT device signals—are sent back and forth, consuming significant bandwidth. Edge computing minimizes this burden by processing only relevant data locally and sending only essential insights to cloud servers for further analysis. This not only lowers data transfer costs but also enhances operational efficiency, making edge-powered marketing solutions more scalable for businesses operating across multiple locations (Nozari & Irani, 2024).

Beyond performance improvements, data security and privacy compliance are major advantages of edge computing in marketing. With growing concerns over data breaches and regulatory requirements such as GDPR and CCPA, edge computing allows businesses to keep sensitive customer data closer to its source, reducing exposure to cyber threats. Traditional cloud models centralize data storage, making them attractive targets for cyberattacks, whereas edge computing processes much of the data locally, minimizing the risk of unauthorized access. Additionally, processing data at the edge ensures that businesses can maintain greater control over customer information, strengthening compliance with privacy regulations.

To better illustrate these advantages, the Table 2 compares the key benefits of edge computing with traditional cloud computing approaches:

Table 2. Advantages of Edge Computing vs. Cloud Computing in Marketing

Feature	Edge Computing	Cloud Computing
Latency	Ultra-low, real-time responses	Noticeable delay due to remote processing
Bandwidth Usage	Lower, processes data locally	Higher, requires continuous data transfer
Security & Privacy	Enhanced, localized data storage	More vulnerable due to centralized storage
Personalization Speed	Instant, real-time adjustments	Delayed, dependent on server response
Scalability	Ideal for decentralized marketing campaigns	More suited for centralized data management

Despite these advantages, the challenges of implementing edge computing in marketing cannot be ignored. One of the most pressing issues is the high initial cost of infrastructure. Deploying edge computing requires businesses to invest in localized processing hardware, edge servers, and IoT-enabled devices, which can be costly compared to cloud-based SaaS (Software-as-a-Service) models. Smaller companies with limited budgets may struggle to justify the upfront investment, even though the long-term benefits of edge computing often outweigh these costs (Nozari et al., 2023).

Another challenge businesses face is the complexity of managing decentralized data processing systems. Unlike cloud computing, where data is stored and processed in a centralized manner, edge computing distributes data processing across multiple locations. This requires a more sophisticated IT infrastructure, including robust synchronization mechanisms, real-time monitoring, and AI-driven automation to ensure seamless operations across different edge nodes. Companies must adopt advanced AI algorithms and machine learning models to manage and analyze decentralized data effectively. Security, while improved in some aspects, also presents new risks associated with distributed edge devices. While edge computing reduces reliance on centralized cloud storage, it expands the attack surface by increasing the number of entry points in a network. Each edge device—whether a smart sensor, an IoT beacon, or an AI-powered digital display—becomes a potential target for cyberattacks. Securing these devices requires end-to-end encryption, real-time threat detection, and continuous updates, which can add complexity to deployment and maintenance (Nozari &Chobar, 2024).

By weighing these advantages and challenges, businesses can make informed decisions on whether and how to integrate edge computing into their marketing ecosystems. Those that successfully implement edge solutions will gain a competitive edge by delivering real-time, hyper-personalized marketing experiences, while also navigating the complexities of infrastructure investment, security, and scalability. In an era where consumers demand instant engagement and tailored experiences, edge computing is set to become a cornerstone of next-generation marketing strategies, but only for organizations that can strategically manage its implementation.

To conclude, while edge computing offers unmatched speed, efficiency, and security benefits, its infrastructure requirements, management complexity, and cybersecurity challenges must be carefully addressed to maximize its potential. Businesses that adopt a well-planned approach to edge computing will be better positioned to create real-time, intelligent marketing campaigns that enhance customer satisfaction, increase brand loyalty, and drive sustained business growth.

6- THE FUTURE OF EDGE COMPUTING IN MARKETING

As digital transformation accelerates, edge computing is poised to play an even more significant role in reshaping the future of marketing. Businesses are increasingly prioritizing speed, personalization, and seamless customer experiences, all of which require real-time data processing and rapid decision-making. The limitations of traditional cloud computing, such as latency, bandwidth constraints, and growing concerns over data privacy, are driving organizations to embrace edge computing as a fundamental component of their marketing strategies. As this technology evolves, its influence on marketing will extend beyond current applications, unlocking new capabilities that redefine how brands interact with consumers.

One of the most impactful developments in the future of edge computing is the deeper integration of artificial intelligence at the edge. AI-powered analytics will be embedded directly into edge devices, allowing businesses to process consumer data instantly and autonomously adapt marketing strategies. With edge AI, personalized advertising will become even more dynamic, as smart retail systems, IoT-enabled devices, and AI-driven chatbots will be able to assess consumer preferences and behaviors in real-time without needing to communicate with remote servers. This shift will lead to hyper-responsive marketing environments where product recommendations, promotional offers, and digital content dynamically adjust based on immediate user interactions, significantly improving engagement rates (Aliahmadi & Nozari, 2023).

The emergence of 5G networks will further amplify the impact of edge computing in marketing, enabling ultra-fast data transfer and seamless connectivity between edge devices and consumer applications. With near-instantaneous communication between smart sensors, mobile apps, and digital advertisements, businesses will be able to create marketing experiences that are more immersive and interactive than ever before. Augmented reality (AR) and virtual reality (VR) campaigns will benefit tremendously from this evolution, as edge-powered processing will eliminate lag, ensuring real-time rendering of AR-based product try-ons or VR-enhanced shopping experiences. Brands will be able to offer personalized, real-time interactions without delays, making marketing content feel more natural and engaging to consumers.

As privacy regulations become more stringent and consumers grow more concerned about data security, edge computing will also be instrumental in ensuring compliance with global privacy laws such as GDPR and CCPA. By processing sensitive customer data locally rather than transmitting it to centralized cloud servers, businesses will be able to reduce the risk of data breaches and improve transparency in how consumer information is handled. Decentralized data storage will help companies build trust with customers, who will have greater control over their personal data while still benefiting from personalized marketing experiences. This will push brands to adopt privacy-first marketing approaches, where edge computing serves as the backbone for ethical, permission-based data processing (Nozari et al., 2024).

The integration of blockchain technology with edge computing is another area that will shape the future of marketing. Blockchain's decentralized ledger system can be used to enhance transparency and security in marketing transactions, particularly in digital advertising and influencer marketing. Smart contracts, powered by blockchain at the edge, will automate advertising transactions, ensuring that brands and influencers engage in secure, verifiable partnerships without intermediaries. Additionally, by integrating blockchain with edge-powered IoT devices, companies will be able to create fully traceable, real-time marketing campaigns, where customer interactions with smart billboards, personalized ads, or location-based offers are securely logged and authenticated.

In addition to AI, 5G, and blockchain, the evolution of autonomous marketing systems will be significantly driven by edge computing. Businesses will increasingly rely on self-learning algorithms and predictive analytics at the edge, allowing marketing systems to optimize campaigns in real-time without human intervention. Autonomous marketing platforms will be capable of adjusting ad placements, modifying pricing strategies, and identifying emerging consumer trends based on edge-generated insights. These self-optimizing marketing ecosystems will make digital advertising more efficient, reducing wasted ad spend and ensuring that brands deliver the right message to the right audience at the right time.

As more businesses embrace edge computing, the retail and e-commerce industries will likely be among the biggest beneficiaries. Smart stores, powered by edge AI, will become more common, offering consumers frictionless shopping experiences where physical and digital commerce merge seamlessly. Interactive displays, voice assistants, and facial recognition-enabled payment systems will create fully personalized shopping environments, adjusting in real-time to each customer's preferences and needs. Meanwhile, e-commerce platforms will leverage edge-powered recommendation engines to deliver instant product suggestions, optimize search results, and create dynamic pricing strategies based on live consumer demand (Nozari et al., 2021).

The continued advancement of edge computing in marketing will also open doors to new types of real-time customer engagement strategies. Digital twins—virtual replicas of physical stores, products, or entire customer segments—will leverage edge computing to simulate consumer interactions and optimize marketing campaigns before deployment. By using real-time consumer behavior data, businesses will be able to test marketing strategies in a digital twin environment and refine them for maximum effectiveness before rolling them out in the real world.

Looking ahead, edge computing will not just complement marketing strategies but will become a foundational pillar of next-generation marketing architectures. As AI, 5G, blockchain, and IoT technologies continue to evolve, businesses that integrate edge computing into their marketing ecosystems will gain a substantial competitive advantage. The ability to process data at the source, adapt marketing strategies instantly, and ensure data privacy will define the future of digital engagement. In this new era, brands that harness the full potential of edge computing will be able to create marketing experiences that are not only faster and more efficient but also more intelligent, secure, and personalized than ever before.

7- CONCLUSION

The integration of edge computing into marketing represents a transformative shift in how businesses engage with consumers, analyze data, and optimize their strategies. By decentralizing data processing and enabling real-time decision-making, edge computing has introduced a new era of hyper-personalized marketing, reduced latency, and enhanced consumer experiences. As digital interactions become increasingly fast-paced, brands that embrace this technology will gain a significant competitive advantage by offering responsive, intelligent, and seamless customer engagement.

Throughout this research, we explored the role of edge computing in marketing, its key applications, the advantages and challenges it presents, and its future potential in shaping digital marketing landscapes. Edge computing has already demonstrated its ability to enhance hyper-personalization, optimize location-based marketing, improve chatbot responsiveness, and revolutionize smart retail environments. By shifting data processing closer to the source, businesses can analyze customer behavior instantaneously, ensuring that marketing messages, promotions, and product recommendations are delivered with maximum relevance and impact.

However, while edge computing solves several limitations of traditional cloud-based marketing, it also presents challenges, including high infrastructure costs, complex data management, and security risks associated with decentralized systems. Addressing these challenges will require businesses to invest in robust cybersecurity measures, scalable edge infrastructure, and AI-driven automation to efficiently manage decentralized data networks. Despite these hurdles, the long-term benefits of edge computing—including lower bandwidth costs, improved data security, and real-time engagement capabilities—make it an essential tool for the future of marketing.

Looking ahead, the convergence of edge computing with emerging technologies such as AI, 5G, blockchain, and digital twins will further redefine marketing ecosystems. Smart advertising, autonomous marketing platforms, and fully immersive consumer experiences will become the norm, offering brands unprecedented opportunities to connect with their audiences. Companies that proactively integrate edge computing into their digital strategies will be better equipped to navigate the evolving landscape of real-time, data-driven marketing. In an era where consumer expectations continue to rise, edge computing is not just an option but a necessity for businesses seeking to remain agile, innovative, and competitive in the modern digital economy.

REFERENCES

Aliahmadi, A., & Nozari, H. (2023, January). Evaluation of security metrics in AIoT and blockchain-based supply chain by Neutrosophic decision-making method. In *Supply chain forum: an international journal* (Vol. 24, No. 1, pp. 31-42). Taylor & Francis. DOI: 10.1080/16258312.2022.2101898

Anozie, U. C., Dada, S. A., Okonkwo, F. C., Egunlae, O., Animasahun, B., & Mazino, O. (2024). The convergence of edge computing and supply chain resilience in retail marketing. *International Journal of Science and Research Archive*, 12(02), 2769–2779. DOI: 10.30574/ijsra.2024.12.2.1574

Fallah, M., & Nozari, H. (2021). Neutrosophic mathematical programming for optimization of multi-objective sustainable biomass supply chain network design. *Computer Modeling in Engineering & Sciences*, 129(2), 927–951. DOI: 10.32604/cmes.2021.017511

Gupta, S., & Vyas, S. (2022). Contemporary role of edge-AI in IoT and IoE in healthcare and digital marketing. In *Edge-AI in Healthcare* (pp. 75–84). CRC Press.

Hornik, J., Ofir, C., & Rachamim, M. (2024). Out of the fog: fog computing-enabled AI to support smart marketing management. *Management Review Quarterly*, 1-33.

Hu, S., Huang, S., Huang, J., & Su, J. (2021). Blockchain and edge computing technology enabling organic agricultural supply chain: A framework solution to trust crisis. *Computers & Industrial Engineering*, 153, 107079. DOI: 10.1016/j.cie.2020.107079

Irani, H. R., & Nozari, H. (Eds.). (2024). *Smart and Sustainable Interactive Marketing*. IGI Global. DOI: 10.4018/979-8-3693-1339-8

Jayadeva, S. M., Al Ayub Ahmed, A., Malik, R., Shaikh, A. A., Siddique, M. N. E. A., & Naved, M. (2022, June). Roles of Cloud Computing and Internet of Things in Marketing Management: A Critical Review and Future Trends. In *Proceedings of Second International Conference in Mechanical and Energy Technology: ICMET 2021,India* (pp. 165-173). Singapore: Springer Nature Singapore.

Movahed, A. B., Movahed, A. B., & Nozari, H. (a)(2024). Opportunities and Challenges of Marketing 5.0. *Smart and Sustainable Interactive Marketing*, 1-21.

Movahed, A. B., Movahed, A. B., & Nozari, H. (b)(2024). Marketing 6.0 Conceptualization. In *Advanced Businesses in Industry 6.0* (pp. 15-31). IGI Global.

Najafi, S. E., Nozari, H., & Edalatpanah, S. A. (2022). Investigating the key parameters affecting sustainable IoT-based marketing. In *Computational Intelligence Methodologies Applied to Sustainable Development Goals* (pp. 51–61). Springer International Publishing. DOI: 10.1007/978-3-030-97344-5_4

Nozari, H., & Chobar, A. P. (2024). The Dimensions and Components of Marketing 5.0: Introduction to Marketing 6.0. In *Advanced Businesses in Industry 6.0* (pp. 75-86). IGI Global.

Nozari, H., Irani, H. R., & Rahmaty, M. (2023, November). Investigating Critical Success Factors in IoT-Based Marketing Systems. In *International Conference on Optimization and Data Science in Industrial Engineering* (pp. 259-271). Cham: Springer Nature Switzerland.

Nozari, H., Rahmaty, M., & Szmelter-Jarosz, A. (2024). A framework for AIoT-based smart sustainable marketing system. In *Artificial Intelligence of Things for Achieving Sustainable Development Goals* (pp. 255–271). Springer Nature Switzerland. DOI: 10.1007/978-3-031-53433-1_13

Nozari, H., Szmelter-Jarosz, A., & Ghahremani-Nahr, J. (2021). The ideas of sustainable and green marketing based on the internet of everything—The case of the dairy industry. *Future Internet*, 13(10), 266. DOI: 10.3390/fi13100266

Nozari, H., Szmelter-Jarosz, A., & Rahmaty, M. (2024). Smart Marketing Based on Artificial Intelligence of Things (AIoT) and Blockchain and Evaluating Critical Success Factors. In *Smart and Sustainable Interactive Marketing* (pp. 68-82). IGI Global.

Sharipov, K., Abdurashidova, N., Valiyeva, A., Tuychieva, V., Kholmatova, M., & Minarova, M. (2022, December). A systematic mapping study of using the cutting-edge technologies in marketing: the state of the art of four key new-age technologies. In *International Conference on Next Generation Wired/Wireless Networking* (pp. 381-389). Cham: Springer Nature Switzerland.

Wang, G., & Wang, Y. (2021). Innovative Marketing Framework for Enterprises Using Edge-Enabled Data Analysis. *Mobile Information Systems*, 2021(1), 6699420. DOI: 10.1155/2021/6699420

Yu, Y. (2021). Application of mobile edge computing technology in civil aviation express marketing. *Wireless Communications and Mobile Computing*, 2021(1), 9932977. DOI: 10.1155/2021/9932977

Zhang, X., Cao, Z., & Dong, W. (2020). Overview of edge computing in the agricultural internet of things: Key technologies, applications, challenges. *IEEE Access : Practical Innovations, Open Solutions*, 8, 141748–141761. DOI: 10.1109/ACCESS.2020.3013005

Chapter 13

Financial Innovations in the Era of Industry 5.0: Opportunities and Challenges

Amirhosein Emami
https://orcid.org/0000-0003-4551-9992
Arden University, Germany

Mohamad Afshar
Islamic Azad University, Tehran, Iran

Mahdi Aliyari
https://orcid.org/0009-0005-1325-6800
Islamic Azad University, Shabestar, Iran

ABSTRACT

The integration of Industry 5.0 technologies into financial services is revolutionizing the sector, emphasizing human-centric innovation, sustainability, and digital transformation. This research explores the role of Artificial Intelligence, Blockchain, the Internet of Things (IoT), and Green FinTech in reshaping financial ecosystems. While these technologies offer enhanced efficiency, security, and sustainability, they also introduce challenges related to regulatory compliance, cybersecurity, and ethical AI. The study highlights the opportunities and risks associated with financial innovations in Industry 5.0 and their long-term implications.

DOI: 10.4018/979-8-3693-4369-2.ch013

1- INTRODUCTION

The rapid technological advancements of the 21st century have ushered in a new industrial paradigm known as Industry 5.0, which seeks to harmonize human intelligence with cutting-edge digital technologies. While Industry 4.0 primarily focused on automation, data-driven decision-making, and cyber-physical systems, Industry 5.0 places an emphasis on human-centric innovation, sustainability, and resilience. This paradigm shift has profound implications for the financial sector, where innovations driven by artificial intelligence (AI), blockchain, quantum computing, and the Internet of Things (IoT) are redefining how financial transactions, investments, and risk assessments are conducted. The intersection of these transformative technologies with finance has given rise to financial innovations that offer unprecedented opportunities while simultaneously introducing new challenges (Muzaffar et al., 2024).

In traditional financial systems, efficiency, accuracy, and security have always been critical concerns. However, with the rise of Industry 5.0 technologies, the financial sector is moving beyond merely optimizing processes toward creating intelligent, adaptive, and more personalized financial services. AI-driven algorithms now have the ability to analyze vast amounts of financial data, providing predictive insights that assist in decision-making for businesses, investors, and policymakers. Meanwhile, blockchain technology is revolutionizing transactions by introducing decentralized and trustless systems, reducing the reliance on intermediaries and enhancing security. The integration of IoT devices into financial services has further expanded the scope of innovation, allowing real-time monitoring of assets, transactions, and financial behaviors on a global scale (Najafi et al., 2022).

One of the defining aspects of financial innovations in the Industry 5.0 era is the shift toward a more inclusive and ethical financial ecosystem. The emergence of decentralized finance (DeFi) has challenged traditional banking models, enabling individuals and businesses to access financial services without the need for intermediaries. Smart contracts, built on blockchain networks, facilitate self-executing agreements that enhance transparency and reduce transaction costs. Moreover, AI-driven risk assessment models have improved access to credit by evaluating alternative data sources beyond conventional credit scores, allowing a broader segment of the population to participate in the global financial system. These advancements align with the broader goals of Industry 5.0, which emphasize human collaboration with technology rather than complete automation, ensuring that financial systems remain resilient, ethical, and human-centric (Mahawar et al., 2024).

Despite the vast opportunities, financial innovations in the Industry 5.0 era also present significant challenges. One of the most pressing concerns is cybersecurity and data privacy. As financial systems become increasingly digitized and interconnected, they become more vulnerable to cyber threats, fraud, and hacking. AI-powered financial services rely on massive datasets, raising ethical questions about data ownership, bias in algorithmic decision-making, and potential misuse of personal information. Additionally, blockchain, while offering decentralized security, poses regulatory challenges as governments and financial institutions struggle to establish clear frameworks for its integration into traditional financial systems (George et al., 2024).

Regulatory adaptation is another critical challenge. Financial authorities worldwide must keep pace with the rapid evolution of technology to ensure that new financial innovations do not lead to systemic risks, market manipulations, or economic inequalities. For instance, the growing influence of AI in financial decision-making raises concerns about accountability, as AI-driven investment algorithms can lead to unintended consequences in financial markets. Similarly, the rise of digital currencies and DeFi platforms challenges traditional monetary policies, forcing regulators to reconsider how financial stability can be maintained in a decentralized landscape.

Another major consideration is the ethical implications of financial automation. While AI and machine learning have enabled sophisticated risk modeling, automated trading, and fraud detection, their deployment must be carefully managed to prevent biases and unintended consequences. Algorithmic trading, for example, has the potential to create flash crashes in stock markets if not properly regulated. The need for explainable AI in financial decision-making is growing, as stakeholders demand transparency in how AI models make predictions and influence economic outcomes.

Furthermore, Industry 5.0 emphasizes sustainability and environmental responsibility, and financial innovations must align with these objectives. The concept of Green FinTech is gaining momentum, leveraging AI, blockchain, and big data analytics to promote sustainable investing, carbon credit trading, and climate risk assessment. Financial institutions are now incorporating Environmental, Social, and Governance (ESG) factors into their investment strategies, reflecting the broader societal shift toward ethical finance. This shift not only improves corporate responsibility but also ensures long-term financial stability in an era of increasing climate-related risks.

Looking ahead, the financial sector will continue to evolve as it embraces emerging technologies in Industry 5.0. The convergence of AI, blockchain, quantum computing, and IoT will lead to even more sophisticated, secure, and efficient financial systems. However, the success of these innovations will depend on regulatory foresight, ethical considerations, and the ability to balance technological advancements with human values. As we move further into the era of Industry 5.0, the challenge for financial institutions, policymakers, and technology developers will be to create an ecosystem where technological progress enhances rather than disrupts financial stability, trust, and inclusivity.

This book chapter explores the key opportunities and challenges posed by financial innovations in Industry 5.0, examining how they reshape the financial landscape while addressing the ethical, regulatory, and security concerns that accompany them. By understanding these dynamics, we can navigate the complexities of the evolving financial ecosystem and harness its full potential for a more sustainable and inclusive global economy.

2- THE ROLE OF ARTIFICIAL INTELLIGENCE AND MACHINE LEARNING IN FINANCE

The financial sector has long relied on technology to optimize processes, reduce risks, and enhance decision-making. However, the introduction of Artificial Intelligence (AI) and Machine Learning (ML) in finance has revolutionized the industry by enabling systems to learn from data, detect patterns, and make informed predictions with unprecedented accuracy. These technologies are reshaping everything from investment strategies and credit scoring to fraud detection and customer service, offering both immense opportunities and significant challenges.

One of the most impactful applications of AI in finance is algorithmic trading. Traditional trading strategies often require extensive human analysis, but AI-powered algorithms can now process vast datasets, recognize market trends, and execute trades at speeds far beyond human capability. High-frequency trading (HFT), which relies on ML models, allows financial institutions to capitalize on minor price fluctuations, optimizing portfolio performance (Rahmaty & Nozari, 2023). While this has enhanced market efficiency, it has also raised concerns regarding market stability, as AI-driven trading can lead to volatility and unexpected crashes.

Another crucial area where AI is making a difference is credit risk assessment. Conventional credit scoring models rely heavily on historical financial data and standardized criteria. AI-based credit analysis, however, can integrate alternative data sources such as transaction behavior, social media activity, and even smartphone usage patterns to determine an individual's creditworthiness. This has expanded financial inclusion by enabling access to loans for individuals and businesses that might otherwise be excluded from traditional banking systems. Nevertheless, AI-driven credit decisions must be carefully monitored to prevent algorithmic biases that could unintentionally discriminate against certain demographic groups.

AI is also revolutionizing fraud detection and risk management. Traditional fraud detection methods are largely rule-based, requiring manual updates to keep up with evolving threats. Machine learning models, on the other hand, can continuously learn from historical fraud patterns, flagging suspicious activities in real-time. AI-powered fraud detection systems analyze customer behavior, transaction histories, and device metadata to identify anomalies indicative of fraudulent activities. This has significantly improved the security of financial transactions, reducing fraud-related losses. However, as fraudsters also leverage AI to create more sophisticated attacks, financial institutions must continually refine their models to stay ahead of emerging threats.

In the field of personalized financial services, AI has led to the rise of robo-advisors, digital platforms that provide automated investment recommendations based on individual preferences and risk tolerance. These advisors use ML algorithms to analyze market conditions and tailor investment portfolios for users, offering cost-effective and data-driven financial planning. The increasing reliance on robo-advisors highlights the shift toward AI-driven decision-making, but it also raises concerns about the loss of human judgment in financial advisory services. While AI can optimize investment strategies, it cannot fully replace human intuition and emotional intelligence, which play a crucial role in financial decision-making (Movahed et al., 2024).

Customer experience has also been enhanced through AI-powered chatbots and virtual assistants, which provide instant responses to customer inquiries, assist with transactions, and guide users through banking processes. Unlike traditional customer service, AI chatbots operate 24/7, reducing operational costs while improving efficiency. These systems are now capable of understanding natural language, adapting to user behavior, and providing increasingly sophisticated financial guidance.

Despite these advancements, AI in finance presents several challenges, particularly concerning explainability and transparency. Many machine learning models operate as "black boxes," making it difficult for financial institutions to justify their decisions to regulators and customers. If an AI model rejects a loan application or executes a high-value trade, financial institutions must be able to explain why and how the decision was made. The push for explainable AI (XAI) aims to make these decision-making processes more transparent and accountable, ensuring that AI-driven financial systems remain fair and ethical.

The key applications, benefits, and challenges of AI in finance are summarized in Table 1, which provides an overview of how AI is transforming financial operations and the potential risks associated with its adoption.

Table 1. Key AI and ML Applications in Finance

Application	Benefits	Challenges
Algorithmic Trading	High-speed execution, data-driven investment strategies	Market volatility, risk of AI-driven crashes
Credit Risk Assessment	Improved access to credit, alternative data integration	Potential biases in AI-driven scoring models
Fraud Detection	Real-time anomaly detection, reduced financial losses	AI-powered fraud evolving alongside defenses
Robo-Advisors	Personalized, low-cost investment strategies	Lack of human intuition in financial advising
Chatbots & Virtual Assistants	24/7 customer support, reduced operational costs	Limited emotional intelligence, risk of misinterpretation
Risk Management	Predictive analytics for financial stability	Complexity of AI-driven decision-making models

Looking ahead, the role of AI in finance will continue to expand as models become more sophisticated and capable of handling larger and more complex datasets. Quantum computing is expected to further enhance AI's capabilities in financial modeling, cryptographic security, and risk analysis. However, financial institutions must navigate the fine balance between technological efficiency and ethical responsibility. Ensuring regulatory compliance, addressing biases, and enhancing transparency will be critical for building trust in AI-powered financial systems.

While AI and machine learning offer remarkable improvements in financial innovation, their integration into the industry must be guided by human oversight and responsible development. If managed correctly, these technologies have the potential to create a more efficient, secure, and inclusive financial ecosystem, in alignment with the principles of Industry 5.0.

3- INTERNET OF THINGS (IOT) AND SMART FINANCIAL SERVICES

The Internet of Things (IoT) is rapidly transforming financial services, creating a more interconnected, efficient, and intelligent ecosystem that enhances the way businesses and individuals interact with financial institutions. As a key enabler of Industry 5.0, IoT integrates smart devices, sensors, and real-time data analytics to optimize financial transactions, risk management, and personalized banking experiences. By leveraging IoT, financial services are becoming more responsive, data-driven, and secure, ushering in an era of seamless automation, predictive decision-making, and enhanced customer engagement (Movahed et al., 2024).

One of the most significant contributions of IoT in finance is its ability to facilitate real-time data collection and processing, leading to more accurate risk assessments and personalized financial services. Traditionally, financial institutions relied on historical data and credit reports to assess loan applicants or predict market trends. With IoT-enabled devices, financial institutions can now access live data streams, such as transaction histories, geolocation patterns, spending behaviors, and even biometric authentication, to gain deeper insights into customer financial behavior (Nozari et al., 2021). This shift has led to more dynamic credit scoring models, where lenders analyze real-time financial data from wearables, smart home devices, or IoT-connected vehicles to make more precise and fair lending decisions.

IoT has also revolutionized the insurance industry, particularly in risk assessment and fraud prevention. Insurers are increasingly adopting IoT-driven solutions to collect real-time data from smart devices, such as connected vehicles, home security systems, and health-monitoring wearables. For instance, auto insurers now offer usage-based insurance (UBI) programs that track driving behavior through IoT-enabled sensors, adjusting premiums based on real-time driving patterns rather than fixed risk categories. Similarly, health insurers can incentivize policyholders to maintain a healthy lifestyle by monitoring fitness data through wearable devices, offering reduced premiums to individuals who meet certain health metrics. These advancements not only create more personalized and fair insurance pricing but also encourage safer behavior among policyholders (Tavakkoli-Moghaddam et al., 2024).

Another major application of IoT in financial services is its role in enhancing security and fraud detection. The financial industry has long battled cyber threats, identity theft, and fraudulent transactions, making security a top priority. IoT plays a crucial role in strengthening security measures through biometric authentication, AI-driven anomaly detection, and real-time monitoring of financial transactions. Banks and payment processors now use IoT-powered security features such as fingerprint recognition, facial authentication, and voice biometrics to validate transactions and prevent unauthorized access. Moreover, IoT-driven geolocation tracking helps financial institutions detect suspicious activities, such as credit card transactions occurring in different locations within short timeframes, enabling instant fraud alerts and automated security protocols (Aliahmadi et al., 2024).

Beyond security, IoT is also transforming smart payments and contactless transactions, reducing friction in everyday financial interactions. With the rise of IoT-enabled payment systems, customers can now make seamless transactions using wearable devices, smart cars, and even IoT-connected household appliances. The integration of contactless payment technologies with IoT has streamlined retail experiences, allowing customers to complete purchases using voice-activated assistants, smart refrigerators that reorder groceries automatically, or connected cars that handle fuel payments without requiring physical contact. These advancements are making financial transactions faster, more convenient, and deeply embedded into daily activities.

The banking sector is also benefiting from IoT-driven automation and smart infrastructure. Many banks are adopting IoT-enabled smart branches, where real-time analytics, facial recognition, and sensor-based tracking optimize customer experiences. Banks use IoT devices to analyze foot traffic, adjust staffing based on real-time demand, and enhance security by monitoring customer movements. Smart ATMs powered by IoT can perform advanced self-diagnosis, detecting potential malfunctions before they occur and automatically requesting maintenance, reducing downtime and operational costs (Nozari et al., 2024).

While IoT brings undeniable advantages to financial services, its widespread adoption also raises concerns regarding data privacy, cybersecurity, and regulatory compliance. The massive influx of real-time data generated by IoT devices requires robust security frameworks to protect sensitive financial information from cyber threats. Financial institutions must navigate regulatory challenges related to data collection, storage, and sharing, ensuring compliance with global data protection laws. Moreover, as IoT devices become more integrated into financial operations, cybersecurity risks increase, necessitating the implementation of end-to-end encryption, multi-factor authentication, and AI-driven threat detection systems.

Despite these challenges, the future of IoT in financial services is promising. As 5G technology expands IoT connectivity and advances in AI-driven analytics enhance real-time decision-making, financial institutions will continue to leverage IoT to create more personalized, secure, and efficient financial solutions. The integration of IoT with blockchain technology could further enhance transparency and security in financial transactions, mitigating fraud risks and ensuring trust in digital payments. Additionally, IoT-enabled sustainable finance initiatives are gaining traction, where smart sensors track energy consumption, carbon emissions, and ESG (Environmental, Social, and Governance) metrics to promote ethical investing and green finance (Movahed et al., 2024).

As we move deeper into the Industry 5.0 era, IoT will redefine how financial services operate, shifting from static, rule-based systems to intelligent, adaptive ecosystems driven by real-time data. Financial institutions that embrace IoT will be better equipped to provide personalized, automated, and secure financial experiences, paving the way for a more connected and intelligent financial ecosystem that benefits businesses, consumers, and society as a whole.

4- SUSTAINABLE FINANCE AND GREEN FINTECH IN INDUSTRY 5.0

The intersection of sustainable finance and Green FinTech is gaining significant traction in the Industry 5.0 era, where technology-driven financial solutions align with environmental and social responsibility. Unlike Industry 4.0, which primarily emphasized automation and efficiency, Industry 5.0 places a stronger focus on human-centric innovation, sustainability, and ethical economic growth. This paradigm shift is driving financial institutions, investors, and policymakers to integrate environmental, social, and governance (ESG) principles into financial decision-making, ensuring that economic progress does not come at the expense of environmental degradation or social inequality.

One of the most significant advancements in sustainable finance is the use of artificial intelligence (AI) and big data analytics to assess and predict the environmental impact of investments. Traditional financial models often relied on historical data and static metrics to evaluate risk, but modern AI-driven tools now provide real-time ESG analytics, helping investors make data-driven decisions that promote sustainability. These AI-powered platforms aggregate data from multiple sources, including corporate sustainability reports, government policies, and satellite imagery, to offer a comprehensive assessment of an organization's environmental footprint. The ability to analyze carbon emissions, energy consumption, and supply chain sustainability in real-time has made it easier for investors to align their portfolios with green finance principles.

The adoption of blockchain technology in Green FinTech has further enhanced transparency and accountability in sustainable finance. One of the key challenges in ESG investing has been the lack of reliable and standardized data, leading to concerns about greenwashing—where companies falsely claim to be environmentally responsible. Blockchain offers a decentralized and immutable ledger where ESG data can be securely stored and verified, eliminating the risk of data manipulation. This ensures that financial institutions, investors, and regulators have access to trustworthy, tamper-proof records of environmental performance metrics. Additionally, blockchain-based carbon credit trading platforms have emerged, allowing businesses to buy, sell, and track carbon offsets with full transparency, ensuring compliance with global climate policies.

The role of IoT and smart sensors in sustainable finance is also growing rapidly. These technologies provide real-time monitoring of energy usage, water consumption, and carbon footprints, allowing financial institutions to design green loans and sustainable investment products. Banks and insurers are now leveraging IoT-driven data to offer dynamic sustainability-linked financial incentives, where companies demonstrating lower carbon emissions or higher energy efficiency receive preferential interest rates and lower insurance premiums. The integration of IoT in financial services ensures that sustainability is not just a theoretical concept but an actionable, measurable reality.

One of the fastest-growing segments of Green FinTech is the rise of sustainable digital banking solutions, where financial institutions integrate eco-friendly financial products and services. Many banks are now offering green bonds, ESG-compliant investment portfolios, and carbon-neutral credit cards that allow consumers to track and offset their carbon footprint with every purchase. Digital banking platforms are also implementing AI-driven personal finance tools that encourage users to adopt more sustainable spending habits by offering insights into their ecological impact.

Table 2 highlights key technological advancements in Green FinTech, their benefits, and the challenges associated with their implementation:

Table 2. Key Innovations in Green FinTech and Their Impact

Technology	Benefits	Challenges
AI and Big Data in ESG Analysis	Real-time monitoring, accurate sustainability assessment	Data availability and standardization issues
Blockchain for ESG Compliance	Tamper-proof sustainability reporting, carbon credit trading	High energy consumption of some blockchain systems
IoT and Smart Sensors	Real-time tracking of energy and carbon footprint	Cybersecurity risks and data privacy concerns
Sustainable Digital Banking	Personalized green financial products, carbon tracking	Integration with traditional banking infrastructure
Green Bonds & Sustainable Investments	Financial incentives for eco-friendly projects	Regulatory challenges and evolving ESG metrics

As Green FinTech continues to evolve, regulatory frameworks and global financial policies must adapt to ensure that sustainability-driven finance remains transparent, ethical, and scalable. While the financial sector is making significant progress in integrating sustainable technologies, challenges such as data reliability, regulatory inconsistencies, and financial accessibility remain critical barriers. Governments and financial institutions must work collaboratively to establish standardized ESG reporting frameworks, ensuring that sustainability data is consistent, comparable, and verifiable across industries and regions.

The future of sustainable finance and Green FinTech in Industry 5.0 will be defined by its ability to balance economic growth with environmental responsibility. Emerging technologies such as quantum computing hold the potential to revolutionize ESG analytics, enabling hyper-accurate climate risk modeling and sustainability forecasting. Additionally, advancements in decentralized finance (DeFi) and tokenized ESG assets may further democratize access to green finance, allowing individuals and businesses worldwide to participate in sustainable economic activities without reliance on traditional banking institutions.

Ultimately, the integration of AI, blockchain, IoT, and other disruptive technologies into financial services is shaping a future where sustainability is no longer a secondary concern but a core pillar of financial decision-making. As Green FinTech continues to mature, financial institutions that embrace technological innovation and ethical finance practices will not only drive long-term economic stability but also contribute to a more resilient, sustainable, and inclusive global economy.

5- CONCLUSION

The convergence of Industry 5.0 technologies and financial innovations is reshaping the financial sector, driving a fundamental transformation in how transactions, investments, and risk management are conducted. Unlike its predecessor, which primarily emphasized automation and efficiency, Industry 5.0 places a strong emphasis on human-centric, sustainable, and intelligent financial solutions. The integration of Artificial Intelligence (AI), Machine Learning (ML), Blockchain, the Internet of Things (IoT), and Quantum Computing has enabled financial institutions to offer more personalized, efficient, and secure financial services, but it has also introduced new regulatory, ethical, and cybersecurity challenges.

AI and ML have significantly enhanced financial operations by improving risk assessment, automating trading strategies, and optimizing fraud detection mechanisms. However, concerns over algorithmic biases, transparency, and accountability highlight the need for regulatory oversight and the development of explainable AI models. Similarly, blockchain and decentralized finance (DeFi) are transforming banking, lending, and investment by enabling transparent, trustless financial ecosystems, but their widespread adoption is still hindered by regulatory uncertainties and scalability limitations. Meanwhile, IoT-driven financial services have introduced real-time monitoring capabilities, improving security, customer experiences, and data-driven decision-making, yet they also raise significant concerns over data privacy and cybersecurity vulnerabilities.

A key component of financial innovation in Industry 5.0 is its alignment with sustainability and ethical finance. The rise of Green FinTech has facilitated the integration of Environmental, Social, and Governance (ESG) principles into financial decision-making. AI-powered ESG analytics, blockchain-based carbon credit trading, and IoT-driven sustainability tracking are providing investors and policymakers with real-time insights into environmental impact. However, despite these advancements, regulatory inconsistencies, data standardization issues, and the risk of greenwashing remain critical barriers to achieving a truly sustainable financial system.

As financial technologies continue to evolve, the biggest challenge will be to balance innovation with regulatory compliance, ethical considerations, and financial stability. Governments, financial institutions, and technology developers must work together to develop robust frameworks that ensure transparency, security, and fairness in AI-driven and blockchain-based financial systems. The financial sector must also address data privacy concerns, cybersecurity risks, and the ethical implications of AI-driven decision-making to build public trust in emerging financial technologies.

Looking forward, the future of financial innovation in Industry 5.0 will depend on its ability to create a resilient, inclusive, and sustainable global financial ecosystem. By leveraging cutting-edge technologies responsibly and ethically, financial institutions can drive long-term economic growth while ensuring that technological progress serves both financial and societal well-being.

REFERENCES

Aliahmadi, M. H., Movahed, A. B., Movahed, A. B., Nozari, H., & Bayanati, M. (2024). Hospital 6.0 Components and Dimensions. In *Advanced Businesses in Industry 6.0* (pp. 46-61). IGI Global.

George, A. S., & Baskar, T. (2024). The Transformational Impact of AI Innovation on Financial Sectors in the Industry 5.0 Era. *Partners Universal International Innovation Journal, 2*(6), 09-13.

Mahawar, P., Bajaj, S., & Kashyap, S. V. (2024). Banking in the Age of Industry 5.0: Charting a Path to Technological Transformation. In *Industry 5.0 and Emerging Technologies: Transformation Through Technology and Innovations* (pp. 393–408). Springer Nature Switzerland. DOI: 10.1007/978-3-031-70996-8_19

Movahed, A. B., Movahed, A. B., Aliahmadi, B., & Nozari, H. (2024). Green and Sustainable Supply Chain in Agriculture 6.0. In *Advanced Businesses in Industry 6.0* (pp. 32-45). IGI Global.

Movahed, A. B., Movahed, A. B., & Nozari, H. (2024). Opportunities and challenges of smart supply chain in Industry 5.0. *Information Logistics for Organizational Empowerment and Effective Supply Chain Management*, 108-138.

Movahed, A. B., Movahed, A. B., Nozari, H., & Rahmaty, M. (2024). Security Criteria in Financial Systems in Industry 6.0. In *Advanced Businesses in Industry 6.0* (pp. 62-74). IGI Global.

Muzaffar, M., Ghouse, G., & Alahmad, F. A. (2024). Assessing the Interplay of Financial Development, Human Capital, Democracy, and Industry 5.0 in Environmental Dynamics. *Sustainability (Basel)*, 16(16), 6846. DOI: 10.3390/su16166846

Najafi, S. E., Nozari, H., & Edalatpanah, S. A. (2022). Artificial Intelligence of Things (AIoT) and Industry 4.0–Based Supply Chain (FMCG Industry). *A Roadmap for Enabling Industry 4.0 by Artificial Intelligence*, 31-41.

Nozari, H., Szmelter-Jarosz, A., & Ghahremani-Nahr, J. (2021). The ideas of sustainable and green marketing based on the internet of everything—The case of the dairy industry. *Future Internet*, 13(10), 266. DOI: 10.3390/fi13100266

Nozari, H., Tavakkoli-Moghaddam, R., & Dolgui, A. (2024, September). Analysis of Critical Success Factors of Sustainable and Resilient Aioe-based Supply Chain in Industry 5.0. In *IFIP International Conference on Advances in Production Management Systems* (pp. 76-90). Cham: Springer Nature Switzerland. DOI: 10.1007/978-3-031-65894-5_6

Rahmaty, M., & Nozari, H. (2023). Optimization of the hierarchical supply chain in the pharmaceutical industry. *Edelweiss Applied Science and Technology*, 7(2), 104–123. DOI: 10.55214/25768484.v7i2.376

Tavakkoli-Moghaddam, R., Nozari, H., Bakhshi-Movahed, A., & Bakhshi-Movahed, A. (2024). A Conceptual Framework for the Smart Factory 6.0. In *Advanced Businesses in Industry 6.0* (pp. 1–14). IGI Global. DOI: 10.4018/979-8-3693-3108-8.ch001

Chapter 14
The Role of the Internet of Everything (IoE) in Smart Economic Ecosystems

Maryam Rahmaty
https://orcid.org/0000-0003-3772-4216
Islamic Azad University, Chalous, Iran

ABSTRACT

The Internet of Everything (IoE) is transforming smart economies by integrating people, devices, processes, and data into intelligent, interconnected ecosystems. This research explores the economic impact, key applications, and challenges of IoE-driven smart economies, emphasizing real-time decision-making, automation, and blockchain-based transactions. While IoE enhances efficiency, cybersecurity risks, data privacy concerns, and workforce disruptions remain major challenges. Addressing these issues through policy frameworks and advanced security measures is crucial for sustainable IoE adoption and economic resilience.

1- INTRODUCTION

The global economy is undergoing a profound transformation, driven by the rapid advancement of digital technologies and the increasing integration of intelligent systems into everyday life. At the heart of this transformation lies the Internet of Everything (IoE)—a concept that extends beyond the Internet of Things (IoT) by incorporating not just devices, but also people, processes, and data into a seamless, interconnected ecosystem. Unlike traditional IoT systems, which focus primarily on

DOI: 10.4018/979-8-3693-4369-2.ch014

machine-to-machine (M2M) communication, IoE leverages artificial intelligence (AI), big data analytics, and real-time automation to create a truly dynamic economic landscape where businesses, governments, and individuals can make data-driven decisions with unprecedented efficiency (Tavakkoli-Moghaddam et al., 2024).

The rise of smart economic ecosystems, powered by IoE, marks a shift from conventional economic structures to highly adaptive, automated, and self-regulating systems. These ecosystems harness vast amounts of real-time data from interconnected sensors, intelligent networks, and cloud-based infrastructures to optimize supply chains, enhance financial transactions, improve public services, and drive sustainable development. Whether in smart cities, digital finance, manufacturing, or healthcare, IoE enables economic actors to engage in hyper-efficient resource allocation, predictive decision-making, and seamless interactions across multiple domains. In this new paradigm, traditional economic models, which relied on static policies and human intuition, are rapidly being replaced by intelligent, self-optimizing systems that continuously evolve based on data-driven insights (Movahed et al., 2024).

Despite its vast potential, the implementation of IoE-driven economic systems presents numerous challenges and risks. Concerns over cybersecurity, data privacy, regulatory policies, and workforce disruptions pose significant hurdles that must be addressed to ensure sustainable economic growth. As more industries embrace automation, AI-driven decision-making, and blockchain-powered transactions, the need for robust governance frameworks and ethical AI integration becomes increasingly critical. Moreover, the disparity between technologically advanced regions and developing economies raises questions about digital inclusion and equitable access to smart economic opportunities (Ghahremani-Nahr et al., 2022).

This chapter explores the foundational principles of IoE, its key components, and the transformative impact it has on modern economic systems. It examines the ways in which IoE is reshaping industries, optimizing financial structures, and fostering sustainable economic ecosystems. Additionally, the discussion delves into the challenges, risks, and regulatory considerations associated with large-scale IoE adoption. Finally, the chapter highlights emerging technological trends and future opportunities, paving the way for a smarter, more connected global economy. By the end of this discussion, it will be evident that the Internet of Everything is not merely a technological advancement—it is a paradigm shift that is redefining how economies function in the digital age.

2- LITERATURE REVIEW

The concept of the Internet of Everything (IoE) has emerged as a fundamental driver of the digital economy, transforming traditional economic structures into smart, interconnected ecosystems. Building upon the foundation of the Internet of Things (IoT), IoE extends beyond machine-to-machine communication by integrating people, processes, and data into intelligent networks. This transition has been examined across various disciplines, including industrial automation, smart cities, digital finance, and supply chain optimization, highlighting its role in enhancing operational efficiency, decision-making capabilities, and economic sustainability (Movahed et al., 2023).

Early discussions on digital connectivity predominantly focused on IoT, which revolved around connecting physical devices through networked communication. The expansion toward IoE marked a shift from device-centric automation to a human-centric, process-driven, and data-integrated model. Unlike IoT, which primarily enables passive data collection, IoE employs artificial intelligence (AI), edge computing, and big data analytics to facilitate active decision-making and predictive automation. The literature suggests that this advancement has significantly improved real-time responsiveness across multiple industries, leading to greater adaptability and efficiency in economic systems.

The role of IoE in smart economies has been widely explored, emphasizing its capacity to optimize business operations, streamline financial transactions, and enhance service delivery. Within smart economic ecosystems, interconnected devices and intelligent networks provide continuous data streams that facilitate automated decision-making and real-time analytics. This connectivity enables businesses to predict market trends, governments to implement data-driven policies, and consumers to engage in personalized economic interactions. Studies indicate that industries leveraging IoE-based systems experience improved productivity, cost reductions, and enhanced customer engagement, as smart economic models prioritize efficiency and personalization over traditional rigid frameworks.

A key area of focus within smart economies is IoE-driven financial ecosystems, where the integration of blockchain, AI-driven financial analytics, and decentralized finance (DeFi) has transformed traditional banking and investment mechanisms. Digital payment infrastructures powered by IoE facilitate secure, transparent, and frictionless transactions, reducing dependence on intermediaries and increasing financial inclusion. Literature in this domain underscores the shift toward algorithmic trading, AI-powered risk assessments, and smart contract automation, all of which are revolutionizing economic transactions in the digital era (Das et al., 2024).

The industrial sector has witnessed a significant transformation with the adoption of IoE in smart manufacturing and supply chain management. The literature highlights the shift from conventional production models to intelligent, data-driven manufacturing systems enabled by cyber-physical integration, digital twins, and real-time monitoring. These advancements facilitate predictive maintenance, automated resource allocation, and supply chain optimization, reducing inefficiencies and minimizing operational disruptions (Ghahremani-Nahr et al., 2023).

Smart logistics has also been a major beneficiary of IoE-driven automation, with autonomous delivery systems, AI-powered fleet management, and predictive demand forecasting reshaping supply chain operations. Studies suggest that integrating IoE with blockchain enhances transparency and traceability, addressing longstanding challenges in logistics such as counterfeit goods, supply chain fraud, and inventory mismanagement. These innovations contribute to the emergence of fully automated, self-regulating supply chains, which optimize efficiency while reducing environmental impact (Nozari, 2023).

Governments and public institutions have increasingly turned to IoE-powered governance models, which leverage real-time data analytics, AI-driven policy-making, and automated public service systems. Literature in this domain explores the implementation of smart infrastructure, digital identification systems, and AI-enhanced decision-making, all of which contribute to responsive governance and efficient urban management.

Smart cities serve as a prime example of IoE integration in governance, where sensor-based urban planning, AI-powered traffic management, and intelligent energy grids enhance public service delivery. Studies highlight the ability of IoE to reduce urban congestion, optimize energy consumption, and improve public safety through interconnected, adaptive systems. Additionally, the use of IoE in emergency response management has been recognized for its role in enabling real-time crisis prediction, automated resource deployment, and AI-assisted disaster mitigation strategies (Lata et al., 2021).

Despite its numerous advantages, IoE adoption presents several challenges and risks, which have been widely debated in the literature. One of the most pressing concerns is cybersecurity, as the expansion of interconnected systems increases vulnerability to cyberattacks, data breaches, and malicious interventions. The interconnected nature of IoE amplifies potential risks, requiring the development of advanced encryption protocols, decentralized security models, and AI-powered threat detection systems (Fallah & Nozari, 2021).

Another challenge frequently discussed is data privacy and ethical considerations in IoE deployment. The vast amount of real-time, continuously collected personal data raises concerns over consumer consent, data ownership, and surveillance risks. Regulatory discussions highlight the need for comprehensive data governance frameworks, transparent AI regulations, and consumer protection mechanisms to ensure responsible data utilization (Aliahmadi et al., 2022).

Economic and workforce implications also form a crucial part of the discourse surrounding IoE. While IoE-driven automation enhances efficiency, it has also led to concerns over job displacement, skill gaps, and socioeconomic inequalities. The literature suggests that addressing these challenges requires retraining programs, policy interventions, and inclusive digital economy strategies to mitigate the risks associated with widespread automation (Solanki et al., 2022).

Recent discussions in the field highlight several emerging trends that will shape the future of IoE in smart economies. The convergence of IoE with AI, blockchain, and quantum computing is expected to enhance economic decision-making, increase security, and drive greater efficiency in global markets. 6G networks and edge computing are also projected to redefine real-time connectivity and data processing, enabling faster, more intelligent economic interactions (Nozari & Nahr, 2022).

As digital transformation continues, literature suggests that policy development, ethical considerations, and cybersecurity advancements will play a critical role in shaping IoE's future trajectory. Governments, businesses, and technology developers must collaborate to create a secure, scalable, and sustainable IoE-driven economic ecosystem, ensuring that the benefits of digital interconnectivity are accessible, equitable, and resilient against emerging risks.

The literature on IoE and smart economic ecosystems provides a comprehensive understanding of how interconnected systems are reshaping industries, governance, and financial infrastructures. From enhancing industrial automation to redefining digital finance and public services, IoE stands at the forefront of economic transformation. However, as with any technological evolution, its widespread adoption necessitates robust security frameworks, regulatory oversight, and strategic policy implementations. Future research and development in this field will continue to refine IoE's role in driving efficiency, inclusivity, and sustainability in the digital economy.

3- UNDERSTANDING THE INTERNET OF EVERYTHING

The Internet of Everything (IoE) represents an advanced stage of digital connectivity, where not only devices but also people, processes, and data are seamlessly integrated into a single intelligent network. It expands beyond the traditional Internet of Things (IoT) by fostering a more comprehensive and interactive environment where automation, real-time decision-making, and predictive analytics drive efficiency across industries. Unlike IoT, which primarily focuses on machine-to-machine (M2M) communication, IoE incorporates human interaction, intelligent automation, and real-time adaptability, enabling a more dynamic and responsive digital ecosystem.

At its core, IoE consists of four primary components—people, devices, processes, and data—each playing a crucial role in establishing an interconnected system that fosters continuous communication and intelligent decision-making. People, as active participants, interact with smart systems through wearable devices, AI-driven virtual assistants, and digital platforms that personalize experiences based on real-time inputs. Devices, embedded with sensors and connected through the cloud, function as the foundation of IoE by collecting, transmitting, and responding to vast amounts of data. Processes, powered by artificial intelligence and machine learning, orchestrate interactions between people and devices, optimizing workflows, automating tasks, and facilitating seamless communication between different entities. Data, which serves as the lifeblood of IoE, is continuously generated, analyzed, and transformed into actionable insights that improve decision-making in various economic sectors (Nozari & Edalatpanah, 2023).

One of the defining characteristics of IoE is its ability to transition from passive data collection to proactive decision-making. Unlike IoT, where devices primarily transmit information without actively influencing economic processes, IoE enables smart systems to anticipate needs, make autonomous adjustments, and enhance user experiences. For instance, in a smart economic ecosystem, an interconnected supply chain can detect real-time fluctuations in demand, adjust production schedules accordingly, and optimize logistics routes, all without direct human intervention. Similarly, financial institutions leveraging IoE can utilize AI-driven algorithms to predict market trends, automate trading, and detect fraudulent activities with greater accuracy.

The shift from IoT to IoE marks a fundamental evolution in economic connectivity and automation. IoT introduced a world where devices could communicate and perform automated tasks based on predefined parameters. However, IoE enhances this connectivity by integrating human intelligence, advanced AI, and predictive analytics, allowing for more fluid, responsive, and efficient operations. This transformation has led to the emergence of self-learning systems, where networks continuously evolve based on real-time data, improving their ability to optimize resources, enhance security, and drive sustainable economic growth (Nozari et al., 2023).

The potential of IoE is most evident in smart economic ecosystems, where interconnected devices, people, and processes work together to create a highly efficient and adaptable digital infrastructure. In smart cities, for example, traffic management systems analyze data from sensors, GPS devices, and mobile applications to dynamically adjust signals, reduce congestion, and optimize public transportation routes. In healthcare, IoE-driven systems enable remote monitoring of patients, allowing for real-time diagnostics and automated adjustments to treatment plans. Similarly, in digital finance, AI-powered algorithms use IoE-generated insights to facilitate faster, more secure, and more personalized banking services (Najafi et al., 2022).

Despite its vast potential, the widespread adoption of IoE presents challenges related to cybersecurity, data privacy, and regulatory compliance. The interconnectivity of billions of devices increases the risk of cyberattacks, data breaches, and unauthorized access, necessitating the development of advanced encryption protocols, decentralized security models, and AI-driven threat detection mechanisms. Additionally, ethical concerns surrounding data ownership, user consent, and automated decision-making require policymakers to establish comprehensive legal frameworks that protect individuals while enabling continued innovation.

As technological advancements continue to push the boundaries of IoE, its integration with emerging technologies such as quantum computing, edge computing, and blockchain will further enhance its capabilities. Future IoE systems are expected to become even more autonomous, self-optimizing, and resilient against cybersecurity threats, paving the way for a fully interconnected, intelligent economic environment.

Ultimately, the Internet of Everything is not just a technological development but a paradigm shift in how digital connectivity influences economic activity. By enabling seamless interactions between people, devices, processes, and data, IoE is shaping a future where smart economic ecosystems operate autonomously, efficiently, and sustainably, redefining the way businesses, governments, and individuals engage with the digital world.

4- SMART ECONOMIC ECOSYSTEMS IN THE DIGITAL AGE

The modern economy is undergoing a digital revolution, transforming from traditional linear models into highly interconnected, intelligent, and adaptive ecosystems. At the core of this transformation is the Internet of Everything (IoE), which integrates people, devices, data, and processes into a unified network that fosters real-time decision-making, automation, and personalized economic interactions. Smart economic ecosystems leverage AI, blockchain, big data, and cloud computing to create self-optimizing environments where businesses, governments, and consumers can engage seamlessly in a digital-first economy.

One of the defining characteristics of smart economic ecosystems is their ability to process and analyze vast amounts of real-time data to optimize financial transactions, supply chain operations, governance models, and consumer experiences. For example, in financial markets, AI-driven trading algorithms utilize IoE data to predict trends, automate transactions, and reduce market volatility. In smart supply chains, interconnected IoE sensors track goods in real time, optimize logistics routes, and minimize waste, resulting in cost-efficient and sustainable operations.

A crucial aspect of this transformation is the shift toward decentralized financial transactions through blockchain and smart contracts. Unlike traditional centralized banking systems, blockchain-powered ecosystems offer secure, transparent, and autonomous transactions, reducing the dependency on intermediaries and lowering operational costs. The use of smart contracts in economic transactions further enhances automation, allowing for self-executing agreements based on predefined conditions, significantly improving transaction efficiency and reducing fraud (Aliahmadi & Nozari, 2023).

The adoption of IoE in various economic sectors has been growing rapidly. The financial sector leads in IoE implementation, with 85% adoption of AI-driven financial analytics and blockchain solutions. Manufacturing, supply chain, and smart cities follow closely, as businesses integrate IoE technologies to enhance efficiency, reduce operational risks, and transition toward sustainable economic models. The healthcare industry, while slower in adoption, is increasingly utilizing IoE-driven remote patient monitoring, AI diagnostics, and predictive healthcare analytics, ensuring more personalized and preventive medical solutions. This trend is illustrated in Figure 1, which shows the adoption of IoE in various economic sectors.

Figure 1. Adoption of IoE in Various Economic Sectors

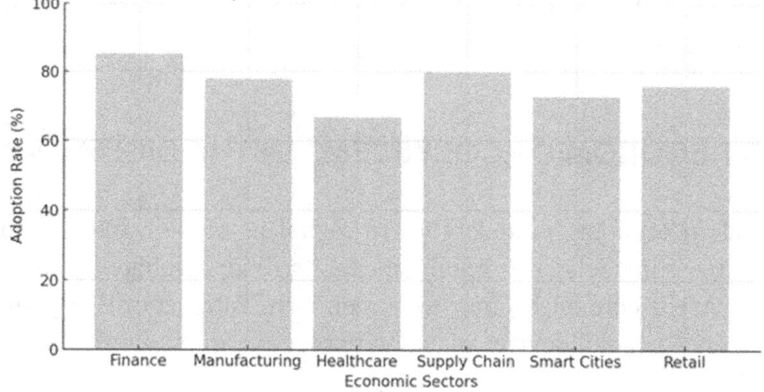

The key features of smart economic ecosystems are summarized in Table 1, highlighting how IoE enhances various sectors through real-time data processing, AI-driven decision-making, and blockchain-based transactions. These components work together to create highly adaptive and self-regulating digital economies.

Table 1. Key Features of Smart Economic Ecosystems

Feature	Description
Real-Time Data Processing	Continuous monitoring and analysis of economic activities for efficiency.
AI-Driven Decision Making	Machine learning and AI-driven insights for adaptive economic strategies.
Blockchain-Based Transactions	Decentralized, secure, and transparent economic transactions.
Automated Supply Chain Management	Optimization of logistics, inventory, and distribution through IoE.
Smart Infrastructure & Governance	AI-powered governance models for public services and economic policies.
IoE-Powered Personalization	Personalized user experiences through interconnected smart services.
Cybersecurity & Risk Mitigation	AI-driven security frameworks to prevent fraud and cyber threats.

As smart economic ecosystems continue to evolve, governance and public sector services are also undergoing a digital transformation. Governments are leveraging IoE to implement AI-driven policymaking, intelligent taxation systems, and automated public service delivery. Smart infrastructure, powered by IoE, enables real-time traffic management, dynamic energy distribution, and AI-enhanced urban planning, improving the overall quality of life for citizens.

Despite its vast potential, the expansion of smart economic ecosystems is accompanied by challenges related to cybersecurity, data privacy, and regulatory compliance. The interconnected nature of IoE-based economies increases exposure to cyber threats, necessitating advanced encryption, decentralized security protocols, and AI-driven risk mitigation strategies. Moreover, ethical concerns regarding data ownership, user consent, and automation-driven job displacement require comprehensive policy interventions to ensure inclusivity, security, and economic sustainability (Aliahmadi et al., 2022).

The transition toward smart economic ecosystems is not just a technological advancement—it is a paradigm shift in how economic interactions take place. As digital connectivity continues to accelerate, businesses, policymakers, and consumers must embrace agile, data-driven, and AI-empowered models to harness the full potential of IoE-driven economies. By overcoming regulatory and cybersecurity challenges, the world can move toward a future where economic transactions, governance, and industries operate in a seamlessly connected, intelligent, and sustainable ecosystem.

5- CHALLENGES AND RISKS OF IOE IN SMART ECONOMIES

As the Internet of Everything (IoE) continues to reshape economic landscapes by integrating people, devices, processes, and data into interconnected ecosystems, several challenges and risks have emerged that could hinder its full potential. These challenges span across cybersecurity, data privacy, economic disruptions, regulatory frameworks, and infrastructure limitations, posing significant concerns for policymakers, businesses, and consumers alike. Understanding and addressing these challenges is essential to ensuring the sustainable and secure adoption of IoE in smart economies (Nozari et al., 2022).

One of the most pressing concerns in the implementation of IoE is cybersecurity. The interconnected nature of IoE expands the attack surface, making smart economies vulnerable to cyberattacks, hacking, and data breaches. As more devices and processes are connected, the risk of malware, ransomware, and unauthorized access increases, necessitating robust encryption protocols, multi-factor authentication, and AI-driven threat detection systems. Cybersecurity threats account for a significant portion of the challenges, as depicted in Figure 1, which illustrates the distribution of challenges in IoE implementation.

Figure 2. Distribution of Challenges in IoE Implementation in Smart Economies

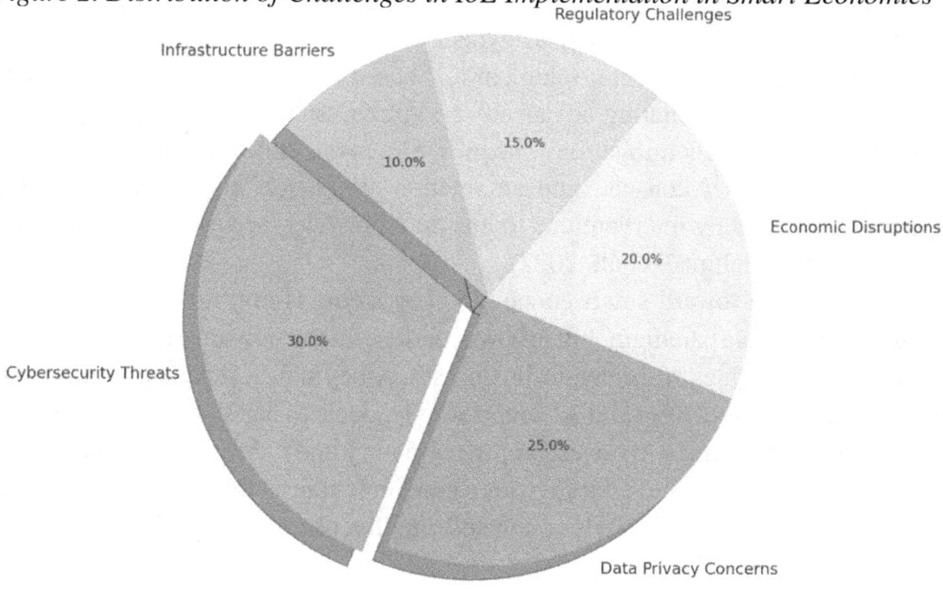

Data privacy is another critical issue, as IoE systems continuously collect and process vast amounts of personal and sensitive information. Concerns over user consent, data ownership, and surveillance have raised questions about the ethical use of data in smart economies. Without clear data governance policies, there is a risk of misuse or overreach, leading to a loss of consumer trust and potential legal repercussions. The need for transparent data handling practices and strict compliance with global privacy regulations such as the General Data Protection Regulation (GDPR) is paramount to building a secure and trustworthy IoE environment (Kumar et al., 2025).

Economic disruptions pose additional challenges, particularly in terms of workforce displacement and market volatility. As automation and AI-driven decision-making become more prevalent, traditional jobs may be rendered obsolete, leading to unemployment and socio-economic disparities. The transition to IoE-enabled economies requires retraining programs, skill development initiatives, and inclusive policies to ensure that the workforce can adapt to new roles within a digital-first economy. Moreover, the reliance on real-time data and automated systems can exacerbate market fluctuations, as rapid decision-making in financial markets may lead to unintended economic consequences (Shahinzadeh et al., 2019).

Regulatory and policy challenges also play a significant role in the adoption of IoE. The lack of standardized regulations and international cooperation can create barriers to the seamless implementation of IoE technologies. Varying legal frameworks, compliance requirements, and governance models across countries hinder the development of a unified smart economy. Effective regulation must balance innovation and consumer protection, ensuring that IoE can thrive while safeguarding the rights and interests of all stakeholders.

Infrastructure limitations, especially in developing regions, represent another significant hurdle. The deployment of IoE requires reliable internet connectivity, advanced telecommunications networks, and robust cloud infrastructure. In areas lacking these foundational elements, the benefits of IoE remain out of reach, creating a digital divide that exacerbates global inequalities. Investments in telecommunications, data centers, and edge computing are essential to making IoE accessible and functional across diverse geographic regions.

Despite these challenges, the path toward integrating IoE into smart economies remains promising. Addressing cybersecurity risks through advanced encryption and AI-driven security measures, ensuring data privacy with transparent governance frameworks, mitigating economic disruptions with proactive workforce development, and harmonizing regulatory policies are crucial steps in overcoming barriers. Additionally, enhancing infrastructure through public-private partnerships and international cooperation can provide the foundation necessary for a secure, inclusive, and resilient IoE ecosystem.

In conclusion, while the adoption of IoE in smart economies presents unprecedented opportunities for efficiency, innovation, and personalization, it also brings forth substantial challenges that must be strategically managed. By developing comprehensive policies, investing in secure infrastructure, and fostering a culture of digital literacy, smart economies can leverage the transformative power of IoE while mitigating its inherent risks.

6- CONCLUSION

The Internet of Everything (IoE) is revolutionizing the way economy's function, enabling a highly interconnected, intelligent, and automated economic landscape. As digital transformation accelerates, IoE has emerged as a fundamental driver of smart economic ecosystems, facilitating seamless interaction between people, devices, processes, and data. From financial systems and industrial automation to healthcare and public governance, the integration of IoE has introduced unprecedented levels of efficiency, adaptability, and predictive intelligence. However, while IoE offers remarkable opportunities for economic growth, innovation, and sustainability, its adoption also brings critical challenges and risks that must be carefully managed.

One of the most significant contributions of IoE to smart economies is its ability to leverage real-time data analytics and AI-driven decision-making to optimize business operations and public services. By enhancing automation, personalization, and self-regulation, IoE is reshaping industries, reducing inefficiencies, and fostering economic growth in ways that were previously unimaginable. The integration of blockchain, AI, and cloud computing within IoE ecosystems further strengthens transparency, security, and operational efficiency, making digital transactions more seamless and secure. The adoption of smart contracts, AI-driven financial modeling, and automated supply chain logistics is already transforming industries, demonstrating the immense economic potential of IoE in an increasingly digital world.

Despite these advancements, the widespread implementation of IoE is not without risks. Cybersecurity vulnerabilities, data privacy concerns, workforce disruptions, regulatory gaps, and infrastructure limitations pose significant challenges to the seamless integration of IoE within smart economic ecosystems. As the number of interconnected devices continues to grow, the risk of cyberattacks, data breaches, and unauthorized access increases, requiring robust security measures, encryption protocols, and AI-enhanced cybersecurity frameworks. Moreover, ethical concerns related to data ownership, user consent, and algorithmic bias demand transparent governance frameworks and stricter compliance measures to protect consumer rights and prevent misuse of personal data.

From an economic perspective, the transition to IoE-powered smart economies raises concerns about job displacement and socio-economic inequalities. Automation and AI-driven decision-making processes, while improving efficiency, may lead to a reduction in traditional employment opportunities, necessitating workforce reskilling and policy interventions to ensure economic inclusivity. Additionally, the digital divide between developed and developing economies underscores the need for infrastructure investments and international cooperation to create a globally inclusive digital economy.

Looking ahead, the success of IoE in smart economies will depend on how effectively stakeholders address these challenges while harnessing its potential for innovation and economic advancement. Governments, businesses, and policymakers must collaborate to develop secure, scalable, and sustainable IoE frameworks that balance efficiency with security, innovation with regulation, and automation with workforce development. Investments in AI-driven cybersecurity, ethical AI governance, and smart infrastructure will be essential in building a resilient, adaptive, and intelligent digital economy.

In conclusion, while the Internet of Everything represents a transformative force in economic development, its impact will ultimately be shaped by the ability to manage risks, ensure equitable access, and implement responsible governance frameworks. By striking a balance between technological progress and regulatory oversight, smart economic ecosystems can evolve into sustainable, intelligent, and secure digital environments that enhance both economic prosperity and social well-being. The future of IoE in smart economies is promising, but realizing its full potential will require strategic innovation, policy coordination, and a commitment to ethical and sustainable digital transformation.

REFERENCES

Aliahmadi, A., & Nozari, H. (2023, January). Evaluation of security metrics in AIoT and blockchain-based supply chain by Neutrosophic decision-making method. In *Supply chain forum: an international journal* (Vol. 24, No. 1, pp. 31-42). Taylor & Francis. DOI: 10.1080/16258312.2022.2101898

Aliahmadi, A., Nozari, H., & Ghahremani-Nahr, J. (2022). A framework for IoT and Blockchain based on marketing systems with an emphasis on big data analysis. *International journal of Innovation in Marketing Elements, 2*(1), 25-34.

Aliahmadi, A., Nozari, H., Ghahremani-Nahr, J., & Szmelter-Jarosz, A. (2022). Evaluation of key impression of resilient supply chain based on artificial intelligence of things (AIoT). *arXiv preprint arXiv:2207.13174.*

Das, P., Jain, C., & Singh, M. (2024). Toward a trusted smart city ecosystem: IoE and blockchain-enabled cognitive frameworks for shared business Services. In *Industrial Internet of Things Security* (pp. 208–228). CRC Press. DOI: 10.1201/9781003466284-11

Fallah, M., & Nozari, H. (2021). Neutrosophic mathematical programming for optimization of multi-objective sustainable biomass supply chain network design. *Computer Modeling in Engineering & Sciences*, 129(2), 927–951. DOI: 10.32604/cmes.2021.017511

Ghahremani-Nahr, J., Najafi, S. E., & Nozari, H. (2022). A combined transportation model for the fruit and vegetable supply chain network. *Journal of Optimization in Industrial Engineering*, 15(2), 131–145.

Ghahremani-Nahr, J., Nozari, H., Rahmaty, M., Zeraati Foukolaei, P., & Sherejsharifi, A. (2023). Development of a novel fuzzy hierarchical location-routing optimization model considering reliability. *Logistics (Basel)*, 7(3), 64. DOI: 10.3390/logistics7030064

Kumar, M. S., Nagalakshmi, M. V. N., Reddy, C., Charan, Y. S. S., Kataria, A., & George, A. S. (2025). AI-Enhanced Real-Time Economic Data Analysis Using IoE. In *Role of Internet of Everything (IOE), VLSI Architecture, and AI in Real-Time Systems* (pp. 33-44). IGI Global Scientific Publishing.

Lata, M., & Kumar, V. (2021). 5 IoE Applications for Smart. *Internet of Energy for Smart Cities: Machine Learning Models and Techniques*, 127.

Movahed, A. B., Aliahmadi, A., Parsanejad, M., & Nozari, H. (2023). A systematic review of collaboration in supply chain 4.0 with meta-synthesis method. *Supply Chain Analytics*, 100052.

Movahed, A. B., Movahed, A. B., & Nozari, H. (2024). Opportunities and challenges of smart supply chain in Industry 5.0. *Information Logistics for Organizational Empowerment and Effective Supply Chain Management*, 108-138.

Najafi, S. E., Nozari, H., & Edalatpanah, S. A. (2022). Artificial Intelligence of Things (AIoT) and Industry 4.0–Based Supply Chain (FMCG Industry). *A Roadmap for Enabling Industry 4.0 by Artificial Intelligence*, 31-41.

Nozari, H. (Ed.). (2023). *Building Smart and Sustainable Businesses with Transformative Technologies*. IGI Global. DOI: 10.4018/979-8-3693-0210-1

Nozari, H., & Edalatpanah, S. A. (2023). Smart Systems Risk Management in IoT-Based Supply Chain. In *Advances in Reliability, Failure and Risk Analysis* (pp. 251–268). Springer Nature Singapore. DOI: 10.1007/978-981-19-9909-3_11

Nozari, H., Ghahremani-Nahr, J., & Najafi, E. (2023). The role of Internet of things and Blockchain in the development of agile and sustainable supply chains. In *Digital Supply Chain, Disruptive Environments, and the Impact on Retailers* (pp. 271-282). IGI Global. DOI: 10.4018/978-1-6684-7298-9.ch015

Nozari, H., & Nahr, J. G. (2022). The impact of blockchain technology and the internet of things on the agile and sustainable supply chain. *International Journal of Innovation in Engineering*, 2(2), 33–41. DOI: 10.59615/ijie.2.2.33

Nozari, H., Szmelter-Jarosz, A., & Ghahremani-Nahr, J. (2022). Analysis of the challenges of artificial intelligence of things (AIoT) for the smart supply chain (case study: FMCG industries). *Sensors (Basel)*, 22(8), 2931. DOI: 10.3390/s22082931 PMID: 35458916

Shahinzadeh, H., Moradi, J., Gharehpetian, G. B., Nafisi, H., & Abedi, M. (2019, February). Internet of Energy (IoE) in smart power systems. In *2019 5th Conference on Knowledge Based Engineering and Innovation (KBEI)* (pp. 627-636). IEEE.

Solanki, A. (Ed.). (2023). *Intelligent Systems for IoE Based Smart Cities*. Bentham Science Publishers. DOI: 10.2174/97898151249651230101

Tavakkoli-Moghaddam, R., Nozari, H., Bakhshi-Movahed, A., & Bakhshi-Movahed, A. (2024). A Conceptual Framework for the Smart Factory 6.0. In *Advanced Businesses in Industry 6.0* (pp. 1–14). IGI Global. DOI: 10.4018/979-8-3693-3108-8.ch001

Chapter 15
Transformation of SME Financing Models Using Disruptive Technologies

Farshad Kaveh
Islamic Azad University, Najafabad, Iran

Majid Mehrabi Delshad
Islamic Azad University, Parand, Iran

Adel Pourghader Chobar
https://orcid.org/0000-0002-8377-5906
Islamic Azad University, Qazvin, Iran

ABSTRACT

The evolution of SME financing is being reshaped by disruptive technologies such as blockchain, artificial intelligence, big data, and the Internet of Things. These innovations enhance financial accessibility, streamline credit assessment, and enable decentralized finance solutions. However, challenges such as regulatory uncertainties, cybersecurity risks, and algorithmic biases persist. This research explores the transformative impact of these technologies, addressing both opportunities and risks while proposing policy recommendations to ensure secure, inclusive, and efficient SME financing in an increasingly digital economy.

DOI: 10.4018/979-8-3693-4369-2.ch015

1- INTRODUCTION

Small and medium-sized enterprises (SMEs) form the backbone of economies worldwide, contributing significantly to employment, innovation, and economic stability. Despite their crucial role, SMEs have historically faced persistent challenges in securing adequate financing. Traditional financing mechanisms, primarily driven by banks and financial institutions, impose rigid requirements that often act as barriers for SMEs, particularly those in emerging markets. High collateral demands, lengthy credit approval processes, and stringent regulatory frameworks make it difficult for these businesses to access the funds they need to sustain operations and expand. The lack of comprehensive credit histories and financial transparency further exacerbates these challenges, leaving many SMEs financially underserved (Smuts et al., 2024).

The advent of disruptive technologies has initiated a paradigm shift in financial ecosystems, offering new avenues for SMEs to overcome these longstanding obstacles. The digital transformation of financial services has ushered in an era where alternative financing models, powered by technologies such as artificial intelligence (AI), blockchain, big data, and the Internet of Things (IoT), are reshaping access to capital. These innovations are dismantling traditional financial barriers by enabling decentralized, efficient, and data-driven decision-making processes. Fintech companies, leveraging cutting-edge technologies, are providing SMEs with alternative credit scoring mechanisms, peer-to-peer (P2P) lending platforms, and automated financing solutions that operate with greater flexibility and inclusivity.

Blockchain technology has emerged as a particularly disruptive force in SME financing. Through decentralized finance (DeFi) solutions, businesses can access funding without relying on traditional intermediaries. Smart contracts facilitate trustless transactions, ensuring transparency and security while reducing operational costs. The tokenization of assets allows SMEs to diversify their financing options, attracting investors globally without the need for complex legal frameworks. Moreover, blockchain-based financing mechanisms mitigate fraud risks, enhance transactional security, and increase liquidity in capital markets. As a result, SMEs that previously struggled to obtain bank loans are now finding alternative funding channels through decentralized platforms (Soni et al., 2022).

Artificial intelligence plays an equally transformative role in addressing the credit assessment challenges faced by SMEs. Conventional credit scoring models rely heavily on historical financial data, often excluding businesses with limited formal financial records. AI-driven algorithms, on the other hand, leverage alternative data sources, including transactional behaviors, market trends, and even real-time operational metrics, to assess creditworthiness with greater accuracy. By integrating machine learning models, financial institutions and fintech startups can offer SMEs more personalized and dynamic financing solutions. AI also enhances fraud detection capabilities, minimizing risks for both lenders and borrowers, while streamlining loan approval processes to make them more efficient and accessible (Soluk et al., 2023).

Big data analytics further strengthens SME financing by enabling more informed and predictive financial decision-making. By aggregating vast amounts of structured and unstructured data, financial entities can gain deeper insights into SME performance, industry trends, and risk factors. This data-driven approach allows for the creation of tailored financial products that align with the specific needs of businesses. Predictive analytics also enables lenders to proactively identify potential risks and adjust financing terms accordingly, fostering a more sustainable financial ecosystem. The ability to analyze market conditions in real-time ensures that SMEs receive timely financial support, reducing the likelihood of liquidity crises and business failures.

The Internet of Things (IoT) is also contributing to the evolution of SME financing, particularly in asset-backed lending and real-time financial tracking. IoT-enabled devices provide verifiable and real-time data on supply chain activities, inventory levels, and operational efficiency. Lenders can use this data to assess the financial health of SMEs more accurately and offer financing solutions that align with real-time business performance. By integrating IoT data with AI and blockchain, financial institutions can create highly adaptive and responsive financing models that cater to the dynamic nature of SME operations (Lijuan, 2025).

While disruptive technologies present immense opportunities for enhancing SME financing, their adoption is not without challenges. Issues related to regulatory compliance, data privacy, cybersecurity, and technological infrastructure remain key concerns that must be addressed. Governments and financial regulators are grappling with how to create policies that support innovation while ensuring financial stability and consumer protection. Additionally, SMEs themselves must adapt to these technological shifts, investing in digital literacy and infrastructure to fully leverage the benefits of emerging financial solutions.

The transformation of SME financing models through disruptive technologies marks a significant departure from conventional banking-driven approaches. As these technologies continue to evolve, they will play a pivotal role in bridging the financial inclusion gap, fostering innovation, and driving economic growth. The intersection of AI, blockchain, big data, and IoT is redefining the financial landscape, creating new opportunities for SMEs to thrive in an increasingly digital economy. This chapter explores the key technological advancements shaping SME financing, their practical applications, the challenges they present, and the future implications for financial ecosystems. By understanding these dynamics, policymakers, financial institutions, and business leaders can navigate the changing financial landscape and harness the full potential of disruptive technologies to empower SMEs (Masenya, 2023).

2- DISRUPTIVE TECHNOLOGIES RESHAPING SME FINANCING

The evolution of technology has fundamentally altered the financial landscape, introducing innovations that have redefined how small and medium-sized enterprises (SMEs) access capital. Traditional financing models, which rely heavily on credit histories, collateral requirements, and lengthy approval processes, have proven inadequate in addressing the dynamic needs of SMEs. The emergence of disruptive technologies, including blockchain, artificial intelligence (AI), big data analytics, and the Internet of Things (IoT), has provided alternative financing solutions that offer efficiency, inclusivity, and security. These technologies have not only lowered the barriers to accessing finance but have also introduced novel mechanisms for credit evaluation, transaction security, and real-time financial management (Lamperti et al., 2023).

One of the most transformative innovations in SME financing is blockchain technology. By eliminating the need for intermediaries, blockchain facilitates faster, more secure, and transparent financial transactions. The implementation of smart contracts automates agreements, reducing the reliance on manual verification and administrative costs. Additionally, decentralized finance (DeFi) platforms have provided SMEs with access to funding through peer-to-peer lending and asset tokenization. Unlike traditional financing, which requires a centralized authority, DeFi leverages blockchain to create trustless transactions, ensuring greater financial inclusion for businesses that struggle to secure conventional loans (Jibril et al., 2024).

Artificial intelligence has also emerged as a game-changer in credit assessment and risk management. Traditional credit evaluation methods primarily depend on financial records and past transactions, often excluding SMEs with limited formal documentation. AI-driven algorithms, on the other hand, analyze alternative data sources, including transaction patterns, social media activity, and industry trends, to generate comprehensive creditworthiness profiles. Machine learning models continuously adapt to new data, improving the accuracy of risk assessments and enabling lenders to offer customized financing solutions. Additionally, AI-powered chatbots and virtual financial advisors have enhanced customer interactions, providing SMEs with instant insights into their financial health and investment options.

Big data analytics complements AI by harnessing vast amounts of information to create predictive financial models. SMEs often face fluctuating market conditions that can impact their cash flow and financial stability. Through big data, lenders can assess industry-specific risks, monitor economic indicators, and tailor financing solutions based on real-time insights. The ability to analyze behavioral patterns and transaction histories allows financial institutions to detect fraud, prevent default risks, and offer more flexible repayment structures. The integration of big data into SME financing ensures that lending decisions are data-driven rather than based on rigid traditional assessments.

Another technological breakthrough transforming SME financing is the Internet of Things (IoT). IoT devices collect real-time data from business operations, allowing financial institutions to assess the performance and creditworthiness of SMEs more accurately. For instance, in asset-backed lending, IoT-enabled tracking systems provide lenders with visibility into inventory levels, equipment usage, and supply chain movements. This transparency minimizes the risks associated with lending, as financial institutions can monitor assets and adjust credit terms based on real-time business activity. Furthermore, IoT enhances financial automation by enabling real-time transactions and reducing operational delays (Kashif et al., 2024).

Table 1 summarizes the key disruptive technologies revolutionizing SME financing, along with their primary benefits:

Table 1. Key Disruptive Technologies in SME Financing and Their Benefits

Technology	Key Applications in SME Financing	Benefits for SMEs
Blockchain	Decentralized finance (DeFi), smart contracts, asset tokenization	Faster transactions, enhanced security, lower costs
Artificial Intelligence	Credit scoring, risk assessment, fraud detection	Improved credit access, personalized financial solutions
Big Data Analytics	Predictive modeling, behavioral analysis, fraud prevention	Better risk management, real-time financing solutions
Internet of Things (IoT)	Asset tracking, real-time financial monitoring, automated transactions	Transparent lending, optimized financial operations

The practical implications of these technologies are already visible in various sectors. Fintech companies leveraging blockchain have introduced platforms that facilitate seamless cross-border payments for SMEs, reducing transaction costs and eliminating the complexities of currency conversions. AI-powered lending platforms have enabled businesses with limited financial histories to access capital through alternative credit scoring models. Additionally, big data-driven risk assessment tools have allowed financial institutions to refine their lending criteria, offering tailored repayment plans that align with the cash flow patterns of SMEs (Mărăcine et al., 2020).

Despite these advancements, the integration of disruptive technologies in SME financing is not without challenges. Regulatory uncertainties, cybersecurity threats, and technological literacy gaps among SMEs remain significant hurdles. Many SMEs, particularly in developing economies, lack the necessary infrastructure to adopt blockchain-based financing models or implement AI-driven financial management systems. Moreover, the decentralized nature of blockchain poses challenges for regulatory oversight, raising concerns about fraud and compliance. Similarly, while AI enhances credit assessments, it also introduces ethical considerations regarding data privacy and algorithmic bias (Albats et al., 2023).

Nonetheless, the long-term potential of these technologies in shaping SME financing is undeniable. As financial ecosystems continue to evolve, policymakers and financial institutions must work collaboratively to establish regulatory frameworks that promote innovation while ensuring security and transparency. Investment in digital literacy programs for SMEs can further accelerate the adoption of these technologies, empowering businesses to leverage fintech solutions effectively.

In conclusion, the rise of disruptive technologies has redefined SME financing, introducing alternative funding mechanisms that are more inclusive, efficient, and adaptive to market dynamics. Blockchain, AI, big data, and IoT have collectively paved the way for a more transparent and data-driven financial ecosystem. While challenges persist, the ongoing digital transformation of financial services presents unprecedented opportunities for SMEs to overcome traditional barriers and achieve sustainable growth. As the financial industry continues to embrace technological advancements, SMEs must position themselves to harness the full potential of these innovations, ensuring long-term financial resilience in an increasingly digital economy.

3- CHALLENGES AND RISKS IN TECHNOLOGY-DRIVEN SME FINANCING

The integration of disruptive technologies into SME financing has introduced new opportunities for financial inclusion, efficiency, and transparency. However, these advancements also come with significant challenges and risks that must be carefully managed. While blockchain, artificial intelligence, big data, and the Internet of Things (IoT) have redefined financial accessibility, the transition to technology-driven financing is far from seamless. Issues related to regulatory compliance, cybersecurity threats, algorithmic bias, and the technological divide continue to pose barriers to widespread adoption. Addressing these challenges is critical to ensuring that SMEs can fully leverage the benefits of financial technologies while mitigating associated risks (Łasak, 2022).

One of the most pressing challenges in technology-driven SME financing is regulatory uncertainty. Many of the emerging financial models, particularly decentralized finance (DeFi) and blockchain-based lending, operate in a regulatory gray area. Governments and financial regulators struggle to keep pace with the rapid evolution of these technologies, leading to inconsistencies in regulatory frameworks across different jurisdictions. The lack of clear guidelines for smart contracts, digital asset tokenization, and peer-to-peer lending creates ambiguity for both SMEs and financial institutions. In some cases, overly restrictive regulations stifle innovation, preventing SMEs from accessing novel financing solutions. In others, the absence of oversight increases the risk of fraud, market manipulation, and financial instability.

Cybersecurity concerns present another significant risk in the adoption of financial technologies. As financial transactions become increasingly digitized, SMEs are more vulnerable to cyberattacks, data breaches, and identity theft. Blockchain technology, despite its promise of security, is not immune to risks, as smart contract vulnerabilities and hacking incidents have demonstrated. AI-driven financial platforms also rely on vast amounts of sensitive data, making them attractive targets for cybercriminals. Many SMEs lack the resources to implement robust cybersecurity measures, leaving them exposed to financial and reputational damage. Without adequate protections, the digital transformation of SME financing could lead to unintended consequences, including financial fraud and the loss of critical business information.

Algorithmic bias in AI-driven financing models poses another substantial risk. AI-based credit scoring systems, while designed to improve access to capital, may inadvertently reinforce existing biases. Machine learning algorithms are trained on historical data, which may reflect discriminatory lending practices or socio-economic disparities. As a result, certain SMEs, particularly those in underrepresented markets or industries, may face unjustified loan denials or unfavorable financing terms. The opacity of AI decision-making further complicates this issue, as businesses may struggle to understand why their loan applications were rejected. Ensuring fairness and transparency in AI-driven financial models requires continuous monitoring, diverse data training sets, and ethical AI governance frameworks (Gomber et al., 2018).

The technological divide between SMEs also contributes to disparities in financial access. While larger SMEs with advanced digital capabilities can seamlessly adopt fintech solutions, smaller businesses, particularly in developing economies, may struggle with technological literacy and infrastructure limitations. Many SMEs lack access to high-speed internet, digital payment systems, or cloud-based financial tools, creating a gap in their ability to engage with technology-driven financing models. Additionally, the upfront costs of implementing AI-driven financial management systems or blockchain-based payment solutions can be prohibitive for small businesses with limited capital. Bridging this gap requires investment in digital education, financial technology training programs, and affordable technological solutions tailored to SMEs' specific needs.

Another challenge in technology-driven SME financing is the volatility of digital assets. With the rise of blockchain-based financing models, some SMEs have turned to cryptocurrencies and tokenized assets as alternative funding sources. However, the high price volatility of digital currencies creates financial instability, making it difficult for SMEs to rely on these assets for long-term financing. A sudden drop in the value of a cryptocurrency-backed loan could result in financial distress, particularly for SMEs operating with tight profit margins. This uncertainty deters many businesses from adopting blockchain-based financial solutions, limiting the scalability of these innovations.

Table 2 provides an overview of the key challenges and risks associated with technology-driven SME financing, highlighting the primary concerns and potential implications for businesses.

Table 2. Challenges and Risks in Technology-Driven SME Financing

Challenge	Key Concerns	Potential Impact on SMEs
Regulatory Uncertainty	Lack of clear regulations for blockchain and AI-driven financing	Increased legal risks, barriers to adoption, inconsistent financial access
Cybersecurity Threats	Data breaches, hacking, identity theft	Financial loss, reputational damage, fraud risks
Algorithmic Bias in AI	Discriminatory credit scoring, lack of transparency	Unfair lending practices, reduced access to financing
Technological Divide	Limited digital infrastructure, lack of fintech literacy	Exclusion from digital financing, difficulty adopting fintech solutions
Volatility of Digital Assets	Unstable cryptocurrency valuations, market fluctuations	Financial instability, difficulty in securing stable funding sources

These challenges highlight the complexity of integrating emerging technologies into SME financing. While fintech solutions offer substantial benefits, they must be implemented with caution to avoid unintended financial risks. Addressing these issues requires a multi-stakeholder approach, involving policymakers, financial institutions, and technology developers. Regulatory bodies must establish comprehensive frameworks that balance innovation with security, ensuring that technology-driven financing remains both accessible and trustworthy. SMEs must also be equipped with the necessary tools and knowledge to navigate the digital financial ecosystem, ensuring that they can fully leverage new financing opportunities without exposing themselves to undue risks.

In conclusion, while disruptive technologies have the potential to transform SME financing, the associated challenges and risks must be carefully managed. Regulatory uncertainties, cybersecurity vulnerabilities, AI biases, technological disparities, and digital asset volatility all pose significant obstacles to widespread adoption. Overcoming these challenges requires a coordinated effort from financial regulators, technology developers, and SME stakeholders. By addressing these risks proactively, the financial industry can create a more inclusive, efficient, and secure ecosystem that enables SMEs to thrive in an increasingly digitized economy. As financial technologies continue to evolve, ensuring responsible and sustainable adoption will be crucial in unlocking their full potential for SME financing.

4- FUTURE TRENDS AND POLICY RECOMMENDATIONS

The landscape of SME financing is undergoing a profound transformation driven by the continuous evolution of disruptive technologies. As digital financial ecosystems mature, the future of SME financing will be characterized by increased automation, enhanced accessibility, and improved security. Emerging trends indicate that artificial intelligence, blockchain, decentralized finance, and embedded financial services will play an even greater role in shaping how small and medium-sized enterprises access capital. Alongside these advancements, policymakers and regulatory bodies must implement strategies that foster financial innovation while ensuring stability, inclusivity, and transparency.

One of the most promising future trends in SME financing is the growing adoption of AI-powered decision-making systems. As machine learning algorithms become more sophisticated, credit assessment models will rely on an even wider range of alternative data sources to evaluate creditworthiness. The expansion of AI-driven financial inclusion will enable SMEs in underserved regions to access credit based on real-time transactional data, supply chain activity, and customer feedback rather than traditional financial statements. The continuous refinement of AI models will lead to more dynamic and personalized financial products, allowing SMEs to secure funding tailored to their specific cash flow patterns and risk profiles (Oguanobi et al., 2024).

Blockchain technology will continue to revolutionize SME financing through the expansion of decentralized finance platforms. The rise of tokenized assets and smart contracts will enable businesses to raise funds through global crowdfunding initiatives without the need for traditional banking intermediaries. As regulatory clarity around digital assets improves, institutional investors are expected to become more involved in blockchain-based financing, providing SMEs with more liquidity options. The integration of central bank digital currencies (CBDCs) into SME financing ecosystems may also emerge as a stabilizing force, offering secure and government-backed digital payment methods that bridge the gap between traditional finance and decentralized financial models.

Another key trend shaping the future of SME financing is the proliferation of embedded financial services. Rather than seeking financing through traditional banking channels, SMEs will increasingly access financial products directly within the platforms they use for daily operations. E-commerce marketplaces, supply chain management software, and business-to-business (B2B) platforms will integrate financing solutions powered by AI and blockchain, allowing businesses to secure loans, manage cash flow, and access working capital without leaving their operational ecosystems. This shift toward embedded finance will streamline access to capital, reducing administrative burdens and improving the efficiency of financial transactions.

Despite these promising advancements, the successful integration of disruptive technologies into SME financing requires proactive policy interventions. Regulatory bodies must establish clear and adaptive frameworks that accommodate emerging financial models while safeguarding businesses from risks such as fraud, cyber threats, and algorithmic biases. Policymakers should work towards harmonizing regulations across jurisdictions to ensure that SMEs operating in global markets can leverage decentralized financing solutions without facing compliance complexities. Regulatory sandboxes, which allow fintech startups to test innovative financial products under supervised conditions, should be expanded to encourage responsible innovation in SME financing.

Cybersecurity and data protection must also be prioritized in financial policy reforms. As SMEs increasingly rely on digital financial platforms, robust cybersecurity standards should be mandated to protect sensitive business data from breaches and cyberattacks. Governments and financial institutions should collaborate to establish industry-wide best practices for data privacy, ensuring that AI-driven credit assessment models operate transparently and fairly. SME owners must be equipped with the necessary digital literacy skills to navigate fintech ecosystems safely, reducing their exposure to financial fraud and misinformation.

Another critical policy area is the promotion of financial inclusion through technology-driven financing models. Governments should incentivize financial institutions to adopt AI-driven credit assessment tools that accommodate SMEs with limited formal financial records. Initiatives such as alternative credit scoring frameworks and government-backed digital financing platforms can help bridge the gap for businesses that remain excluded from traditional financial systems. Additionally, fostering partnerships between fintech firms and traditional banks can enhance SME financing options by combining technological innovation with the trust and regulatory security offered by established financial institutions.

The integration of sustainability principles into SME financing policies is also gaining traction as businesses increasingly align their financial strategies with environmental, social, and governance (ESG) criteria. Future policy recommendations should encourage the development of green financing initiatives that leverage AI and blockchain to fund sustainable business practices. Tokenized carbon credit markets and blockchain-based supply chain transparency solutions can help SMEs secure financing based on their sustainability efforts, creating incentives for environmentally responsible business operations.

Looking ahead, the role of public-private collaborations in shaping the future of SME financing will be crucial. Governments, financial institutions, and technology firms must work together to design inclusive, secure, and scalable financing models that cater to the diverse needs of SMEs. Investment in research and development for AI-driven financial solutions, the establishment of digital identity frameworks for secure transactions, and the promotion of interoperable fintech ecosystems are all essential steps in fostering a resilient and future-ready financial landscape.

As digital finance continues to evolve, SMEs must remain adaptable and proactive in embracing technological advancements. While disruptive technologies present challenges, they also offer unprecedented opportunities for businesses to access flexible, transparent, and efficient financing solutions. Policymakers and industry leaders must strike a balance between innovation and regulation, ensuring that SME financing remains inclusive, secure, and responsive to the rapidly changing global economic environment. The coming years will witness the convergence of financial technologies, regulatory frameworks, and market dynamics, shaping a new era of SME financing that is smarter, more inclusive, and better equipped to support entrepreneurial growth.

5- CONCLUSION

The transformation of SME financing through disruptive technologies marks a significant shift from traditional, rigid financial systems to more flexible, inclusive, and efficient models. Emerging technologies such as blockchain, artificial intelligence, big data, and the Internet of Things have created new pathways for small and medium-sized enterprises to access capital, streamline financial operations, and improve creditworthiness. These innovations have addressed longstanding barriers, including limited credit access, high transaction costs, and lengthy approval processes, allowing SMEs to compete in an increasingly digital and globalized economy.

Despite these advancements, challenges such as regulatory uncertainty, cybersecurity risks, algorithmic biases, and the technological divide remain critical concerns. The integration of financial technologies must be accompanied by robust policies that ensure security, transparency, and fairness. Governments, financial institutions, and technology providers must collaborate to create regulatory frameworks that foster innovation while mitigating risks.

Looking ahead, the future of SME financing will be driven by the continued adoption of AI-powered decision-making, blockchain-based decentralized finance, and embedded financial services. As SMEs embrace these technologies, they must also develop digital capabilities to navigate the evolving financial landscape. By balancing innovation with responsible governance, the financial ecosystem can create a more resilient and inclusive environment that empowers SMEs to thrive.

REFERENCES

Albats, E., Podmetina, D., & Vanhaverbeke, W. (2023). Open innovation in SMEs: A process view towards business model innovation. *Journal of Small Business Management*, 61(6), 2519–2560. DOI: 10.1080/00472778.2021.1913595

Gomber, P., Kauffman, R. J., Parker, C., & Weber, B. W. (2018). On the fintech revolution: Interpreting the forces of innovation, disruption, and transformation in financial services. *Journal of Management Information Systems*, 35(1), 220–265. DOI: 10.1080/07421222.2018.1440766

Jibril, A. B., Amoah, J., Panigrahi, R. R., & Gochhait, S. (2024). Digital transformation in emerging markets: The role of technology adoption and innovative marketing strategies among SMEs in the post–pandemic era. *The International Journal of Organizational Analysis*. Advance online publication. DOI: 10.1108/IJOA-05-2024-4509

Kashif, M., Kumar, P., Ghai, S., & Kumar, S. (2024). Disruptive Technologies in Computational Finance. In *Algorithmic Approaches to Financial Technology: Forecasting, Trading, and Optimization* (pp. 46-60). IGI Global. DOI: 10.4018/979-8-3693-1746-4.ch003

Lamperti, S., Cavallo, A., & Sassanelli, C. (2023). Digital servitization and business model innovation in SMEs: A model to escape from market disruption. *IEEE Transactions on Engineering Management*, 71, 4619–4633. DOI: 10.1109/TEM.2022.3233132

Łasak, P. (2022). The role of financial technology and entrepreneurial finance practices in funding small and medium-sized enterprises. *Journal of Entrepreneurship. Management and Innovation*, 18(1), 7–34.

Lijuan, H. (2025). Enhancing SMEs Development Through Fintech: Insights from China's Economic Transformation. *International Journal of Education and Humanities*, 5(2), 257–265.

Mărăcine, V., Voican, O., & Scarlat, E. (2020, July). The digital transformation and disruption in business models of the banks under the impact of FinTech and BigTech. In *Proceedings of the international conference on business excellence* (Vol. 14, No. 1, pp. 294-305). DOI: 10.2478/picbe-2020-0028

Masenya, T. M. (2023). Digital Transformation in SMEs: Developing Digital Business Model Innovations Artificial Intelligence. *Business Models and Innovative Technologies for SMEs, 62*.

Oguanobi, V. U., & Joel, O. T. (2024). Scalable business models for startups in renewable energy: Strategies for using GIS technology to enhance SME scaling. *Engineering Science & Technology Journal*, 5(5), 1571–1587. DOI: 10.51594/estj.v5i5.1109

Smuts, H., Weilbach, L., Padachi, K., Boolaky, A., Mauree-Narrainen, D., Ramphul, N., & Chittoo, H. (2024). Harnessing Disruptive Innovation: A Conceptual Model for SME Growth and Adaptation. *Businesses*, 4(4), 738–764. DOI: 10.3390/businesses4040041

Soluk, J., Decker-Lange, C., & Hack, A. (2023). Small steps for the big hit: A dynamic capabilities perspective on business networks and non-disruptive digital technologies in SMEs. *Technological Forecasting and Social Change*, 191, 122490. DOI: 10.1016/j.techfore.2023.122490

Soni, G., Kumar, S., Mahto, R. V., Mangla, S. K., Mittal, M. L., & Lim, W. M. (2022). A decision-making framework for Industry 4.0 technology implementation: The case of FinTech and sustainable supply chain finance for SMEs. *Technological Forecasting and Social Change*, 180, 121686. DOI: 10.1016/j.techfore.2022.121686

Chapter 16
The Impact of Gig Economy Trends on Traditional Employment Models:
Evidence From Hotel Industry

Mohammad Badruddoza Talukder
https://orcid.org/0009-0008-1662-9221
International University of Business Agriculture and Technology, Bangladesh

Musfiqur Rahoman Khan
https://orcid.org/0009-0005-7416-2533
Daffodil Institute of IT, Bangladesh

Sanjeev Kumar
https://orcid.org/0000-0002-7375-7341
Lovely Professional University, India

ABSTRACT

The gig economy has changed employment patterns throughout industries, including the dynamic hotel business. This chapter analyzes industrial statistics, scholarly research, and case studies to understand the complex effects of change in labour dynamics. It provides examples of how gig economy developments have altered hotel employment arrangements, bolstering the research conclusions. The gig economy has disturbed hotel employment and spurred innovation. Airbnb and Uber have enabled hoteliers to hire on-demand housekeepers and guest service workers. The inflow of gig workers will change the workforce but also boost efficiency and agility, offering a bright future for the business. Traditional hotels have adopted digital platforms

DOI: 10.4018/979-8-3693-4369-2.ch016

and automation to compete due to the gig economy's focus on technology-driven efficiency. This shift toward gig-driven models emphasizes balancing innovation with hospitality ideals like individualized guest experiences and employee well-being. This unwavering commitment ensures the industry's commitment to quality service, reassuring stakeholders.

INTRODUCTION

According to Tug and Basar (2023), the gig economy, characterized by the proliferation of short-term contracts and freelance labour over traditional full-time employment, is dramatically affecting numerous industries, with the hotel business being at the vanguard of this transformation. Pull on. For most of their history, hotels have relied on a consistent workforce that is employed full-time to maintain high levels of service quality and operational efficiency (Joshi et al., 2024). On the other hand, the proliferation of digital platforms that provide on-demand labour and freelance opportunities substantially impacts conventional employment patterns (Rahman et al., 2024). Within the hospitality sector, this shift toward a gig-based workforce is driven by several factors.

According to Joshi et al. (2024), the flexibility the gig economy offers is among the most significant advantages that hotels may reap. According to Şen (2022), hotels can adjust their staffing levels according to the shifting seasonal demands and availability rates. This flexibility is necessary for an industry where demand can be highly varied due to tourism seasons, economic situations, and weather patterns. This is to manage their labour costs better and avoid the financial pressures of retaining a big permanent staff during off-peak periods. Hotels can better manage their labour costs using gig workers (Shvetsova, 2022).

Additionally, hotels have access to a broader talent pool as a result of the gig economy. According to Joshi et al. (2024), temporary workers and freelancers have the potential to contribute a wide range of professional experiences and one-of-a-kind skills that can enhance the quality of service that is provided to clients. To provide guests with a novel dining experience without the long-term commitment of full-time employment, a hotel might employ the services of a freelance chef specializing in a particular culinary speciality for a limited period. In a similar vein, independent event coordinators or marketing professionals can be brought in for specific projects to give knowledge that may be lacking in the workforce that is currently in place (Filippova, 2023). On the other hand, this shift toward employment based on gigs is difficult. According to Singh and Singh (2023), one of the essential concerns is ensuring that the quality of service provided is maintained consistently. The hotel sector is designed to provide outstanding service, and a staff that is constantly changing could be detrimental to the achievement of this objective (Endress, 2024). Gig workers may have a different level of commitment or acquaintance with the hotel's standards and processes than full-time staff, which can result in anomalies in the delivery of services. Additionally, the continuous onboarding of new employees can burden management resources, as training and integrating these temporary staff members requires a significant amount of time and effort (A. Hassan, 2021).

One of the most critical challenges the gig economy faces is the retention of employees. According to R. Hassan (2023), full-time employees frequently enjoy the benefits of job security, possibilities for professional advancement, and a sense of belonging, all of which have the potential to improve their loyalty and performance. There is a correlation between the absence of these perks and lower levels of engagement and loyalty among gig workers, which in turn leads to higher employee turnover rates. This high turnover will probably result in increased costs associated with recruiting and training new staff and potential operational issues (Syarfina Abu Bakar et al., 2024).

To successfully overcome these challenges, hotels must implement a strategic human management approach. Through comprehensive training programs, it is possible to ensure that gig workers quickly become accustomed to the establishment's procedures and standards (Brown, 2019). Furthermore, even for individuals who are only employed temporarily, establishing a pleasant working environment and offering competitive remuneration can be an effective way to attract top talent and strengthen their commitment. Good management is the most crucial factor in successfully integrating gig workers. This can be accomplished through technology, as digital platforms provide excellent scheduling, communication, and performance tracking (S. Li, 2023). The hotel business is experiencing a transformation in the old employment structures due to the gig economy, which presents both opportunities and disadvantages. By adopting workforce flexibility, hotels can more effectively control labour expenditures and access a broader range of skills (April, 2024a). However, to ensure their continued success over the long term, they must also handle the concerns of maintaining consistent service and retaining employees. To design effective strategies that balance flexibility and service quality, it is vital to have a comprehensive understanding of the subtle relationships between the trends of the gig economy and traditional employment structures (April, 2024b). This will allow the hotel sector to maintain its competitive advantage in an era of exponential change.

There is no such thing as a fleeting trend in the gig economy, characterized by the prevalence of short-term contracts and freelance work concerning traditional permanent employment. It has dramatically reshaped many industries, and the hospitality industry is no exception. Because of this transformation, the old employment models that hotels have relied on are being disrupted, which requires reevaluating workforce management techniques to adapt to the changing landscape (Adekoya et al., 2023). The shift toward a workforce based on gig work, which is affected by several important factors, brings with it a number of potential benefits. According to Singh and Singh (2023), hotels increasingly take advantage of the gig economy's flexibility to change their employment levels in response to shifting seasonal demands and occupancy rates, respectively. This strategy not only makes it possible to save expenses on employee benefits and long-term obligations, but it also makes it possible to allocate resources more actively and flexibly.

Nevertheless, this transformation is not without its difficulties. According to Buchak (2024), ensuring service and sustaining employee retention rates are key challenges when relying on a workforce subject to rotation. According to De Ruyter and Brown (2019), In the current environment, it is vital to have a comprehensive understanding of the intricate relationship between the tendencies of the gig economy and the traditional employment structures in the hotel business. By analyzing the effects that on-demand labour, temporary staffing, and freelance work have on workforce management and labour market trends, we can better understand the future of employment in the hospitality industry. According to Nakka and Chintha (2023), this analysis is essential for developing strategies that successfully address the ever-changing requirements of the sector while also maintaining sustainability and exceeding expectations in terms of service.

LITERATURE REVIEW

The gig economy, characterized by a rise in freelancing and short-term contracts, has drastically changed the nature of work across several industries (Mironova et al., 2022). This development is causing significant changes for the hotel business, which has always relied on a steady and permanent workforce (Mahra, 2023). To give readers a thorough grasp of this dynamically changing field, this literature review analyzes how changes in the gig economy are affecting conventional employment patterns in the hotel business. It does so by referencing both recent research and theoretical viewpoints (Varavva & Lazareva, 2022).

Flexibility and Workforce Management

The requirement for labour flexibility is one of the main factors driving the hotel industry's embrace of gig economy techniques (Kaur, 2024). Because gig work is flexible, companies can respond to changing demand by modifying worker numbers. This is especially useful for industries with seasonal fluctuations and erratic occupancy rates (Barral Valdez, 2023). Because of this flexibility, hotels can save labour expenses by hiring staff as needed and spare themselves the cost of keeping a sizable full-time workforce during off-peak times (Huang & Zhu, 2023). Hotels can also hire specialized specialists for short-term projects or unique events because of the gig economy's access to a varied talent pool (Hadi & Pratono, 2024). This strategy improves them and allows hotels to stand out from the competition in a crowded market. This change necessitates implementing vital workforce management techniques to guarantee that temporary employees are appropriately integrated and taught to uphold service standards (De Ruyter & Brown, 2019).

Service Quality and Consistency

The hotel business faces considerable hurdles in maintaining consistent service quality because of the transient nature of gig work. According to Guduru et al. (2023), providing the high standards of service demanded in the hotel industry requires a stable and dedicated workforce. Gig workers might add to the unpredictability of service delivery because they could require additional training on the unique policies and procedures of hotels. This problem is made worse by the rapid turnover that comes with gig work, which calls for ongoing efforts in hiring and training (Keshminder et al., 2022). Notwithstanding these challenges, research suggests that gig workers could offer fresh perspectives and original ideas that raise the bar for overall service quality. When properly and effectively managed, gig workers—frequently driven by the flexibility and variety of their roles—can demonstrate elevated levels of job satisfaction and performance (Pant & Majumder, 2022). Effective onboarding and training programs are essential to ensure that gig workers are ready to satisfy the expectations of both the employer and the guests (Arriagada et al., 2023).

Employee Retention and Engagement

In the gig economy, employee retention is a crucial problem, especially for sectors like hospitality that mainly depend on human resources. Full-time workers' benefits include job security, chances for career advancement, and a feeling of community that encourages fidelity and sustained commitment. Gig workers, on the other hand, frequently require more incredible perks, which could cause service continuity issues and increase turnover rates (Yunita, 2023). Even though gig employment can present alluring chances for extra money and flexibility, it might not deliver the consistency needed for long-term professional fulfilment (Zalizko et al., 2022). Hotels can lessen these adverse effects by implementing professional development opportunities, recognition programs, and competitive remuneration to increase gig worker engagement and lower turnover. Furthermore, utilizing technology to manage the workforce effectively can simplify procedures and enhance the gig worker experience (Nath, 2020).

Technological Integration and Efficiency

An essential component of efficiently managing gig labour is technology integration. Maintaining operational efficiency and ensuring gig workers can easily integrate into the hotel's workflow require digital tools that make scheduling, communication, and performance tracking easier (M. Rogerson, 2013). By easing administrative burdens, these technologies free up managers to concentrate on crucial responsibilities like quality assurance and training. Furthermore, technology may improve the gig worker experience by offering faster communication channels, instant feedback, and explicit guidelines. Despite their temporary job status, this support can make gig workers feel more a part of the company and more equipped to provide high-quality service (Behl et al., 2022). This literature study offers insights into how hotels might manage this changing landscape by examining these characteristics and highlighting the intricate interactions between traditional employment models and trends of the gig economy in the hotel industry (Singh & Singh, 2023).

Introduction to the Gig Economy in Hospitality

The gig economy has been a powerful force in recent years, changing traditional job patterns in various industries, including hospitality. The gig economy, defined by on-demand labour, freelance employment, and short-term contracts, has completely changed how companies handle their workforces and provide services (Vu & Nguyen, 2024). The gig economy affects the hospitality industry, which includes lodging facilities, dining establishments, resorts, and other associated businesses, regarding hiring policies and operational dynamics. In the past, the hospitality sector has depended on a permanent workforce to fulfil operational and guest service requirements. Employees at hotels and other hospitality companies are employed on long-term contracts, offering them perks, steady pay, and chances for professional growth (Hanivan & Rakhmawan, 2023). However, the emergence of digital platforms and mobile technologies has made it easier for gig workers to flourish, giving them more freedom and flexibility in their daily lives. According to Mudholkar & Prashant (2024), the hospitality gig economy includes a variety of jobs and activities such as housekeeping, food and beverage service, event organizing, concierge services, and more. Depending on the business, freelancers and gig workers may be able to work on a project-by-project basis or supply services hourly or daily. Many workers are drawn to this flexibility, such as students, retirees, and individuals who value autonomy to decide when and where they work (De Ruyter & Brown, 2019). The gig economy presents a variety of options for hospitality firms. According to Dettlaff (2023), gig workers provide hotels and restaurants with the ability to adjust their personnel in response to varying demands, such as seasonal fluctuations in travel or exceptional events. This adaptability offers a potential answer to the industry's ongoing problem of controlling labour expenses by enabling businesses to optimize staffing levels and regulate labour expenditures more efficiently, especially during low occupancy or economic downturns.

However, additional difficulties with personnel management and service quality assurance come with the gig economy (Abu Bakar et al., 2024). Because they are temporary, gig workers might not have the same training and familiarity with the policies and practices of the company as permanent staff, which could result in inconsistent service delivery. Furthermore, because gig workers may not have the same loyalty and belonging as those employed full-time, the temporary nature of their employment may present difficulties for employers trying to retain and engage their workforce. Firms must modify their management practices in response to these issues to maintain constant service quality and employee happiness.

Evolving Employment Models: From Tradition to Flexibility

The changes in employment arrangements within the hospitality sector indicate broader societal trends towards increased worker autonomy and flexibility. To meet the demands of guest service and operational operations, hospitality organizations, such as hotels, resorts, and restaurants, have historically relied on a fixed, full-time workforce. Long-term contracts were used to hire staff members who also received benefits, chances for professional growth, and steady pay. However, as digital technologies and the gig economy have grown, there has been a shift from inflexible structures to more flexible arrangements (Khoiroh & Syakur, 2023).

Flexibility has become increasingly important in the gig economy, characterized by freelance work, on-demand labour, and short-term contracts. Due to the abundance of gig workers, employers in the hotel sector can now adjust staffing levels in response to fluctuations in demand (Diomin & Kireeva, 2023). This adaptability is crucial in a seasonal economy since job needs might change dramatically depending on events, travel patterns, and the status of the economy. Technology has also made it easier for the hotel industry to shift to more flexible employment structures. Businesses can engage with gig workers using digital platforms and smartphone apps, facilitating smooth scheduling, communication, and payment procedures (Barański, 2023). It is now possible for hotels and restaurants to find temporary employees quickly and effectively, either to cover short-term openings or to add more workers during busy times. This workforce management agility makes it easier for companies to adjust to shifting market conditions.

A shifting workforce has also led to a movement in employment paradigms towards greater flexibility. Employees today value independence, work-life balance, and various employment opportunities, especially younger generations like Millennials and Gen Z (Petrova et al., 2021). The flexibility of gig work attracts many people since it lets them follow their other interests—like learning new things, travelling, or starting their own business—while still making money when it suits them. Gig labour appeals to students, retirees, and anyone looking for part-time work or additional income. Although the shift to flexibility has many advantages for employers and employees, some issues must be resolved. To guarantee that gig workers are successfully included in their operations and are taught to maintain service standards, hospitality organizations must create firm workforce management plans. Furthermore, since gig workers could require a different feeling of loyalty and belonging than permanent employees, questions about employee retention, engagement, and job security must be carefully considered (Dobrowolska, 2024).

Workforce Dynamics in the Gig Economy

The gig economy has changed how workers interact with employers in many sectors, including hospitality. The way companies in the hotel industry manage their personnel and provide services has changed due to the move away from traditional employment models and toward more flexible, project-based agreements. Employers and employees must comprehend the peculiarities of the gig economy's workforce to successfully negotiate this changing environment (Vu & Nguyen, 2024). Short-term contracts and freelancing are widely used in the gig economy, which is one of its fundamental characteristics. In the hospitality industry, lodging facilities, eateries, and other businesses can access a pool of independent contractors willing to labour as needed. Because of this flexibility, companies may adapt to changes in demand, seasonal swings, and exceptional, one-of-a-kind events by instantly adjusting their workforce levels.

Additionally, gig workers are free to select their schedule and location, allowing them to balance work obligations with personal inclinations and lifestyle choices (Vardanyan, 2023). Additionally, the gig economy supports the gig worker marketplace, which connects people with possible employers via mobile apps and digital platforms. These platforms provide a quick and efficient way for companies and gig workers to find opportunities for temporary staffing. Technology may help hospitality companies hire more efficiently, communicate better with gig workers, and guarantee that services are paid for on time. Gig workers can also enhance their visibility and access to job possibilities by developing their reputations and profiles in the marketplace (Chan et al., 2024).

Still, other problems with the characteristics of the gig economy's workforce need to be fixed. One of the most critical problems is that gig workers don't receive benefits or job security. Unlike regular employees, gig workers typically do not receive benefits like paid time off, retirement plans, or health insurance. They might also require guarantees regarding steady employment or income in the future. In addition, gig workers might need assistance accessing professional growth and training opportunities, which could harm their prospects of landing a long-term position (Keshminder et al., 2022).

Service Quality Challenges in a Gig-Driven World

Maintaining consistent service quality presents substantial issues for the hotel industry in today's gig-driven world, when firms increasingly rely on temporary workforce and freelancers to meet operational demands (Pant & Majumder, 2022). This chapter examines the difficulties in providing exceptional service in a gig economy setting and considers how these difficulties may affect long-term business success, guest pleasure, and brand reputation. The irregularity of service delivery is one of the main obstacles to high-quality service in a gig economy. Gig workers might need to become just as familiar with SOPs and service standards as full-time employees, who receive extensive training and are fully integrated into the organization's culture and values. Because of this, customers may receive varying service levels from different staff members, which could leave them unhappy and result in bad reviews (Davidson et al., 2023).

Furthermore, problems with service quality may be made worse by the sporadic nature of gig labour. Since they have no stake in the company's long-term survival, gig workers can require dedication or accountability (Nimmagadda et al., 2024). This might show up as habits like being late, late-late, communicating poorly, or not paying attention to details, all of which can harm the business's reputation and its guests' overall experience.

In addition, the gig economy creates coordination and collaboration challenges. To provide visitors with comprehensive and individualized service, hospitality operations frequently necessitate the smooth coordination of personnel from many departments. To integrate into the workflow effectively, gig workers may need assistance familiarizing themselves with the organization's team dynamics and communication channels. Failure to do so could result in fragmented service delivery and missed opportunities to surpass guest expectations (Hibrida & Sunarni, 2023). A further obstacle to service quality in a gig economy is the possibility of skill and knowledge shortages. While gig workers might provide specific knowledge or abilities in some areas, they might lack the competency or experience in others, which could result in inconsistent service across different sections of the visitor experience. For instance, a freelance bartender hired for a particular occasion might be excellent at mixing drinks. However, they might need assistance understanding the wine list or table service protocol (Kaushik, 2024).

In addition, the gig economy brings difficulties in supervision and training. Gig workers need to be trained so that hospitality organizations can be sure they have the know-how to provide high-quality service, which will take time and money. However, due to the sporadic nature of gig employment, offering thorough training or continuing supervision may be challenging, which could result in knowledge gaps or miscommunications regarding expected service levels (Endress, 2024). In the gig economy, hospitality organizations confront various service quality difficulties that call for strategic planning and close attention to detail (Huđek & Širec, 2023). Companies may reduce the risks associated with gig work and maintain high levels of service quality by implementing thorough training, fostering a culture of accountability and teamwork, and utilizing technology to help with communication and coordination. In addition, taking proactive steps to choose and integrate gig workers who share the company's values and service ethos will guarantee a dependable and remarkable visitor experience, fostering customer satisfaction, loyalty, and long-term business success (Joshi et al., 2024).

Employee Retention in the Age of Gig Work

Employee retention has become a significant concern for enterprises across different industries, including the hotel industry, in the modern work landscape marked by the development of gig economy options and freelance agreements (Ali & Sivasubramanian, 2024). This chapter explores the intricacies of employee retention in the gig economy, looking at tactics for improving retention, factors influencing departure rates, and the consequences for organizational success.

The gig economy has significantly changed the nature of the traditional employment relationship by providing workers with more freedom and flexibility to make a living. The ability to select their projects, hours, and clients is a common source of motivation for gig workers, who may value independence over long-term employment with a single company. Because gig workers can try different gigs and follow different career routes, hospitality organizations must contend with increased talent competition (Bewtra et al., 2023). Furthermore, hotel industry staff retention is hampered by gig labour's temporary nature. In contrast to full-time workers who enjoy benefits like job stability and growth chances, gig workers could require a distinct sense of loyalty or devotion to the company. Because gig workers may easily transition to other opportunities that offer better pay, flexibility, or job satisfaction, this could result in higher turnover rates (Vu & Nguyen, 2024).

Moreover, the gig economy brings labour management and engagement complications. To accommodate Workers, hospitality businesses must modify their retention methods (Trí & Anh, 2024). Conventional rewards like pay raises or job promotions might not have the same impact on gig workers since they value flexibility and independence in their work schedules. Alternatively, companies may need to look into other retention strategies, such as providing individualized benefits, acknowledgement initiatives, or networking and skill-building opportunities (Shiml et al., 2023).

Furthermore, the hotel business must foster a favourable work environment and organizational culture to retain gig workers. Employers emphasizing inclusion, communication, and employee well-being are more likely to attract and retain talent, regardless of the employee's status. Additionally, providing gig workers with opportunities for meaningful employment, professional growth, and a sense of belonging can increase their commitment to the organization, reduce attrition, and boost output (Hungary et al., 2023).

CASE STUDIES: GIG ECONOMY INTEGRATION IN LEADING HOTELS

Leading hotels are often incorporating gig economy methods into their workforce management plans to adjust to changing visitor preferences and market realities. This chapter examines case studies of hotels that have embraced the gig economy and used on-demand labour to improve staffing, boost operational flexibility, and provide excellent guest experiences (Tug & Basar, 2023).

Case Study 1: Marriott International

Marriott International, a prominent global hotel operator, has embraced the gig economy to augment its staff in times of high demand and exceptional occasions. Through collaboration with gig economy platforms like Upwork and Wanelo, Marriott can promptly obtain temporary workers for various positions, such as housekeeping, event planning, and front desk services. Because of this, Marriott can adjust its workforce to meet changing demand and maintain optimal staffing numbers and high service standards. Additionally, Marriott offers assistance and training to freelance workers to ensure they know the brand's policies and guidelines, improving visitor satisfaction and encouraging loyalty (Pant & Majumder, 2022).

Case Study 2: Hilton Worldwide

Hilton Worldwide has incorporated creative techniques for integrating the gig economy to improve operational effectiveness and guest pleasure throughout its hotel portfolio. Hilton has access to a wide range of gig workers with specific abilities, such as bartending, culinary arts, and event planning, thanks to collaborations with gig economy platforms like Shift Gig and Interwork. This enables Hilton to provide guests with distinctive and personalized experiences, like exceptional amenities, pop-up restaurants, and themed events. Additionally, Hilton offers gig workers chances for job progression and professional growth, which encourages brand loyalty (Joshi et al., 2024).

Case Study 3: Airbnb

While traditionally known as a disruptor in the hospitality industry, Airbnb has also embraced the gig economy to enhance its service offerings and customer support(Joshi et al., 2024). Through partnerships with gig economy platforms, such as TaskRabbit and Handy, Airbnb can connect hosts with gig workers for various tasks, such as cleaning, maintenance, and guest services. This enables Airbnb hosts to maintain high cleanliness standards, provide personalized experiences to guests, and ensure smooth check-in and check-out processes. Moreover, Airbnb provides gig workers incentives, such as bonuses and discounts, to encourage quality service delivery and promote positive guest reviews(Endress, 2024).

Leading hotels worldwide are leveraging the gig economy to enhance operational flexibility, optimize staffing, and deliver exceptional guest experiences. By partnering with gig economy platforms and integrating gig workers into their workforce management strategies, hotels can adapt to changing market dynamics, meet guest expectations, and maintain a competitive edge in the hospitality industry. Moreover, by providing gig workers with training, support, and opportunities for career advancement, hotels can foster a culture of excellence and innovation, driving long-term success and sustainability(Nimmagadda et al., 2024).

ECONOMIC IMPLICATIONS OF GIG WORK IN HOSPITALITY

Businesses, employees, and the overall economy are all significantly impacted by the surge in gig employment in the hospitality sector. This chapter examines how gig work affects consumer behaviour, labour markets, employment, and overall economic growth in the hotel industry (Li et al., 2023).

1. **Labor Market Flexibility**: Businesses in the hospitality sector benefit from increased workforce management flexibility from gig employment, which enables them to modify staffing levels in response to varying demands. During busy times or unusual occurrences, this flexibility helps businesses reduce personnel expenses and boost productivity (Talukder, 2024). However, it also presents difficulties for workforce management and service quality assurance because

gig workers can require additional training and knowledge of the company's policies and practices than regular employees.

2. **Job Creation and Income Generation**: According to Muhammad and Iva (2024), gig labour enables people to explore flexible employment arrangements that complement their lifestyle choices or supplement their income. Gig work in the hotel industry might open up new job prospects, especially for those looking for temporary or part-time work. Furthermore, gig workers may use their earnings to purchase goods and services in their local areas, which can boost consumer spending and help small businesses (Mohammad et al., 2024).
3. **Income Inequality and Job Insecurity**: Although gig employment gives freedom and flexibility, it also has drawbacks regarding steady income and job security. In the hospitality sector, gig workers could experience erratic work schedules, varying pay, and restricted access to retirement plans or health care benefits. In addition, gig workers might not have the same legal safeguards and job rights as regular employees, which could result in differences in pay and job security among the workforce (Talukder & Kumar, 2024).
4. **Regulatory and Policy Considerations**: To guarantee sufficient rights for gig workers, legislators have been forced to reevaluate labour laws and employment regulations due to the increasing frequency of gig work in the hospitality sector. Stakeholders are arguing for policies to protect gig workers' rights and well-being while balancing the demands of companies and customers on issues including worker classification, minimum wage laws, and benefits access (Jain, 2024).
5. **Consumer Behavior and Service Expectations**: The gig economy has also impacted customer behaviour and service standards in the hospitality industry. Convenience, customization, and flexibility are increasingly important to customers when interacting with hospitality firms. To satisfy these changing demands, businesses must modify their service offerings and customer engagement tactics. They can utilize technology and data analytics to provide personalized experiences and raise customer satisfaction (Seal & Gupta, 2024).

In the hospitality sector, gig employment has wide-ranging and intricate financial ramifications (Kumar et al., 2024). Gig labour brings issues with income inequality, employment insecurity, and regulatory compliance, but it also gives businesses more flexibility and gives individuals additional ways to generate revenue. Stakeholders may promote economic growth and prosperity by comprehending and resolving these implications and working to create a more fair, sustainable, and inclusive labour market within the hotel industry.

FUTURE TRENDS AND THE EVOLUTION OF HOTEL EMPLOYMENT

Hotel employment is changing due to broader cultural trends, evolving consumer tastes, and technology improvements. The future factors influencing the growth of hotel employment are examined in this chapter, including workforce diversity, automation, skill development, and the incorporation of gig work (Das et al., 2024).

1. **Automation and Technological Innovation**: The hospitality industry is adopting automation and technologically advanced solutions faster to enhance visitor experiences and optimize operations (Firoj & Mohammad, 2024). Hotels deploy automated check-in kiosks and robotic room service delivery to increase productivity and reduce labour costs. While some repetitive jobs may be replaced by automation, staff will have more time to focus on higher-value tasks, including interacting with visitors, resolving issues, and offering personalized service (Cichorska & Zielina, 2023).
2. **Skills Development and Lifelong Learning**: There is an increasing need for specific skills and capabilities as the hospitality business develops. To provide their staff with the skills necessary to succeed in a fast-paced and cutthroat industry, hotels are investing in training and development programs (Auguste et al., 2023). Employees can learn new skills, adjust to changing trends, and pursue professional progression within the sector through online training platforms, mentorship programs, and lifelong learning initiatives (Liu et al., 2024).
3. **Workforce Diversity and Inclusion**: To build inclusive work cultures that reflect the diversity of their visitors and communities, hotels find that diversity and inclusion are increasingly important concerns. To attract and retain talent from various backgrounds, promote a culture of respect and belonging, and capitalize on their staff members' distinct perspectives and experiences to stimulate innovation and creativity, hotels are putting diversity and inclusion programs into practice.
4. **Flexible Employment Models and Gig Work Integration**: Hotels are increasingly using gig work to complement their workers and meet fluctuating demand, which is changing the traditional employment structures in the hospitality sector (Filippova, 2023). Part-time, temporary, and remote work choices are examples of flexible employment agreements that allow employees more freedom and flexibility in their work schedules. Furthermore, hotels may adjust to shifting market conditions and provide individualized guest experiences by using gig workers' flexibility in staffing and cost management (Liu et al., 2024).

5. **Sustainability and Corporate Social Responsibility**: Hotels emphasize sustainability and corporate social responsibility in their employment practices due to the growing demand for socially and environmentally conscientious businesses. Fair compensation, employee wellness programs, and community service initiatives are sustainable employment practices that promote hotels' long-term profitability by assisting in talent recruitment and retention (Kucheriava, 2024).

RECOMMENDATIONS

Adopting a hybrid workforce strategy is a sensible, doable, and forward-thinking suggestion for resolving the effects of gig economy trends on conventional employment patterns in the hotel business. This strategy prioritizes employee well-being and visitor pleasure while combining the advantages of traditional employment with the adaptability and agility of gig work, enabling hotels to adjust to shifting market circumstances.

Here's how hotels can put a hybrid workforce strategy into practice:

1. **Strategic Workforce Planning:** Perform a thorough analysis of personnel requirements, considering seasonal fluctuations, occupancy rates, and visitor preferences. Determine how gig workers might improve flexibility and operational efficiency by supplementing the current labour in certain areas.
2. **Develop partnerships with reputable gig economy platforms:** To gain access to a wide range of gig workers with particular knowledge and abilities. Establish thorough hiring and onboarding procedures to ensure gig workers share the organization's values and service requirements.
3. **Training and Development:** Invest in ongoing training and development initiatives to help gig workers advance their careers and acquire the skills necessary to provide superior customer service. Provide chances for professional progression and cross-training to encourage engagement and loyalty among gig workers.
4. **Technology Integration:** Use technological solutions to expedite the scheduling, performance management, and communication procedures for both permanent and contract employees. Use mobile apps and digital platforms to make coordination and communication among the hybrid workforce easier.
5. **Employee Engagement and Recognition**: Put programs in place to honour and compensate gig workers for their services to the company. You can promote an inclusive and collaborative culture by giving gig workers the chance to join regular employees in team meetings, social gatherings, and training sessions.

6. **Compliance and Legal Considerations**: Keep up with the latest labour laws and regulations that apply to gig work to minimize legal risks and maintain compliance. Provide precise rules and regulations for gig work agreements, such as worker classification, pay scales, and eligibility for benefits.

Figure 1. Conceptual model

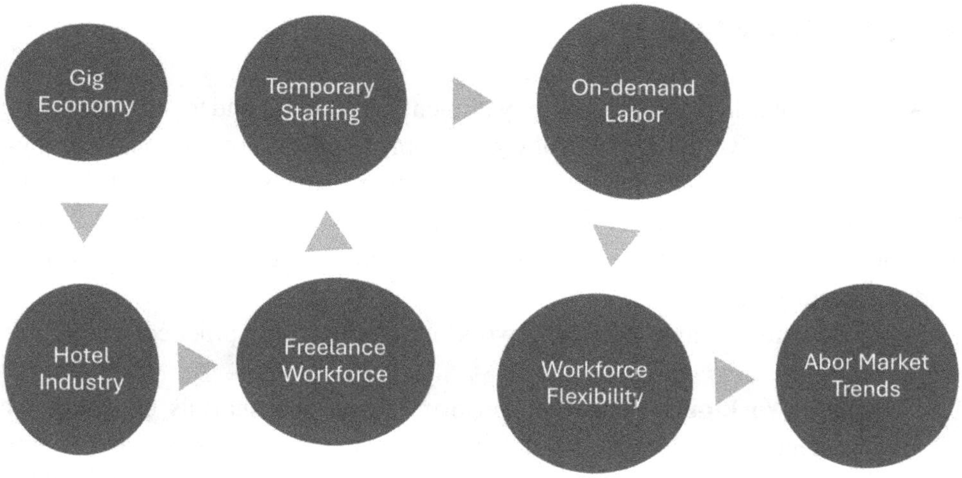

(Author compilation)

7. **Feedback and Performance Evaluation:** Frequent performance reviews and feedback systems should be used to evaluate the performance of gig workers and pinpoint areas for development. Seek feedback from full-time staff members and contract workers to promote acollaborative and ongoing improvement culture. By adopting a hybrid workforce strategy, hotels can capitalize on gig economy developments and maintain the benefits of conventional employment models. With this proactive approach, hotels can better position themselves for long-term success in the hospitality sector by improving operational flexibility, responding to changing market conditions, and providing outstanding guest experiences.

CONCLUSION

The hotel sector faces both opportunities and challenges when it comes to incorporating trends from the gig economy into established employment patterns. Although gig labour provides flexibility and agility, it raises concerns over job security, service quality, and compliance with regulatory requirements. On the other hand, hotels may successfully handle these challenges and exploit the opportunities presented by the shifting labour market by implementing a hybrid workforce approach that combines the benefits of gig work with the advantages of regular employment. Hotels can construct a dynamic and resilient workforce capable of catering to the diverse requirements of guests and adapting to the ever-changing dynamics of the market. This can be accomplished by meticulously organizing their workforce, making use of technology, investing in training and development, and cultivating a culture that is both inclusive and collaborative. In addition, hotels have the potential to develop a profitable and sustainable business model that fosters long-term growth by placing emphasis on the well-being of their employees, recognizing the contributions of gig workers, and ensuring compliance with labour laws and regulations.

To put it another way, the future of hotel employment will consist of striking the right balance between history and innovation, permanence and flexibility, to cultivate a flexible, engaged, and ready staff to create exceptional experiences for guests in a constantly moving sector. Hotels that implement this strategy have the potential to establish themselves as industry leaders, thereby fostering innovation, cultivating human capital, and establishing new standards of excellence in the hospitality industry.

REFERENCES

Adekoya, O. D., Mordi, C., Ajonbadi, H. A., & Chen, W. (2023). Implications of algorithmic management on careers and employment relationships in the gig economy – a developing country perspective. *Information Technology & People*. Advance online publication. DOI: 10.1108/ITP-01-2023-0064

Ali, K. T. M., & Sivasubramanian, R. C. (2024). Understanding the Nexus Between Techno-Stress, Psychological Well-Being, and the Moderating Role of Job Resources in the Gig Economy. *Employee Responsibilities and Rights Journal*. Advance online publication. DOI: 10.1007/s10672-024-09505-5

April, K. (2024). Precarious Work in the Gig Economy: Diversity, Race and Indigeneity Lenses. In Meliou, E., Vassilopoulou, J., & Ozbilgin, M. F. (Eds.), *Diversity and Precarious Work During Socio-Economic Upheaval* (1st ed., pp. 137–162). Cambridge University Press. DOI: 10.1017/9781108933070.008

Arriagada, A., Bonhomme, M., Ibáñez, F., & Leyton, J. (2023). The gig economy in Chile: Examining labor conditions and the nature of gig work in a Global South country. *Digital Geography and Society*, 5, 100063. DOI: 10.1016/j.diggeo.2023.100063

Auguste, D., Roll, S., & Despard, M. (2023). Democratizing the Economy or Introducing Economic Risk? Gig Work During the COVID-19 Pandemic. *Work and Occupations*, 07308884231202032. Advance online publication. DOI: 10.1177/07308884231202032

Barański, M. (2023). Employment flexibility in times of crisis. *Studia Iuridica*, 95(95), 9–29. DOI: 10.31338/2544-3135.si.2022-95.1

Barral Valdez, C. (2023). Manifestation of global trends in hotel industries in baguio city as perceived by hotel guests. *International Journal of Advanced Research*, 11(11), 948–962. DOI: 10.21474/IJAR01/17898

Behl, A., Rajagopal, K., Sheorey, P., & Mahendra, A. (2022). Barriers to entry of gig workers in the gig platforms: Exploring the dark side of the gig economy. *Aslib Journal of Information Management*, 74(5), 818–839. DOI: 10.1108/AJIM-08-2021-0235

Bewtra, P., Kharbanda, S., & Kamna, S. (2023). Gig Economy in India: Growth, Challenges and Way Forward. *International Journal of Indian Culture and Business Management*, 1(1), 1. DOI: 10.1504/IJICBM.2023.10056418

Buchak, G. (2024). Financing the Gig Economy. *The Journal of Finance*, 79(1), 219–256. DOI: 10.1111/jofi.13292

Chan, X. W., Shang, S., & Lu, L. (Eds.). (2024). *Work-Life Research in the Asia-Pacific: Implications for Justice, Equity, Diversity, and Inclusion*. Springer Nature Switzerland. DOI: 10.1007/978-3-031-52795-1

Cichorska, J., & Zielina, K. (2023). Assessment of the Effects of the COVID-19 Pandemic in the HoReCa Industry in the Opinion of Customers and Employees. *Finanse i Prawo Finansowe*, 2(38), 45–73. DOI: 10.18778/2391-6478.2.38.03

Das, I. R., Talukder, M. B., & Kumar, S. (2024). Implication of Artificial Intelligence in Hospitality Marketing. In Kumar, S., Talukder, M. B., & Pego, A. (Eds.), *Advances in Hospitality, Tourism, and the Services Industry* (pp. 291–310). IGI Global. DOI: 10.4018/979-8-3693-1978-9.ch014

Davidson, A., Gleim, M. R., Johnson, C. M., & Stevens, J. L. (2023). Gig worker typology and research agenda: Advancing research for frontline service providers. *Journal of Service Theory and Practice*, 33(5), 647–670. DOI: 10.1108/JSTP-08-2022-0188

De Ruyter, A., & Brown, M. (2019). *The Gig Economy* (1st ed.). Agenda Publishing. DOI: 10.1017/9781788210065

Dettlaff, A. (2023). Professional Activation of Women and Flexible Forms of Employment, as Exemplified by Gig Economy. *WSB Journal of Business and Finance*, 57(1), 12–20. DOI: 10.2478/wsbjbf-2023-0002

Diomin, A., & Kireeva, O. (2023). Personal flexibility and psychological well-being under multiple employment. *World of Science.Pedagogy and Psychology*, 11(5). Advance online publication. DOI: 10.15862/55PSMN523

Dobrowolska, M. (2024). The Role of Employment Flexibility in the Professional Education of Individuals at Risk of Social Exclusion. *Interdisciplinary Journal of Labor and Economics*, 13(1), 1–09. DOI: 10.62693/898pbl41

Endress, T. (2024). Disruption and the Gig Economy: What's Next? In Endress, T., & Badir, Y. F. (Eds.), *Business and Management in Asia: Disruption and Change* (pp. 109–122). Springer Nature Singapore. DOI: 10.1007/978-981-99-9371-0_7

Filippova, O. Yu. (2023). International hotel service industry trends. *Visnyk of Donetsk National University of Economics and Trade named after Mykhailo Tugan-Baranovsky, 2(79) 2023*, 63–68. DOI: 10.33274/2079-4819-2023-79-2-63-68

Firoj, K., & Mohammad, B. T. (2024). Measuring sustainability in the broadcasting media industry in Bangladesh. *I-Manager's. Journal of Management*, 18(3), 51. DOI: 10.26634/jmgt.18.3.20234

Guduru, S., Santhanam, N., & Pushparaj, N. (2023). Comprehending the research on the gig economy: A bibliometric approach. *Global Knowledge, Memory and Communication*. Advance online publication. DOI: 10.1108/GKMC-02-2023-0056

Hadi, A. A. W. K., & Pratono, A. H. (2024). Ethical predicaments of gig economy: Bibliometric approach. *Optimum: Jurnal Ekonomi Dan Pembangunan*, 14(1), 40–48. DOI: 10.12928/optimum.v14i1.9316

Hanivan, H., & Rakhmawan, S. A. (2023). Gig Economy During Pandemic in East Java. *East Java Economic Journal*, 7(1), 69–89. DOI: 10.53572/ejavec.v7i1.88

Hassan, A. (Ed.). (2021). *Technology Application in the Tourism and Hospitality Industry of Bangladesh*. Springer Singapore. DOI: 10.1007/978-981-16-2434-6

Hassan, R. (2023). *Work Arrangements in the Informal Sector and Gig Economy/Digital Platform Economy in Egypt*. Unpublished. DOI: 10.13140/RG.2.2.24113.19041

Hibrida, A. R., & Sunarni, . (2023). The Future of Work: Navigating the Challenges and Opportunities of Automation, Gig Economy, and Skills Evolution in a Post-Pandemic World. *West Science Interdisciplinary Studies*, 1(08), 638–647. DOI: 10.58812/wsis.v1i08.186

Huang, K., & Zhu, F. (2023). ChatGPT and Gig Economy. In Huang, K., Wang, Y., Zhu, F., Chen, X., & Xing, C. (Eds.), *Beyond AI* (pp. 129–158). Springer Nature Switzerland. DOI: 10.1007/978-3-031-45282-6_5

Huđek, I., & Širec, K. (2023). The terminology and the concept of the gig economy. *Ekonomski Pregled*, 74(1), 34–58. DOI: 10.32910/ep.74.1.2

. Jain, P. A. (2024). The Gig Economy: Disruption, Innovation, and Economic Evolution. *Educational Administration: Theory and Practice*, 5133–5140. DOI: 10.53555/kuey.v30i5.3755

Joshi, A., Jain, S., & Gupta, P. K. (2024). Challenges and impact of the gig economy. *Sustainable Economies*, 2(2), 96. DOI: 10.62617/se.v2i2.96

Kabir, F., & Talukder, M. B. (2024). Measuring Sustainability in the Broadcasting Media Industry in Bangladesh. i-manager's. *Journal of Management*, 18(3), 51–63. DOI: 10.26634/jmgt.18.3.20234

Kaur, N. (2024). Employment Opportunities and Work Trends Post-pandemic. In Kamaruddin, N., Idris, A., & Fernandez, K. (Eds.), *The New Normal and Its Impact on Society* (pp. 25–40). Springer Nature Singapore. DOI: 10.1007/978-981-97-0527-6_3

Kaushik, A. (2024). Comprehensive Impact of On-Demand Platforms: Examining the Gig Economy \'s Influence on Specialized Professionals, Work-Life Balance, and Gig Workers\' Perspectives. *International Journal for Research in Applied Science and Engineering Technology*, 12(1), 552–559. DOI: 10.22214/ijraset.2024.58005

Keshminder, J. S., Mia, M. A., Nourani, M., & Zhang, M. (2022). Gig employment in the Malaysian manufacturing industry: A cross-sectional analysis. *Asian-Pacific Economic Literature*, 36(1), 48–66. DOI: 10.1111/apel.12348

Khoiroh, M., & Syakur, A. S. (2023). The flexibility of Islamic law in the Ganjur tradition in Lamongan, Indonesia. *Ijtihad : Jurnal Wacana Hukum Islam Dan Kemanusiaan*, 23(2), 139–159. DOI: 10.18326/ijtihad.v23i2.139-159

Kozak, T., Kasza, L., & Nemeth, P. (2023). Examining the impact of the gig-economy, as a new challenge for supply chain strategy. *The Journal of Business and Retail Management Research*, 18(01). Advance online publication. DOI: 10.24052/JBRMR/V18IS01/ART-01

Kucheriava, H. O. (2024). Hotel industry of Ukraine in crisis conditions: Challenges, trends, prospects. *Вісник Київського Національного Лінгвістичного Університету. Серія Історія, Економіка. Філософія*, 29(29), 60–69. DOI: 10.32589/2412-9321.29.2024.301784

Kumar, S., Talukder, M. B., & Pego, A. (Eds.). (2024). *Utilizing Smart Technology and AI in Hybrid Tourism and Hospitality*. IGI Global. DOI: 10.4018/979-8-3693-1978-9

Li, S. (2023). The Gig Economy and Labour Market Dynamics. *Advances in Economics. Management and Political Sciences*, 61(1), 275–281. DOI: 10.54254/2754-1169/61/20231285

Li, Y., Xu, S., Yu, Y., & Meadows, R. (2023). The well-being of gig workers in the sharing economy during COVID-19. *International Journal of Contemporary Hospitality Management*, 35(4), 1470–1489. DOI: 10.1108/IJCHM-01-2022-0064

Liu, X., Wider, W., Fauzi, M. A., Jiang, L., Udang, L. N., & Hossain, S. F. A. (2024). The evolution of smart hotels: A bibliometric review of the past, present and future trends. *Heliyon*, 10(4), e26472. DOI: 10.1016/j.heliyon.2024.e26472 PMID: 38420486

Mahra, A. K. (2023). A Study On Gig Economy And Redefining Employment In Bhopal District. Open Science Framework. DOI: 10.17605/OSF.IO/KJYRN

Mironova, S. M., Kozhemyakin, D. V., & Ponomarchenko, A. E. (2022). Adaptation of the legal regulation of labor, civil, tax relations to the gig economy. *Law Enforcement Review*, 6(4), 314–329. DOI: 10.52468/2542-1514.2022.6(4).314-329

Mohammad, B. T., & Iva, R. D. (2024). The technology impacts and AI solutions in hospitality. *I-Manager's Journal on Artificial Intelligence &. Machine Learning*, 2(1), 56. DOI: 10.26634/jaim.2.1.20291

Mohammad, B. T., Mushfika, H., & Iva, R. D. (2024). Opportunities of tourism and hospitality education in bangladesh: Career perspectives. *I-Manager's. Journal of Management*, 18(3), 21. DOI: 10.26634/jmgt.18.3.20385

Mudholkar, B. S., & Gaikwad, P. S. (2024). Gig is Big in Indian Industry: Concept and Overview. *International Journal of Advanced Research in Science. Tongxin Jishu*, 115–119, 115–119. Advance online publication. DOI: 10.48175/IJARSCT-18422

Nakka, S., & Chintha, V. (2023). Role of Gig Economy in Generating Urban Employment- A Study on the City of Hyderabad. *KMICS Journal of Commerce and Management*, 1(1), 1–8. DOI: 10.62011/kmicsjcm.2023.1.1.1

Nath, P. (2020). Trust in Gig Economy. *NHRD Network Journal*, 13(4), 480–486. DOI: 10.1177/2631454120974224

Nimmagadda, B., Vangaveti, Y., Aaluri, S., Mallikarjuna Rao, Ch., & Singh, B. (2024). An Analytical study on Navigating Sustainability Challenges and Opportunities in the era of AI and the Gig Economy. *MATEC Web of Conferences, 392*, 01044. DOI: 10.1051/matecconf/202439201044

Pant, J. J., & Majumder, M. G. (2022). Themes and Narratives of Gig Economy: An Indian HR Perspective. *NHRD Network Journal*, 15(1), 83–99. DOI: 10.1177/26314541211064751

Petrova, I., Kravchenko, I., Lisogor, L., & Chuvardynskyi, V. (2021). Employment flexibility in ukraine: Advantages and limitations. *Financial and Credit Activity Problems of Theory and Practice*, 3(38), 490–498. DOI: 10.18371/fcaptp.v3i38.237481

Rogerson, M. (2013). Market segmentation and the changing budget hotel industry in urban South Africa. *Urbani Izziv*, 24(2), 112–123. DOI: 10.5379/urbani-izziv-en-2013-24-01-003

Seal, P. P., & Gupta, P. (2024). Artificial Intelligence in Human Resource Management in Hotels: A Qualitative Approach. In Kumar, S., Talukder, M. B., & Pego, A. (Eds.), *Advances in Hospitality, Tourism, and the Services Industry* (pp. 277–290). IGI Global. DOI: 10.4018/979-8-3693-1978-9.ch013

Şen, G. (2022). Effects of gig economy on employment. *International Journal of Research in Commerce and Management Studies*, 04(05), 57–69. DOI: 10.38193/IJRCMS.2022.4504

Shvetsova, O. (2022). Gig Economy: Trends and Perspectives. How to Define Advantages and Disadvantages of Gig Economy? In Gupta, A., Tewary, T., & Gopalakrishnan, B. N. (Eds.), *Sustainability in the Gig Economy* (pp. 19–31). Springer Nature Singapore. DOI: 10.1007/978-981-16-8406-7_2

Sood, A., & Singh, R. (2023). The New Emerging World of Work: Growth Story of India's Gig Economy. *International Journal of Management and Economics Invention*, 09(10). Advance online publication. DOI: 10.47191/ijmei/v9i10.03

Syarfina Abu Bakar, A., Razeef Abd Razak, M., & Anwar, R. (2024). *Evolution of Digital Platform for Gig Economy in Design Industry*. KnE Engineering. DOI: 10.18502/keg.v6i1.15414

Talukder, M. B. (2024). Implementing Artificial Intelligence and Virtual Experiences in Hospitality. In Manohar, S., Mittal, A., Raju, S., & Nair, A. J. (Eds.), *Advances in Hospitality, Tourism, and the Services Industry* (pp. 145–160). IGI Global. DOI: 10.4018/979-8-3693-2019-8.ch009

Talukder, M. B., & Das, I. R. (2024). The Technology Impacts and AI Solutions in Hospitality. i-manager's Journal on Artificial Intelligence &. *Machine Learning*, 2(1), 56–72. DOI: 10.26634/jaim.2.1.20291

Talukder, M. B., Hoque, M., & Das, I. R. (2024). Opportunities of Tourism and Hospitality Education in Bangladesh: Career Perspectives. i-manager's. *Journal of Management*, 18(3), 21–34. DOI: 10.26634/jmgt.18.3.20385

Talukder, M. B., & Kumar, S. (2024). The Development of ChatGPT and Its Implications for the Future of Customer Service in the Hospitality Industry. In Derbali, A. (Ed.), *Blockchain Applications for Smart Contract Technologies* (pp. 100–126). IGI Global. DOI: 10.4018/979-8-3693-1511-8.ch005

Talukder, M. B., Kumar, S., & Das, I. R. (2024). Mindful Consumers and New Marketing Strategies for the Restaurant Business: Evidence of Bangladesh. In Ramos, C., Costa, T., Severino, F., & Calisto, M. (Eds.), *Social Media Strategies for Tourism Interactivity* (pp. 240–260). IGI Global. DOI: 10.4018/979-8-3693-0960-5.ch010

Talukder, M. B., Kumar, S., Kaiser, F., & Mia, M. N. (2024). Pilgrimage Creative Tourism: A Gateway to Sustainable Development Goals in Bangladesh. In Hamdan, M., Anshari, M., Ahmad, N., & Ali, E. (Eds.), *Global Trends in Governance and Policy Paradigms* (pp. 285–300). IGI Global. DOI: 10.4018/979-8-3693-1742-6.ch016

Talukder, M. B., & Muhsina, K. (2024). Prospect of Smart Tourism Destination in Bangladesh. In Correia, R., Martins, M., & Fontes, R. (Eds.), *AI Innovations for Travel and Tourism* (pp. 163–179). IGI Global. DOI: 10.4018/979-8-3693-2137-9.ch009

Trí, C. M., & Anh, P. N. (2024). Generation differences in the gig economy. *Ho Chi Minh City Open University Journal of Science - Economics and Business Administration, 14*(3). DOI: 10.46223/HCMCOUJS.econ.en.14.3.2730.2024

Tug, M. A., & Basar, P. (2023). Future of the gig economy. *Pressacademia*, 1, 1. Advance online publication. DOI: 10.17261/Pressacademia.2023.1796

Varavva, M. Yu., & Lazareva, O. S. (2022). Platform Gig-Economy as Alternative Model with Non-Standard Labour Relations. *Vestnik of the Plekhanov Russian University of Economics*, 5(5), 108–115. DOI: 10.21686/2413-2829-2022-5-108-115

Vardanyan, T. (2023). Future of Freelancing: How the Gig Economy is Reshaping the International Labor Market? *AMBERD Bulletin*, 48–56. DOI: 10.52174/2579-2989_2023.6-48

Vu, A. N., & Nguyen, D. L. (2024). The gig economy: The precariat in a climate precarious world. *World Development Perspectives*, 34, 100596. DOI: 10.1016/j.wdp.2024.100596

Yunita, F. T. (2023). Embracing the Gig Economy. *Indonesian Journal of Law and Society*, 4(2). Advance online publication. DOI: 10.19184/ijls.v4i2.43628

Zalizko, V. D., Dobrowolski, R. H., Cherniak, A. M., Artemov, V. Y., & Nowak, D. V. (2022). Gig-economy as a safety gradient for sustainable development of the mining industry. *Naukovyi Visnyk Natsionalnoho Hirnychoho Universytetu*, 4(4), 170–175. DOI: 10.33271/nvngu/2022-4/170

Chapter 17
Driving Digital Transformation: A Case Study of ITC Limited's Journey Towards Operational Excellence and Sustainable Growth

A. B. Mishra
https://orcid.org/0000-0003-4429-4058
International Institute of Management Studies, Pune, India

ABSTRACT

This case study delves into the digital transformation journey of ITC Limited, one of India's leading conglomerates, and its profound impact on operational efficiency, customer engagement, and sustainable growth. Through a comprehensive analysis of ITC's digital initiatives, including the adoption of cutting-edge technologies like AI, ML, IoT, and blockchain, this study uncovers the strategic shifts and innovative approaches that have propelled ITC towards becoming an agile, customer-focused, and sustainable business. Key findings reveal how ITC's digital transformation has streamlined supply chain operations, enabled personalized customer experiences, and fostered innovation across its various business divisions. The study highlights the importance of continuous investment in emerging technologies, cybersecurity measures, and talent development to sustain ITC's competitive edge in the digital era. By prioritizing customer-centric digital strategies and remaining agile in adapting to market changes and maintain its leadership position.

DOI: 10.4018/979-8-3693-4369-2.ch017

INTRODUCTION

ITC Limited (formerly Imperial Tobacco Company of India Limited) is one of India's foremost private sector companies with a diversified presence in various industries including FMCG (Fast Moving Consumer Goods), hotels, paperboards and packaging, agribusiness, and information technology. (A. Singh et al., 2011) Established in 1910, ITC has evolved from a single-product company to a multi-business conglomerate. Encouraging wealth through exceptional service delivery is ITC's objective, as it is ranked among India's top 10 most valued and admired organisations. ITC prioritises developing trust and adding value for all its stakeholders because it is a customer-centric business. To increase client happiness and promote steadfast loyalty, the business is committed to innovation and is always creating new and better goods, services, and management techniques.(Mishra & Dodke, 2024) In India, 275 million people use tobacco products, and the country's cigarette market is worth $9 billion. In that country, ITC Ltd sells 81% of the cigarettes consumed there. About 5 percent of women and 37 percent of males between the ages of 17 and 69 smoke in India, where there are an estimated 120 million smokers. The big customer bases result in a big number of tiers in the overall distribution hierarchy and many intermediaries in the system.(Srivastava et al., 2019) This case study aims to provide a comprehensive analysis of ITC Limited's strategies in managing its diverse business portfolio, adapting to digital transformation, meeting changing consumer demands, and implementing sustainable practices. The insights derived from this study will offer valuable lessons for other conglomerates facing similar challenges and seeking to maintain a competitive edge in a rapidly evolving market landscape.

PROBLEM STATEMENT

ITC Limited, an Indian multinational conglomerate, operates across a diverse range of industries including FMCG, hotels, agribusiness, paperboards and packaging, and information technology. As a market leader, ITC has continually sought to innovate and stay ahead of the competition. In the current digital era, the company faces the imperative to undergo digital transformation to maintain its competitive edge, enhance operational efficiencies, and meet evolving consumer expectations. To encounters several key issues that need to be addressed to sustain its market leadership position and ensure continued growth:

Legacy Systems and Processes: Transitioning from traditional business models and legacy systems to modern, digital-first approaches.

Integration Across Business Units: Ensuring seamless digital integration across its diverse business units, each with unique operational dynamics and requirements.

Consumer Expectations: Meeting the heightened expectations of digitally savvy consumers who demand personalized experiences and instant gratification.

Data Management and Analytics: Leveraging big data and analytics to drive decision-making, improve customer insights, and enhance marketing strategies.

Workforce Adaptation: Training and equipping employees with the necessary digital skills to adapt to new technologies and processes.

Sustainability and CSR: Utilizing digital tools to enhance sustainability practices and effectively communicate these efforts to stakeholders.(Mishra, 2022) By examining ITC's strategies and their outcomes, the study will offer valuable insights for other conglomerates seeking to navigate the digital landscape and enhance their competitiveness in an increasingly digital world.

METHODOLOGY

To comprehensively analyze the digital transformation at ITC Limited and its impact on the company's competitiveness, operational efficiency, and customer engagement, the following multi-faceted methodology will be employed:

Literature Review: Review ITC's annual reports and official publications to gather data on the company's financial performance, strategic initiatives, and digital transformation efforts. Examine industry reports, whitepapers, and case studies on digital transformation trends and best practices in the FMCG, hospitality, agribusiness, and packaging sectors. Analyze academic papers and books on digital transformation frameworks and their application in large conglomerates.

Case Study Analysis: Identify key digital transformation initiatives at ITC, such as the e-Choupal initiative, digital marketing campaigns, supply chain digitalization, and ITC's own digital platforms.

Synthesis and Interpretation: Integrate the insights and data into a structured case study report, highlighting key findings, successes, challenges, and areas for improvement. Develop strategic recommendations for ITC to further enhance its digital transformation efforts based on the analysis.

Recommendations and Conclusions: Drawing conclusions based on the analysis and making recommendations for strategic actions or areas of further research.

LITERATURE REVIEW

The literature review provides a foundational understanding of ITC Limited's digital transformation journey, the broader context of digital transformation in conglomerates, and the specific strategies and challenges associated with such initiatives.

This review draws on company reports, industry publications, academic research, and case studies to offer a comprehensive overview.

1. ITC Limited: Company Overview and Historical Context

On August 24, 1910, Imperial Tobacco Company of India Limited was the name under which ITC was formed. With the increasing Indianization of the company's ownership, the company renamed itself from Imperial Tobacco Company of India Limited in 1970 to India Tobacco Company Limited and finally to I.T.C. Limited in 1974. (ITC Portal, 2024) The detail timeline (fig. no. 1) are as follows,

Table 1. Timeline

Year	Activities
1910	Incorporated under the name Imperial Tobacco Company
1925	Packaging and Printing: Backward Integration
1970	Company was renamed as the India Tobacco Company Limited
1974	Company was renamed as I.T.C. Limited
1975	Entry into the Hospitality Sector - A 'Welcome' Move- 'ITC-Welcome group Hotel Chola' (now renamed Welcome hotel by ITC Hotels, Cathedral Road, Chennai).
1979	Paperboards & Specialty Papers - Development of a Backward Area
1985:	Nepal Subsidiary - First Steps beyond National Borders
1990	Paperboards & Specialty Papers - Consolidation and Expansion
1990	Agri Business - Strengthening Farmer Linkages - Choupal initiative
2000	Information Technology - ITC Infotech India Limited,
2000	e-Choupal initiative
2001	Company was renamed as ITC Limited
2001:	Branded Packaged Foods - mint-o, Candyman confectionery and Aashirvaad Atta
2002	Education & Stationery Products: Paperkraft, Classmate
2002:	Agarbattis & Safety Matches - iKno, Mangaldeep and Aim
2005:	Personal Care Products- 'Essenza Di Wills', 'Fiama', 'Vivel' 'Superia', Engage deodorants
2010	Expanding the Tobacco Portfolio hand rolled cigar, Armenteros,

Source: Accumulated Data

Business Diversification and Strategies:

1. FMCG: Cigarettes: ITC remains the market leader in the Indian cigarette industry with brands include Wills Navy Cut, Gold Flake Kings, Gold Flake Premium lights, Gold Flake Super Star, Insignia, India Kings, Classic (Verve, Menthol,

Menthol Rush, Regular, Citric Twist, Mild & Ultra Mild), 555, Silk Cut, Scissors, Capstan, Berkeley, Bristol, Lucky Strike, Players, Flake and Duke & Royal.(BS web, 2023) With fewer than 10% of consumers switching brands every year, cigarette brands have the highest level of brand loyalty of all consumer goods. (Mishra, Goel, et al., 2022) There would be pull demand in this situation, thus availability is more crucial. Fast-moving consumer goods (FMCG) revenue for ITC increased by 20% to Rs 29,000 crore in FY23 from Rs 24,000 crore in FY22. The Revenue generated by ITC Limited in FY 2023 - 78,498 crore (US$9.8 billion) (Bohra et al., 2022) Food Products are ITC's FMCG portfolio includes leading brands such as Aashirvaad (staples), Sunfeast (biscuits and noodles), Bingo! (snacks), and Yippee! (noodles). ITC has ventured into personal care with brands like Fiama, Vivel, and Engage.(BS web, 2023)

2. Hotels: ITC Hotels is one of the largest hotel chains in India, focusing on luxury and sustainability. The group operates premium properties like ITC Maurya in New Delhi and ITC Grand Chola in Chennai.(Anupindi & Sivakumar, 2007)
3. Paperboards and Packagin: ITC is a leading player in the paper and packaging industry. The company focuses on eco-friendly and innovative packaging solutions. (ITC Portal, 2024)
4. Agribusiness: ITC's agribusiness division is a critical segment that sources raw materials for its FMCG products. The e-Choupal initiative is a notable program, which digitally empowers farmers and enhances the agri-value chain.(ITC Portal, 2024)
5. Information Technology: ITC Infotech provides IT services and solutions to clients globally. The IT division focuses on delivering digital solutions across industries.(ITC Portal, 2024)

Digital Transformation in Conglomerates: Digital transformation involves integrating digital technologies into all areas of a business, fundamentally changing how businesses operate and deliver value to customers.(Mishra, Satarkar, et al., 2024) For conglomerates like ITC, digital transformation spans various sectors, each with unique digital adoption needs and challenges. It enables companies to stay competitive in a rapidly evolving market by leveraging technologies such as data analytics, artificial intelligence, and IoT. (Mohseni et al., 2022) ITC's Digital Transformation Initiatives, e-Choupal Initiative was launched in 2000, e-Choupal is one of ITC's most significant digital initiatives, aimed at empowering farmers through digital access to information, products, and services. (Mishra, Ranjan, et al., 2023) The initiative has created a network of digital kiosks in rural areas, enhancing agricultural productivity and supply chain efficiency.(Mishra & Singh, 2024) ITC has increasingly adopted digital marketing strategies to engage with consumers, leveraging social media, SEO, and online advertising. The company's foray into e-commerce includes partnerships with major online retailers and the development of its own digital sales platforms. (Mishra et al., 2021) Global Digital Transformation Trends is a global trend towards adopting digital solutions to enhance customer experience, operational efficiency, and business innovation. Leading companies are leveraging big data, cloud computing, AI, and machine learning to drive digital transformation.(Usman M et al., 2023)

DIGITAL TRANSFORMATION AT ITC

ITC has expedited the use of digital technology at every operational node. The company is using cutting-edge digital technologies like AI/ML, Industry 4.0, Advanced Analytics, Big Data, and the Internet of Things to acquire information, source, manufacture, distribute, and serve customers. These technologies are being utilised to stimulate innovation and expansion, increase productivity, optimise operations and costs, enhance customer service, and boost all around effectiveness.(Ranjan et al., 2023) ITC is evolving into an agile, customer-focused, and sustainable business attributable to this rapid digital transformation. ITC has invested in digital technologies to enhance its supply chain operations, improving transparency, efficiency, and responsiveness. Technologies such as blockchain and IoT are being explored to ensure traceability and sustainability in sourcing and logistics. The implementation of advanced CRM systems has enabled ITC to better understand and engage with its customers, offering personalized experiences and fostering loyalty. The digital adoption nodes are as follows:

Figure 1. Digital adoption across nodes of operations

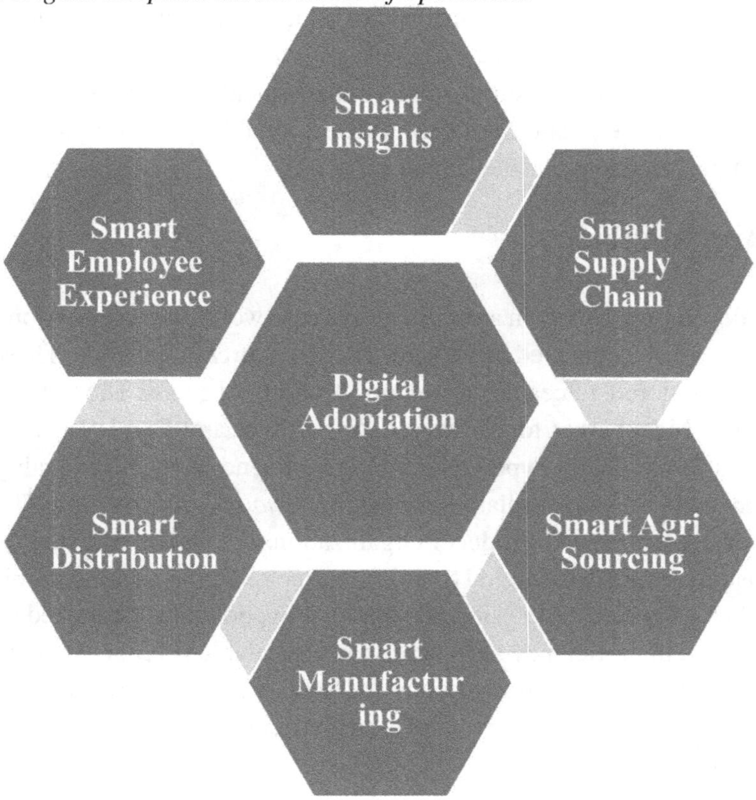

Source: Accumulated Data

Smart Insights:

ITC's digital efforts center around understanding customer needs and preferences. The Sixth Sense marketing command center analyzes unstructured data to create immersive brand storytelling, deliver hyper-personalized recommendations, and gain valuable consumer insights and market knowledge. Using generative AI-based technologies, it helps the business evaluate competitors, track digital performance, and develop adaptable content assets. (S. Singh, 2004)

Smart Supply Chain:

ITC's distribution networks have become more flexible, robust, and efficient due to digital acceleration across the company. An AI/ML-powered integrated planning and supply chain solution optimizes inventory and boosts efficiency, enhancing consumer services and increasing supply chain agility. An IoT-based system tracks inventory movements in real-time, improving vehicle turnaround times and customer experiences through data analytics.(Ahamad et al., 2024) The ITC One collaboration platform facilitates effective supply chain management, cost optimization through data analytics, and the exchange of best practices, enabling the company to identify areas for improvement and achieve better outcomes.

Smart Agri Sourcing:

ITC is developing NextGen agriculture value networks that are environmentally smart and digitally connected to enhance its agri sourcing network. These supply chains feature tailored, traceable, and identity-preserved goods. The state-of-the-art ITCMAARS (Metamarket for Advanced Agriculture and Rural Services) super-app provides farmers with hyperlocal crop recommendations, high-quality inputs, market connections, and ancillary services. (*E-Choupal Initiative by ITC*, 2020) Covering over 1105 Farmer Producer Organizations (FPOs) in nine states, it facilitates precision farming with digital tools like online soil testing and customized crop nutrition. MAARS ensures the smooth supply of hyperlocal, customized solutions, improving sourcing efficiency and creating new, scalable revenue streams. Project Astra, an AI/ML and advanced analytics-based platform, supports ITC's Agribusiness by promoting price discovery, operational efficiency, and informed purchasing decisions.(GOVIND S, 2020)

Smart Manufacturing:

ITC's Paper & Paperboard division has adopted Industry 4.0 techniques, with over 100 use cases created and implemented. The division has achieved smart operations using digital technologies like Industrial IoT, integrated data infrastructure, AI/ML algorithms, computer vision-based solutions, and IoT-based crop monitoring. Robotic Process Automation (RPA) has also been extensively utilized, streamlining procedures, accelerating turnaround times, and ensuring accuracy and compliance. (Rana et al., 2022)Currently, around 830 BOTs are in use for various processes, eliminating repetitive manual tasks, improving accuracy and compliance, and saving substantial time.

Smart Distribution:

The B2B app Unnati has digitized over 520,000 stores in India, offering hyper-local connections, personalized recommendations, and 24/7 ordering capabilities. Big data analytics and machine learning algorithms enhance decision-making at the frontline, providing outlet-level personalized recommendations through Project PACE, which uses over 8000 data points to make precise, tailored store-level suggestions. AI-based tools like Trinetra automate in-outlet display quality inspections, while the online salesperson VIRU streamlines the ordering process, ensuring smooth transactions and strengthening trade relations. The Vistaar mobile application enhances rural sales engagement and execution within the network of rural stockists, enabling digital empowerment and growth in rural markets. ITC's "phygital" model—which involves working with farmer producer organisations (FPOs) and using digital technology to provide individualised solutions to farmers—is likely to bode well for the business as it seeks to maximise procurement costs through broad backward connections and assist producers in price exploration. Project Lighthouse leverages advanced analytics to optimize marketing expenditures through media mix modeling and trade-based promotional spending, ensuring effective resource allocation and improved operational efficiency (Mishra, Satarkar, et al., 2023)

Smart Employee Experience:

The ITC Young Digital Innovators' Forum and the DigiNext Council play crucial roles in advancing digital transformation within ITC by fostering a "digi-first" culture and empowering employees. The Young Digital Innovators' Forum, comprising digital natives from various sectors, crowdsources innovative digital strategies and explores opportunities across the value chain. The DigiNext Council, consisting of senior ITC managers, facilitates idea exchange and sponsors high-impact digital initiatives. Recognizing digital as the decade's biggest trend, ITC is committed to investing in a smart, interconnected ecosystem to gain a competitive advantage and capitalize on new opportunities. (*Digital Transformation at ITC - For a Future Tech Organisation*, 2024)

MARKETING STRATEGY OF ITC LIMITED

ITC Limited employs a multifaceted marketing strategy to maintain its leadership position and drive growth across its diverse business segments. These strategies are tailored to the unique demands and consumer dynamics of each sector. Here are the key elements of ITC's marketing strategy:

1. Brand Portfolio and Positioning

Diverse Brand Portfolio: FMCG: ITC offers a wide range of products under various brands catering to different consumer needs. (Mishra, Raikwar, et al., 2024) Notable brands include Aashirvaad (staples), Sunfeast (biscuits and noodles), Bingo! (snacks), Yippee! (noodles), and personal care products under Fiama, Vivel, and Engage. (A. Singh et al., 2011)

Hotels: ITC Hotels are positioned as luxury and premium, focusing on sustainable luxury and heritage, with flagship properties like ITC Maurya and ITC Grand Chola.(Bohra et al., 2022)

Premium Positioning: ITC positions its FMCG and hotel products as premium to attract a broad spectrum of consumers seeking quality and reliability.

2. Product Innovation and Diversification

Constant Innovation: ITC invests significantly in research and development to drive product innovation, ensuring its offerings align with evolving consumer preferences. This includes introducing new flavors, variants, and entirely new product lines. (Varma & Mishra, 2015)

Category Diversification: ITC continuously explores new categories, such as premium chocolates with the Fabelle brand and dairy products under Aashirvaad Svasti, to tap into emerging markets and consumer demands.

3. Integrated Marketing Communications

Advertising and Promotion: ITC employs an integrated approach combining traditional and digital marketing. They use high-impact TV commercials, print ads, and outdoor advertising, complemented by a robust digital presence on social media platforms like Instagram and Facebook. ITC's influencer marketing campaign was to promote the newly launched Ved Vidya range effectively. (Mishra, Chand, et al., 2022)

Sponsorship and Events: ITC enhances brand visibility and consumer engagement through sponsorship of cultural festivals, sports events, and other significant events. Celebrity Brand endorsement for various products by celebrities such as Kartik Aaryan, Tara Sutaria, Shah Rukh Khan, Yuvraj Singh & Soha ali Khan, Sonam Kapoor, Sachin Tendulkar, Kiara Advani, Saina Nehwal and many more.

4. Sustainability and Corporate Social Responsibility (CSR)

Sustainability as a Marketing Tool: ITC highlights its commitment to sustainability and CSR in its marketing communications. Initiatives in water conservation, solid waste recycling, and sustainable agriculture appeal to environmentally conscious consumers. The "Responsible Luxury" theme in ITC Hotels emphasizes eco-friendly practices, differentiating the brand in the hospitality sector (A. Singh et al., 2011)

5. Distribution and Reach

Extensive Distribution Network: ITC has built a comprehensive distribution network ensuring its products are available in both urban and rural markets. (Varma & Mishra, 2013)This extensive reach is a significant competitive advantage. The company employs a combination of direct distribution and partnerships with wholesalers and retailers. E-commerce and Modern Retail: ITC strengthens its digital presence through e-commerce partnerships with platforms like Amazon and Flipkart and its own online portals. (Mishra, 2015)This ensures accessibility for tech-savvy consumers. Collaborations with modern retail chains further enhance ITC's footprint in urban areas.

6. Consumer Engagement and Loyalty Programs

Consumer-Centric Approach: ITC focuses on understanding consumer needs through market research and direct feedback. This approach informs product development and marketing strategies. Loyalty programs like Club ITC in the hospitality sector offer personalized experiences and rewards, fostering brand loyalty and repeat business (Varma & Mishra, 2015)

7. Strategic Alliances and Partnerships

Collaborations: ITC forms strategic alliances and partnerships to enhance product offerings and market reach. This includes collaborations with international brands for technology transfer and product development. Agri-Business Linkages: The e-Choupal initiative links rural farmers with the market, providing them with information and resources while securing raw material supply for ITC's agribusiness (S. Singh, 2004)

8. Digital Transformation

Embracing Digital Technologies: ITC integrates digital technologies across its operations to enhance efficiency and customer engagement. The e-Choupal initiative is a pioneering effort in leveraging digital solutions in agriculture. The company uses advanced data analytics and digital marketing tools to understand consumer behavior and personalize marketing efforts. Along with its motto of giving farmers "the freedom of choice" to sell their produce through market linkages. (S. Singh, 2004)

THE E-CHOUPAL MODEL:

ITC's Agri Business Division, one of India's leading exporters of agricultural commodities, developed e-Choupal to create a more efficient and sustainable supply chain, delivering enhanced value to its global customers. The e-Choupal model is tailored to address the unique challenges of Indian agriculture, including fragmented farms, inadequate infrastructure, and the presence of numerous intermediaries. (ITC, 2024)

Figure 2. e-Choupal - The Value Chain – Farm to Factory Gate

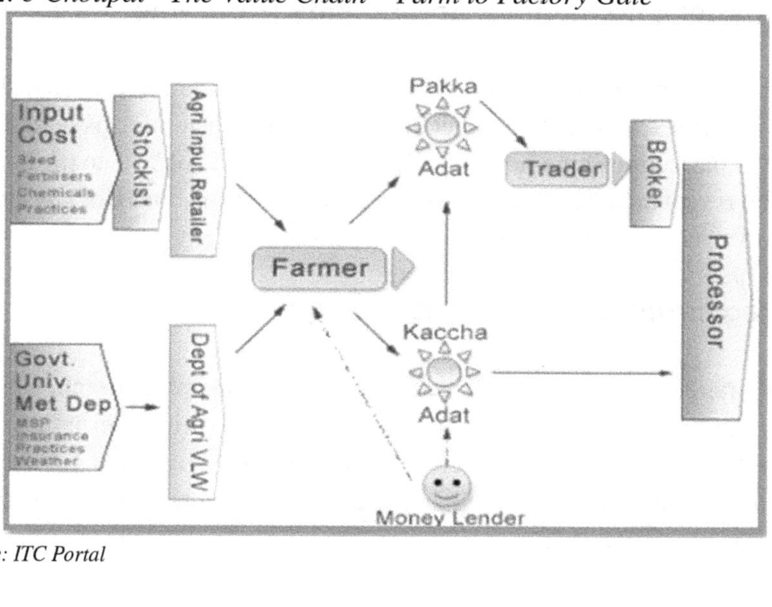

Source: ITC Portal

To disintermediate current intermediaries from the chain of information flow and market signals, e-Choupal leverages their physical transmission capabilities, including aggregation, logistics, counter-party risk, and bridge finance. Village internet kiosks run by farmers themselves, known as sanchalaks, skillfully combine click-and-mortar features. (*E-Choupal Initiative by ITC*, 2020)These kiosks allow the agricultural community to easily access local language information on weather and market prices, share knowledge about scientific farming practices and risk management, and make it easier to buy farm produce straight from the farmers themselves.(Mishra & Ranjan, 2022) The 'e-Choupal' platform offers farmers tailored knowledge and real-time information that improves their decision-making skills and helps them align their farm output with market demand while improving quality and productivity. Individual farmers can obtain high-quality inputs from reputable manufacturers at reasonable prices by pooling their demand for agricultural inputs.

Figure 3. e-chopal

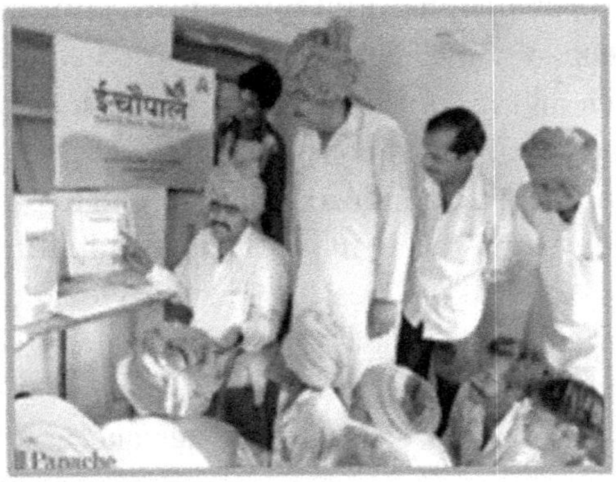

Source: ITC limited

With its direct marketing channel and virtual connection to the "mandi" system for price discovery, "e-Choupal" does away with needless middlemen and multiple handling. As a result, transaction expenses are greatly decreased. (GOVIND S, 2020) By means of many product- and service-specific collaborations with industry experts and ITC's own experience, "e-Choupal" guarantees top-notch quality in the delivery of all these items and services. Farmers gain from increased farm output and higher farm gate prices. Currently, 6100 kiosks spread throughout 10 states provide "e-Choupal" services to over 4 million farmers in over 35,000 villages. Many creative and novel approaches, some of which are costly, are being used to address these issues. A few examples include installing mobile chopals, installing VSAT equipment, upgrading BSNL exchanges with RNS kits, powering backup through batteries charged by solar panels, local caching of static content on websites to stream in fresh material more effectively, and operating a 24/7 help desk. (Goyal Vishnu, 2024) For E-payment, Several initiatives were taken to encourage customers and create extensive awareness.(Mishra, 2020) To move towards cashless transactions across ITC's network of Choupal Saagars. As a result, cashless transactions at Choupal Saagars increased from 8% to 21% post demonetization.

SYNTHESIS AND INTERPRETATION

The digital transformation at ITC Limited reflects a strategic shift towards leveraging advanced technologies to enhance every aspect of its operations. This section synthesizes the key insights from ITC's digital initiatives and interprets their broader implications.

- ITC's implementation of AI/ML-powered integrated planning and IoT-based tracking systems has optimized inventory management, improved real-time tracking of inventory movements, and increased supply chain agility. The use of blockchain and IoT for traceability and sustainability in sourcing ensures transparency and fosters consumer trust. These advancements lead to reduced operational costs, minimized wastage, and improved resource allocation, making ITC's supply chain more efficient and resilient. Enhanced traceability and sustainability practices align with global standards, enhancing ITC's reputation and appeal among environmentally conscious consumers and stakeholders
- The Sixth Sense marketing command center and advanced CRM systems enable ITC to gather deep consumer insights, deliver hyper-personalized recommendations, and create immersive brand experiences. By leveraging big data and AI, ITC can anticipate and respond to market trends and consumer preferences more effectively, maintaining a competitive edge.(Mishra, Allen, et al., 2024)
- Digital transformation in agri sourcing enables ITC to build a more resilient and efficient agricultural supply chain, ensuring consistent quality and supply of raw materials. Empowering farmers with digital tools not only improve their productivity and income but also fosters long-term partnerships and loyalty to ITC.
- ITC's Paper & Paperboard division utilizes Industry 4.0 techniques, including Industrial IoT, AI/ML algorithms, and RPA, to achieve smart operations and streamline processes.
- The use of robotic process automation (RPA) has eliminated repetitive tasks, increased accuracy, and ensured compliance. By adopting Industry 4.0 practices, ITC positions itself at the forefront of manufacturing innovation, capable of rapidly adapting to changes in demand and production requirements.

ITC's digital transformation initiatives demonstrate a strategic and comprehensive approach to integrating advanced technologies across its operations. The resulting enhancements in supply chain efficiency, customer engagement, agri sourcing, manufacturing, and employee empowerment have positioned ITC as a leading, innovative, and sustainable conglomerate. This transformation not only drives operational excellence and growth but also ensures ITC's continued relevance and competitiveness in a rapidly evolving digital landscape. The company's commitment to digital innovation and investment in a smart, interconnected ecosystem lays a strong foundation for future success.

CONCLUSIONS AND RECOMMENDATIONS

ITC Limited's journey from a tobacco company to a diversified conglomerate is marked by strategic diversification, innovation, and sustainability. Despite facing challenges, ITC's robust business model and commitment to sustainable growth position it well for future success. As ITC continues to expand its footprint across various sectors, it remains a quintessential example of a company that balances profitability with social responsibility. ITC's adoption of advanced digital technologies such as AI, ML, IoT, and blockchain has significantly improved its operational efficiency. This has streamlined processes across supply chain management, manufacturing, and agri-sourcing, leading to reduced costs, minimized wastage, and better resource allocation. The use of advanced CRM systems and data analytics has enabled ITC to gain deep insights into consumer behavior, allowing for hyper-personalized marketing and enhanced customer experiences. This has resulted in increased customer satisfaction and loyalty, strengthening ITC's market position. ITC's focus on digital tools for traceability and sustainability, particularly in its agri-business division, has not only ensured higher quality and consistency in sourcing but has also aligned with global standards for environmental responsibility. This has bolstered ITC's reputation among consumers and stakeholders as a responsible and sustainable company. ITC should continue to invest in emerging technologies such as AI, ML, blockchain, and IoT. Exploring these technologies can further enhance operational efficiencies and create new opportunities for innovation and growth. ITC should continue to leverage big data and advanced analytics to inform strategic decision-making. This includes using predictive analytics to anticipate market trends, optimize inventory, and enhance customer personalization efforts. The digital landscape is rapidly evolving, and ITC should remain agile in monitoring market changes and adapting its digital strategies accordingly. Regularly reviewing and updating digital initiatives will ensure ITC stays relevant and competitive in the market. ITC's comprehensive digital transformation has positioned it as a leader in leveraging advanced technologies for operational excellence, customer engagement, and sustainable growth. By continuing to invest in digital innovations, enhancing cybersecurity, and fostering a digi-first culture, ITC can sustain its competitive advantage and drive future success. Emphasizing customer-centric strategies and expanding digital initiatives in rural markets will further consolidate ITC's position as a forward-thinking and inclusive conglomerate.

REFERENCES

Ahamad, S., Mishra, A. B., Raghuram, K. S., Riyazuddin, Y. M., & Alanya-Beltran, J. (2024). *Applications of Internet of Things (IoT) in Maintaining Privacy and Security of Smart Cities*. DOI: 10.1201/9781003405580-30

Anupindi, R., & Sivakumar, S. (2007). ITC's e-Choupal: a platform strategy for rural transformation. *Business Solutions for the Global Poor: Creating Social and Economic Value*, 173–182.

Bohra, D. K., Nagansur, S., & Anute, N. (2022). *Comparative Analysis of FMCG Products with Special Reference to HUL and ITC*. OmniScience A Multi-Disciplinary Journal. DOI: 10.37591/omniscience.v12i2.3395

BS web. (2023). *ITC's FMCG revenue up 20% in FY23 as it aims to de-risk from tobacco biz*. Business Standard. https://www.business-standard.com/companies/news/itc-s-fmcg-revenue-up-20-in-fy23-as-it-aims-to-de-risk-from-tobacco-biz-123061500213_1.html

Digital transformation at ITC - For a Future Tech Organisation. (2024). ITC. https://www.itcportal.com/digital-transformation-at-itc.aspx

e-Choupal initiative by ITC. (2020). https://dmeo.gov.in/sites/default/files/2021-08/Package1_Agriculture_CaseStudy4.pdf

GOVIND S. (2020). *E-Choupal : 20 Glorious Years, One Epic Revolution*. The Fiery Fawkes. https://thefieryfawkes.in/2020/06/23/e-choupal-20-glorious-years-one-epic-revolution/

Goyal Vishnu. (2024). *Success Story: How ITC E-Choupal Initiative Revolutionised the Lives of 4 million+ Farmers*. MyOperator. https://myoperator.com/blog/success-story-how-itc-e-choupal-revolutionized-the-lives-of-4-million-farmers

ITC. (2024). *The e-Choupal model*. ITC. https://www.itcportal.com/businesses/agri-business/e-choupal.aspx

Mishra, A. B. (2015). *Mobile Commerce in Modern Business Era. 3*, 1–80. https://www.researchgate.net/publication/351840817_Mobile_Commerce_in_Modern_Business_Era

Mishra, A. B. (2020). E- PAYMENT SYSTEM: A RISING TREND OF ECONOMY. *New Paradigm in Business and Education.* https://www.researchgate.net/profile/Anitha-K-2/publication/349605501_E-LEARNING_THROUGH_GAMIFICATION-_AN_ITINERARY_TO_GAIN_IN-DEPTH_KNOWLEDGE/links/6037d566299bf1cc26ef9597/E-LEARNING-THROUGH-GAMIFICATION-AN-ITINERARY-TO-GAIN-IN-DEPTH-KNOWLEDGE.pdf#page=10

Mishra, A. B., Varma Anil, & Ranjan Nitin. (2021). PUTSCH BUYER TENDENCY AND CLIMBING SALES OF MOBILE TRADE BUSINESS. *Manager –. British Journal of Administrative Management*, 58(152), 54–60.

Mishra, A. B. (2022). SAHYADRI FARMS: INDIA'S LARGEST FARMER PRODUCER COMPANY. *International Journal of Advance and Applied Research*, 10, 996–998. https://ijaar.co.in/wp-content/uploads/2022/11/1001175.pdf

Mishra, A. B., Allen, M., & Tirkey, P. (2024). *Disruption causes to Micromax by once a Market leader now a Myth*. https://www.iimspune.edu.in/images/pdf/Journal/Vol3I1-Paper11.pdf

Mishra, A. B., Chand, K., & Kaith, K. (2022). Influencer Marketing as Emerging Promotional Tool in Modern Era and Opportunities to Uprising Sales. *International Journal of Emerging Research in Engineering, Science, and Management*, 1(3). Advance online publication. DOI: 10.58482/ijeresm.v1i3.3

Mishra, A. B., & Dodke, S. D. (2024). ZARA: Technological Influence on Becoming the Fashion Industry's Market Leader. In *IGI Global* (pp. 204–215). DOI: 10.4018/979-8-3693-2643-5.ch012

Mishra, A. B., Goel, A., & Jajoo, P. (2022). A Case Study of Amul: Implementation of Extension Strategy to Repositioning Brand During Covid-19 Period. *International Journal of Emerging Research in Engineering, Science, and Management*, 1(4). Advance online publication. DOI: 10.58482/ijeresm.v1i4.3

Mishra, A. B., Raikwar, A., & Tiwari, A. (2024). *BRITANNIA: MARKETING INITIATIVES BOOST A FLEDGLING BUSINESS'S TRANSFORMATION TO ONE OF THE LARGEST FMCG BRANDS*. https://www.iimspune.edu.in/images/pdf/Journal/Vol3I1-Paper12.pdf

Mishra, A. B., & Ranjan, N. (2022). INTERNET OF THINGS BASED EMERGING SMART TOOLS FOR NEW EDGE EDUCATION. *Mukt Shabd Journal*, 11(10), 80–87. DOI: 10.0014.MSJ.2022.V11I10.0086781.1135708

Mishra, A. B., Ranjan, N., Sharma, K. M., Padhye, P., & Chand, K. (2023). Advancement of Digital Transformation to Boost Financial Services Industry. *Journal of Informatics Education and Research*, 3(2), 2435–2440.

Mishra, A. B., Satarkar, M., & Joshi, S. (2023). IKEA - Phygital Transformation in Furniture Manufacturing Industry. *International Journal of Emerging Research in Engineering, Science, and Management*, 2(3), 6–9. DOI: 10.58482/ijeresm.v2i3.2

Mishra, A. B., Satarkar, M., & Joshi, S. (2024). Capitalizing the Retail Industry by Automation and Artificial Intelligence (AI): Case Study of IKEA. In *IGI Global* (pp. 239–251). DOI: 10.4018/979-8-3693-2643-5.ch014

Mishra, A. B., & Singh, A. (2024). The Mumbai Dabbawalas : An Efficient and Sustainable Lunchbox Delivery System. In *IGI Global* (pp. 154–160). DOI: 10.4018/979-8-3693-1544-6.ch007

Mohseni, M., Othman, B. A., Raturi, P., Mishra, A. B., Priya, S. J., & Saravanan, V. (2022). The Role of Parallel Computing Towards Implementation of Enhanced and Effective Industrial Internet of Things (IOT) Through Manova Approach. *2022 2nd International Conference on Advance Computing and Innovative Technologies in Engineering (ICACITE)*, 160–164. DOI: 10.1109/ICACITE53722.2022.9823698

Portal, I. T. C. (2024). *History and Evolution*. Itcportal.Com. https://www.itcportal.com/about-itc/profile/history-and-evolution.aspx

Ranjan, N., Mishra, A. B., & Padhye, P. (2023). Dynamics of Digital Payments Enable the World's Safest Way to Pay. *Journal of Informatics Education and Research*, 3(2). Advance online publication. DOI: 10.52783/jier.v3i2.406

Singh, A., Rishi, M., & Shukla, R. (2011). Green management and environmental sustainability: A case of ITC Green Center. *Emerald Emerging Markets Case Studies*, 1(2), 1–13. DOI: 10.1108/20450621111159859

Singh, S. (2004). Leveraging ICTs for Agricultural Development: A case study of E-choupals of ITC. *Paradigm*, 8(1), 1–6. DOI: 10.1177/0971890720040101

Srivastava, A. K., Jonjua Mehak, & Rana Rajesh. (2019). Status of Communicating CSR to Stakeholders on Social Media : A Case Study on ITC Limited & Nestle India. *Journal of Content. Community & Communication*, 9, 81–92.

Usman M, Sheoliha N, Prabhakar P V, Mishra, A. B., & Dondapati. (2023). Leading Strategies for Organizational Adaptation and Growth in Digital Transformation in Marketing. *Journal of Informatics Education and Research*.

Varma, S. R., & Mishra, A. B. (2013). *Distribution Channels of Indian Insurance Business - A Study*. Abhinavan.

Varma, S. R., & Mishra, A. B. (2015). Study of Consumer Buying Behaviour in General Insurance Industry. In *Excellence through creativity, Research, innovation in field of IT and Management*.

Compilation of References

Abdi, H., & Nozari, H. (2025). Blockchain-Powered Multiobjective Portfolio Optimization under Uncertainty. *Journal of Future Digital Optimization*, 1(1), 62–70.

Adekoya, O. D., Mordi, C., Ajonbadi, H. A., & Chen, W. (2023). Implications of algorithmic management on careers and employment relationships in the gig economy – a developing country perspective. *Information Technology & People*. Advance online publication. DOI: 10.1108/ITP-01-2023-0064

Adeodato, R., & Pournouri, S. (2020). Secure implementation of e-governance: a case study about Estonia. Cyber Defence in the Age of AI, Smart Societies and Augmented Humanity, 397-429.

Admass, W. S., Munaye, Y. Y., & Diro, A. A. (2024). Cyber security: State of the art, challenges and future directions. *Cyber Security and Applications*, 2, 100031. DOI: 10.1016/j.csa.2023.100031

Ahamad, S., Mishra, A. B., Raghuram, K. S., Riyazuddin, Y. M., & Alanya-Beltran, J. (2024). *Applications of Internet of Things (IoT) in Maintaining Privacy and Security of Smart Cities*. DOI: 10.1201/9781003405580-30

Ahmad, W., Rasool, A., Javed, A. R., Baker, T., & Jalil, Z. (2021). Cyber security in iot-based cloud computing: A comprehensive survey. *Electronics (Basel)*, 11(1), 16. DOI: 10.3390/electronics11010016

Ai, J., Brockett, P. L., Cooper, W. W., & Golden, L. L. (2009, July). *An Optimization Approach to Enterprise Risk Management: An Aid to Financial Decision Management for Risk, Crisis and Opportunity.*

Aigner, I., Garai-Fodor, M., & Szemere, T. P. (2022, July). Singapore's journey as a digit-all-sized and innovative smart nation toward sustainability. In *2022 IEEE 10th Jubilee International Conference on Computational Cybernetics and Cyber-Medical Systems (ICCC)* (pp. 000259-000264). IEEE.

Akhtar, Z., & Rawol, A. T. (2024). Harnessing artificial intelligence (AI) for cybersecurity: Challenges, opportunities, risks, future directions. *Computers and Artificial Intelligence*, 2(2), 1485. DOI: 10.59400/cai.v2i2.1485

Akpan, I. J., & Akpan, A. A. (2024). Evolutionary Trends in Decision Sciences Education Research From Simulation and Games to Data Analytics and Generative Artificial Intelligence. DOI: 10.20944/preprints202407.1294.v1

Alaa Hammad, A., Adnan Falih, M., Ali Abd, S., & Rashid Ahmed, A. (2025). Detecting Cyber Threats in IoT Networks: A Machine Learning Approach. *International Journal of Computing and Digital Systems*, 17(1), 1–25. DOI: 10.12785/ijcds/1571020041

Albats, E., Podmetina, D., & Vanhaverbeke, W. (2023). Open innovation in SMEs: A process view towards business model innovation. *Journal of Small Business Management*, 61(6), 2519–2560. DOI: 10.1080/00472778.2021.1913595

Ali, S. (2024). *Investigating the Role of Blockchain Technology in Ireland; Enhancing Trust and Security in Digital Marketing Transactions* (Doctoral dissertation, Dublin Business School).

Aliahmadi, A., & Nozari, H. (2023, January). Evaluation of security metrics in AIoT and blockchain-based supply chain by Neutrosophic decision-making method. In *Supply chain forum: an international journal* (Vol. 24, No. 1, pp. 31-42). Taylor & Francis. DOI: 10.1080/16258312.2022.2101898

Aliahmadi, A., Nozari, H., & Ghahremani-Nahr, J. (2022). A framework for IoT and Blockchain based on marketing systems with an emphasis on big data analysis. *International journal of Innovation in Marketing Elements, 2*(1), 25-34.

Aliahmadi, A., Nozari, H., Ghahremani-Nahr, J., & Szmelter-Jarosz, A. (2022). Evaluation of key impression of resilient supply chain based on artificial intelligence of things (AIoT). *arXiv preprint arXiv:2207.13174.*

Aliahmadi, M. H., Movahed, A. B., Movahed, A. B., Nozari, H., & Bayanati, M. (2024). *Hospital 6.0 Components and Dimensions* (pp. 46–61). DOI: 10.4018/979-8-3693-3108-8.ch004

Aliahmadi, M. H., Movahed, A. B., Movahed, A. B., Nozari, H., & Bayanati, M. (2024). Hospital 6.0 Components and Dimensions. In *Advanced Businesses in Industry 6.0* (pp. 46-61). IGI Global.

Alijoyo, F. A., Kaur, C., Anjum, A., Vuyyuru, V. A., & Bala, B. K. (2024). Enhancing Cyber-Physical Systems Resilience: Adaptive Self-Healing Security Using Long Short-Term Memory Networks. *2024 International Conference on Advances in Computing, Communication and Applied Informatics (ACCAI)*, 1–8. DOI: 10.1109/ACCAI61061.2024.10602467

Ali, K. T. M., & Sivasubramanian, R. C. (2024). Understanding the Nexus Between Techno-Stress, Psychological Well-Being, and the Moderating Role of Job Resources in the Gig Economy. *Employee Responsibilities and Rights Journal*. Advance online publication. DOI: 10.1007/s10672-024-09505-5

Ameedeen, M. A., Hamid, R. A., Aldhyani, T. H. H., Al-Nassr, L. A. K. M., Olatunji, S. O., & Subramanian, P. (2024). A Framework for Automated Big Data Analytics in Cybersecurity Threat Detection. *Mesopotamian Journal of Big Data*, 2024, 175–184. DOI: 10.58496/MJBD/2024/012

Amit Bhardwaj, P. (2024). The Rise of Cyber Physical Systems: A Retrospective and Prospective Analysis of Applications. *International IT Journal of Research, ISSN: 3007-6706, 2*(3), 11-22.

Andronie, M., Lăzăroiu, G., tefănescu, R., U ă, C., & Dijmărescu, I. (2021). Sustainable, smart, and sensing technologies for cyber-physical manufacturing systems: A systematic literature review. *Sustainability (Basel)*, 13(10), 5495. DOI: 10.3390/su13105495

Anozie, U. C., Dada, S. A., Okonkwo, F. C., Egunlae, O., Animasahun, B., & Mazino, O. (2024). The convergence of edge computing and supply chain resilience in retail marketing. *International Journal of Science and Research Archive*, 12(02), 2769–2779. DOI: 10.30574/ijsra.2024.12.2.1574

Anupindi, R., & Sivakumar, S. (2007). ITC's e-Choupal: a platform strategy for rural transformation. *Business Solutions for the Global Poor: Creating Social and Economic Value*, 173–182.

April, K. (2024). Precarious Work in the Gig Economy: Diversity, Race and Indigeneity Lenses. In Meliou, E., Vassilopoulou, J., & Ozbilgin, M. F. (Eds.), *Diversity and Precarious Work During Socio-Economic Upheaval* (1st ed., pp. 137–162). Cambridge University Press. DOI: 10.1017/9781108933070.008

Arriagada, A., Bonhomme, M., Ibáñez, F., & Leyton, J. (2023). The gig economy in Chile: Examining labor conditions and the nature of gig work in a Global South country. *Digital Geography and Society*, 5, 100063. DOI: 10.1016/j.diggeo.2023.100063

Arutyunov, V. S., & Lisichkin, G. V. (2017). Energy resources of the 21st century: Problems and forecasts. Can renewable energy sources replace fossil fuels. *Russian Chemical Reviews*, 86(8), 777–804. DOI: 10.1070/RCR4723

Ashrafi, A., Constantinides, P., Mehandjiev, N., & Thatcher, J. B. (2025). Mobilising new frontiers in digital transformation research: A problematization review. *Information Systems Journal*, 35(1), 97–139. DOI: 10.1111/isj.12531

Attaran, S., Attaran, M., & Celik, B. G. (2024). Digital Twins and Industrial Internet of Things: Uncovering operational intelligence in industry 4.0. *Decision Analytics Journal*, 10, 100398. DOI: 10.1016/j.dajour.2024.100398

Auguste, D., Roll, S., & Despard, M. (2023). Democratizing the Economy or Introducing Economic Risk? Gig Work During the COVID-19 Pandemic. *Work and Occupations*, 07308884231202032. Advance online publication. DOI: 10.1177/07308884231202032

Baldassarre, B., Schepers, M., Bocken, N., Cuppen, E., Korevaar, G., & Calabretta, G. (2019). Industrial Symbiosis: Towards a design process for eco-industrial clusters by integrating Circular Economy and Industrial Ecology perspectives. *Journal of Cleaner Production*, 216, 446–460. DOI: 10.1016/j.jclepro.2019.01.091

Barański, M. (2023). Employment flexibility in times of crisis. *Studia Iuridica*, 95(95), 9–29. DOI: 10.31338/2544-3135.si.2022-95.1

Barral Valdez, C. (2023). Manifestation of global trends in hotel industries in baguio city as perceived by hotel guests. *International Journal of Advanced Research*, 11(11), 948–962. DOI: 10.21474/IJAR01/17898

Bathaee, M., Nozari, H., & Szmelter-Jarosz, A. (2023). Designing a new location-allocation and routing model with simultaneous pick-up and delivery in a closed-loop supply chain network under uncertainty. *Logistics (Basel)*, 7(1), 3. DOI: 10.3390/logistics7010003

Bechara, F. R., & Schuch, S. B. (2021). Cybersecurity and global regulatory challenges. *Journal of Financial Crime*, 28(2), 359–374. DOI: 10.1108/JFC-07-2020-0149

Behl, A., Rajagopal, K., Sheorey, P., & Mahendra, A. (2022). Barriers to entry of gig workers in the gig platforms: Exploring the dark side of the gig economy. *Aslib Journal of Information Management*, 74(5), 818–839. DOI: 10.1108/AJIM-08-2021-0235

Bewtra, P., Kharbanda, S., & Kamna, S. (2023). Gig Economy in India: Growth, Challenges and Way Forward. *International Journal of Indian Culture and Business Management*, 1(1), 1. DOI: 10.1504/IJICBM.2023.10056418

Bhambri, P., Rani, S., & Khang, A. (2024). Al-driven Digital Twin and Resource Optimization in Industry 4.0 Ecosystem. *Intelligent Techniques for Predictive Data Analytics*, 47.

Bhat, A. K. (2024). Application And Impact of Artificial Intelligence in Financial Decision Making. *International Journal of Scientific Research in Science, Engineering and Technology*, 11(5), 57–63. DOI: 10.32628/IJSRSET2411417

Bhattacharya, S., & Sachdev, B. K. Implementation of renewable technologies in energy-efficient urban infrastructure: Development to promote sustainable socio-economic growth. In *Sustainable Technologies for Energy Efficient Buildings* (pp. 337–357). CRC Press.

Bloom, P. (2020). *Identity, Institutions and Governance in an AI World*. Springer International Publishing., DOI: 10.1007/978-3-030-36181-5

Bohra, D. K., Nagansur, S., & Anute, N. (2022). *Comparative Analysis of FMCG Products with Special Reference to HUL and ITC*. OmniScience A Multi-Disciplinary Journal. DOI: 10.37591/omniscience.v12i2.3395

Bonfanti, M. E. (2022). *Artificial intelligence and the offence-defence balance in cyber security. Cyber Security: Socio-Technological Uncertainty and Political Fragmentation*. Routledge.

Bongomin, O., Mwape, M. C., Mpofu, N. S., Bahunde, B. K., Kidega, R., Mpungu, I. L., & Ngulube, G. (2024). Digital Twin technology advancing Industry 4.0 and Industry 5.0 across Sectors. *Available atSSRN* 5072457.

Boye, J. I., & Arcand, Y. (2013). Current trends in green technologies in food production and processing. *Food Engineering Reviews*, 5(1), 1–17. DOI: 10.1007/s12393-012-9062-z

Broo, D. G., & Schooling, J. (2021). A framework for using data as an engineering tool for sustainable cyber-physical systems. *IEEE Access : Practical Innovations, Open Solutions*, 9, 22876–22882. DOI: 10.1109/ACCESS.2021.3055652

Brown, M. A., Zhou, S., & Ahmadi, M. (2018). Smart grid governance: An international review of evolving policy issues and innovations. *Wiley Interdisciplinary Reviews. Energy and Environment*, 7(5), e290. Advance online publication. DOI: 10.1002/wene.290

BS web. (2023). *ITC's FMCG revenue up 20% in FY23 as it aims to de-risk from tobacco biz*. Business Standard. https://www.business-standard.com/companies/news/itc-s-fmcg-revenue-up-20-in-fy23-as-it-aims-to-de-risk-from-tobacco-biz-123061500213_1.html

Buchak, G. (2024). Financing the Gig Economy. *The Journal of Finance*, 79(1), 219–256. DOI: 10.1111/jofi.13292

Camacho, N. G. (2024). The Role of AI in Cybersecurity: Addressing Threats in the Digital Age. *Journal of Artificial Intelligence General Science (JAIGS) ISSN:3006-4023, 3*(1), 143–154. DOI: 10.60087/jaigs.v3i1.75

Chahal, S. (2023). Navigating Financial Evolution: Business process optimization and digital transformation in the finance sector. *International Journal of Finance*, 8(5), 67–81. DOI: 10.47941/ijf.1475

Chan, X. W., Shang, S., & Lu, L. (Eds.). (2024). *Work-Life Research in the Asia-Pacific: Implications for Justice, Equity, Diversity, and Inclusion*. Springer Nature Switzerland. DOI: 10.1007/978-3-031-52795-1

Chen, Y., Yang, O., Sampat, C., Bhalode, P., Ramachandran, R., & Ierapetritou, M. (2020). Digital twins in pharmaceutical and biopharmaceutical manufacturing: A literature review. *Processes (Basel, Switzerland)*, 8(9), 1088. DOI: 10.3390/pr8091088

Chowdhry, D. G., Verma, R., & Mathur, M. (Eds.). (2020). *The Evolution of Business in the Cyber Age: Digital Transformation, Threats, and Security*. CRC Press. DOI: 10.1201/9780429276484

Cichorska, J., & Zielina, K. (2023). Assessment of the Effects of the COVID-19 Pandemic in the HoReCa Industry in the Opinion of Customers and Employees. *Finanse i Prawo Finansowe*, 2(38), 45–73. DOI: 10.18778/2391-6478.2.38.03

Cordeiro, C. M., & Sindhøj, E. (2024). Situating the discourse of recycled nutrient fertilisers in circular economy principles for sustainable agriculture. *Frontiers in Sustainability*, 5, 1465752. DOI: 10.3389/frsus.2024.1465752

Cyber Security Agency of Singapore. (2021). Singapore's National Cybersecurity Strategy. Retrieved from: https://www.csa.gov.sg

da Costa Fernandes, S., Pigosso, D. C., McAloone, T. C., & Rozenfeld, H. (2020). Towards product-service system oriented to circular economy: A systematic review of value proposition design approaches. *Journal of Cleaner Production*, 257, 120507. DOI: 10.1016/j.jclepro.2020.120507

Dana, L.-P., Salamzadeh, A., Mortazavi, S., & Hadizadeh, M. (2022). Investigating the Impact of International Markets and New Digital Technologies on Business Innovation in Emerging Markets. *Sustainability (Basel)*, 14(2), 983. DOI: 10.3390/su14020983

Darem, A. A., Alhashmi, A. A., Alkhaldi, T. M., Alashjaee, A. M., Alanazi, S. M., & Ebad, S. A. (2023). Cyber Threats Classifications and Countermeasures in Banking and Financial Sector. *IEEE Access : Practical Innovations, Open Solutions*, 11(2), 125138–125158. DOI: 10.1109/ACCESS.2023.3327016

Das, I. R., Talukder, M. B., & Kumar, S. (2024). Implication of Artificial Intelligence in Hospitality Marketing. In Kumar, S., Talukder, M. B., & Pego, A. (Eds.), *Advances in Hospitality, Tourism, and the Services Industry* (pp. 291–310). IGI Global. DOI: 10.4018/979-8-3693-1978-9.ch014

Das, P., Jain, C., & Singh, M. (2024). Toward a trusted smart city ecosystem: IoE and blockchain-enabled cognitive frameworks for shared business Services. In *Industrial Internet ofThings Security* (pp. 208–228). CRC Press. DOI: 10.1201/9781003466284-11

Davidson, A., Gleim, M. R., Johnson, C. M., & Stevens, J. L. (2023). Gig worker typology and research agenda: Advancing research for frontline service providers. *Journal of Service Theory and Practice*, 33(5), 647–670. DOI: 10.1108/JSTP-08-2022-0188

De Ruyter, A., & Brown, M. (2019). *The Gig Economy* (1st ed.). Agenda Publishing. DOI: 10.1017/9781788210065

Demertzi, V., Demertzis, S., & Demertzis, K. (2023). An Overview of Cyber Threats, Attacks and Countermeasures on the Primary Domains of Smart Cities. In *Applied Sciences (Switzerland)* (Vol. 13, Issue 2). DOI: 10.3390/app13020790

Dettlaff, A. (2023). Professional Activation of Women and Flexible Forms of Employment, as Exemplified by Gig Economy. *WSB Journal of Business and Finance*, 57(1), 12–20. DOI: 10.2478/wsbjbf-2023-0002

Di Renzo, B., Hillairet, M., Picard, M., Rifaut, A., Bernard, C., Hagen, D., Maar, P., & Reinard, D. (2007). Operational risk management in financial institutions: Process assessment in concordance with Basel II. *Software Process Improvement and Practice*, 12(4), 321–330. DOI: 10.1002/spip.322

Diagne, M. (2002). *Financial Risk Management and Portfolio Optimization Using Artificial Neural Networks and Extreme Value Theory* (Doctoral dissertation, Technische Universität Kaiserslautern).

Digital transformation at ITC - For a Future Tech Organisation. (2024). ITC. https://www.itcportal.com/digital-transformation-at-itc.aspx

Diomin, A., & Kireeva, O. (2023). Personal flexibility and psychological well-being under multiple employment. *World of Science.Pedagogy and Psychology*, 11(5). Advance online publication. DOI: 10.15862/55PSMN523

Dobrowolska, M. (2024). The Role of Employment Flexibility in the Professional Education of Individuals at Risk of Social Exclusion. *Interdisciplinary Journal of Labor and Economics*, 13(1), 1–09. DOI: 10.62693/898pbl41

Dos Santos, S., Singh, J., Thulasiram, R. K., Kamali, S., Sirico, L., & Loud, L. (2022, June). A new era of blockchain-powered decentralized finance (DeFi)-a review. In *2022 IEEE 46th Annual Computers, Software, and Applications Conference (COMPSAC)* (pp. 1286-1292). IEEE.

Dupont, B. (2019). The cyber-resilience of financial institutions: Significance and applicability. *Journal of Cybersecurity*, 5(1), tyz013. Advance online publication. DOI: 10.1093/cybsec/tyz013

e-Choupal initiative by ITC. (2020). https://dmeo.gov.in/sites/default/files/2021-08/Package1_Agriculture_CaseStudy4.pdf

el Harrouti, T., Abouabdellah, A., & Serrou, D. (2020, December). Impact of electric mobility on the sustainable development of the country, Case study in Morocco. In *2020 IEEE 13th International Colloquium of Logistics and Supply Chain Management (LOGISTIQUA)* (pp. 1-6). IEEE.

El Mrabet, Z., Kaabouch, N., El Ghazi, H., & El Ghazi, H. (2018). Cyber-security in smart grid: Survey and challenges. *Computers & Electrical Engineering*, 67, 469–482. DOI: 10.1016/j.compeleceng.2018.01.015

ElMamy, S. B., Mrabet, H., Gharbi, H., Jemai, A., & Trentesaux, D. (2020). A Survey on the Usage of Blockchain Technology for Cyber-Threats in the Context of Industry 4.0. *Sustainability (Basel)*, 12(21), 9179. DOI: 10.3390/su12219179

Endress, T. (2024). Disruption and the Gig Economy: What's Next? In Endress, T., & Badir, Y. F. (Eds.), *Business and Management in Asia: Disruption and Change* (pp. 109–122). Springer Nature Singapore. DOI: 10.1007/978-981-99-9371-0_7

Fahrul, M., Rusliati, E., Hosseini, S. H., Jannati Mashkani, A., Abdellahi, S. A., & Ilvira, Rifka Fitri, D. (2016). Document (3).Pdf. In *Agri Ekonomi* (Vol. 25, Issue Analisis Usaha dan Strategi Pengembangan Agribisnis Buah Naga CV. Kusumo Wanadri Kulon Progo, p. 20).

Fallah, M., & Nozari, H. (2021). Neutrosophic mathematical programming for optimization of multi-objective sustainable biomass supply chain network design. *Computer Modeling in Engineering & Sciences*, 129(2), 927–951. DOI: 10.32604/cmes.2021.017511

Familoni, B. T. (2024). Cybersecurity challenges in the age of AI: Theoretical approaches and practical solutions. *Computer Science & IT Research Journal*, 5(3), 703–724.

Feng, S., Mao, Y., Li, G., & Bai, J. (2025). Enterprise digital transformation, biased technological progress and carbon total factor productivity. *Journal of Environmental Planning and Management*, 68(1), 154–184. DOI: 10.1080/09640568.2023.2239493

Filip, F. G. (2020). *DSS—A Class of Evolving Information Systems*. Springer., DOI: 10.1007/978-3-030-39250-5_14

Filippova, O. Yu. (2023). International hotel service industry trends. *Visnyk of Donetsk National University of Economics and Trade named after Mykhailo Tugan-Baranovsky, 2(79) 2023*, 63–68. DOI: 10.33274/2079-4819-2023-79-2-63-68

Firoj, K., & Mohammad, B. T. (2024). Measuring sustainability in the broadcasting media industry in Bangladesh. *I-Manager's. Journal of Management*, 18(3), 51. DOI: 10.26634/jmgt.18.3.20234

Fragiadakis, G., Diou, C., Kousiouris, G., & Νικολαΐδου, M. (2024). Evaluating Human-AI Collaboration: A Review and Methodological Framework. https://doi.org//arxiv.2407.19098DOI: 10.48550

Gamero, E., Shoshi, A., Full, J., Sauer, A., & Miehe, R. (2024). Data Management in Biorefineries: Conceptual Thoughts on Lean Digital Twinning. *Procedia CIRP*, 125, 48–53. DOI: 10.1016/j.procir.2024.08.009

Gedam, V. V., Raut, R. D., de Sousa Jabbour, A. B. L., Tanksale, A. N., & Narkhede, B. E. (2021). Circular economy practices in a developing economy: Barriers to be defeated. *Journal of Cleaner Production*, 311, 127670. DOI: 10.1016/j.jclepro.2021.127670

Geissdoerfer, M., Pieroni, M. P., Pigosso, D. C., & Soufani, K. (2020). Circular business models: A review. *Journal of Cleaner Production*, 277, 123741. DOI: 10.1016/j.jclepro.2020.123741

Geissdoerfer, M., Savaget, P., Bocken, N. M., & Hultink, E. J. (2017). The Circular Economy–A New Sustainability Paradigm? *Journal of Cleaner Production*, 143, 757–768. DOI: 10.1016/j.jclepro.2016.12.048

George, A. S., & Baskar, T. (2024). The Transformational Impact of AI Innovation on Financial Sectors in the Industry 5.0 Era. *Partners Universal International Innovation Journal, 2*(6), 09-13.

Ghahremani-Nahr, J., Najafi, S. E., & Nozari, H. (2022). A combined transportation model for the fruit and vegetable supply chain network. *Journal of Optimization in Industrial Engineering*, 15(2), 131–145.

Ghahremani-Nahr, J., Nozari, H., & Aliahmadi, A. (2023). Contract Design for Return Products in a Cooperative Closed-Loop Supply Chain. *Global Business Review*, 09721509221148892. DOI: 10.1177/09721509221148892

Ghahremani-Nahr, J., Nozari, H., Rahmaty, M., Zeraati Foukolaei, P., & Sherejsharifi, A. (2023). Development of a novel fuzzy hierarchical location-routing optimization model considering reliability. *Logistics (Basel)*, 7(3), 64. DOI: 10.3390/logistics7030064

Ghanbari, H., Mohammadi, E., Fooeik, A. M. L., Kumar, R. R., Stauvermann, P. J., & Shabani, M. (2024). Cryptocurrency Portfolio Allocation under Credibilistic CVaR Criterion and Practical Constraints. *Risks*, 12(10), 163. DOI: 10.3390/risks12100163

Ghansah, F. A., & Lu, W. (2023). Cyber-physical systems and digital twins for "cognitive building" in the construction industry. *Construction Innovation*. Advance online publication. DOI: 10.1108/CI-07-2022-0164

Ghobakhloo, M., Iranmanesh, M., Foroughi, B., Tseng, M. L., Nikbin, D., & Khanfar, A. A. (2025). Industry 4.0 digital transformation and opportunities for supply chain resilience: A comprehensive review and a strategic roadmap. *Production Planning and Control*, 36(1), 61–91. DOI: 10.1080/09537287.2023.2252376

Gisladottir, V., Ganin, A. A., Keisler, J. M., Kepner, J., & Linkov, I. (2017). Resilience of Cyber Systems with Over- and Underregulation. *Risk Analysis*, 37(9), 1644–1651. DOI: 10.1111/risa.12729 PMID: 27935146

Glarum, J., & Adrianopoli, C. (2020). *A short history of the study of decision making*. Butterworth-Heinemann., DOI: 10.1016/B978-0-12-815769-5.00003-8

Gomber, P., Kauffman, R. J., Parker, C., & Weber, B. W. (2018). On the fintech revolution: Interpreting the forces of innovation, disruption, and transformation in financial services. *Journal of Management Information Systems*, 35(1), 220–265. DOI: 10.1080/07421222.2018.1440766

GOVIND S. (2020). *E-Choupal : 20 Glorious Years, One Epic Revolution*. The Fiery Fawkes. https://thefieryfawkes.in/2020/06/23/e-choupal-20-glorious-years-one-epic-revolution/

Goyal Vishnu. (2024). *Success Story: How ITC E-Choupal Initiative Revolutionised the Lives of 4 million+ Farmers*. MyOperator. https://myoperator.com/blog/success-story-how-itc-e-choupal-revolutionized-the-lives-of-4-million-farmers

Grigorievich, T. A. (2025). METHODOLOGICAL APPROACH TO THE DEVELOPMENT OF DIGITAL TRANSFORMATION OF AN ENTERPRISE.

Guduru, S., Santhanam, N., & Pushparaj, N. (2023). Comprehending the research on the gig economy: A bibliometric approach. *Global Knowledge, Memory and Communication*. Advance online publication. DOI: 10.1108/GKMC-02-2023-0056

Guembe, B., Azeta, A., Misra, S., Osamor, V. C., Fernandez-Sanz, L., & Pospelova, V. (2022). The Emerging Threat of Ai-driven Cyber Attacks: A Review. *Applied Artificial Intelligence*, 36(1), 9–62. DOI: 10.1080/08839514.2022.2037254

Gunduz, M. Z., & Das, R. (2020). Cyber-security on smart grid: Threats and potential solutions. *Computer Networks*, 169, 107094. DOI: 10.1016/j.comnet.2019.107094

Guo, R., Lv, S., Liao, T., Xi, F., Zhang, J., Zuo, X., Cao, X., Feng, Z., & Zhang, Y. (2020). Classifying green technologies for sustainable innovation and investment. *Resources, Conservation and Recycling*, 153, 104580. DOI: 10.1016/j.resconrec.2019.104580

Gupta, S., & Vyas, S. (2022). Contemporary role of edge-AI in IoT and IoE in healthcare and digital marketing. In *Edge-AI in Healthcare* (pp. 75–84). CRC Press.

Habibzadeh, H., Nussbaum, B. H., Anjomshoa, F., Kantarci, B., & Soyata, T. (2019). A survey on cybersecurity, data privacy, and policy issues in cyber-physical system deployments in smart cities. *Sustainable Cities and Society*, 50, 101660. DOI: 10.1016/j.scs.2019.101660

Hadi, A. A. W. K., & Pratono, A. H. (2024). Ethical predicaments of gig economy: Bibliometric approach. *Optimum: Jurnal Ekonomi Dan Pembangunan*, 14(1), 40–48. DOI: 10.12928/optimum.v14i1.9316

Hailemariam, A., & Erdiaw-Kwasie, M. O. (2023). Towards a circular economy: Implications for emission reduction and environmental sustainability. *Business Strategy and the Environment*, 32(4), 1951–1965. DOI: 10.1002/bse.3229

Hamel, C., Ahsan, M. M., & Raman, S. (2024). PMI-DT: Leveraging Digital Twins and Machine Learning for Predictive Modeling and Inspection in Manufacturing. *arXiv preprint arXiv:2411.01299*.

Han, X., Wang, N., Che, S., Yang, H., Zhang, K., & Xu, S. X. (2024). Enhancing Investment Analysis: Optimizing AI-Agent Collaboration in Financial Research. 538–546. DOI: 10.1145/3677052.3698645

Hanivan, H., & Rakhmawan, S. A. (2023). Gig Economy During Pandemic in East Java. *East Java Economic Journal*, 7(1), 69–89. DOI: 10.53572/ejavec.v7i1.88

Han, M. J. N., & Kim, M. J. (2021). A critical review of the smart city about citizen adoption towards sustainable smart living. *Habitat International*, 108, 102312. DOI: 10.1016/j.habitatint.2021.102312

Haque, A., Bharath, K. V. S., & Mateen, S. (2024). Smart grid concept and technologies for smart cities. In *Smart Cities: Power Electronics, Renewable Energy, and Internet of Things* (pp. 96-129). CRC Press.

Harsono, I., Hatim, F., Sumastuti, E., Thalib, B., & Sya'rani, R. (2024). Poverty statistics of South Sulawesi Province based on Human Development Index and GRDP using panel data. International Journal on Social Science. *Economics and Art*, 13(4), 234–239.

Hassan, A. (Ed.). (2021). *Technology Application in the Tourism and Hospitality Industry of Bangladesh*. Springer Singapore. DOI: 10.1007/978-981-16-2434-6

Hassan, R. (2023). *Work Arrangements in the Informal Sector and Gig Economy/Digital Platform Economy in Egypt*. Unpublished. DOI: 10.13140/RG.2.2.24113.19041

Hawkins, T. R., & Dente, S. M. (2010). Greenhouse gas emissions driven by the transportation of goods associated with French consumption. *Environmental Science & Technology*, 44(22), 8656–8664. DOI: 10.1021/es9025529 PMID: 20886825

Heshmati, A. (2017). A review of the circular economy and its implementation. *International Journal of Green Economics*, 11(3-4), 251–288. DOI: 10.1504/IJGE.2017.089856

Hibrida, A. R., & Sunarni, . (2023). The Future of Work: Navigating the Challenges and Opportunities of Automation, Gig Economy, and Skills Evolution in a Post-Pandemic World. *West Science Interdisciplinary Studies*, 1(08), 638–647. DOI: 10.58812/wsis.v1i08.186

Hödl, K. (2023). Artificial Intelligence for Decision Making. [Dodaj do projektu Citavi wg DOI]DOI: 10.59646/edbookc2/009

Ho, J.-Y., & O'Sullivan, E. (2019). Addressing the evolving standardisation challenges of 'smart systems' innovation: Emerging roles for government? *Science & Public Policy*, 46(4), 552–569. DOI: 10.1093/scipol/scz008

Hong, D. (2023). *Decision-Making Intelligence*. Springer Nature., DOI: 10.1007/978-981-99-4299-2_20

Hornik, J., Ofir, C., & Rachamim, M. (2024). Out of the fog: fog computing-enabled AI to support smart marketing management. *Management Review Quarterly*, 1-33.

Huang, K., & Zhu, F. (2023). ChatGPT and Gig Economy. In Huang, K., Wang, Y., Zhu, F., Chen, X., & Xing, C. (Eds.), *Beyond AI* (pp. 129–158). Springer Nature Switzerland. DOI: 10.1007/978-3-031-45282-6_5

Huđek, I., & Širec, K. (2023). The terminology and the concept of the gig economy. *Ekonomski Pregled*, 74(1), 34–58. DOI: 10.32910/ep.74.1.2

Huovila, A., Siikavirta, H., Rozado, C. A., Rökman, J., Tuominen, P., Paiho, S., & Ylén, P. (2022). Carbon-neutral cities: Critical review of theory and practice. *Journal of Cleaner Production*, 341, 130912. DOI: 10.1016/j.jclepro.2022.130912

Hu, S., Huang, S., Huang, J., & Su, J. (2021). Blockchain and edge computing technology enabling organic agricultural supply chain: A framework solution to trust crisis. *Computers & Industrial Engineering*, 153, 107079. DOI: 10.1016/j.cie.2020.107079

Ijiga, O. M., Idoko, I. P., Ebiega, G. I., Olajide, F. I., Olatunde, T. I., & Ukaegbu, C. (2024). Harnessing adversarial machine learning for advanced threat detection: AI-driven strategies in cybersecurity risk assessment and fraud prevention.

Ingle, M., Khati, K., & Dahiya, K. (2025). The Rise of Product-as-a-Service Models in the Digital Era: Redesigning Business Models for Circular Innovation. In *Innovating Sustainability Through Digital Circular Economy* (pp. 107–132). IGI Global Scientific Publishing.

Institute for AI Policy and Strategy (IAPS). (2023). *Adapting cybersecurity frameworks to manage frontier AI risks*. https://doi.org/https://doi.org/10.48550/arXiv.2408.07933

Irani, H. R., & Nozari, H. (Eds.). (2024). *Smart and Sustainable Interactive Marketing*. IGI Global. DOI: 10.4018/979-8-3693-1339-8

Islam, M. A., Khan, R. H., & Syeed, M. (2020, January). A smart and integrated surface water monitor system architecture: Bangladesh perspective. In *Proceedings of the International Conference on Computing Advancements* (pp. 1-6). DOI: 10.1145/3377049.3377103

ITC. (2024). *The e-Choupal model*. ITC. https://www.itcportal.com/businesses/agri-business/e-choupal.aspx

Jayadeva, S. M., Al Ayub Ahmed, A., Malik, R., Shaikh, A. A., Siddique, M. N. E. A., & Naved, M. (2022, June). Roles of Cloud Computing and Internet of Things in Marketing Management: A Critical Review and Future Trends. In *Proceedings of Second International Conference in Mechanical and Energy Technology: ICMET 2021,India* (pp. 165-173). Singapore: Springer Nature Singapore.

Jibril, A. B., Amoah, J., Panigrahi, R. R., & Gochhait, S. (2024). Digital transformation in emerging markets: The role of technology adoption and innovative marketing strategies among SMEs in the post–pandemic era. *The International Journal of Organizational Analysis*. Advance online publication. DOI: 10.1108/IJOA-05-2024-4509

Joel, O. T., & Oguanobi, V. U. (2024). Navigating business transformation and strategic decision-making in multinational energy corporations with geodata. *International Journal of Applied Research in Social Sciences*, 6(5), 801–818. DOI: 10.51594/ijarss.v6i5.1103

Jogarao, M., Lakshmana, B. C., & Naidu, S. T. (2024). AI-enabled circular economy management for sustainable smart cities: integrating artificial intelligence in resource optimisation and waste reduction. In *Smart Cities and Circular Economy* (pp. 83–96). Emerald Publishing Limited. DOI: 10.1108/978-1-83797-957-820241008

Joshi, A., Jain, S., & Gupta, P. K. (2024). Challenges and impact of the gig economy. *Sustainable Economies*, 2(2), 96. DOI: 10.62617/se.v2i2.96

Juneja, A., Goswami, S. S., & Mondal, S. (2024). Cyber security and digital economy: opportunities, growth and challenges. Journal of technology innovations and energy, 3(2), 1-22.

Kabanda, S., Tanner, M., & Kent, C. (2018). Exploring SME cybersecurity practices in developing countries. *Journal of Organizational Computing and Electronic Commerce*, 28(3), 269–282. DOI: 10.1080/10919392.2018.1484598

Kaloudi, N., & Li, J. (2021). The AI-Based Cyber Threat Landscape. *ACM Computing Surveys*, 53(1), 1–34. DOI: 10.1145/3372823

Kaneko, T. (2023). Naturally decision intelligence: Perfect algorithm generated by the hypothetical and synchronizing model for life system. *Intelligent Decision Technologies*, 17(1), 195–210. DOI: 10.3233/IDT-220231

Kashif, M., Kumar, P., Ghai, S., & Kumar, S. (2024). Disruptive Technologies in Computational Finance. In *Algorithmic Approaches to Financial Technology: Forecasting, Trading, and Optimization* (pp. 46-60). IGI Global. DOI: 10.4018/979-8-3693-1746-4.ch003

Kaspersky (2023). Global Cybersecurity Trends Report. *Kaspersky Cybersecurity Insights*. Retrieved from: https://www.kaspersky.com

Katsoulakis, E., Wang, Q., Wu, H., Shahriyari, L., Fletcher, R., Liu, J., Achenie, L., Liu, H., Jackson, P., Xiao, Y., Syeda-Mahmood, T., Tuli, R., & Deng, J. (2024). Digital twins for health: A scoping review. *NPJ Digital Medicine*, 7(1), 77. DOI: 10.1038/s41746-024-01073-0 PMID: 38519626

Kaur, N. (2024). Employment Opportunities and Work Trends Post-pandemic. In Kamaruddin, N., Idris, A., & Fernandez, K. (Eds.), *The New Normal and Its Impact on Society* (pp. 25–40). Springer Nature Singapore. DOI: 10.1007/978-981-97-0527-6_3

Kaushik, A. (2024). Comprehensive Impact of On-Demand Platforms: Examining the Gig Economy \'s Influence on Specialized Professionals, Work-Life Balance, and Gig Workers\' Perspectives. *International Journal for Research in Applied Science and Engineering Technology*, 12(1), 552–559. DOI: 10.22214/ijraset.2024.58005

Keshminder, J. S., Mia, M. A., Nourani, M., & Zhang, M. (2022). Gig employment in the Malaysian manufacturing industry: A cross-sectional analysis. *Asian-Pacific Economic Literature*, 36(1), 48–66. DOI: 10.1111/apel.12348

Khoiroh, M., & Syakur, A. S. (2023). The flexibility of Islamic law in the Ganjur tradition in Lamongan, Indonesia. *Ijtihad : Jurnal Wacana Hukum Islam Dan Kemanusiaan*, 23(2), 139–159. DOI: 10.18326/ijtihad.v23i2.139-159

Khor, C. S., Giarola, S., Chachuat, B., & Shah, N. (2011). An optimization-based framework for process planning under uncertainty with risk management. *Chemical Product and Process Modeling*, 6(2). Advance online publication. DOI: 10.2202/1934-2659.1597

Kozak, T., Kasza, L., & Nemeth, P. (2023). Examining the impact of the gig-economy, as a new challenge for supply chain strategy. *The Journal of Business and Retail Management Research*, 18(01). Advance online publication. DOI: 10.24052/JBRMR/V18IS01/ART-01

Kucheriava, H. O. (2024). Hotel industry of Ukraine in crisis conditions: Challenges, trends, prospects. *Вісник Київського Національного Лінгвістичного Університету. Серія Історія, Економіка. Філософія*, 29(29), 60–69. DOI: 10.32589/2412-9321.29.2024.301784

Kumar, M. S., Nagalakshmi, M. V. N., Reddy, C., Charan, Y. S. S., Kataria, A., & George, A. S. (2025). AI-Enhanced Real-Time Economic Data Analysis Using IoE. In *Role of Internet of Everything (IOE), VLSI Architecture, and AI in Real-Time Systems* (pp. 33-44). IGI Global Scientific Publishing.

Kumar, P., Sharma, L., & Sharma, N. C. (2024). Sustainable Development Balancing Economic Viability, Environmental Protection, and Social Equity. In *Sustainable Partnership and Investment Strategies for Startups and SMEs* (pp. 212–234). IGI Global. DOI: 10.4018/979-8-3693-2197-3.ch012

Kumar, R., & Agrawal, N. (2024). Shaping the future of industry: Understanding the dynamics of industrial digital twins. *Computers & Industrial Engineering*, 191, 110172. DOI: 10.1016/j.cie.2024.110172

Kumar, S., Talukder, M. B., & Pego, A. (Eds.). (2024). *Utilizing Smart Technology and AI in Hybrid Tourism and Hospitality*. IGI Global. DOI: 10.4018/979-8-3693-1978-9

Kuppa, V. K. P., Hegadi, R., Sajjan, K., Chowdary, K. D., Vanga, M. S. R., & Kumar, P. (2024, January). Investopolis: Decentralized customer loyalty tokenization on the blockchain. In *2024 IEEE International Conference on Consumer Electronics (ICCE)* (pp. 1-5). IEEE. DOI: 10.1109/ICCE59016.2024.10444326

Kuzma, E., & Sehnem, S. (2023). Propose a structural model for business value creation based on circular business models, innovation, and resource recovery in the pet industry. *Business Strategy and the Environment*, 32(1), 516–537. DOI: 10.1002/bse.3158

Lamperti, S., Cavallo, A., & Sassanelli, C. (2023). Digital servitization and business model innovation in SMEs: A model to escape from market disruption. *IEEE Transactions on Engineering Management*, 71, 4619–4633. DOI: 10.1109/TEM.2022.3233132

Lampropoulos, G., & Siakas, K. (2023). Enhancing and securing cyber-physical systems and Industry 4.0 through digital twins: A critical review. *Journal of Software (Malden, MA)*, 35(7), e2494. DOI: 10.1002/smr.2494

Łasak, P. (2022). The role of financial technology and entrepreneurial finance practices in funding small and medium-sized enterprises. *Journal of Entrepreneurship. Management and Innovation*, 18(1), 7–34.

Lata, M., & Kumar, V. (2021). 5 IoE Applications for Smart. *Internet of Energy for Smart Cities: Machine Learning Models and Techniques*, 127.

Laxmi, S., & Kumar, S. (2024). Improving Cyber Security: Artificial Intelligence's Ability to Detect and Stop Threats. *International Journal of Advanced Engineering Research and Science*, 11(6), 19–24. DOI: 10.22161/ijaers.116.3

Liang, H., Moya, B., Seah, E., Weng, A. N. K., Baillargeat, D., Joerin, J., ... & Chatzi, E. (2024). Harnessing Hybrid Digital Twinning for Decision-Support in Smart Infrastructures.

Lijuan, H. (2025). Enhancing SMEs Development Through Fintech: Insights from China's Economic Transformation. *International Journal of Education and Humanities*, 5(2), 257–265.

Li, S. (2023). The Gig Economy and Labour Market Dynamics. *Advances in Economics. Management and Political Sciences*, 61(1), 275–281. DOI: 10.54254/2754-1169/61/20231285

Liu, J., Zhang, Y., & Qian, X. (2009, June). Modeling chlorophyll-a in Taihu Lake with machine learning models. In 2009 3rd International Conference on Bioinformatics and Biomedical Engineering (pp. 1-6). IEEE. DOI: 10.1109/ICBBE.2009.5163072

Liu, M., Teng, F., Zhang, Z., Ge, P., Sun, M., Deng, R., Cheng, P., & Chen, J. (2024). Enhancing Cyber-Resiliency of DER-Based Smart Grid: A Survey. *IEEE Transactions on Smart Grid*, 15(5), 4998–5030. DOI: 10.1109/TSG.2024.3373008

Liu, X., Wider, W., Fauzi, M. A., Jiang, L., Udang, L. N., & Hossain, S. F. A. (2024). The evolution of smart hotels: A bibliometric review of the past, present and future trends. *Heliyon*, 10(4), e26472. DOI: 10.1016/j.heliyon.2024.e26472 PMID: 38420486

Li, X., Wang, J., & Yang, C. (2023). Risk prediction in financial management of listed companies based on optimized BP neural network under digital economy. *Neural Computing & Applications*, 35(3), 2045–2058. DOI: 10.1007/s00521-022-07377-0

Li, Y., Xu, S., Yu, Y., & Meadows, R. (2023). The well-being of gig workers in the sharing economy during COVID-19. *International Journal of Contemporary Hospitality Management*, 35(4), 1470–1489. DOI: 10.1108/IJCHM-01-2022-0064

Li, Z., & Liao, Q. (2018). Economic solutions to improve cybersecurity of governments and smart cities via vulnerability markets. *Government Information Quarterly*, 35(1), 151–160. DOI: 10.1016/j.giq.2017.10.006

Lundgren, R., Kyrö, R., & Olander, S. (2024). The lifecycle impact and value capture of circular business models in the built environment. *Construction Management and Economics*, 42(6), 527–544. DOI: 10.1080/01446193.2023.2279743

Luo, Y., & Ball, P. (2023, September). Digital Twins as a Catalyst for Sustainability and Resilience in Manufacturing Systems: A Review from the Supply Chain Perspective. In *International Conference on Sustainable Design and Manufacturing* (pp. 263-273). Springer Nature Singapore.

Mahawar, P., Bajaj, S., & Kashyap, S. V. (2024). Banking in the Age of Industry 5.0: Charting a Path to Technological Transformation. In *Industry 5.0 and Emerging Technologies: Transformation Through Technology and Innovations* (pp. 393–408). Springer Nature Switzerland. DOI: 10.1007/978-3-031-70996-8_19

Mahra, A. K. (2023). A Study On Gig Economy And Redefining Employment In Bhopal District. Open Science Framework. DOI: 10.17605/OSF.IO/KJYRN

Mamchur, R., Minochkina, O., Ianushevych, I., & Khrystenko, L. (2023). Optimization of operational and financial risks of conducting business activities under the conditions of changes and sustainable development. *Economic Affairs*, 68(1s), 91–98. DOI: 10.46852/0424-2513.1s.2023.11

Mangal, U., Mogha, S. K., & Malik, S. (2024). Data-Driven Decision Making: Maximizing Insights Through Business Intelligence, Artificial Intelligence and Big Data Analytics. 1–7. DOI: 10.1109/ACROSET62108.2024.10743399

Mărăcine, V., Voican, O., & Scarlat, E. (2020, July). The digital transformation and disruption in business models of the banks under the impact of FinTech and BigTech. In *Proceedings of the international conference on business excellence* (Vol. 14, No. 1, pp. 294-305). DOI: 10.2478/picbe-2020-0028

Masenya, T. M. (2023). Digital Transformation in SMEs: Developing Digital Business Model Innovations Artificial Intelligence. *Business Models and Innovative Technologies for SMEs, 62*.

Ma, Y. (2024). Exploring the synergy of human-computer interaction in financial decision-making. *Applied and Computational Engineering*, 42(1), 111–121. DOI: 10.54254/2755-2721/42/20230697

Milhem, M., Ateeq, A., Al Astal, A., Alzoraiki, M., Ateeq, R. A., Shafie, D. I., & Santhanamery, T. (2024). Advancing Sustainability: Embracing the Circular Economy for Environmental and Economic Resilience. In *Business Sustainability with Artificial Intelligence (AI): Challenges and Opportunities* (Vol. 2, pp. 57–68). Springer Nature Switzerland.

Mironova, S. M., Kozhemyakin, D. V., & Ponomarchenko, A. E. (2022). Adaptation of the legal regulation of labor, civil, tax relations to the gig economy. *Law Enforcement Review*, 6(4), 314–329. DOI: 10.52468/2542-1514.2022.6(4).314-329

Mishra, A. B. (2015). *Mobile Commerce in Modern Business Era. 3*, 1–80. https://www.researchgate.net/publication/351840817_Mobile_Commerce_in_Modern_Business_Era

Mishra, A. B. (2020). E- PAYMENT SYSTEM: A RISING TREND OF ECONOMY. *New Paradigm in Business and Education*. https://www.researchgate.net/profile/Anitha-K-2/publication/349605501_E-LEARNING_THROUGH_GAMIFICATION-_AN_ITINERARY_TO_GAIN_IN-DEPTH_KNOWLEDGE/links/6037d566299bf1cc26ef9597/E-LEARNING-THROUGH-GAMIFICATION-AN-ITINERARY-TO-GAIN-IN-DEPTH-KNOWLEDGE.pdf#page=10

Mishra, A. B., & Dodke, S. D. (2024). ZARA: Technological Influence on Becoming the Fashion Industry's Market Leader. In *IGI Global* (pp. 204–215). DOI: 10.4018/979-8-3693-2643-5.ch012

Mishra, A. B., & Singh, A. (2024). The Mumbai Dabbawalas : An Efficient and Sustainable Lunchbox Delivery System. In *IGI Global* (pp. 154–160). DOI: 10.4018/979-8-3693-1544-6.ch007

Mishra, A. B., Allen, M., & Tirkey, P. (2024). *Disruption causes to Micromax by once a Market leader now a Myth*. https://www.iimspune.edu.in/images/pdf/Journal/Vol3I1-Paper11.pdf

Mishra, A. B., Raikwar, A., & Tiwari, A. (2024). *BRITANNIA: MARKETING INITIATIVES BOOST A FLEDGLING BUSINESS'S TRANSFORMATION TO ONE OF THE LARGEST FMCG BRANDS*. https://www.iimspune.edu.in/images/pdf/Journal/Vol3I1-Paper12.pdf

Mishra, A. B., Satarkar, M., & Joshi, S. (2024). Capitalizing the Retail Industry by Automation and Artificial Intelligence (AI): Case Study of IKEA. In *IGI Global* (pp. 239–251). DOI: 10.4018/979-8-3693-2643-5.ch014

Mishra, A. B. (2022). SAHYADRI FARMS: INDIA'S LARGEST FARMER PRODUCER COMPANY. *International Journal of Advance and Applied Research*, 10, 996–998. https://ijaar.co.in/wp-content/uploads/2022/11/1001175.pdf

Mishra, A. B., Varma Anil, & Ranjan Nitin. (2021). PUTSCH BUYER TENDENCY AND CLIMBING SALES OF MOBILE TRADE BUSINESS. *Manager –. British Journal of Administrative Management*, 58(152), 54–60.

Mishra, A. B., Chand, K., & Kaith, K. (2022). Influencer Marketing as Emerging Promotional Tool in Modern Era and Opportunities to Uprising Sales. *International Journal of Emerging Research in Engineering, Science, and Management*, 1(3). Advance online publication. DOI: 10.58482/ijeresm.v1i3.3

Mishra, A. B., Goel, A., & Jajoo, P. (2022). A Case Study of Amul: Implementation of Extension Strategy to Repositioning Brand During Covid-19 Period. *International Journal of Emerging Research in Engineering, Science, and Management*, 1(4). Advance online publication. DOI: 10.58482/ijeresm.v1i4.3

Mishra, A. B., & Ranjan, N. (2022). INTERNET OF THINGS BASED EMERGING SMART TOOLS FOR NEW EDGE EDUCATION. *Mukt Shabd Journal*, 11(10), 80–87. DOI: 10.0014.MSJ.2022.V11I10.0086781.1135708

Mishra, A. B., Ranjan, N., Sharma, K. M., Padhye, P., & Chand, K. (2023). Advancement of Digital Transformation to Boost Financial Services Industry. *Journal of Informatics Education and Research*, 3(2), 2435–2440.

Mishra, A. B., Satarkar, M., & Joshi, S. (2023). IKEA - Phygital Transformation in Furniture Manufacturing Industry. *International Journal of Emerging Research in Engineering, Science, and Management*, 2(3), 6–9. DOI: 10.58482/ijeresm.v2i3.2

Mishra, A., Alzoubi, Y. I., Anwar, M. J., & Gill, A. Q. (2022). Attributes impacting cybersecurity policy development: An evidence from seven nations. *Computers & Security*, 120, 102820. DOI: 10.1016/j.cose.2022.102820

Mohammad, B. T., & Iva, R. D. (2024). The technology impacts and AI solutions in hospitality. *I-Manager's Journal on Artificial Intelligence &. Machine Learning*, 2(1), 56. DOI: 10.26634/jaim.2.1.20291

Mohammad, B. T., Mushfika, H., & Iva, R. D. (2024). Opportunities of tourism and hospitality education in bangladesh: Career perspectives. *I-Manager's. Journal of Management*, 18(3), 21. DOI: 10.26634/jmgt.18.3.20385

Mohseni, M., Othman, B. A., Raturi, P., Mishra, A. B., Priya, S. J., & Saravanan, V. (2022). The Role of Parallel Computing Towards Implementation of Enhanced and Effective Industrial Internet of Things (IOT) Through Manova Approach. *2022 2nd International Conference on Advance Computing and Innovative Technologies in Engineering (ICACITE)*, 160–164. DOI: 10.1109/ICACITE53722.2022.9823698

Molina, D. A., Kharlov, V., & Chen, J. (2024). Towards Effective Human-AI Collaboration in Decision-Making: A Comprehensive Review and Conceptual Framework. 96, 1–6. DOI: 10.23919/PICMET64035.2024.10653303

Moser, R., Rengarajan, S., & Narayanamurthy, G. (2021). Decision intelligence: Creating a fit between intelligence requirements and intelligence processing capacities. *IIM Kozhikode Society & Management Review*, 10(2), 160–177. DOI: 10.1177/22779752211017386

Mountassir, Y. (2020). Economic Intelligence system and decision making: Proposal of a theoretical model. 2(3), 137–152. DOI: 10.48379/IMIST.PRSM/MJQR-V2I3.22005

Movahed, A. B., Aliahmadi, A., Parsanejad, M., & Nozari, H. (2023). A systematic review of collaboration in supply chain 4.0 with meta-synthesis method. Supply Chain Analytics, 100052.

Movahed, A. B., Movahed, A. B., & Nozari, H. (2024). *Marketing 6.0 Conceptualization* (pp. 15–31). DOI: 10.4018/979-8-3693-3108-8.ch002

Movahed, A. B., Movahed, A. B., & Nozari, H. (2024). Marketing 6.0 Conceptualization. In *Advanced Businesses in Industry 6.0* (pp. 15-31). IGI Global.

Movahed, A. B., Movahed, A. B., & Nozari, H. (2024). Opportunities and Challenges of Marketing 5.0. *Smart and Sustainable Interactive Marketing*, 1-21.

Movahed, A. B., Movahed, A. B., & Nozari, H. (2024). Opportunities and challenges of smart supply chain in Industry 5.0. *Information Logistics for Organizational Empowerment and Effective Supply Chain Management*, 108-138.

Movahed, A. B., Movahed, A. B., & Nozari, H. (2024a). Marketing 6.0 Conceptualization. In *Advanced Businesses in Industry 6.0* (pp. 15-31). IGI Global.

Movahed, A. B., Movahed, A. B., & Nozari, H. (2024b). Opportunities and Challenges of Marketing 5.0. *Smart and Sustainable Interactive Marketing*, 1-21.

Movahed, A. B., Movahed, A. B., & Nozari, H. (a)(2024). Opportunities and Challenges of Marketing 5.0. *Smart and Sustainable Interactive Marketing*, 1-21.

Movahed, A. B., Movahed, A. B., & Nozari, H. (b)(2024). Marketing 6.0 Conceptualization. In *Advanced Businesses in Industry 6.0* (pp. 15-31). IGI Global.

Movahed, A. B., Movahed, A. B., Aliahmadi, B., & Nozari, H. (2024). *Green and Sustainable Supply Chain in Agriculture 6.0* (pp. 32–45). DOI: 10.4018/979-8-3693-3108-8.ch003

Movahed, A. B., Movahed, A. B., Aliahmadi, B., & Nozari, H. (2024). Green and Sustainable Supply Chain in Agriculture 6.0. In *Advanced Businesses in Industry 6.0* (pp. 32-45). IGI Global.

Movahed, A. B., Movahed, A. B., Nozari, H., & Rahmaty, M. (2024). *Security Criteria in Financial Systems in Industry 6.0* (pp. 62–74). DOI: 10.4018/979-8-3693-3108-8.ch005

Movahed, A. B., Movahed, A. B., Nozari, H., & Rahmaty, M. (2024). Security Criteria in Financial Systems in Industry 6.0. In *Advanced Businesses in Industry 6.0* (pp. 62-74). IGI Global.

Mudholkar, B. S., & Gaikwad, P. S. (2024). Gig is Big in Indian Industry: Concept and Overview. *International Journal of Advanced Research in Science. Tongxin Jishu*, 115–119, 115–119. Advance online publication. DOI: 10.48175/IJARSCT-18422

Muzaffar, M., Ghouse, G., & Alahmad, F. A. (2024). Assessing the Interplay of Financial Development, Human Capital, Democracy, and Industry 5.0 in Environmental Dynamics. *Sustainability (Basel)*, 16(16), 6846. DOI: 10.3390/su16166846

Najafi, S. E., Nozari, H., & Edalatpanah, S. A. (2022). Artificial Intelligence of Things (AIoT) and Industry 4.0–Based Supply Chain (FMCG Industry). *A Roadmap for Enabling Industry 4.0 by Artificial Intelligence*, 31-41.

Najafi, S. E., Nozari, H., & Edalatpanah, S. A. (b)(2022). Investigating the key parameters affecting sustainable IoT-based marketing. In Computational Intelligence Methodologies Applied to Sustainable Development Goals (pp. 51-61). Cham: Springer International Publishing.

Najafi, E., & Nozari, H. (2024). Examining Dimensions and Critical Success Factors of Supply Chains Based on the Blockchain and Internet of Things (B-IoT). In *Analytical Decision Making and Data Envelopment Analysis: Advances and Challenges* (pp. 281–294). Springer Nature Singapore. DOI: 10.1007/978-981-97-6972-8_13

Najafi, S. E., Nozari, H., & Edalatpanah, S. A. (2022). Investigating the key parameters affecting sustainable IoT-based marketing. In *Computational Intelligence Methodologies Applied to Sustainable Development Goals* (pp. 51–61). Springer International Publishing. DOI: 10.1007/978-3-030-97344-5_4

Nakka, S., & Chintha, V. (2023). Role of Gig Economy in Generating Urban Employment- A Study on the City of Hyderabad. *KMICS Journal of Commerce and Management*, 1(1), 1–8. DOI: 10.62011/kmicsjcm.2023.1.1.1

Nanda, P., & Kumar, V. (2022). Information Processing and Data Analytics for Decision Making: A Journey From Traditional to Modern Approaches. *Information Resources Management Journal*, 35(2), 1–14. DOI: 10.4018/IRMJ.291693

Nath, P. (2020). Trust in Gig Economy. *NHRD Network Journal*, 13(4), 480–486. DOI: 10.1177/2631454120974224

Nejabatkhah, F., Li, Y. W., Liang, H., & Reza Ahrabi, R. (2020). Cyber-Security of Smart Microgrids: A Survey. *Energies*, 14(1), 27. DOI: 10.3390/en14010027

Nimmagadda, B., Vangaveti, Y., Aaluri, S., Mallikarjuna Rao, Ch., & Singh, B. (2024). An Analytical study on Navigating Sustainability Challenges and Opportunities in the era of AI and the Gig Economy. *MATEC Web of Conferences, 392*, 01044. DOI: 10.1051/matecconf/202439201044

Nozari, H. (2024a). Investigating Key Dimensions and Key Indicators of AIoT-Based Supply Chain in Sustainable Business Development. In *Artificial Intelligence of Things for Achieving Sustainable Development Goals* (pp. 293-310). Cham: Springer Nature Switzerland.

Nozari, H. (2024b). Investigating Key Dimensions and Key Indicators of AIoT-Based Supply Chain in Sustainable Business Development. In *Artificial Intelligence of Things for Achieving Sustainable Development Goals* (pp. 293-310). Cham: Springer Nature Switzerland.

Nozari, H. (2024c). Supply Chain 6.0 and Moving Towards Hyper-Intelligent Processes. In *Information Logistics for Organizational Empowerment and Effective Supply Chain Management* (pp. 1-13). IGI Global.

Nozari, H., & Chobar, A. P. (2024). The Dimensions and Components of Marketing 5.0: Introduction to Marketing 6.0. In *Advanced Businesses in Industry 6.0* (pp. 75-86). IGI Global.

Nozari, H., Fallah, M., Szmelter-Jarosz, A., & Krzemiński, M. (2021). Analysis of security criteria for IoT-based supply chain: a case study of FMCG industries. *Central European Management Journal, 29*(4).

Nozari, H., Ghahremani-Nahr, J., & Najafi, E. (2023). The role of Internet of things and Blockchain in the development of agile and sustainable supply chains. In Digital Supply Chain, Disruptive Environments, and the Impact on Retailers (pp. 271-282). IGI Global. DOI: 10.4018/978-1-6684-7298-9.ch015

Nozari, H., Ghahremani-Nahr, J., & Najafi, E. (2023a). The role of Internet of things and Blockchain in the development of agile and sustainable supply chains. In *Digital Supply Chain, Disruptive Environments, and the Impact on Retailers* (pp. 271-282). IGI Global.

Nozari, H., Ghahremani-Nahr, J., Fallah, M., & Szmelter-Jarosz, A. (2022). Assessment of cyber risks in an IoT-based supply chain using a fuzzy decision-making method. *International Journal of Innovation in Management, Economics and Social Sciences, 2*(1).

Nozari, H., Ghahremani-Nahr, J., Rahmaty, M., & Bayanati, M. (2024). A Framework for Smart and Resilient Supply Chains Based on Blockchain and the Internet of Things. In *Blockchain-based Internet of Things* (pp. 73-86). Chapman and Hall/CRC.

Nozari, H., Irani, H. R., & Rahmaty, M. (2023, November). Investigating Critical Success Factors in IoT-Based Marketing Systems. In *International Conference on Optimization and Data Science in Industrial Engineering* (pp. 259-271). Cham: Springer Nature Switzerland.

Nozari, H., Irani, H. R., & Rahmaty, M. (2023b, November). Investigating Critical Success Factors in IoT-Based Marketing Systems. In *International Conference on Optimization and Data Science in Industrial Engineering* (pp. 259-271). Cham: Springer Nature Switzerland.

Nozari, H., Rahmaty, M., & Szmelter-Jarosz, A. (2024a). A framework for AIoT-based smart sustainable marketing system. In *Artificial Intelligence of Things for Achieving Sustainable Development Goals* (pp. 255-271). Cham: Springer Nature Switzerland.

Nozari, H., Szmelter-Jarosz, A., & Rahmaty, M. (2024). Smart Marketing Based on Artificial Intelligence of Things (AIoT) and Blockchain and Evaluating Critical Success Factors. In *Smart and Sustainable Interactive Marketing* (pp. 68-82). IGI Global.

Nozari, H., Szmelter-Jarosz, A., & Rahmaty, M. (2024b). Smart Marketing Based on Artificial Intelligence of Things (AIoT) and Blockchain and Evaluating Critical Success Factors. In *Smart and Sustainable Interactive Marketing* (pp. 68-82). IGI Global.

Nozari, H., Tavakkoli-Moghaddam, R., & Dolgui, A. (2024, September). Analysis of Critical Success Factors of Sustainable and Resilient Aioe-based Supply Chain in Industry 5.0. In *IFIP International Conference on Advances in Production Management Systems* (pp. 76-90). Cham: Springer Nature Switzerland. DOI: 10.1007/978-3-031-65894-5_6

Nozari, H. (2024a). Green Supply Chain Management based on Artificial Intelligence of Everything. *Journal of Economics and Management*, 46, 171–188. DOI: 10.22367/jem.2024.46.07

Nozari, H. (Ed.). (2023). *Building Smart and Sustainable Businesses with Transformative Technologies*. IGI Global. DOI: 10.4018/979-8-3693-0210-1

Nozari, H., & Abdi, H. (2024). Greedy Man Optimization Algorithm (GMOA): A Novel Approach to Problem Solving with Resistant Parasites. *Journal of Industrial and Systems Engineering*, 16(3), 106–117.

Nozari, H., & Edalatpanah, S. A. (2023). Smart Systems Risk Management in IoT-Based Supply Chain. In *Advances in Reliability, Failure and Risk Analysis* (pp. 251–268). Springer Nature Singapore. DOI: 10.1007/978-981-19-9909-3_11

Nozari, H., Fallah, M., Kazemipoor, H., & Najafi, S. E. (2021). Big data analysis of IoT-based supply chain management considering FMCG industries. *Бизнес-информатика*, 15(1, 1 (eng)), 78–96. DOI: 10.17323/2587-814X.2021.1.78.96

Nozari, H., Ghahremani-Nahr, J., & Szmelter-Jarosz, A. (2024). AI and machine learning for real-world problems. []. Elsevier.]. *Advances in Computers*, 134, 1–12. DOI: 10.1016/bs.adcom.2023.02.001

Nozari, H., & Nahr, J. G. (2022). The impact of blockchain technology and the internet of things on the agile and sustainable supply chain. *International Journal of Innovation in Engineering*, 2(2), 33–41. DOI: 10.59615/ijie.2.2.33

Nozari, H., Najafi, E., Fallah, M., & Hosseinzadeh Lotfi, F. (2019). Quantitative analysis of key performance indicators of green supply chain in FMCG industries using non-linear fuzzy method. *Mathematics*, 7(11), 1020. DOI: 10.3390/math7111020

Nozari, H., Rahmaty, M., & Szmelter-Jarosz, A. (2024). A framework for AIoT-based smart sustainable marketing system. In *Artificial Intelligence of Things for Achieving Sustainable Development Goals* (pp. 255–271). Springer Nature Switzerland. DOI: 10.1007/978-3-031-53433-1_13

Nozari, H., & Szmelter-Jarosz, A. (2024). An Analytical Framework for Smart Supply Chains 5.0. In *Building Smart and Sustainable Businesses With Transformative Technologies* (pp. 1–15). IGI Global.

Nozari, H., Szmelter-Jarosz, A., & Ghahremani-Nahr, J. (2021). The ideas of sustainable and green marketing based on the internet of everything—The case of the dairy industry. *Future Internet*, 13(10), 266. DOI: 10.3390/fi13100266

Nozari, H., Szmelter-Jarosz, A., & Ghahremani-Nahr, J. (2022). Analysis of the challenges of artificial intelligence of things (AIoT) for the smart supply chain (case study: FMCG industries). *Sensors (Basel)*, 22(8), 2931. DOI: 10.3390/s22082931 PMID: 35458916

Nwafor, K. C., Ikudabo, A. O., Onyeje, C. C., & Ihenacho, D. O. T. (2024). Mitigating cybersecurity risks in financial institutions: The role of AI and data analytics. *International Journal of Science and Research Archive*, 13(1), 2895–2910. DOI: 10.30574/ijsra.2024.13.1.2014

Oguanobi, V. U., & Joel, O. T. (2024). Scalable business models for startups in renewable energy: Strategies for using GIS technology to enhance SME scaling. *Engineering Science & Technology Journal*, 5(5), 1571–1587. DOI: 10.51594/estj.v5i5.1109

Onesi-Ozigagun, O., Ololade, Y. J., Eyo-Udo, N. L., & Ogundipe, D. O. (2024). Leading digital transformation in non-digital sectors: A strategic review. *International Journal of Management & Entrepreneurship Research*, 6(4), 1157–1175. DOI: 10.51594/ijmer.v6i4.1005

Öz, B., Karran, A.-J., Beringer, J., Coursaris, C. K., & Léger, P.-M. (2023). The Dynamics of Collaborative Decision-Making with Intelligent Systems (pp. 167–172). Springer Science+Business Media. DOI: 10.1007/978-3-031-49215-0_20

Pant, J. J., & Majumder, M. G. (2022). Themes and Narratives of Gig Economy: An Indian HR Perspective. *NHRD Network Journal*, 15(1), 83–99. DOI: 10.1177/26314541211064751

Parra, X., Tort-Martorell, X., Alvarez-Gomez, F., & Ruiz-Viñals, C. (2022). Chronological Evolution of the Information-Driven Decision-Making Process (1950–2020). *Journal of the Knowledge Economy*. Advance online publication. DOI: 10.1007/s13132-022-00917-y

Petrova, I., Kravchenko, I., Lisogor, L., & Chuvardynskyi, V. (2021). Employment flexibility in ukraine: Advantages and limitations. *Financial and Credit Activity Problems of Theory and Practice*, 3(38), 490–498. DOI: 10.18371/fcaptp.v3i38.237481

Petrovskaya, M. V., Zaitseva, N. A., Bondarchuk, N. V., Grigorieva, E. M., & Vasilieva, L. S. (2016). Scientific methodological basis of the risk management implementation for companies' capital structure optimization. *International Electronic Journal of Mathematics Education*, 11(7), 2571–2580.

Pires, F., ... (2019) Digital twin in industry 4.0: Technologies, applications and challenges., 2019 IEEE 17th International Conference on Industrial Informatics, INDIN, Vol. 1., 721-726.

Popova, Y., & Popovs, S. (2022). Impact of smart economy on smart areas and mediation effect of national economy. *Sustainability (Basel)*, 14(5), 2789. DOI: 10.3390/su14052789

Portal, I. T. C. (2024). *History and Evolution*. Itcportal.Com. https://www.itcportal.com/about-itc/profile/history-and-evolution.aspx

Prebilič, V., Može, M., & Golobič, I. (2024). Waste-to-Energy Processes as a Municipality-Level Waste Management Strategy: A Case Study of Kočevje, Slovenia. *Processes (Basel, Switzerland)*, 12(5), 1010. DOI: 10.3390/pr12051010

Prince, N. U., Faheem, M. A., Khan, O. U., Hossain, K., Alkhayyat, A., Hamdache, A., & Elmouki, I. (2024). AI-Powered Data-Driven Cybersecurity Techniques: Boosting Threat Identification and Reaction. *Nanotechnology Perceptions*, 20, 332–353.

Raffak, H., Lakhouili, A., & Mansouri, M. (2024). Continuous Integration of Risk Management in a Business Process Reengineering: Towards Optimization through Machine Learning. *Emerging Science Journal*, 8(3), 1118–1135. DOI: 10.28991/ESJ-2024-08-03-019

Raheem, D., Raposo, A., Oluwole, O. B., Nieuwland, M., Saraiva, A., & Carrascosa, C. (2019). Entomophagy: Nutritional, ecological, safety and legislation aspects. *Food Research International*, 126, 108672. DOI: 10.1016/j.foodres.2019.108672 PMID: 31732082

Rahmaty, M., & Nozari, H. (2023). Optimization of the hierarchical supply chain in the pharmaceutical industry. *Edelweiss Applied Science and Technology*, 7(2), 104–123. DOI: 10.55214/25768484.v7i2.376

Ranawaka, A., Alahakoon, D., Sun, Y., & Hewapathirana, K. (2024). Leveraging the Synergy of Digital Twins and Artificial Intelligence for Sustainable Power Grids: A Scoping Review. *Energies*, 17(21), 5342. DOI: 10.3390/en17215342

Rane, N., Choudhary, S., & Rane, J. (2024). Artificial intelligence for enhancing resilience. *Journal of Applied Artificial Intelligence*, 5(2), 1–33. DOI: 10.48185/jaai.v5i2.1053

Ranjan, N., Mishra, A. B., & Padhye, P. (2023). Dynamics of Digital Payments Enable the World's Safest Way to Pay. *Journal of Informatics Education and Research*, 3(2). Advance online publication. DOI: 10.52783/jier.v3i2.406

Ren, S. (2022). Optimization of Enterprise Financial Management and Decision-Making Systems Based on Big Data. *Journal of Mathematics*, 2022(1), 1708506. DOI: 10.1155/2022/1708506

Rogerson, M. (2013). Market segmentation and the changing budget hotel industry in urban South Africa. *Urbani Izziv*, 24(2), 112–123. DOI: 10.5379/urbani-izziv-en-2013-24-01-003

Sachan, S., Almaghrabi, F., Yang, J.-B., & Xu, D.-L. (2024). Human-AI collaboration to mitigate decision noise in financial underwriting: A study on FinTech innovation in a lending firm. *International Review of Financial Analysis*, 93, 103149. Advance online publication. DOI: 10.1016/j.irfa.2024.103149

Sadeghi, M. E., Nozari, H., Dezfoli, H. K., & Khajezadeh, M. (2021). Ranking of different of investment risk in high-tech projects using TOPSIS method in fuzzy environment based on linguistic variables. *arXiv preprint arXiv:2111.14665.*

Sagi, S., & Yadav, A. (2024). Blockchain in Advertising and Marketing. *New Trends in Marketing and Consumer Science*, 89.

Sanni, B. (2024). Human-AI Collaboration in Supply Chains: Coordination Impacts and Challenges.

Sarker, I. H., Furhad, M. H., & Nowrozy, R. (2021). AI-Driven Cybersecurity: An Overview, Security Intelligence Modeling and Research Directions. *SN Computer Science*, 2(3), 173. DOI: 10.1007/s42979-021-00557-0 PMID: 33778771

Şen, G. (2022). Effects of gig economy on employment. *International Journal of Research in Commerce and Management Studies*, 04(05), 57–69. DOI: 10.38193/IJRCMS.2022.4504

Shahana, A., Hasan, R., Farabi, S. F., Akter, J., Al Mahmud, M. A., Johora, F. T., & Suzer, G. (2024). AI-Driven Cybersecurity: Balancing Advancements and Safeguards. *Journal of Computer Science and Technology Studies*, 6(2), 76–85. DOI: 10.32996/jcsts.2024.6.2.9

Shahinzadeh, H., Moradi, J., Gharehpetian, G. B., Nafisi, H., & Abedi, M. (2019, February). Internet of Energy (IoE) in smart power systems. In *2019 5th Conference on Knowledge Based Engineering and Innovation (KBEI)* (pp. 627-636). IEEE.

Sharipov, K., Abdurashidova, N., Valiyeva, A., Tuychieva, V., Kholmatova, M., & Minarova, M. (2022, December). A systematic mapping study of using the cutting-edge technologies in marketing: the state of the art of four key new-age technologies. In *International Conference on Next Generation Wired/Wireless Networking* (pp. 381-389). Cham: Springer Nature Switzerland.

Shen, Y. (2022). Application of internet of things in online teaching of adult education based on android voice assistant. *Mobile Information Systems*, 2022(1), 8915889. DOI: 10.1155/2022/8915889

Shvetsova, O. (2022). Gig Economy: Trends and Perspectives. How to Define Advantages and Disadvantages of Gig Economy? In Gupta, A., Tewary, T., & Gopalakrishnan, B. N. (Eds.), *Sustainability in the Gig Economy* (pp. 19–31). Springer Nature Singapore. DOI: 10.1007/978-981-16-8406-7_2

Sikki, N., Aripin, Z., & Fitrianti, N. G. (2024). Business innovation and critical success factors in digital transformation and challenging times: An econometric analysis of startup viability and success. *KRIEZ ACADEMY: Journal of development and community service, 1*(2), 1-15.

Silvestri, M., Rodríguez González, S., & Bucciarelli, E. (2016). Decision Economics, In Commemoration of the Birth Centennial of Herbert A. Simon 1916-2016 (Nobel Prize in Economics 1978) : Distributed Computing and Artificial Intelligence, 13th International Conference. Springer International Publishing

Singh, A., Rishi, M., & Shukla, R. (2011). Green management and environmental sustainability: A case of ITC Green Center. *Emerald Emerging Markets Case Studies*, 1(2), 1–13. DOI: 10.1108/20450621111159859

Singh, S. (2004). Leveraging ICTs for Agricultural Development: A case study of E-choupals of ITC. *Paradigm*, 8(1), 1–6. DOI: 10.1177/0971890720040101

Smuts, H., Weilbach, L., Padachi, K., Boolaky, A., Mauree-Narrainen, D., Ramphul, N., & Chittoo, H. (2024). Harnessing Disruptive Innovation: A Conceptual Model for SME Growth and Adaptation. *Businesses*, 4(4), 738–764. DOI: 10.3390/businesses4040041

Solanki, A. (Ed.). (2023). *Intelligent Systems for IoE Based Smart Cities*. Bentham Science Publishers. DOI: 10.2174/97898151249651230101

Soluk, J., Decker-Lange, C., & Hack, A. (2023). Small steps for the big hit: A dynamic capabilities perspective on business networks and non-disruptive digital technologies in SMEs. *Technological Forecasting and Social Change*, 191, 122490. DOI: 10.1016/j.techfore.2023.122490

Soni, G., Kumar, S., Mahto, R. V., Mangla, S. K., Mittal, M. L., & Lim, W. M. (2022). A decision-making framework for Industry 4.0 technology implementation: The case of FinTech and sustainable supply chain finance for SMEs. *Technological Forecasting and Social Change*, 180, 121686. DOI: 10.1016/j.techfore.2022.121686

Sood, A., & Singh, R. (2023). The New Emerging World of Work: Growth Story of India's Gig Economy. *International Journal of Management and Economics Invention*, 09(10). Advance online publication. DOI: 10.47191/ijmei/v9i10.03

Srinivas, J., Das, A. K., & Kumar, N. (2019). Government regulations in cyber security: Framework, standards and recommendations. *Future Generation Computer Systems*, 92, 178–188. DOI: 10.1016/j.future.2018.09.063

Srivastava, A. K., Jonjua Mehak, & Rana Rajesh. (2019). Status of Communicating CSR to Stakeholders on Social Media : A Case Study on ITC Limited & Nestle India. *Journal of Content. Community & Communication*, 9, 81–92.

Sudarsan, A., & Chithra, K. (2024). The role of energy management in transition towards green cities: A review. *Environment, Development and Sustainability*, •••, 1–23. DOI: 10.1007/s10668-024-04830-z

Sun, X., & Song, Y. (2025). Unlocking the Synergy: Increasing productivity through Human-AI collaboration in the industry 5.0 Era. *Computers & Industrial Engineering*, 200, 110657. DOI: 10.1016/j.cie.2024.110657

Sutherland, E. (2018). Trends in Regulating the Global Digital Economy. SSRN *Electronic Journal*. DOI: 10.2139/ssrn.3216772

Su, Y., & Wu, J. (2024). Digital transformation and enterprise sustainable development. *Finance Research Letters*, 60, 104902. DOI: 10.1016/j.frl.2023.104902

Syarfina Abu Bakar, A., Razeef Abd Razak, M., & Anwar, R. (2024). *Evolution of Digital Platform for Gig Economy in Design Industry*. KnE Engineering. DOI: 10.18502/keg.v6i1.15414

Szmelter-Jarosz, A., Ghahremani-Nahr, J., & Nozari, H. (2021). A neutrosophic fuzzy optimisation model for optimal sustainable closed-loop supply chain network during COVID-19. *Journal of Risk and Financial Management*, 14(11), 519. DOI: 10.3390/jrfm14110519

Talarico, C., Chang, H., Annamalai, A., & Roveda, J. (2013, August). Energy management design for smart homes using green technology. In 2013 IEEE 56th International Midwest Symposium on Circuits and Systems (MWSCAS) (pp. 517-520). IEEE. DOI: 10.1109/MWSCAS.2013.6674699

Talukder, M. B., & Kumar, S. (2024). The Development of ChatGPT and Its Implications for the Future of Customer Service in the Hospitality Industry. In Derbali, A. (Ed.), *Blockchain Applications for Smart Contract Technologies* (pp. 100–126). IGI Global. DOI: 10.4018/979-8-3693-1511-8.ch005

Talukder, M. B., Kumar, S., & Das, I. R. (2024). Mindful Consumers and New Marketing Strategies for the Restaurant Business: Evidence of Bangladesh. In Ramos, C., Costa, T., Severino, F., & Calisto, M. (Eds.), *Social Media Strategies for Tourism Interactivity* (pp. 240–260). IGI Global. DOI: 10.4018/979-8-3693-0960-5.ch010

Talukder, M. B., Kumar, S., Kaiser, F., & Mia, M. N. (2024). Pilgrimage Creative Tourism: A Gateway to Sustainable Development Goals in Bangladesh. In Hamdan, M., Anshari, M., Ahmad, N., & Ali, E. (Eds.), *Global Trends in Governance and Policy Paradigms* (pp. 285–300). IGI Global. DOI: 10.4018/979-8-3693-1742-6.ch016

Talukder, M. B., & Muhsina, K. (2024). Prospect of Smart Tourism Destination in Bangladesh. In Correia, R., Martins, M., & Fontes, R. (Eds.), *AI Innovations for Travel and Tourism* (pp. 163–179). IGI Global. DOI: 10.4018/979-8-3693-2137-9.ch009

Tanaka, M., Kameda, T., Kawamoto, T., Sugihara, S., & Kambayashi, R. (2025). Managing long working hours: Evidence from a management practice survey. *The Journal of Human Resources*, 60(1), 37–69. DOI: 10.3368/jhr.0421-11605R2

Tang, J., Li, W., Hu, J., & Ren, Y. (2025). Can government digital transformation improve corporate energy efficiency in resource-based cities? *Energy Economics*, 141, 108043. DOI: 10.1016/j.eneco.2024.108043

Tarr, D. G., Kuznetsov, D. E., Overland, I., & Vakulchuk, R. (2023). Why carbon border adjustment mechanisms will not save the planet, but a climate club and subsidies for transformative green technologies may. *Energy Economics*, 122, 106695. DOI: 10.1016/j.eneco.2023.106695

Tavakkoli-Moghaddam, R., Nozari, H., Bakhshi-Movahed, A., & Bakhshi-Movahed, A. (2024). A conceptual framework for the smart factory 6.0. In *Advanced Businesses in Industry 6.0* (pp. 1–14). DOI: 10.4018/979-8-3693-3108-8.ch001

Temara, S. (2024). Harnessing the power of artificial intelligence to enhance next-generation cybersecurity. *World Journal of Advanced Research and Reviews*, 23(2), 797–811. DOI: 10.30574/wjarr.2024.23.2.2428

Tiirmaa-Klaar, H. (2016). Building national cyber resilience and protecting critical information infrastructure. *Journal of Cyber Policy*, 1(1), 94–106. DOI: 10.1080/23738871.2016.1165716

Trí, C. M., & Anh, P. N. (2024). Generation differences in the gig economy. *Ho Chi Minh City Open University Journal of Science - Economics and Business Administration, 14*(3). DOI: 10.46223/HCMCOUJS.econ.en.14.3.2730.2024

Tug, M. A., & Basar, P. (2023). Future of the gig economy. *Pressacademia*, 1, 1. Advance online publication. DOI: 10.17261/Pressacademia.2023.1796

Tweedale, J., Phillips-Wren, G., & Jain, L. C. (2016). *Advances in Intelligent Decision-Making Technology Support*. Springer International Publishing., DOI: 10.1007/978-3-319-21209-8_1

Ünal, E., Urbinati, A., Chiaroni, D., & Manzini, R. (2019). Value Creation in Circular Business Models: The case of a US small medium enterprise in the building sector. *Resources, Conservation and Recycling*, 146, 291–307. DOI: 10.1016/j.resconrec.2018.12.034

Usman M, Sheoliha N, Prabhakar P V, Mishra, A. B., & Dondapati. (2023). Leading Strategies for Organizational Adaptation and Growth in Digital Transformation in Marketing. *Journal of Informatics Education and Research.*

Uzoka, A., Cadet, E., & Ojukwu, P. U. (2024). Applying artificial intelligence in Cybersecurity to enhance threat detection, response, and risk management. *Computer Science & IT Research Journal*, 5(10), 2511–2538. DOI: 10.51594/csitrj.v5i10.1677

van Langen, S. K., Vassillo, C., Ghisellini, P., Restaino, D., Passaro, R., & Ulgiati, S. (2021). Promoting circular economy transition: A study about different stakeholder groups' perceptions and awareness. *Journal of Cleaner Production*, 316, 128166. DOI: 10.1016/j.jclepro.2021.128166

Varavva, M. Yu., & Lazareva, O. S. (2022). Platform Gig-Economy as Alternative Model with Non-Standard Labour Relations. *Vestnik of the Plekhanov Russian University of Economics*, 5(5), 108–115. DOI: 10.21686/2413-2829-2022-5-108-115

Vardanyan, T. (2023). Future of Freelancing: How the Gig Economy is Reshaping the International Labor Market? *AMBERD Bulletin*, 48–56. DOI: 10.52174/2579-2989_2023.6-48

Varma, S. R., & Mishra, A. B. (2015). Study of Consumer Buying Behaviour in General Insurance Industry. In *Excellence through creativity, Research, innovation in field of IT and Management.*

Varma, S. R., & Mishra, A. B. (2013). *Distribution Channels of Indian Insurance Business - A Study*. Abhinavan.

Vu, A. N., & Nguyen, D. L. (2024). The gig economy: The precariat in a climate precarious world. *World Development Perspectives*, 34, 100596. DOI: 10.1016/j.wdp.2024.100596

Wang, B., Kanwar, B., Byrnes, W., Casteleiro Costa, P., Filan, C., Bowles-Welch, A. C., ... & Roy, K. (2024). Digital twin-enabled feedback-controlled bioreactors with integrated process analytics for biomanufacturing of cell therapies.

Wang, G., & Wang, Y. (2021). Innovative Marketing Framework for Enterprises Using Edge-Enabled Data Analysis. *Mobile Information Systems*, 2021(1), 6699420. DOI: 10.1155/2021/6699420

Wongwas, W., Wongsim, M., & Satchawatee, N. (2024). The Role of Digital Transformation in Enhancing Business Performance and Smart Economy Integration: A Case Study of Thailand's Retail Industry. *International Journal of Analysis and Applications*, 22, 173. DOI: 10.28924/2291-8639-22-2024-173

Xiao, J., Chen, S., Han, J., Tan, Z., Mu, S., & Jiayi, W. (2024). The carbon emission reduction effect of renewable resource utilisation: From the perspective of green innovation. *Atmospheric Pollution Research*, 15(6), 102121. DOI: 10.1016/j.apr.2024.102121

Yang, X., Li, N., Ahmad, M., & Mu, H. (2022). Natural resources, population aging, and environmental quality: Analyzing the role of green technologies. *Environmental Science and Pollution Research International*, 29(31), 46665–46679. DOI: 10.1007/s11356-022-19219-6 PMID: 35171429

Yang, Y., Ren, H., Liu, Y., & Yang, Y. (2025). Integration of technology and finance, digital transformation and corporate green innovation. *Finance Research Letters*, 71, 106444. DOI: 10.1016/j.frl.2024.106444

Yunita, F. T. (2023). Embracing the Gig Economy. *Indonesian Journal of Law and Society*, 4(2). Advance online publication. DOI: 10.19184/ijls.v4i2.43628

Yun, W. S., Pinjaman, S. B., Yassin, J., & Taasim, S. I. (2023). The Role of Green Technologies in the Transition Towards a Circular Economy. In *Handbook of Research on Designing Sustainable Supply Chains to Achieve a Circular Economy* (pp. 121–141). IGI Global. DOI: 10.4018/978-1-6684-7664-2.ch007

Yu, P.-L. (2001). *Evolution Toward a New State of Multi-criteria Decision Making* (Vol. 507). Springer., DOI: 10.1007/978-3-642-56680-6_1

Yu, Y. (2021). Application of mobile edge computing technology in civil aviation express marketing. *Wireless Communications and Mobile Computing*, 2021(1), 9932977. DOI: 10.1155/2021/9932977

Zalizko, V. D., Dobrowolski, R. H., Cherniak, A. M., Artemov, V. Y., & Nowak, D. V. (2022). Gig-economy as a safety gradient for sustainable development of the mining industry. *Naukovyi Visnyk Natsionalnoho Hirnychoho Universytetu*, 4(4), 170–175. DOI: 10.33271/nvngu/2022-4/170

Żebrowski, P., Couce-Vieira, A., & Mancuso, A. (2022). A Bayesian Framework for the Analysis and Optimal Mitigation of Cyber Threats to Cyber-Physical Systems. *Risk Analysis*, 42(10), 2275–2290. DOI: 10.1111/risa.13900 PMID: 35229333

Zhang, D. (2024). Leveraging artificial intelligence in economics and finance: Enhancing decision-making and market efficiency. *Applied and Computational Engineering*, 82(1), 118–123. DOI: 10.54254/2755-2721/82/20240980

Zhang, H. (2020). Optimization of risk control in financial markets based on particle swarm optimization algorithm. *Journal of Computational and Applied Mathematics*, 368, 112530. DOI: 10.1016/j.cam.2019.112530

Zhang, X., Cao, Z., & Dong, W. (2020). Overview of edge computing in the agricultural internet of things: Key technologies, applications, challenges. *IEEE Access : Practical Innovations, Open Solutions*, 8, 141748–141761. DOI: 10.1109/ACCESS.2020.3013005

Zhang, Y., & Wang, J. (2024). Research on influencing factors and path of digital transformation of manufacturing enterprises. *Kybernetes*, 53(2), 752–762. DOI: 10.1108/K-06-2023-1042

Zia, Z., Shuming, L., Akbar, M. W., & Ahmed, T. (2023). Environmental sustainability and green technologies across BRICS countries: The role of institutional quality. *Environmental Science and Pollution Research International*, 30(11), 30155–30166. DOI: 10.1007/s11356-022-24331-8 PMID: 36427128

About the Contributors

Hamed Nozari is a distinguished researcher and innovator in industrial engineering, supply chain optimization, and artificial intelligence applications. Holding a Ph.D. in Industrial Engineering, he has made significant contributions to the fields of multi-objective decision-making, smart supply chains, and digital twin technologies. As the developer of the Greedy Man Optimization Algorithm (GMOA), Dr. Nozari has introduced a novel approach to problem-solving inspired by human behavior and parasitic resistance. His research spans various interdisciplinary areas, including predictive maintenance in green supply chains, AI-driven marketing optimization, cybersecurity in smart economies, and autonomous AI for sustainable last-mile delivery.

***

Ali Bakhshi Movahed is a researcher in the field of industrial engineering. He holds a master's degree in industrial engineering from Iran University of Science and Technology (IUST).

Amirhosein Emami is a seasoned business and process development specialist with extensive expertise in project management, operational strategy, and organizational transformation. With a strong background in process optimization, strategic planning, and risk management, he has successfully led high-impact initiatives across various industries, driving efficiency and sustainable growth. His ability to analyze complex business challenges, implement data-driven solutions, and foster cross-functional collaboration has enabled organizations to enhance their performance and competitiveness. Amirhosein holds a Master's degree in Industrial Engineering (Engineering Management) and is currently pursuing an MBA at Arden University in Berlin, Germany. His academic background has provided him with a deep understanding of business intelligence, decision-making models, and agile methodologies, further strengthening his ability to drive transformative change. In addition to his professional and academic achievements, Amirhosein has published several works in the fields of business process management, project governance, strategic development, and process optimization, contributing valuable insights to industry professionals and researchers. His dedication to continuous learning, innovation, and business excellence makes him a key asset in shaping the future of organizations and industries.

Ali Jahanian is a Chemical Engineer holding a PhD in Bioprocess Engineering and a Master of Chemical Engineering (Biotechnology). His doctoral research, supported by the Australian Research Council and conducted in collaboration with the University of Melbourne and Sun Pharma as an industry partner, provided him with extensive expertise in developing a novel biocatalytic process for synthesizing morphinan alkaloids. His work included optimizing upstream microbial fermentation and downstream processing techniques. Currently, Ali's research is focused on mechanistic and data-driven modelling in bioprocessing, as well as the optimization and control of systems. As an active member of the ARC Centre of Excellence in Synthetic Biology and the Centre for Agriculture and the Bioeconomy at QUT, he engages in collaborative efforts with industry partners, contributing to high-impact research and consulting projects in the following areas: Industrial biotechnology Bioprocess modelling and optimisation Precision fermentation Downstream processing Scale up and commercialisation through QUT's Mackay Renewable Biocommodities Pilot Plant (MRBPP) Techno-economic assessment Bioeconomy

Sanjeev Kumar is an accomplished expert in Food and Beverage. He currently holds the positions of Professor in Lovely Professional University, Punjab, India. With over a decade of experience in the field, food Service Industry, his research focuses on Alcoholic beverages, Event management and Sustainable Management Practices, Metaverse and Artificial Intelligence. He has published more than 50 research papers, articles and chapters in Scopus Indexed, UGC Approved and peer reviewed Journals and books. Dr. Sanjeev Kumar participated and acted as resource person in various National and International conferences, seminars, research workshops and industry talks and his work has been widely cited.

A. B. Mishra Presently serving as an Associate Professor in International Institute of Management Studies, Pune. India. Dr. Mishra earned his PhD in Business Management and brings a wealth of corporate experience from renowned Multinational Companies in Sales & Marketing. With extensive tenure in both academia and industry, he blends practical insights with scholarly rigor. Dr. Mishra has actively participated in a myriad of seminars, conferences, and workshops hosted by eminent educational and corporate platforms. His research endeavors have left an indelible mark, with publications gracing the pages of reputable journals like SCOPUS, ABDC, and Web of Science and other leading journals. Not stopping there, he is also credited as an author of books and holds patents, showcasing his multifaceted contributions to the field. Not content with merely domestic endeavors, Dr. Mishra has broadened his horizons through participation in an International Immersion Program. His research interests are as diverse as they are cutting-edge, encompassing areas such as Phygital, Banking & Insurance, E-business, M-commerce, Artificial Intelligence (AI), Internet of Things (IoT), Consumer Perception of sustainable practices, and more. Beyond research, Dr. Mishra is deeply committed to nurturing the next generation of leaders, imparting invaluable knowledge in core subjects such as Marketing Management, Sales Management, Consumer Behavior, Advertisement & Sales Promotion, and beyond. Through his holistic approach to education, Dr. Mishra inspires students to excel and innovate in the ever-evolving landscape of business and academia.

Sepideh Samadi is the Director of the MA Marketing (Hons) Program and a course leader, teaching undergraduate and postgraduate courses at Edinburg Business School, Heriot-Watt University. As a marketing professor, she focuses on enhancing pedagogical practices, managing courses, and fostering student engagement. Dr. Sepideh also supervises undergraduate and postgraduate students in their research dissertations. Her area of specialization is in Marketing Psychology, Digital Marketing, and Consumer Behavior on Digital Platforms. She has published research papers in these areas, contributing to well-known local and international conferences and journals.

Agnieszka Szmelter, PhD, is a researcher working at the Department of Logistics, Faculty of Economics since 2012. She is an author and co-author of over 60 scientific papers in English and Polish. Her major scientific interests are logistics strategies and mobility cultures. She is a Lean Six Sigma Black Belt, ISO 9001 and 14001 internal auditor, SAP Certified Application Associate and Design Thinking Moderator.

Mohammad Badruddoza Talukder is an Associate Professor, College of Tourism and Hospitality Management, IUBAT - International University of Business Agriculture and Technology, Dhaka-1230, Bangladesh. He holds PhD in Hotel Management from Lovely Professional University, India. He has been teaching various courses in the Department of Tourism and Hospitality at various universities in Bangladesh since 2008. His research areas include tourism management, hotel management, hospitality management, food & beverage management, and accommodation management, where he has published research papers in well-known journals in Bangladesh and abroad. Mr. Talukder is one of the executive members of the Tourism Educators Association of Bangladesh. He has led training and consulting for a wide range of hospitality organizations in Bangladesh. He just became an honorary facilitator at the Bangladesh Tourism Board's Bangabandhu international tourism and hospitality training institution.

Zornitsa Yordanova is both an academic and business professional with experience in Digital Transformation, AI, Innovation Management, ICT and project management. In academia, she is an Associate Professor at the largest economic university in the Balkans, the University of National and World Economy, Sofia, where she teaches Innovation and Technology Management. She has published over 80 articles and papers, including 40 publications, indexed by Scopus & Web of Science. She has led six national research projects in the fields of education and innovation / digitalization management. In business, she plays three roles: (1) project manager for international large-scale ICT projects, (2) trainer and consultant in projects focused on innovation management and digital transformation, and (3) startup founder of: GAPideaz - a software solution for digitalization of organizational innovation processes of corporates and schools/universities and ZoYo Cards - digital contact / business cards. She started the first YouTube channel in Bulgaria for technical innovations in 2020, called The Future is right now. She is also regularly participating in TV interviews in the field of AI in education and business.

Index

E

F

G

H

I

www.ingramcontent.com/pod-product-compliance
Lightning Source LLC
LaVergne TN
LVHW081340300926
849161LV00008B/2035
* 9 7 9 8 3 6 9 3 4 3 6 9 2 *